CONCISE
SIXTH EDITION

# CORNERSTONE

# Creating Success
# Through Positive Change

ROBERT M. SHERFIELD
*College of Southern Nevada*

PATRICIA G. MOODY
*University of South Carolina*

**PEARSON**

Boston • Columbus • Indianapolis • New York • San Francisco • Upper Saddle River
Amsterdam • Cape Town • Dubai • London • Madrid • Milan • Munich • Paris • Montreal • Toronto
Delhi • Mexico City • Sao Paulo • Sydney • Hong Kong • Seoul • Singapore • Taipei • Tokyo

Executive Editor: Sande Johnson
Development Editor: Jennifer Gessner
Editorial Assistant: Clara Ciminelli
Vice President, Director of Marketing:
  Quinn Perkson
Marketing Manager: Amy Judd
Production Editor: Janet Domingo

Editorial Production Service: Elm Street
  Publishing Services
Manufacturing Buyer: Megan Cochran
Electronic Composition: Integra Software Services
  Pvt. Ltd.
Interior Design: Carol Somberg
Cover Designer: Linda Knowles

For related titles and support materials, visit our online catalog at www.pearsonhighered.com

Printed in the United States of America

Credits appear on page 305, which constitutes an extension of the copyright page.

10 9 8 7 6 5 4  V011  13

www.pearsonhighered.com

ISBN 13: 978-0-13-700762-2
ISBN 10:  0-13-700762-0

# Dedication

We would like to dedicate this book to the ***many teachers*** throughout our lives who taught us about life, responsibility, and our role in the world. We carry you with us every day.

| | | |
|---|---|---|
| Louise Lymas | Neely Beaty | Beverly Jordan |
| Kitty Carson | Betty Griffin | Dick Smith |
| Steve Brannon | Frank Jackson | Dr. Harvey Jeffreys |
| Dr. Marilyn Kameen | Dr. Lars Bjork | Ann Wenz |
| Phil Lynn | Dr. Howard Jackson | Dr. Leonard Maiden |
| Mary Alice Roughton | Dr. Marilyn Neidig | Audrey Fulford |

# TABLE OF CONTENTS

## PART ONE
## CHANGING YOUR THOUGHTS

/**CHAPTER 1**
## CHANGE
ADJUSTING TO THE CULTURE OF
COLLEGE, NURTURING
CHANGE, AND SETTING
GOALS,
*page 2*

/**CHAPTER 2**
## ENGAGE
DEVELOPING YOUR PERSONAL
AND ACADEMIC PASSION TO
PERSIST IN COLLEGE,
*page 28*

/**CHAPTER 3**
## COMMUNICATE
IMPROVING YOUR
PERSONAL
COMMUNICATION,
CULTIVATING RELATIONSHIPS,
AND MANAGING CONFLICT,
*page 58*

/**CHAPTER 4**
## THINK
EXPANDING YOUR APTITUDE
FOR CRITICAL THINKING,
EMOTIONAL INTELLIGENCE,
AND INFORMATION LITERACY
SKILLS,
*page 82*

# PART THREE
## CHANGING YOUR LIFE

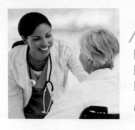

# CHAPTER 11
# PLAN

FOCUSING ON YOUR
PROFESSIONAL CAREER AND
LIVING WELL,
*page 278*

# ABOUT YOUR AUTHORS

## Robert M. Sherfield, Ph.D.

Robert Sherfield has been teaching public speaking, theatre, and student success and working with first-year orientation programs for over 25 years. Currently, he is a professor at the College of Southern Nevada, teaching student success, professional communication, public speaking, and drama.

An award-winning educator, Robb was named **Educator of the Year** at the College of Southern Nevada. He twice received the **Distinguished Teacher of the Year Award** from the University of South Carolina Union, and has received numerous other awards and nominations for outstanding classroom instruction and advisement.

Robb's extensive work with student success programs includes experience with the design and implementation of these programs—including one program that was presented at the International Conference on the First-Year Experience in Newcastle upon Tyne, England. He has conducted faculty development keynotes and workshops at over 350 institutions of higher education across the United States. He has spoken in 46 states and several foreign countries.

In addition to his co-authorship of *Cornerstone, Opening Doors to Career Success* (Prentice Hall, 2009), he has authored or co-authored *Solving the Professional Development Puzzle: 101 Solutions for Career and Life Planning* (Prentice Hall, 2009), *Cornerstone: Discovering Your Potential, Learning Actively, and Living Well* (Prentice Hall, 2008), *Roadways to Success* (Prentice Hall, 2001), the trade book *365 Things I Learned in College* (Allyn & Bacon, 1996), *Capstone: Succeeding Beyond College* (Prentice Hall, 2001), *Case Studies for the First Year: An Odyssey into Critical Thinking and Problem Solving* (Prentice Hall, 2004), *The Everything® Self-Esteem Book* (Adams Media, 2004), and *Cornerstone: Building On Your Best for Career Success* (Prentice Hall, 2006)

Robb's interest in student success began with his own first year in college. Low SAT scores and a dismal high school ranking denied him entrance into college. With the help of a success program, Robb was granted entrance into college, and went on to earn five college degrees, including a doctorate. He has always been interested in the social, academic, and cultural development of students and sees this book as his way to help students enter the world of work and establishing lasting, rewarding careers. Visit www.robertsherfield.com.

## Patricia G. Moody, Ph.D.

Patricia G. Moody is Dean Emerita of the College of Hospitality, Retail and Sport Management at the University of South Carolina, where she served on the faculty and in administration for over 30 years. An award-winning educator, Pat was honored as **Distinguished Educator of the Year** at her college and as **Collegiate Teacher of the Year** by the National Business Education Association. She was also a top-five finalist for the **Amoco Teaching Award** at the University of South Carolina. She received the prestigious **John Robert Gregg Award**, the highest honor in her field of over 100,000 educators.

Pat has co-authored many texts and simulations including: *Solving the Professional Development Puzzle: 101 Solutions for Career and Life Planning, Cornerstone: Discovering Your Potential, Learning Actively, and Living Well, 365 Things I Learned in College, Capstone: Succeeding Beyond College, Case Studies for the First Year: An Odyssey into Critical Thinking and Problem Solving,* and *Cornerstone: Opening Doors to Career Success.*

A nationally known motivational speaker, consultant, and author, Pat has spoken in most states, has been invited to speak in several foreign countries, and frequently keynotes national and regional conventions. She has presented her signature, motivational keynote address, *"Fly Like an Eagle"* to tens of thousands of people, from Olympic athletes to corporate executives to high school students.

As the Dean of her college, Dr. Moody led international trips to build relationships and establish joint research projects in hospitality. Under her direction, faculty members in her college began a landmark study of Chinese Tourists. Pat now travels the country delivering workshops, keynotes, and presentations on topics such as Managing Change, Working in the New Global Community, The Future of the Future, Student Motivation, and Emotional Intelligence. She also serves as a personal coach for business executives.

Filled with stories of inspiration and activities with immediate impact, this book is founded on the hope that comes with education, goal-setting, and determination. *Cornerstone* motivates students by concentrating on concrete academic and personal strategies which will help them navigate the personal and professional changes they face. Using the overriding theme of change and utilizing Bloom's Taxonomy and SQ3R throughout, it is a text that actually uses reading and critical thinking strategies rather than just talking about them. The sixth edition reflects a deeper focus on self-responsibility, active learning (which is reinforced by its interactive design), and building academic and personal success through positive change. Thoroughly updated, *Cornerstone* now includes a new chapter on Interpersonal Communication (with information on communicating effectively in the digital age), updated and expanded information on money and debt management, and a stronger focus on self-engagement and personal responsibility. A totally revised chapter on critical thinking now uses a "Critical Thinking Wheel" to assist students in understanding and using critical thinking more effectively. The sixth edition also boasts a new and exciting section on "HOW we learn," and "HOW to learn" in the learning styles chapter. *Cornerstone* also now extensively covers the ever-popular and timely topic of information literacy and how to apply the concepts to every class. The final chapter on planning for a career and your future now includes information on writing a winning resume, cover letter, and interviewing with confidence and assertiveness.

# NEW TO THIS EDITION:

▶ **10 ESSENTIAL CORNERSTONES**—focuses on the 10 most important aspects of one's personal and professional life. These 10 Essential Cornerstones show up throughout the text to help students apply them to everyday situations at school and work.

▶ **ETHICAL BEHAVIOR**—A new section and diagram on the Six Ethical Questions asks students to review his or her thoughts and actions on ethical behavior to ensure successful transitions.

▶ **HOW TO APPROACH CHANGE IN YOUR LIFE**—a six-step process that allows students to implement change into their lives in a practical and concrete fashion.

▶ **INTERPERSONAL COMMUNICATION**—a totally new chapter on interpersonal communication, self-disclosure, getting along with others, and communicating in the digital age.

▶ **SELF-DISCIPLINE AND PROCRASTINATION**—new information on self-discipline as related to time management and a new section on simplifying your life, saying no, and a new focus on beating procrastination.

▶ **MONEY AND DEBT MANAGEMENT**—totally updated and revised information to reflect today's "new" economy. Includes a new economic readiness assessment that asks students to estimate next semester's costs. New information on loans and how much it costs to repay them. New section called "The Big IF's" offers tips for *if* you have to buy a car; *if* you have to purchase furniture; *if* you have to cut your food expenses; *if* you have to watch how much you spend on family; and *if* you need to cut your fuel costs.

▶ **SUCCESS STICKERS**—*Cornerstone* will include a sheet of success stickers so that students can tag important information throughout the text to reread, study for a test, mark a great quote, or just tag information he or she finds informative and interesting.

# ACKNOWLEDGMENTS AND GRATITUDE

We would like to thank the following individuals at **The College of Southern Nevada** for their support:

Dr. Michael Richards, President
Dr. Darren Divine, Interim Vice President for Academic Affairs
Professor Rose Hawkins, Interim Dean, School of Arts and Letters
Professor John Ziebell, Department Chair—English
Professor Kathy Baker, Assistant Chair—English

We would like to thank individuals at the University of South Carolina, and faculty members at the College of Hospitality, Retail and Sport Management.

Our fondest gratitude to the following **colleagues and friends** who recommended individuals for the features, *Why Read This Chapter . . . from My Perspective* and *from Ordinary To Extraordinary—Real People. Real Lives. Real Change.*

Elaine Richardson, Clemson University
Melanie Deffendall, Delgado Community College
Al Dornbach, ITT Technical Institute, Bensalem, PA
Doug Paddock, Louisville Technical College
Bill Rinkenbaugh, Butler Community College
Lea Redmond, Art Institute of Philadelphia
Tim Quezada , El Paso Community College
Arthur Webb, Oklahoma State University-Stillwater
David Housel, Houston Community College
Nancy Stiller, University of Arizona-Tucson
Kathy Nelson, University of Nevada, Las Vegas
Brian Maitland, Pittsburgh Technical Institute
JoAnne Credle, Northern Virginia Community College
Wistar Withers, Northern Virginia Community College
Cheryl Rohrbaugh, Northern Virginia Community College
Charlie Dy, Northern Virginia Community College
Everett Vann Eberhardt, Northern Virginia Community College
Antionette Payne, Pearson Education
Wendy DiLeonardo, Pearson Education

To the **amazing individuals** who shared their life stories with us for the feature, *From Ordinary to Extraordinary: Real People. Real Lives. Real Change.*

Bill Clayton
Lydia Hausler Lebovic
Dino Gonzalez, M.D.
Vivian Wong
Dr. Wayne A. Jones
Maureen Riopelle
Chef Odette Smith-Ransome
Sylvia Eberhardt

Catherine Schleigh
H.P. Rama
Leo G. Borges
Ricky Britner
Matthew Karres
Mark Jones

To **the marvellous students** who shared their advice and experiences for *Why Read This Chapter . . . from My Perspective:*

Crystal Johnson, College of Southern Nevada, Nevada
Brannon Sulka, Clemson University, South Carolina
Stacy Seals, Delgado Community College, Louisiana
Martin Cram, Butler Community College, Kansas
Eric Despinis, ITT Technical Institute, Pennsylvania
Sakinah Pendergrass, The Art Institute of Philadelphia, Pennsylvania
Thomas Paddock, Louisville Technical Institute, Kentucky
Griffin Jones, Point Park University, Pennsylvania
Fernando Machado, El Paso Community College, Texas
Melissa Von Aschen, University of Oklahoma-Stillwater, Oklahoma
Acacia Jamison, University of South Carolina, South Carolina
Perscilla Renew, Houston Community College, Texas
Kendra Hernandez, University of Arizona-Tucson, Arizona
Alyssa Bucchianeri, University of Nevada, Las Vegas

Our **wonderful and insightful reviewers for the Sixth Edition:**

Kristina Leonard, Daytona Beach College
Kim Long, Valencia Community College
Taunya Paul, York Technical College
Charlie L. Dy, Northern Virginia Community College
Gary H. Wanamamker, Ph. D., Houston Community College
Jo Ann Jenkins, Moraine Valley Community College
Judith Lynch, Kansas State University
Timothy J. Quezada, El Paso Community College
Cathy Hall, Indiana University NW
Beverly J. Slaughter, Brevard Community College
Peg Adams, Northern Kentucky University
Sheryl Duquette, Erie Community College
Melanie Deffendall, Delgado Community College
Arthur Webb, Oklahoma State University
Stephanie Young, Butler Community College
Tara Wertz, MTI College
Diana Clennan, College of Southern Nevada
Jennifer Huss-Basquiat, College of Southern Nevada
Wayne A. Jones of Virginia State University

**Reviewers for Previous Editions whom we recognize with deep appreciation.**

Barbara Auris, Montgomery County Community College; Betty Fortune, Houston Community College; Joel V. McGee, Texas A & M University; Jan Norton, University of Wisconsin–OshKosh; Todd Phillips, East Central College, Christian M. Blum, Bryan and Stratton College; James Briski, Katherine Gibbs School; Pela Selene Terry, Art Institute of NYC; Christina Donnelly, York Technical College; Connie Egelman, Nassau Community College; Amy Hickman, Collins College; Beth Humes, Pennsylvania Culinary Institute; Kim Joyce, Art Institute of Philadelphia; Lawrence Ludwig, Sanford-Brown College; Bethany Marcus, ECPI College of Technology; Kate Saywer, Pittsburg Technical Institute; Patricia Sell, National College of Business and Technology; Janis Stiewing, PIMA Medical Institute; June Sullivan, Florida Metropolitan University; Fred Amador, Phoenix College; Kathy Bryan, Daytona Beach Community College; Dorothy Chase, Community College of Southern Nevada; JoAnn Credle, Northern Virginia Community College; Betty Fortune, Houston Community College; Doroteo Franco Jr., El Paso Community College; Cynthia Garrard, Massasoit Community College; Joel Jessen, Eastfield College; Peter Johnston, Massasoit Community College; Steve Konowalow, Community College of Southern Nevada; Janet Lindner, Midlands Technical College; Carmen McNeil, Solano College; Joan O'Connor, New York Institute of Technology; Mary Pepe, Valencia Community College; Bennie Perdue, Miami-Dade Community College; Ginny Peterson-Tennant, Miami-Dade Community College; Anna E. Ward, Miami-Dade Community College; Wistar M. Withers, Northern Virginia Community College; and Marie Zander, New York Institute of Technology; Joanne Bassett, Shelby State Community College; Sandra M. Bovain-Lowe, Cumberland Community College; Carol Brooks, GMI Engineering and Management Institute; Elaine H. Byrd, Utah Valley State College; Janet Cutshall, Sussex County Community College; Deborah Daiek, Wayne State University; David DeFrain, Central Missouri State University; Leslie L. Duckworth, Florida Community College at Jacksonville; Marnell Hayes, Lake City Community College; Elzora Holland, University of Michigan, Ann Arbor; Earlyn G. Jordan, Fayetteville State University; John Lowry-King, Eastern New Mexico University; Charlene Latimer; Michael Laven, University of Southwestern Louisiana; Judith Lynch, Kansas State University; Susan Magun-Jackson, The University of Memphis; Charles William Martin, California State University, San Bernardino; Jeffrey A. Miller; Ronald W. Johnsrud, Lake City Community College; Joseph R. Krzyzanowski, Albuquerque TVI; Ellen Oppenberg, Glendale Community College; Lee Pelton, Charles S. Mott Community College; Robert Rozzelle, Wichita State University; Penny Schempp, Western Iowa Community College; Betty Smith, University of Nebraska at Kearney; James Stepp, University of Maine at Presque Isle; Charles Washington, Indiana University–Purdue University; and Katherine A. Wenen-Nesbit, Chippewa Valley Technical College.

**Our Creative and Supportive Team at Pearson**

Without the support and encouragement of the following people at Pearson, this book would not be possible. Our sincere thanks to:

Susan Badger   Nancy Forsyth   Sande Johnson
Amy Judd   Quinn Perkson   Janet Domingo

Your constant belief in us over the years has been a most cherished gift. We are lucky to know you and are better people because of you. Thank you!

**We also thank the following friends at Pearson for their support, dedication and exceptional work:** Jenny Gessner, Clara Ciminelli, Antionette Payne, Walt Kirby, Debbie Ogilvie, Alan Hensley, Pam Jeffries, Barbara Donlon, Cathy Bennett, Meredith Chandler, Jeff McIlroy, Matt Mesaros, Connie James, Wendy DiLeonardo, Dave Gessell, Eric Hackanson, Deborah Wilson, Eric Weiss, Julie Morel, Julie Hilderbrand, Dana Dodge, Andrea Iorio, and Richard Rowe.

# PEARSON
# mystudentsuccesslab™

## Succeed in college and beyond!
## Connect, practice, and personalize with MyStudentSuccessLab.

### www.mystudentsuccesslab.com

**MyStudentSuccessLab** is an online solution designed to help students acquire the skills they need to succeed. They will have access to peer-led video presentations and develop core skills through interactive exercises and projects that provide academic, life, and career skills that will transfer to ANY course.

**It can accompany any Student Success text, or be sold as a stand-alone course offering.** Often students try to learn material without applying the information. To become a successful learner, they must consistently apply techniques to their daily activities.

## MyStudentSuccessLab provides students with opportunities to become successful learners:

### Connect:
• Engage with real students through video interviews on key issues.

### Practice:
• Three skill-building exercises per topic provide interactive experience and practice.

### Personalize:
• Apply what is learned to your life.
• Create a personal project that will be graded and can be posted to your portfolio.
• Journal online and set short- and long-term goals.

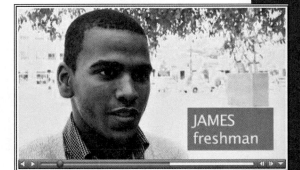

### Resources
• Tools to use: Plagiarism Guide, Dictionary, Calculators, and a Multimedia index of Interactive case studies and activities.

### Text-Specific Study Plan
• Chapter Objectives provide clear expectations.
• Practice Tests for each chapter of your text assess your current understanding.
 - Completion of each practice test generates a study plan that is unique to you.
• Enrichment activities identify strengths and weaknesses, provide immediate feedback, and link to additional media.
• Flashcards help you study and review.

### Assessments
• Includes Career Assessment tool, Learning Styles, and Personality Styles.

# BEGIN

## THE GOAL OF CORNERSTONE AND OUR COMMITMENT TO YOU

*Talent alone won't make you a success. Neither will being in the right place at the right time, unless you are ready. The most important question is: 'Are you ready?'*

—Johnny Carson

If you look at the figure printed here you will see the Chinese symbol (verb) for "***to change.***" It is made up of two symbols— the first means ***to transform*** or to be flexible. The second means ***to do*** or ***to deliver***. In its purest form, the symbol means to ***deliver transformation***. That is what *Cornerstone* is all about, helping you deliver or bring about transformation, positive change if you will, to your life. It is about helping you discover ways to change your thoughts, change your performance, and change your life.

Our goal in writing *Cornerstone* is to help you discover your academic, social, and personal strengths so that you can build on them and to provide **concrete and useful tools** that will help you make the changes that might be necessary for your success. We believe that in helping you identify and transform areas that have challenged you in the past, you can ***discover your true potential, learn more actively, and have the career you want and deserve***.

***Cornerstone: Creating Success through Positive Change*** is devoted to three specific areas where positive change can help you become the individual you would like to be. The book is divided into three parts:

### Changing Your Thoughts
### Changing Your Performance
### Changing Your Life

**PART ONE, Changing Your Thoughts,** addresses a broad spectrum of topics that begins with a focus on change as it relates to becoming a college student in a different culture and setting than you may have known before. In this section, you will be introduced to tools of self-management as they relate to college life. You will be exposed to a variety of new terms, ideas, and thoughts—all of which begin your journey of change. You will learn to enhance your communication skills, improve your self-concept, and manage conflict, all valuable tools on the road to change. You will become more adept at critical thinking and problem solving as you study this section. When you have completed this section, you should notice a difference in the way you approach tasks and think about subjects, challenges, and people.

**PART TWO, Changing Your Performance,** focuses on you and how you physically and mentally manage yourself. You will begin this part of the journey to change by learning to manage your time and control the inherent stress that accompanies being a college student. You will realize that you have a dominant intelligence, learning style, and personality type and how to use them to your advantage. Even though you have been reading for some time, you will be shown strategies to improve both your speed and comprehension since reading is a major part of college studies. You will be shown several note-taking systems designed to improve your ability to record what your professors are teaching. Finally, you will be taught strategies for empowering your memory, learning to study more effectively, and taking tests with confidence. When you complete this section, you should be able to perform most tasks more effectively and confidently.

**PART THREE, Changing Your Life,** is a culmination of the journey you have embarked on as a first-year student. This section is designed to round out your total personal profile and springboard you to success as you move into a different realm. Many college students do well on the topics covered in the first two sections and fall short when they arrive to this point. To be the complete successful college student, you need to address all these areas because they are significant to the changes you need to embrace. You will learn to manage your money and your debts wisely. So many college students are burdened with astronomical college debts when they graduate; our desire is for you to have accumulated as little debt as possible at the same time you are taking advantage of all that college has to offer. You will study the important emerging topic of information literacy and improve your writing and speaking skills. On this important journey to change, you will be shown how to immerse yourself in many categories of diversity while you learn to celebrate all kinds of people. You will be taught to be responsible for your own wellness and how to exercise personal responsibility. Finally, you will be introduced to techniques for planning your professional career in the face of dramatic global changes. When you finish this section, you should be prepared to move through the next few years of college and beyond with confidence and optimism.

We know that your **time is valuable** and that you are pulled in countless directions with work, family, school, previous obligations, and many other tasks. For this reason, we have tried to provide only the most concrete, useful strategies and ideas to help you succeed in this class and beyond.

We have spent over 55 years collectively gathering the information, advice, suggestions, and activities on the following pages. This advice and these activities have come from trial and error, colleagues, former students, instructors across the United States, and solid research. We hope that you will enjoy them, learn from them, and most of all, use them to change your life and move closer to your dreams.

Let the journey to positive change begin!

Robb and Pat

# SQ3R

## What Is It and Why Do I Need to Know It?

You may be asking, "*What does SQ3R mean and what could it possibly have to do with me, my text, this course, and my success?*" The answer: *SQ3R* (**S = Scan, Q = Question, 3 R = Read, Recite, Review**) is one of the most successful and widely used learning and study tools ever introduced.

This simple, yet highly effective mnemonic (memory trick) asks that ***before you actually read the chapter***, you look over the contents, check out the figures and photos, look at section headings, and review any graphs or charts. This is called **scanning**. Step two, **question**, asks that you jot down questions that you think you will need to answer about the chapter's content in order to master the material. These questions might come from charts or figures, but most commonly, they come from the chapter's section headings. Examine the example below of a section heading from: *Criminal Justice, A Brief Introduction*, 6th Edition by Frank Schmalleger (Prentice Hall, 2006).

(1) *What are the categories of crime?*
(2) *Why do they matter?*
(3) *What is crime typology?* or
(4) *When are categories of crime most often used?*

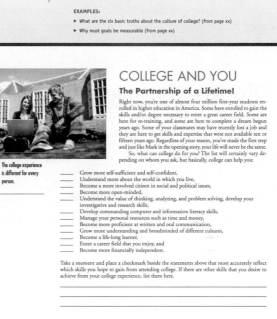

### COLLEGE AND YOU

**The Partnership of a Lifetime!**

Right now, you're one of almost four million first-year students enrolled in higher education in America. Some have enrolled to gain the skills and/or degree necessary to enter a great career field. Some are here for re-training, and some are here to complete a dream begun years ago. Some of your classmates may have recently lost a job and they are here to get skills and expertise that were not available ten or fifteen years ago. Regardless of your reason, you've made the first step and just like Mark in the opening story, your life will never be the same. So, what can college do for you? The list will certainly vary depending on whom you ask, but basically, college can help you:

The college experience is different for every person.

_____ Grow more self-sufficient and self-confident,
_____ Understand more about the world in which you live,
_____ Become a more involved citizen in social and political issues,
_____ Become more open-minded,
_____ Understand the value of thinking, analyzing, and problem solving, develop your investigative and research skills,
_____ Develop commanding computer and information literacy skills,
_____ Manage your personal resources such as time and money,
_____ Become more proficient at written and oral communication,
_____ Grow more understanding and broadminded of different cultures,
_____ Become a life-long learner,
_____ Enter a career field that you enjoy, and
_____ Become more financially independent.

Take a moment and place a checkmark beside the statements above that most accurately reflect which skills you hope to gain from attending college. If there are other skills that you desire to achieve from your college experience, list them here.

_____
_____
_____

133b

---

reported data.[64] Crimes that result from an anomalous event, but which are excluded from reported data, highlight the arbitrary nature of the data-collection process itself.

### Special Categories of Crime

**crime typology**

A classification of crimes along a particular dimension, such as legal categories, offender motivation, victim behavior, or the characteristics of individual offenders.

A **crime typology** is a classification scheme that is useful in the study and description of criminal behavior. All crime typologies have an underlying logic, and the system of classification that derives from any particular typology may be based on legal criteria, offender motivation, victim behavior, the characteristics of individual offenders, or the like. Criminologists Terance D. Miethe and Richard C. McCorkle note that crime typologies "are designed primarily to simplify social reality by identifying homogeneous groups of crime behaviors that are different from other clusters of crime behaviors."[65] Hence one common but simple typology contains only two categories of crime: violent and property. In fact, many crime typologies contain overlapping or nonexclusive categories—just as violent crimes may involve property offenses, and property offenses may lead to violent crimes. Thus no one typology is likely to capture all of the nuances of criminal offending.

---

After writing these questions from the section heading, you will read this section and then answer those questions. This technique gives you more focus and purpose for your reading. Each chapter in *Cornerstone* begins with this technique through a feature called **Scan and Question.**

We included this feature in *Cornerstone* to help you become a more active reader with greater comprehension skills in all of your other classes. This technique is fully discussed in Chapter 7 of this text.

# BLOOM'S TAXONOMY

## What Are All of Those Little Triangles Throughout My Book?

Another feature that you will notice in your text is small triangles throughout followed by questions pertaining to the content. These triangles help you recognize which of the

BLOOM LEVEL 3 QUESTION

six levels of learning is being used from Bloom's Taxonomy. A quick reference chart of Bloom's Taxonomy (Revised) is on the inside front cover of this text and on page xxi.

**Bloom's Taxonomy** (also called Levels of Thinking and Learning) is simply a way of explaining the stages at which we all acquire information. These levels, explained in detail on the next page, progress from simple learning and thinking (levels 1, 2, 3) to more complex learning and thinking (levels 4, 5, 6). In addition to having questions from Bloom's Taxonomy throughout your text, each chapter will end with an exercise called *Knowledge in Bloom*. This chapter-end activity is included to help you process and apply the information from the chapter.

## So, Why Use Bloom in the *Cornerstone* Text?

Bloom's Taxonomy is important to us all because it helps us determine the level at which we understand important information. For example, it is important to be able to answer questions at Level 1 such as:

▶ *Abraham Lincoln was the _____ President of the United States.*

or

▶ *Abraham Lincoln's wife's name was _____ Lincoln.*

However, it is also important to be able to answer questions at levels 5 and 6 such as:

▶ *Based on your knowledge of the Civil War era, predict what would have happened to the United States without the Emancipation Proclamation. Justify your answer.*

or

▶ *Summarize the main events that led to President Lincoln's assassination.*

As you can clearly see, there is a great difference between these levels of learning. The higher the level, the more information and knowledge you need to be able to understand and respond to the question or problem.

The chapter-end activity, **Knowledge in Bloom,** will help you process and demonstrate your knowledge at different levels. This is important because you will have professors who **teach and test** at levels 1, 2, and 3 and those who **teach and test** at levels 4, 5, and 6. Learning to process and demonstrate your knowledge at every level can assist you in:

- doing well in other classes by providing a foundation for effective studying/learning,
- learning to solve problems more thoroughly,
- predicting exam questions,
- learning how to critically evaluate and assess ideas and issues,
- learning to thoroughly and objectively research topics for papers and presentations, and
- testing your own reading comprehension.

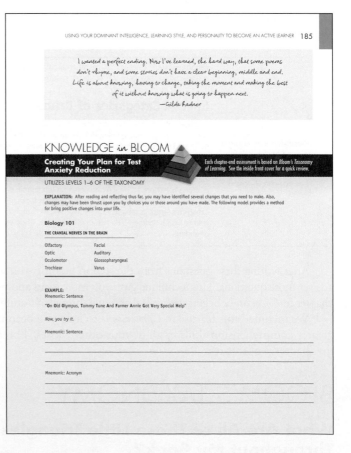

Examine the following chart for Bloom's Taxonomy (Levels of Thinking and Learning).

# BLOOM'S TAXONOMY (Revised)
## Examining the Levels of Thinking and Learning

| **LEVELS** OF *THINKING AND LEARNING.* | WHAT **SKILLS** YOU SHOULD HAVE AT THIS LEVEL. | **EXAMPLES** OF *QUESTIONS* OR *ACTIVITIES* YOU MIGHT ANTICIPATE OR *PRODUCTS* YOU MAY HAVE TO GENERATE |
|---|---|---|
| **1—REMEMBERING** This level is based on simple recall of information. This type of knowledge usually comes from being told or from basic reading. It is the "lowest" or most simple type of learning. | write, list, label, name, state, define, describe, identify, recognize, recall, draw, select, locate, recite, quote, order, state, reproduce, match, tell, and the five standards, who, what, when, where, and how | What is . . . , When did . . . , Why did . . . , Who were . . . , Describe the . . . , Which of the following . . . , Define the . . . , Name the . . . , Identify who . . . , Describe what happened after . . . **SAMPLE:** What are the six levels of learning in Bloom's Taxonomy? |
| **2—UNDERSTANDING** This level determines your grasp or comprehension level of the information presented. It asks, "Do you understand the meaning?" and "Can you explain the ideas or concepts?" | summarize, describe, interpret, contrast, predict, associate, distinguish, estimate, differentiate, discuss, extend, convert, explain, generalize, give examples, rewrite, restate, classify, translate, paraphrase, illustrate, visualize, retell | How would you contrast . . . , Explain why the . . . , Summarize the main . . . , What facts show . . . , Predict the outcome of . . . , Restate the story in your own words . . . , prepare a flow chart to illustrate . . . **SAMPLE:** Explain why Bloom's Taxonomy is being used in *Cornerstone* and describe its importance. |
| **3—APPLYING** This level asks you to "use" the information you have by solving, showing, or applying that information in "real-world" or workplace situations. Can you use the information in a new way? | apply, demonstrate, discover, modify, operate, predict, solve, draw, dramatize, model, sketch, paint, produce, prepare, make, calculate, record, compute, manipulate, modify, use, employ | How could you use . . . , How could you solve . . . , What approach would you take . . . , Write an essay to explain why . . . , Prepare a timeline of . . . , Predict what would happen if . . . **SAMPLE:** Prepare a plan to show how you could use Bloom's Taxonomy to get a better grade in your history class? |
| **4—ANALYZING** This level asks you to "take apart" the information for clarification, classification, and prioritizing. It also asks you to recognize what is "not" said, i.e., . . . hidden meanings and unstated assumptions. This level requires that you distinguish between facts and inferences. | break down, distinguish, infer, arrange, prioritize, order, divide, categorize, appraise, test, examine, separate, deduce, choose, compare/contrast, detect, group, sequence, scrutinize, connect, outlines, research, point out | How is ___ related to ___?, What conclusions can be drawn . . . , What is the relationship between . . . , Categorize the main . . . , Based on X, why is Y . . . , What were the motives behind . . . , What was the turning point in . . . , Write a survey to find out if . . . **SAMPLE:** What assumptions can be made about the rest of the term if your history teacher's first two exams included 20 questions, all from level six? |
| **5—EVALUATING** This level of thinking and learning asks you to make personal judgments about the value of issues, ideas, policies, and evidence based on your complete understanding of the information AND based on stated judging criteria. Basically, it asks that you justify a decision, idea, or belief that you have formulated. | decide, rank, test, measure, recommend, defend, conclude, appraise, assess, judge, predict, rate, select, critique, justify, estimate, validate, measure, discriminate, probe, award, rank, reject, grade, convince, weigh, support | Defend your position about . . . , How would you have handled "X"? Why? Debate the issue of . . . , Prepare a paper or speech to present your ideas of . . . , What is your opinion of . . . , How would you rate . . . , What judgment could you make . . . , Justify your opinion of . . . , Based on your research, convince the reader of your paper or speech that . . . , What criteria would you use to assess the . . . **SAMPLE:** Assess how effective Bloom's Taxonomy was when used to study for your history exam. Recommend two ways to improve the use of Bloom's for the next test. |
| **6—CREATING** This level asks you to integrate your previous knowledge with your new knowledge and come up with new ideas, plans, and solutions. It also asks you to be able to predict outcomes based on what you have learned. This level asks you to be innovative and creative. | compose, combine, compile, create, design, generate, construct, revise, write, rewrite, tell, role play, formulate, invent, develop, modify, arrange, rearrange, prepare, assemble, set-up, forecast, imagine, act, improvise, propose, substitute, integrate, incorporate | Design a plan to . . . , Write a speech or paper that . . . , Create a marketing plan that . . . , Devise a way to . . . , Compose a mnemonic that . . . , Generate a list of questions that . . . , Propose a solution to . . . , Revise the story of . . . **SAMPLE:** Write two possible test questions from each level of Bloom's Taxonomy from Chapter 1 of *Cornerstone*. |

# STICKERS FOR SUCCESS

## What Are Those Colorful Stickers in the Back of My Book?

In the back of this text, you will find a sheet of peel off stickers to help you "tag" pages and content that (1) you need to study for a quiz, (2) review for mastery, (3) seek help with, or (4) mark as important. We have also included a row of blank stickers for your personal use (5). We encourage you to use them to help you locate information easily. The tabs include:

**Study for Quiz** Use to tag information that your instructor tells you will be on the test.

**Review This** Use to identify key terms, definitions, or difficult material that you need to revisit.

**ASK for HELP** Use to remind you to ask questions about the content you may not understand.

**Important** Use to tag important information.

Create your own tab to mark important quotes, charts, or other material you would like to reference quickly.

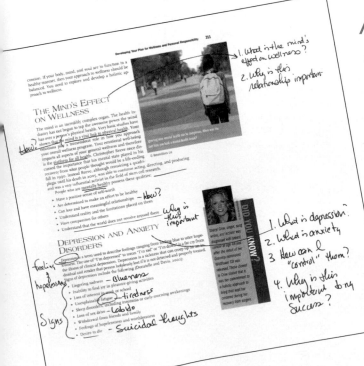

# A WORD ABOUT *READING* AND *USING CORNERSTONE*

We encourage you to read this text (and every text) with great care so that you can learn from the ideas presented within its pages. We also encourage you to USE this book –

- write in the margins,
- circle important terms,
- highlight key phrases,
- jot down word definitions in the margins,
- dog-ear the pages, and
- write questions that you have in the white spaces provided.

By treating this book like your "foundation to success," you will begin to see remarkable progress in your study practices, reading comprehension, and learning skills. Review the example from another *Cornerstone* text.

# CORNERSTONE

# CHAPTER 1
# CHANGE

ADJUSTING TO
THE CULTURE
OF COLLEGE,
NURTURING
CHANGE,
AND SETTING
YOUR GOALS

"The greatest reward of an education is to be able to face the world with an open mind, a caring heart, and a willing soul."

—R. M. Sherfield

# WHY READ THIS CHAPTER?

## What's in it for me?

WHY read this stuff on positive change? WHY will a chapter on change and goal setting help me in college, at work, with my friends, and beyond? WHY spend my time reading something that I'm not sure will help me at all? WHY is it important to understand the "Culture of College"?

Why? Because this chapter, indeed this whole book and course in which you are enrolled, is about helping you become the best college student, thinker, citizen, leader, and lifelong learner that you can possibly be. The information in this chapter is included to help you understand some of the basic truths about college life and academic survival. Quite simply, this chapter was written to help you learn how to adjust to college life, discover your potential, build on your strengths, and bring about positive change in your life through self-analysis, reflection, and goal setting. By reading this chapter and working through the activities, you will begin to see how important change is to your life, your growth, and your future, and more importantly, how to bring about that positive change.

*By carefully reading this chapter and taking the information provided seriously, you will be able to:*

1. Understand the relationship between your education and the new world economy.
2. Identify and apply the Ten Essential Cornerstones for Success in a Changing World.
3. Understand the basic truths about how college can help you beyond the classroom.
4. Understand the differences among high school, college, and career.
5. Understand why change is important and how to bring about change through goal setting.

## CHAPTER 1 / CHANGE

*"When it comes to the future, there are three kinds of people: those who let it happen, those who make it happen, and those who wonder what happened."*

—John Richardson, Jr.

# WHY READ THIS CHAPTER?

## . . . FROM MY PERSPECTIVE

**NAME:** Mark
**INSTITUTION:** Spartanburg Methodist College, Spartanburg, SC
**MAJOR:** Associate of Arts—Theatre and Speech
**AGE:** 18

Change has been a major part of my life, and learning how to transform myself was a very important tool that helped me succeed in my first year of college. A major change in my life was learning how to overcome years of self-defeating behaviors, a horrible academic background, a negative attitude, and terrible study skills. I quickly learned that my success depended on my becoming an open-minded person who knew how to set goals, work to achieve those goals, develop self-motivation skills, and study effectively. These were not easy steps for me after 12 years of failure and disappointment.

I am the son of textile workers. Both of my parents worked in a cotton mill for over 30 years. My hometown is in the rural south about 35 miles from the nearest metropolitan area. I attended a small high school and was never a good student. Because of my poor performance through the years, working full time, and family commitments, I decided to attend a community college and then transfer to a four-year college.

I barely finished high school with a D– average and my SAT scores and class rank were so bad that I was denied entrance to a community college. The college granted me provisional acceptance with the stipulation that I enroll in, and successfully complete, a summer preparatory program. I graduated high school on a Friday night and began my college studies the very next Monday morning enrolled in the prep program. I never realized what lay ahead. I never realized how my life was about to change forever. I never realized at that point how much I would have to change.

My first class that semester was English. Professor Brannon walked in, handed out the syllabus, called the roll, and began to lecture. Lord Byron was the topic for the day. The class ended and after an hour's break, I headed across campus for history. Professor Wilkerson entered with a dust storm behind her. She went over the syllabus, and before we had a chance to blink, she was involved in the first lecture. "The cradle of civilization," she began, "was Mesopotamia."

We all scurried to find notebooks and pens to begin taking notes. I could not believe I was already behind on the first day. "Who teaches on the first day?" I thought.

One minute before class ended, she closed her book, looked directly at us, and said, "You are in history now. You elected to take this class and you will follow my rules. You are not to be late, you are to come to this class prepared, and you are to do your homework assignments. If you do what I ask you to do, read what I've assigned to you, and do your homework activities, you will learn more about Western civilization than you ever thought possible. If you don't keep up with me, you won't know if you are in Egypt, Mesopotamia, or pure Hell! Now get out!"

On the 30-mile trip home, my mind was filled with new thoughts . . . *Lord Byron, Mesopotamia, professors who talked too fast, tuition, parking, and the size of the library*. I knew that something was different, *something had changed in me*. I couldn't put my finger on it. It would be years before I realized that the change had not been my classes, not my schedule, not the people, not the professors—but me; *I had changed*. In one day, I had tasted something intoxicating, something that was addictive. *I had tasted a new world*.

I had to go to work that afternoon at the mill, and even my job and my coworkers had changed. I had always known that I did not want to spend the rest of my life in the factory, but this day the feeling was stronger. My job was not enough, my family was not enough, the farm on which I had been raised was not enough anymore. *There was a new light in me, and I knew that because of that one day in college, I would never be the same.* It was like tasting Godiva chocolate for the first time— Hershey's kisses were no longer enough. It was like seeing the ocean for the first time and knowing that the millpond would never be the same. *I couldn't go back. What I'd known before was simply no longer enough.*

My name is Robert **Mark** Sherfield, and 34 years later, as I coauthor your *Cornerstone* text, I am still addicted to that new world. College changed my life, and I am still changing—with every day I live, every new book I read, every new class I teach, every new person I meet, and every new place to which I travel, I am changing. I wish the same for you.

## SCAN & QUESTION

In the preface of this book (page xix), you read about the **SQ3R Study Method**. Right now, take a few moments, **scan this chapter**, and on page 27, write **five of your own questions** that you think will be important to your mastery of this material. In addition to the two questions below, you will find five questions from your authors. Use one of your *"On The Test"* stickers to flag this page for easy reference.

**EXAMPLES:**

▶ **What are the six basic truths about the culture of college?** (from page 11)

▶ **Why must goals be measurable?** (from page 21)

# THE TIMES . . . THEY ARE A-CHANGIN'

## What Is the Relationship Between Your Education and the New World Economy?

Composer, singer, and activist Bob Dylan once wrote, *"The times, they are a-changin'."* Truer words have never been spoken—especially for anyone living at this moment. This is not your daddy's economy. It is not your mama's workplace, and it certainly is not your grandfather's job market. To glide over this simple truth *could be the most costly decision of your life.*

*"New world economy,"* you might say, *"who cares about a world economy?"*

*"China? Who cares about the fluctuating but growing economy in China, Russia, Dubai, or India? I live in Kansas and I'm worried about America's future."*

*"An iPhone? A Blackberry? A podcast? Twittering? I can't even afford my bus ticket this month,"* you may be thinking.

While you may not be alone in thinking, *"This does not matter to me,"* you would be very wrong and exceptionally foolish to think that today's world affairs do not concern **you**, your **education**, and your **future**. Yes, it may be true that you are simply trying to get a degree in medical assisting to work in a small doctor's office in Spokane, Washington—or to obtain a degree in criminal justice to work at the local police department in Union, South Carolina—or to earn a degree in education so that you can teach first grade in Stockton, California. However, no certificate, no degree, no job, and certainly no person will be exempt from the changes and challenges of "the new world economy."

*"So, where does this leave ME?"* you might be asking. It leaves you in an exciting, vulnerable, challenging, scary, and wonderful place. We did NOT include this information to scare you or to turn you off, but rather to give you a jolt, to open your eyes to the world in which you live and the workforce for which you are preparing. We included it to encourage you to use ***every tool*** available, ***every resource*** possible, ***every connection*** imaginable, and ***every ethical, moral, and legal means*** possible to prepare yourself for this ever-changing world in which you live today. The present and the future may not be as rosy as you had hoped, but the future is here, and it is yours. However, you must know this: If you make strategic changes in your life now, you can have a much brighter future. No workplace will be immune from the changes facing our world today, and your very survival depends on your being prepared and knowing how to quickly adapt to and change in a variety of situations.

In his book *The 2010 Meltdown* (2005), Edward Gordon writes, *"Simply stated, today in America, there are just too many people trained for the wrong jobs. Many jobs have become unnecessary, technically obsolete . . . or worse yet, the job/career aspirations of too many current and future workers are at serious odds with the changing needs of the U.S. labor market"* (p. 17).

However, all is not lost to you or your future. People who are well-skilled, possess superb oral and written communication skills, know how to solve problems, have the capacity to change, and can work well with others will *be in high demand* for many years to come.

## What Employers Are Saying

According to the report *College Learning for the New Global Century* (2008), "Employers want college graduates to acquire versatile knowledge and skills. Fully sixty-three percent of employers believe that too many recent college graduates do not have the skills they need to succeed in the global economy and a majority of employers believe that only half or fewer recent graduates have the skills or knowledge needed to advance or to be promoted in their companies." Skills listed as vitally important to employers include:

| | |
|---|---|
| computer literacy | attention to detail |
| accuracy | tact |
| self-confidence | character |
| humor | the ability to learn new skills quickly |

Whether we like it or not, a massive transformation is going on all around us in this country, as well as all over the world. Thriving in the coming years is going to be more difficult than in the past and will require certain new and different abilities and attitudes for us to be successful. You will need to learn and acquire the skills that will make you competitive, give you an edge, and help you master a life filled with changes and challenges. Many of these skills are outlined in the **Ten Essential Cornerstones for Success in a Changing World** (Figure 1.1). These skills will be needed for your success, personal independence, and growth in the new millennium. Study them carefully, as you will see them throughout the text and be asked to reflect upon each one.

By learning to develop these enduring skills, you will be able to carry them with you on your first job, your 10th job, and well into your future. By learning how to change and reinvent yourself with the times and demands of the world, you will position yourself to become—AND remain—competitive.

Why is it important to learn as much as possible about technology?

## 1.1    *Ten Essential Cornerstones for Success in a Changing World*

**PASSION**—The ability to show the world a person who is passionate about his or her mission and who has aligned his or her goals with his or her education, talents, experiences, and skills. A person who cares not only about his or her own success, but also about the world and his or her surroundings—a person who possesses *Civic Literacy* and sees himself or herself as "a citizen of the world."

**MOTIVATION**—The ability to find the *inner strength and personal drive* to get up each day and face the world with an "I can, I will" attitude. The ability to develop a strong personal value and belief system that motivates you when the going gets tough. The ability to know who you are and to never let anyone steal your identity or erode your personal ethics.

**KNOWLEDGE**—The ability to become *highly skilled in a profession* or craft that will enable you to make a good living for yourself and your family in a rapidly changing workplace and to use lifelong learning to maintain your marketable skill sets. The ability to master important academic information beyond that of your major field in areas such as math, science, psychology, history, technology, economics, and communication and to practically apply that information in an evolving and highly technical work environment.

**RESOURCEFULNESS**—The ability to apply *information literacy*—to know WHERE to find information and the resources that will help you be successful in your academic studies and your chosen profession, and HOW to evaluate that information to determine if it is useful and accurate. The ability to look for and to seek new opportunities, options, and outcomes. The ability to imagine, integrate, and implement new ways of solving old problems.

**CREATIVITY**—The ability to use *creativity and innovation* in solving problems, which will enable you to anticipate new and emerging issues and to communicate and use what you know and what you have learned and discovered to answer critical questions and solve complex and demanding problems.

**ADAPTABILITY**—The ability to make good choices based on future opportunities and a changing workplace and to constantly *reinvent yourself* as change brings about necessity and opportunity. The ability to work effectively in a climate of changing priorities and uncertainty.

**OPEN-MINDEDNESS**—The ability to *accept and appreciate a highly diverse workplace* and the inherent differences and cultures that will be commonplace. The ability to listen to others with whom you disagree or with whom you may have little in common and to learn from them and their experiences. The ability to learn a new language, even if your mastery is only at a primitive, broken, conversational level. The ability to conduct yourself in a respectable and professional manner.

**COMMUNICATION**—The ability to develop and maintain healthy, *supportive personal and professional relationships* and to build a solid network of well-connected professionals who can help you and who YOU can help in return.

**ACCOUNTABILITY**—The ability to *accept responsibility and be accountable* for all aspects of your future including your psychological well-being, your spiritual well-being, your relationships, your health, your finances, and your overall survival skills. Basically, you must develop a plan for the future that states, "If this fails, I'll do this," or "If this job is phased out, I'll do this," or "If this resource is gone, I'll use this," or "If this person won't help me, this one will."

**VISION**—The ability to guide your career path in a new global economy and to understand and take advantage of the inherent impact of worldwide competition—even if you live in a small town and work for a small "mom and pop" company. The ability to *"see" what is coming* and prepare for the changes, adapt to circumstances, and grow with grace and style.

# THE M & M THEORY

## What Have Your Money and Your Mama Got to Do with It?

What is the M & M Theory? It is quite simple really. We all pay attention to and try to protect the things that matter most to us. Your "**m**oney and your **m**ama" are symbolic of what you care about. Most people care deeply about what happens to their families, their income, their friends, their careers, and the environment, and most people do care and are concerned about world events and what is happening around them.

However, in the hustle and bustle of finding day care, studying for classes, working a full-time job, cleaning the house, helping the kids with homework, and trying to prepare a meal from time to time, we may lose sight of some of the most important things in our lives. Try to keep this thought in mind: *Your EDUCATION is important, too.* In fact, it is of paramount importance to your future on many levels—culturally, socially, intellectually, and in preparing you for the future. Your education is a part of the M & M Theory because it involves your money—the future financial health of you and your family.

According to one of the leading research sources in higher education, *The Chronicle of Higher Education* (August 29, 2008, p. 18), first-year students have a variety of thoughts regarding a college education and money. Of the 272,000 students who responded to the survey, 74% said that *"being very well-off financially"* was an essential or very important objective; 66% responded that *"the chief benefit of a college education is that it increases one's earning power."* Another interesting finding was that 79% of those responding to the survey stated that they believed that *"through hard work, everybody can succeed in American society."*

How can your friends, classmates and peers help you achieve your goals?

According to the U.S. Census Bureau in their annual report *Education and Training Pay* (2007), people with college degrees can earn considerably more than those who do not have a degree. For a complete look at the earning power of U.S. citizens age 25 and older, look at the Education, Pay, and Unemployment chart in Figure 1.2.

By focusing on money in this section, we do not mean to suggest that the only reason to attend college is to make more money. As a matter of fact, we feel that it is a secondary reason. Many people *without college degrees* earn huge salaries each year. However, as the data in Figure 1.2 suggests, those with college degrees traditionally **earn MORE** money and **experience LESS**

## FIGURE 1.2 *Education, Pay, and Unemployment Statistics of Full-Time Workers, 25 and Over*

| Unemployment Rate | Degree | Mean Earnings |
|---|---|---|
| 1.35% | Professional Degree | $122,480 |
| 1.40% | Doctorate Degree | $108,563 |
| 1.85% | Master's Degree | $80,407 |
| 2.20% | Bachelor's Degree | $66,133 |
| 3.15% | Associate Degree | $47,196 |
| 3.85% | Some College, No Degree | $44,488 |
| 4.35% | High School Graduate | $37,424 |
| 7.40% | Less than High School Graduate | $28,539 |

*Source:* Department of the Census, Department of Labor, 2007.

unemployment. Basically, college should make the road to financial security easier, but college should also be a place where you learn to make decisions about your values, your character, and your future. College can also be a place where you make decisions about the changes that need to occur in your life so that you can effectively manage and prosper in an ever-changing world.

# COLLEGE AND YOU

## Why Is It the Partnership of a Lifetime?

What can college do for you? The list will certainly vary depending on whom you ask, but basically, college can help you develop in the areas listed below. As you read through the list, place a checkmark beside the statements that most accurately reflect which skills you hope to gain from attending college. If there are other skills that you desire to achieve from your college experience, write them at the end of the list.

_____ Grow more self-sufficient and self-confident
_____ Establish and strengthen your personal identity
_____ Understand more about the global world in which you live
_____ Become a more involved citizen in social and political issues
_____ Become more open-minded
_____ Learn to manage your emotions and reactions more effectively
_____ Understand the value of thinking, analyzing, and problem solving
_____ Expand and use your ethical and moral thinking and reasoning skills
_____ Develop commanding computer and information literacy skills
_____ Manage your personal resources such as time and money

How can your college classes help you grow, change, and prosper?

_____ Become more proficient in written, oral, nonverbal, and technical communication
_____ Grow more understanding and accepting of different cultures
_____ Become a lifelong learner
_____ Become more financially independent
_____ Enter a career field that you enjoy

_____ _____

_____ _____

Which skill is THE most important to you? _____

_Discuss_ how you think this skill will help you in your college classes, in your profession, and in your personal life. _____

_____

**2**

BLOOM LEVEL 2
QUESTION

    _The Chronicle of Higher Education's_ annual report mentioned earlier on first-year students does not list _"I want to change"_ as one of the reasons for attending college. However, you are going to experience changes in your attitudes, your values, your actions, and your intellectual character. You are going to notice changes in old relationships and even in the relationships with your family members. Many of the changes will be positive and rewarding. Sure, there will be a few changes that test your nature and temperament, but that is why this chapter is included in this book—to help you understand how to navigate difficult changes and create positive changes in your life by goal setting, planning, hard work, and persistence.

# THE CULTURE OF COLLEGE

## What Are the Basic Truths about College Success?

> *"Forget mistakes. Forget failures. Forget everything except what you're going to do now . . . and do it."*
> —Will Durant

In your lifetime, you will experience many things that influence and alter your views, goals, and livelihood. These may include travel, relationships, and personal victories or setbacks. However, few experiences will have a greater influence than your college experience. College can mean hopes realized, dreams fulfilled, and the breaking down of social and economic walls. To get the most from your college experience and to lay a path to success, it will be important for you to look at your expectations and the vast differences among high school, jobs you may have held, and the culture of college. This section will introduce you to some of the changes you can expect and give you a brief introduction into the "culture of college."

## Basic Truth #1

### SUCCESS IS ABOUT CHOICES, SACRIFICES, AND CHANGE

Life is a series of choices. Hard choices. Easy choices. Right choices. Wrong choices. Nevertheless, the quality of *your life* is determined by the *choices you make* and your willingness to evaluate your life and determine if changes are in order. You will have many important and hard choices in the near future such as deciding whether to devote your time to studying or partying; whether to ask for help in classes that challenge you or give up and drop out; whether to get involved in campus life or "go it alone"; and/or whether to make the sacrifices needed for your future success or take the easy road. Those choices will determine the quality of your future. Some of the choices that you make will force you to step beyond your comfort zone—to move to places that may frighten you or make you uncomfortable. That's OK. That's good. In fact, that's very good.

So what is a *Comfort Zone?* It sounds cozy, doesn't it? Warm and fuzzy. However, do not let the term fool you. A comfort zone is not necessarily a happy and comfortable place. It is simply a place where you are familiar with your surroundings and don't have to work too hard. It is where you feel confident of your abilities, but it is also a place where your growth stops. *It can be a prison and staying there is a cop-out.* Successful people who have won personal and professional victories know that moving beyond one's comfort zone helps in nurturing change, reaching one's potential, and creating opportunities for positive growth.

What sacrifices do you think you'll need to make in your personal life to be academically successful?

## Basic Truth #2

### HIGHER EDUCATION IS A TWO-WAY STREET

Perhaps the first thing that you will notice about higher education is that you have to **give** in order to **receive**. Not only do you have expectations of your institution and instructors, but your institution and instructors have expectations—great expectations—of you. To be successful, you will need to accept substantially more responsibility for your education than you may have in the past. By attending your college of choice, you have agreed to become a part of its community, values, and policies. You now have the responsibility to stand by its code of academic and moral conduct, and you also have the responsibility to give your very best to every class and organization in which you are involved. And, you have a responsibility to YOURSELF to approach this new world with an

# THINKING *for* CHANGE: An Activity for Critical Reflection

After the first week of classes, Devon was very disheartened about the difficulty of the classes for which he was registered. He had not thought that he was going to have so much reading or homework, and he never thought the instructors would be so demanding. He had never been strong at math, but he was just floored at how difficult his beginning math course had become. He failed his first test. He passed his first essay in English, but only with a grade of C. He seriously considered dropping out. It was just too much. It was more than he had expected.

Devon knew, however, that he had to succeed. He looked at his current financial situation, his dead-end job, and his desire to work in the health profession. Dropping out would never get him there. Dropping out would never make him a better, more prepared person. Dropping out would never afford him the opportunity to

provide a better life for his family. However, Devon felt that he was just too far behind to catch up. He was at a loss as to what to do.

Pretend that Devon is enrolled at your institution. In your own words, what would you suggest that Devon do at this point? List at least two things that he could do to ensure his success and that would help him change his mind about dropping out. Think about what services are offered and what people might be of assistance to him.

1. _____
_____

2. _____
_____

open mind, curiosity and enthusiasm. In return, your institution will be responsible for helping you reach your fullest potential and live the life you desire.

So, what are your thoughts at the moment? Respond to the following questions honestly and personally.

1. Thus far, I think my most rewarding class is _____ taught by Mr./Mrs./Ms./Dr. _____

2. I believe this because _____
_____
_____

3. To date, I've learned that he or she expects me to _____
_____

4. To meet this expectation, how will my academic habits have to change?
_____
_____

BLOOM LEVEL 3
QUESTION

## Basic Truth #3

**YOU'RE IN CHARGE HERE—IT'S ALL ABOUT SELF-MOTIVATION AND SELF-RESPONSIBILITY**
ONE person and ONLY one person has the power to determine your thoughts and the direction of your future. It is YOU! You will decide the direction of your future. You are NOT a victim and you will not be treated as a victim at this institution. You will not be allowed to use "Victim Excuses" or employ the "Victim Mentality." This is all about you and your desire to change your life. Higher education is not about others doing the work, but rather about you finding internal motivation and accepting responsibility for your actions, your decisions, your choices, and yourself. It is

## FIGURE 1.3    *Victim and Winner Chart*

| The VICTIM | The WINNER |
|---|---|
| The victim blames others for his or her problems. | The winner accepts responsibility for what happens in his or her life. |
| The victim procrastinates and makes excuses for not doing a good job. | The winner thinks ahead and plans for success. |
| The victim sees adversity as a permanent obstacle. | The winner sees adversity as a way to get stronger. |
| The victim constantly complains and has a negative mentality about most things. | The winner has an optimistic attitude and is pleasant to be with most of the time. |
| The victim does just enough to get by and is happy with poor grades and mediocre accomplishments. | The winner works hard to raise his or her level of achievement and constantly seeks to improve. |
| The victim lets life happen without trying to make things happen. | The winner has a plan and sets goals and works every day to make positive things happen. |
| The victim is always late and often absent and always has an excuse. | The winner is on time, prepared, and rarely ever negligent regarding his or her responsibilities. |
| The victim hangs out with negative people who are troublemakers and party animals and have low ambition and a poor work ethic. | The winner surrounds himself or herself with people who are working hard to make something of themselves and who are encouraging and motivating. |

not about making excuses and blaming others. *You are in charge here.* This is YOUR education, and no one else will be responsible for acquiring the knowledge and skills you will need to survive and thrive. No one else will be able to "give you" personal motivation.

Regardless of your circumstances, that **late paper** for English is not your husband's fault. That **missed lab report** is not your child's problem. Your **tardiness** is not your mother's mistake. That **unread chapter** is not your partner's liability. Likewise, that **98 you scored** on your Drug Calculation Test is yours. That **A you got** on your paper about the criminal justice system is yours. That **B+ you got** on your first math test is yours. This is about YOU! Your life. Your future. Your attitude is going to greatly affect your possibility of success.

Consider the preceding chart (Figure 1.3) describing the differences between a "Victim" and a "Winner."

1. Name one person available to you (personally or professionally) who can offer you support, encourage you, and to whom you can turn when things get tough. _____

   _____

2. Why do you respect and/or admire this person enough to ask him or her for help? _____

   _____

3. Generate a list of three questions you would like to ask this person about his or her life, how he or she "made it," and how he or she overcame adversity.

   1. _____

   2. _____

   3. _____

BLOOM LEVEL 6 QUESTION

## Basic Truth #4

### SELF-MANAGEMENT WILL BE YOUR KEY TO SUCCESS

A major change coming your way involves the workload for your courses and the choices YOU will need to make regarding your schedule and time. You may be assigned a significant amount of reading as homework; in fact, the amount of reading that college classes demand is usually a shock to many students. Although you may have only two or three classes in one day, the basic guideline is that for every hour spent in class, a minimum of 2–3 hours should be spent in review and preparation for the next class.

**QUICK MATH:** If you are taking five classes and are in class for 15 hours per week, you need to spend 30 hours studying; this makes a 45-hour week—5 hours more than a normal workweek for most people! "Not I," you may say, and you may be right. It all depends on how wisely you use your time, how difficult the work is, and how strong your academic background is. We will discuss time management and study techniques later in this text.

## Basic Truth #5

### THIS IS NOT HIGH SCHOOL

It sounds so simple, but this is perhaps the most universal and important truth discussed here: College is very different from high school OR the world of work and perhaps one of the most different places you'll ever encounter. The expectations for four different areas are outlined on the following chart (Figure 1.4). Review each area carefully and consider your past experiences as you study the differences.

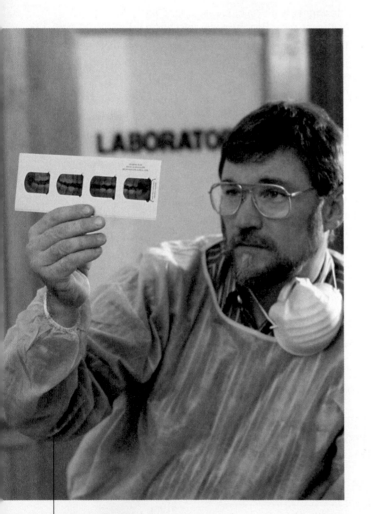

What is the most surprising thing you have learned about your institution's curriculum thus far?

## Basic Truth #6

### ELIMINATING THE "THIS ISN'T HARVARD SYNDROME" WILL BE ESSENTIAL TO YOUR SUCCESS

Some students enter college with little or no perception of how much work is involved or how much effort it is going to take to be successful. They do not think that the local community college or state university they are attending could possibly be *"that difficult."* Many even perceive their college or university to be less rigorous than it actually is. *"It's only Maple State University,"* or *"It's just Trion Technical College,"* some might reason. They do not think that the college they are attending has the academic standards of a Harvard, a Yale, or a Stanford University. The truth is that your college education is what *YOU make of it.* When you graduate and you are interviewing for a job, the name of your institution may hold some weight, but your skills, your passion, your experiences, your knowledge, and your thinking abilities will be the paramount "tipping point."

True, you may not be at Harvard or Yale, but the rigor of your programs, the amount of reading required, the level of math skills needed, and the degree to which critical thinking, communication, and information literacy skills will be required may surprise you. We thus think that it is important for you to dispel the *"This Isn't Harvard Syndrome"* as quickly as possible so that you can prepare yourself for the coursework and requirements ahead and make the most of your college experience.

You've probably already attended a few of your classes and received syllabi from those classes as you read this. Examine the syllabi of two of your current classes. What surprises you the most about what is going to be required of you this semester? Enter your response in the chart on page 17. By embracing these truths about college life, learning, self-motivation, and education in general, you will have taken some very important steps toward your success.

FIGURE

## 1.4  *A Guide to Understanding Expectations*

|  | HIGH SCHOOL | COLLEGE | WORK |
|---|---|---|---|
| **PUNCTUALITY AND ATTENDANCE** | **Expectations:**<br>• State law requires a certain number of days you must attend<br>• The hours in the day are managed for you<br>• There may be some leeway in project dates<br><br>**Penalties:**<br>• You may get detention<br>• You may not graduate<br>• You may be considered a truant<br>• Your grades may suffer | **Expectations:**<br>• Attendance and participation in class are strictly enforced by many professors<br>• Most professors will not give you an extension on due dates<br>• You decide your own schedule and plan your own day<br><br>**Penalties:**<br>• You may not be admitted to class if you are late<br>• You may fail the assignment if it is late<br>• Repeated tardiness is some times counted as an absence<br>• Most professors do not take late assignments | **Expectations:**<br>• You are expected to be at work and on time on a daily basis<br><br>**Penalties:**<br>• Your salary and promotions may depend on your daily attendance and punctuality<br>• You will most likely be fired for abusing either |
| **TEAMWORK AND PARTICIPATION** | **Expectations:**<br>• Most teamwork is assigned and carried out in class<br>• You may be able to choose teams with your friends<br>• Your grade may reflect your participation<br><br>**Penalties:**<br>• If you don't participate, you may get a poor grade<br>• You may jeopardize the grade of the entire team | **Expectations:**<br>• Many professors require teamwork and cooperative learning teams or learning communities<br>• Your grade will depend on your participation<br>• Your grade may depend on your entire team's performance<br>• You will probably have to work on the project outside of class<br><br>**Penalties:**<br>• Lack of participation and cooperation will probably cost you a good grade<br>• Your team members will likely report you to the professor if you do not participate and their grades suffer as a result | **Expectations:**<br>• You will be expected to participate fully in any assigned task<br>• You will be expected to rely on coworkers to help solve problems and increase profits<br>• You will be required to attend and participate in meetings and sharing sessions<br>• You will be required to participate in formal teams and possess the ability to work with a diverse workforce<br><br>**Penalties:**<br>• You will be tagged" as a non-team player<br>• Your lack of participation and teamwork will cost you raises and promotions<br>• You will most likely be terminated |

*(continued)*

## 1.4 *A Guide to Understanding Expectations (continued)*

|  | HIGH SCHOOL | COLLEGE | WORK |
|---|---|---|---|
| **PERSONAL RESPONSIBILITY AND ATTITUDE** | **Expectations:**<br>• Teachers may coach you and try to motivate you<br>• You are required by law to be in high school regardless of your attitude or responsibility level<br><br>Penalties:<br>• You may be reprimanded for certain attitudes<br>• If your attitude prevents you from participating you may fail the class | **Expectations:**<br>• You are responsible for your own learning<br>• Professors will assist you, but there is little "hand holding" or personal coaching for motivation<br>• College did not choose you, you chose it and you will be expected to hold this attitude toward your work<br><br>Penalties:<br>• You may fail the class if your attitude and motivation prevent you from participating | **Expectations:**<br>• You are hired to do certain tasks and the company or institution fully expects this of you<br>• You are expected to be positive and self-motivated<br>• You are expected to model good behavior and uphold the company's work standards<br><br>Penalties:<br>• You will be passed over for promotions and raises<br>• You may be reprimanded<br>• You may be terminated |
| **ETHICS AND CREDIBILITY** | **Expectations:**<br>• You are expected to turn in your own work<br>• You are expected to avoid plagiarism<br>• You are expected to write your own papers<br>• Poor ethical decisions in high school may result in detention or suspension<br><br>Penalties:<br>• You may get detention or suspension<br>• You will probably fail the project | **Expectations:**<br>• You are expected to turn in your own work<br>• You are expected to avoid plagiarism<br>• You are expected to write your own papers<br>• You are expected to conduct research and complete projects based on college and societal standards<br><br>Penalties:<br>• Poor ethical decisions may land you in front of a student ethics committee or a faculty ethics committee or result in expulsion from the college<br>• You will fail the project<br>• You will fail the class<br>• You may face deportation if your visa is dependent on your student status | **Expectations:**<br>• You will be required to carry out your job in accordance with company policies, laws, and moral standards<br>• You will be expected to use adult vision and standards<br><br>Penalties:<br>• Poor ethical decisions may cause you to be severely reprimanded, terminated, or in some cases could even result in a prison sentence |

## Activity

| CLASS | SURPRISING REQUIREMENT | YOUR PLAN FOR SUCCESS |
|-------|------------------------|------------------------|
| #1 | | |
| #2 | | |

# CREATING SUCCESS THROUGH POSITIVE CHANGE

## How Can You Bring Change to Your Daily Life?

Why is change so important to you and your future? Quite simply, change that you direct creates opportunities for you to grow and prosper in ways you may have never imagined. It allows you to become and remain competitive. It allows you to actively live in a world that is fluid and unpredictable. There are several things you need to know about creating success in your life through positive change. Consider the following ideas:

1. **Change is a skill.**   Change is a LEARNED SKILL that any willing person can engage in. Period. Public speaking is a skill. Learning how to drive a car is a skill, and just like those activities, change is a skill, too. You'll need to familiarize yourself with the tools and skills discussed below to bring positive change to your life.

2. **Change takes time.**   Change does not happen immediately at the snap of your fingers. If you've ever taken piano, guitar, or drum lessons, you know it takes time to learn how to play an instrument because it is a skill—just like change. You did not learn to play overnight just as you won't learn everything about math or history or nursing in one semester. Often, change is a slow, systematic series of events that eventually lead you to your desired end.

3. **Change requires an "attitude adjustment."**   As corny or hokey as the following example may sound, a recent contestant on *America's Got Talent* was being interviewed about her chances of success on the show. Queen Emily was an African-American single mother working full time. She had given up her dream of being a professional singer years earlier to raise her children. She stated that before her audition, she stood and looked in the mirror crying. Her only thought was, *"My time has passed; this is never going to happen for me. Never!"* Then she looked herself in the eyes and said, *"Why NOT me? I'm talented. I'm good at performing, and I KNOW I can sing. **WHY NOT ME?**"* Her attitude adjustment was the key to her being able to change her life. She auditioned for the show, surpassed thousands of contestants, and was invited to Los Angeles as one of five finalists. She now performs in a major show in Las Vegas, Nevada.

How can surrounding yourself with positive, upbeat, optimistic people help you with personal change?

"The key to change . . . is to let go of fear."
—Rosanne Cash

# From Ordinary to Extraordinary

## REAL PEOPLE | REAL LIVES | REAL CHANGE

**BILL CLAYTON**
ACE Certified Personal Trainer / Post-Rehabilitation Specialist
Owner/Operator, Clayton Personal Fitness – Las Vegas, NV

*"I was..."* Those are powerful words. For example, *I was* the manager of the gardening department of a major retail chain. *I was* an employee in a shop that prints and mails inserts and flyers. *I was* a rock band drummer for several bands. *I was* a crystal meth addict. Yes . . . *I was!*

It seems strange to write that now, but the term, "I was...." is impossible to erase. My friends and clients often ask me how I managed to go from the life of a meth addict to a personal trainer. The journey was a strange one and often difficult.

I began playing the drums when I was six years old and by the time I was eight, I had my first "garage band." Writing and playing music were my only passions. They were my life. After high school, I worked many odd jobs, but my love of performing never waned.

In my 20's, I had a band that steadily played gigs and I was living the life of a rocker. We traveled. We sang. We partied. We traveled some more and we partied some more . . . and more. Before I really realized what was happening with me, I had become addicted to meth. It was my life. I hung around people who used with me and they became my family. I met Kathy, the woman I would eventually marry, while performing with my band. She and I hit it off even though she knew of my addiction. One evening after we were married, Kathy and I were talking and she mentioned that she would like to have children one day. I wanted children, too. At that moment, the strangest thing came to my mind. I thought, "If she gets pregnant, I'll stop doing meth." How could I be so messed up that I would work to abolish my addiction for a child not yet born, BUT I would not consider trying to stop *just for ME*? That was my wake-up call. I knew I had to change my life. I was 29 years old.

I was one of the lucky ones. I was able to stop "cold turkey" on my own. I know that others are not so lucky. I began to look at my life and tried to determine what I wanted to do. I had to seriously evaluate every aspect of who and what I was. I knew that I had to set goals to get my life back on track.

I had been in a life-threatening motorcycle accident years earlier and remembered the great care I received from my physical therapist. So, I began to look at PT programs and that is when I found the Personal Trainer Program at our local college. Something about this was very attractive to me. Again, I was lucky. I happened to find my passion and my life's vocation without much struggle.

Today, after working through my addiction, surviving a divorce, and mourning the death of my mom, I can say without a doubt that I am one of the luckiest people on earth. Because I was willing to change and stay committed to finding a better life, I own my own gym, hold certifications from every major fitness and rehabilitation organization in America, and count each day as a true gift.

> My friends and clients often ask me how I managed to go from the life of a meth addict to a personal trainer.

## EXTRAORDINARY REFLECTION

**Read the following statement and respond to it in your online journal or class notebook.**

Mr. Clayton mentions that he was one of the "lucky ones." What role do you think luck plays in one's success? Is there a difference among luck, readiness, and action? If so, what is it?

4. **Change demands action.** While circumstances and desire may drive the need for change in your life, don't lose sight of the fact that ultimately, change is an action. It is something you must do—mentally, physically, spiritually, and intellectually. Just as Queen Emily in the previous example knew, without action by her, her life was not going to change.

5. **Change is about working toward something, not running away from something.** If you want true, lasting, meaningful change in your life, you have to think about it as working toward good, positive, useful things, not as running away from bad, negative, unpleasant things. "Working toward" is *positive and internal*. "Running away from" is *negative and external*. Try to work **toward a goal** and not **run from a problem**.

6. **Change is about letting go and holding on.** As with any new endeavor, you will have to decide what is working in your life and what is not. By doing so, you can decide what you need to hold onto and what you finally need to let go of. You will want to hold onto the positive strengths and talents you have while letting go of the negative, destructive attitudes that you may have held in the past.

# ELIMINATING ROADBLOCKS TO YOUR SUCCESS

## What Should You Do if Your Fears and Self-Talk Try to Derail Your Efforts to Change?

Try as you might, sometimes harmful emotions, fear of the unknown, and that nagging little voice inside your head (negative self-talk) can cause you problems. Negative self-talk usually appears when you are afraid, uneasy, hurt, angry, depressed, or lonely. By the time you read this, you may have experienced these feelings. When you experience change, your body, mind, and soul typically go through a process of physical and emotional change as well. Learning to recognize these symptoms of change in order to control them can help you control the stress that can accompany change.

**LISTEN TO YOURSELF FOR A FEW DAYS.** Are you more of an optimist or a pessimist? Do you hear yourself whining, complaining, griping, and finding fault with everything and everybody around you? Do you blame others for things that are wrong in your life? Do you blame your bad grades on your professors? Do you feel that someone else is responsible for your unhappiness? If these thoughts or comments are in your head, you are suffering from the *"I CAN'T Syndrome"* (**I**rritated, **C**ontaminated, **A**ngry, **N**egative **T**houghts). This pessimistic condition can negatively influence every aspect of your life, from your self-esteem to your motivation level to your academic performance, your relationships, and your career success.

If you want to eliminate *I CAN'T* from your life, consider the following tips:

- ☑ Think about the many positive aspects of your life and show gratitude for them.
- ☑ Work every day to find the good in people, places, and things.
- ☑ Eliminate negative thoughts that enter your mind before you begin your day.
- ☑ Discover what is holding you back and what you need to push yourself forward.
- ☑ Visualize your success—visualize yourself actually being who and what you want to be.
- ☑ Locate and observe positive, optimistic people and things in your life.

**DID YOU KNOW**

**ABRAHAM LINCOLN** was born on February 12, 1809, in Hardin, Kentucky, to two uneducated farmers. They lived in a one-room log cabin. His mother died when he was 10 years old, just a few years after his father had moved the family to Illinois.

He was raised in great poverty and had only 18 months of formal schooling. He studied very hard on his own and learned to read, write, and do mathematical problems. He went on to become a lawyer. One of his law partners once said of him, *"His ambition was a great engine that knew no rest."*

He lost the love of his life when he was 26, suffered a nervous breakdown at age 27, failed in business twice, lost eight elections, and suffered the death of three children all BEFORE he became our president and changed the course of our nation. On Good Friday, April 14, 1865, Lincoln was assassinated at Ford's Theatre in Washington, D.C., by John Wilkes Booth. (Adapted from whitehouse.gov)

*"You gain strength, experience, and confidence by every experience where you stop to look fear in the face. You must do the thing you think you cannot."*
—Eleanor Roosevelt

**Tips for Personal Success**

Consider the following tips for adjusting to the many changes in the days to come:

► Approach change with an open mind.

► Don't be afraid to ask people in your class or your professor questions about things that are confusing or unclear.

► If you are not technologically savvy, find out what other resources are available to you.

Now it is your turn. Create a list of at least three more tips that you would offer a fellow classmate to assist him or her in bringing about positive change in his or her life.

1. _____

2. _____

3. _____

☑ Make a list of who helps you, supports you, and helps you feel positive—then make a point to be around them more often.

☑ Take responsibility for your own actions and their consequences.

☑ Force yourself to find five positive things a day for which to be thankful.

You've seen the differences between an optimist and a pessimist. They are both everywhere—at work, at school, and maybe in your own family. Think of the optimist for a moment. You've probably sat next to him or her in one of your classes or seen him or her at work—the person who always seems to be happy, motivated, bubbling with personality, organized, and ready for whatever comes his or her way. Optimists greet people as they enter the room, respond in class, volunteer for projects, and have a presence about them that is positive and lively. You may even look at an optimist out of the corner of your eye and wonder, "What is he on?"

Positive, upbeat, and motivated people are easy to spot. You can see their attitude in the way they walk, the way they carry themselves, the way they approach people, and the way they treat others.

Be wary, however, of *"the others,"* the ones you need to avoid. Whiners. Degraders. Attackers. Manipulators. Pessimists. Backstabbers. Abusers. Cowards. Two-faced racists, sexists, ageists, and people who are homophobic or ethnocentric. These people carry around an aura so negative that it can almost be seen as a dark cloud above them. They degrade others because they do not like themselves. They find fault with everything because their own lives are a mess. They do nothing and then attack you for being motivated and trying to improve your life. We call them ***contaminated people***. Contaminated people are unhappy with who they are. To make themselves feel better, they try to tear down people who are the opposite of what they are. They belittle positive actions and try to make others' lives as miserable as their own.

Sure, everyone has bad days and bad stretches in his or her life. ***This is not the person*** we are talking about here. With contaminated people, being negative and trying to bring you down is epidemic in their lives. It is the way they operate all the time. It is constant. Having a bad day and complaining is normal for some people at various times, but contaminated people see life (and you) as negative and bad on an hourly and daily basis.

# BUILDING A NEW YOU

## How Can You Change Your Life Through Goal Setting?

Positive change can be brought about in several ways, but the most effective way is through goal setting and having a "change plan." Think about what you really want or need to change in your life. More importantly, think about why you want "this thing" and what it is going to mean to your life. By thinking about what you want, what needs to change, and where you want to be, goals become easier to achieve.

## Characteristics of Attainable Goals

The following characteristics will help you in your quest to bring about change through effective goal setting. Goals should be:

► **Reasonable**    Your goal should be a challenge for you, but also within reason based on your abilities.

▶ **Believable**     To achieve a goal, you must really believe it is within your capacity to achieve it.

▶ **Measurable**     Your goal needs to be concrete and measurable in some way.
Avoid such terms as "earn a lot" or "lose some weight."

▶ **Adaptable**     Your goals may need to be adapted to changing circumstances in your life.

▶ **Controllable**     Your goals should be within your own control; they should not depend on the whims and opinions of anyone else.

▶ **Desirable**     To attain a difficult goal, you must want it very badly. You should never work toward something just because *someone else* wants it.

## ESSENTIAL CORNERSTONE

**Vision:**
How can having a clear vision of your future and what you want help you become a more optimistic person?

**Social Networking Moment:**
Share your response to this Essential Cornerstone with peers in your social network. Choose two responses from your peers and respond to their postings.

## How to Write Your Goals to Bring about Positive Change

*"I will pass my next math test with a B or better"* is an example of a short-term goal. *"I will purchase my first home in 7 to 10 years"* is probably a long-term goal. During college, more of your goals may be short term than long term, but you can certainly begin setting both. Goals can be lofty and soaring, but great goals can also be as simple as *"I will spend two hours at the park with my children tomorrow afternoon."*

Well-written, exciting, and effective goals include:

▶ a goal statement with a target date,

▶ action steps,

▶ a narrative statement,

▶ an "I deserve it" statement, and

▶ a personal signature.

The **goal statement** should be specific and measurable; that is, it should entail some tangible evidence of the goal's achievement and have a **target date** and a timeline for accomplishing your goal. Your goal statement MUST also use an action verb. An example of a goal statement with an action verb and target date is: "*I will* lose 10 pounds in six weeks" or "*I am going to* join a campus club by the fifth week of this term." These are much more powerful statements than: "I am thinking about joining a club" or "I wanna have a new car."

After you write the goal statement, you'll need to create **specific action steps** that explain exactly what you are going to do to reach your goal. There is no certain number of steps; it all depends on your goal and your personal commitment. An example of action steps for weight loss might be: (1) I WILL join the campus health center, (2) I WILL meet with a personal trainer on campus, (3) I WILL set an appointment with a nutrition counselor in the health center, (4) I WILL . . .

The next step is to write a **narrative statement** about what your goal accomplishment will mean to you and how your life will change after you reach this goal. For example, if

What exactly is it going to take to achieve your biggest, most important goals?

your goal is to lose 30 pounds, paint a "verbal picture" of how your life is going to look once this goal has been reached. Your verbal picture may include statements such as: "I'll be able to wear nicer clothes." "I'll feel better." "I'll be able to ride my bicycle again." "My self-esteem will be stronger." If your goals don't offer you significant rewards, you are not likely to stick to your plan.

Next, write two reasons why you deserve this goal. This is called your **"I Deserve It Statement."** It may seem simple, but this is a complex issue. Many people do not follow through on their goals because deep down, they don't feel they deserve them. The narrative statement helps you understand how your life will look once the goal is met, but your "I deserve it statement" asks you to consider *why* you deserve this goal.

Finally, **sign your goal statement**. This is an imperative step in that your signature shows that you are making a personal commitment to see this goal to fruition. This is your name. Use it with pride. Use the goal sheet in on page 23 to build your goals.

CHANGING IDEAS TO *Reality*

**REFLECTIONS ON CHANGE AND GOAL SETTING**

The transition from one place to another is seldom easy, even when the change is one you want. Entering college has given you the opportunity to assume new roles, develop new friendships, meet new people, work under different circumstances, and perhaps adjust your lifestyle. It is an opportunity to improve who you are at this moment or to build an entirely new person. College helps you do this. Going to college gives you the opportunity to reflect on your strengths and consider areas where you might need to change. These changes form the very essence of the college experience; they create wonderful new experiences and help you discover who you really are and what you have to offer the world.

As you reflect upon this chapter, keep the following pointers in mind:

▶ Evaluate your reason(s) for attending college and what it means to your life.

▶ Use goal setting to help you direct changes in your life.

▶ Don't just let change happen; get involved in your own life and learning.

▶ Focus on the positive by eliminating your negative self-talk.

▶ Keep your sense of humor.

▶ Be courageous by facing your fears, before they derail you.

"A possibility was born the day you were born,
and it will live as long as you live."
—R. Burak

# My Personal Goal

To help you get started, use this goal-setting sheet as a template for this and future goals.

**Name** _____

**Goal Statement** (with action verb and target date)   _____

_____

_____

**Action Steps** (concrete things you plan to do to reach your goal)

1. _____

2. _____

3. _____

4. _____

5. _____

**Narrative Statement** (how your life will look when you reach your goal) _____

_____

_____

_____

_____

_____

_____

**I deserve this goal because:**

1. _____

_____

2. _____

_____

**I hereby make this commitment to myself.**

_____                    _____
My Signature                                              Date

# KNOWLEDGE in BLOOM

## Bringing Positive Change to Your Life

Each chapter-end assessment is based on *Bloom's Taxonomy of Learning.* See the inside front cover for a quick review.

### UTILIZES LEVELS 1–6 OF THE TAXONOMY

**EXPLANATION:** After reading and reflecting thus far, you may have identified several changes that you need to make in your academic or personal life. Also, changes may have been thrust upon you by choices you or those around you have made. The following model provides a method for bringing positive changes into your life and/or reshaping the changes over which you had little control.

**PROCESS:** Based on Bloom's Taxonomy, the **Change Implementation Model** asks you to consider questions and recommends actions at each level of learning. The chart moves from less difficult questions (Levels 1, 2, 3) to more challenging questions (Levels 4, 5, 6). To begin the change process in your life, follow the steps in this chapter-end activity.

**Step 1:** Review the steps of the **Change Implementation Model** based on **Bloom's Taxonomy.**

| | |
|---|---|
| **LEVEL 1 — REMEMBER** | *Describe* one behavior, belief, or action that you need to change in your life. Also, *list* the possible obstacles that you might encounter. |
| **LEVEL 2 — UNDERSTAND** | *Explain* why this change needs to occur in order for you to be successful. Also, *give two examples* of the options available to you at college, at home, or in the community for making the desired change. |
| **LEVEL 3 — APPLY** | *Using* the information from Levels 1 and 2, *show* your plan (action steps) to overcome the obstacles listed above. |
| **LEVEL 4 — ANALYZE** | *Compare* your current action steps to the steps you have previously taken to overcome obstacles and enact change. What conclusions can be drawn from this comparison? |
| **LEVEL 5 — EVALUATE** | Pretend that someone very close to you asks what you are doing with this plan and why. Write a detailed paragraph *justifying* what you are doing, why you need to do it, and how it is going to positively affect your life. |
| **LEVEL 6 — CREATE** | Based on the information you have gathered above from investigation and reflection, *design your plan* to bring about this change in your life. Consider using the goal-setting format illustrated in this chapter to create a plan and action steps that are truly unique to you. |

**Step 2:** After studying the change model above, read the following fictional scenario in which you encounter difficulty in Accounting 101.

You enter your Accounting 101 class eager to take the first course in your major field. You are shocked to find that the professor begins lecturing on the first day. Not only is the material difficult to understand, so is the professor, whose first language is not English.

For homework, the professor assigns two chapters to read per class, but the lectures are not based on material found in the textbook. You try to study as you had in high school but now you feel overwhelmed and isolated. The material is much harder.

After three weeks and a failed first test, you notice that the students who passed the test have formed study groups, something that you once thought only the brightest students did.

Using the **Change Implementation Model,** you decide to make positive changes in your study habits. As an example, plans for change are shown in Step 3.

**Step 3:** Review this EXAMPLE and determine how you might use the **Change Implementation Model** to enact changes to save your grade in Accounting 101.

## LEVEL 1—REMEMBERING

*Identify* one behavior, belief, or action that you need to change in your life. Also, *list* the possible obstacles that you might encounter.

If I could, I would change my study habits in accounting and become stronger in my math skills.

Obstacles: fear of change, shyness, pride, and time constraints

## LEVEL 2—UNDERSTANDING

*Explain* why this change needs to occur in order for you to be successful. Also, *give two examples* of the options available to you at your college, home, or in the community for making the desired change.

Why change is needed: Weak math skills are causing me to fail accounting.

Campus: tutoring center and math lab

Professor's office hours

Community: Aunt works in accounting office

## LEVEL 3—APPLYING

*Using* the information from Levels 1 and 2, *show* your plan (action steps) to overcome the obstacles listed above.

Step 1—I will join a study group.

Step 2—I will make an appointment for tutoring in the math lab.

Step 3—I will talk to my advisor about services available.

Step 4—I will plan at least five hours per week to study for my accounting class.

Step 5—I will seek help from my aunt who is an accountant.

## LEVEL 4—ANALYZING

*Compare* your current action steps to the steps you have previously taken to overcome obstacles and enact change. What conclusions can be drawn from this comparison?

Past: I took notes in class, looked them over before a test.

New: Join study group, go to tutoring center and math lab

New: Talk with advisor

New: Meet with my aunt for advice and assistance

Conclusion: In taking personal responsibility for my education, taking calculated risks to bring about change, and asking for help, I'm more likely to pass accounting.

## LEVEL 5—EVALUATING

Pretend that someone very close to you asks what you are doing with this plan and why. Write a detailed paragraph justifying what you are doing, why you need to do it, and how it is going to positively affect your life.

I am working so hard to pass accounting because I want this degree and I want the knowledge of how to run my own business. If I don't change my habits, I will not pass accounting and I will not have this degree. Without this degree, I will most likely have to work in low-paying jobs for the rest of my life. By asking for help, spending more time studying, and spending more time around people who have some of the same interests, I can develop the skills to graduate, start my own business, and help my family out financially.

## LEVEL 6—CREATING

Based on the information you have gathered above from investigation and reflection, *design your plan* to bring about this change in your life. Consider using the goal-setting format illustrated in this chapter to create a plan and action steps that are truly unique to you.

**Goal:** I WILL get involved with a study group, schedule a tutor, and spend at least five hours per week studying for accounting. I will do this by the *end of this week.*

**Action Steps:**

Step 1—I will join a study group/get an accounting tutor.

Step 2—I will talk to my advisor about services available.

Step 3—I will study five hours per week for accounting class.

Step 4—I will work w/ my boss to design a plan for more study time.

Step 5—I will meet with my aunt once a week to get her help.

**Narrative Statement:** Basically, by getting involved and not trying to do this alone, I will begin to enjoy college more and do better in my classes.

**I DESERVE this goal because** I have the courage to ask for help and the intelligence to put my pride aside and seek assistance. I deserve to learn this material so that I can successfully run my own business.

**Step 4:** After studying the **Change Implementation** example, focus on a few things that you might want to change about your own academic life such as study habits, motivation level, financial or time management, or your attitude. Now, choose **one** of the major changes you wish to incorporate into your life from the list. Using the Change Implementation Model, devise a strategy to effect this change.

---

### LEVEL 1—REMEMBERING

*Identify* one behavior, belief, or action that you need to change in your life. Also, *list* the possible obstacles that you might encounter.

---

### LEVEL 2—UNDERSTANDING

*Explain* why this change needs to occur in order for you to be successful. Also, *give two examples* of the options available to you at college, at home, or in the community for making the desired change.

---

### LEVEL 3—APPLYING

*Using* the information from Levels 1 and 2, *show* your plan (action steps) to overcome the obstacles listed above.

---

### LEVEL 4—ANALYZING

*Compare* your current action steps to the steps you have previously taken to overcome obstacles and enact change. What conclusions can be drawn from this comparison?

---

### LEVEL 5—EVALUATING

Pretend that someone very close to you asks what you are doing with this plan and why. Write a detailed paragraph justifying what you are doing, why you need to do it, and how it is going to positively affect your life.

---

### LEVEL 6—CREATING

Based on the information you have gathered above from investigation and reflection, *design your plan* to bring about this change in your life. Consider using the goal-setting format illustrated in this chapter to create a plan and action steps that are truly unique to you.

# SQ3R *Mastery* STUDY SHEET

| | |
|---|---|
| **EXAMPLE QUESTION** *(from page 11)*<br>What are the six basic truths about the culture of college? | **ANSWER:** |
| **EXAMPLE QUESTION** *(from page 21)*<br>Why must goals be measurable? | **ANSWER:** |
| **AUTHOR QUESTION** *(from page 11)*<br>Why is it important to know and understand the basic "truths" about college success? | **ANSWER:** |
| **AUTHOR QUESTION** *(from page 14)*<br>What is the "This Isn't Harvard" syndrome? | **ANSWER:** |
| **AUTHOR QUESTION** *(from page 17)*<br>Why does change take time? | **ANSWER:** |
| **AUTHOR QUESTION** *(from page 22)*<br>Explain the "I can't" syndrome (from page 19). | **ANSWER:** |
| **AUTHOR QUESTION** *(from page 21)*<br>What is a narrative statement? | **ANSWER:** |
| **YOUR QUESTION** *(from page ____)* | **ANSWER:** |
| **YOUR QUESTION** *(from page ____)* | **ANSWER:** |
| **YOUR QUESTION** *(from page ____)* | **ANSWER:** |
| **YOUR QUESTION** *(from page ____)* | **ANSWER:** |
| **YOUR QUESTION** *(from page ____)* | **ANSWER:** |

Finally, after answering these questions, recite this chapter's major points in your mind. Consider the following general questions to help you master this material.

▶ What was it about?
▶ What does it mean?
▶ What was the most important thing I learned? Why?
▶ What were the key points to remember?

# CHAPTER 2
# ENGAGE

## DEVELOPING YOUR PERSONAL AND ACADEMIC PASSION TO PERSIST IN COLLEGE

"To be successful you need to find something to hold on to, something to motivate you, something to inspire you."

—Tony Dorsett

**PART ONE** CHANGING YOUR THOUGHTS

# WHY READ THIS CHAPTER?

## What's in it for me?

WHY is personal motivation so vital to my success and persistence? WHY is it important to understand and work with my professors, advisors, and counselors? WHY is self-esteem important to my personal motivation? WHY will information on ethics and academic integrity help me at school, at work, or at home?

Why? Because your success depends—to a great extent—on personal motivation and learned optimism. First, you have to decide what you want in life, learn to put past failures and challenges aside, and focus on what you are becoming. You have to physically, mentally, and emotionally engage in motivating yourself to accomplish your goals and dreams. No one else can do that for you. Right now—and for the next few years of college—you are literally laying the foundation for the person you will become. You are deciding to excel or just get by. You are deciding to pay the price to graduate with a college degree or to become a dropout. You are deciding to either take control of your life or let life control you. Developing a passion for learning and personal development can be a critical tool for expanding your internal motivation and drive.

*By carefully reading this chapter and taking the information provided seriously, you will be able to:*

1. Understand the power of motivation and the difference between internal and external motivation.
2. Define, discuss, and use the Cornerstones of Personal and Professional Success.
3. Understand the value of developing a positive, optimistic attitude in overcoming your doubts and fears.
4. Develop a strong and enduring "Guiding Life Statement" based on your values.
5. Understand the impact of self-esteem on your values, motivation, attitude, and performance.

# CHAPTER 2 / ENGAGE

*"The moment you begin to do what you really want to do, your life becomes a totally different kind of life."*

—B. Fuller

**NAME:** Brannon Sulka
**INSTITUTION:** Clemson University, Clemson, SC
**MAJOR:** History
**AGE:** 19

Being in college is very different from being in high school and the transition can be quite difficult for a lot of people, myself included. Knowing how to "stick with it" is going to be a monumental asset to you. Persistence means *pushing on*—even when times get tough and you feel like giving up. While in college, if you don't learn how to face challenges, deal with them head-on, take care of your body and mind, and tell yourself, "I am not going to quit," the rest of your life may be very difficult. Your future may not hold all of the things you want and need. That is what this chapter is all about: learning how to hold on, how to push yourself, and where to go for assistance. It is also about never being afraid to ask for help.

I am not only a full-time student, but also an athlete. Practice as an athlete is extremely physical, mentally grueling, and at times, not much fun. But just like studying something that you don't want to study or writing a paper you don't want to write, it's what has to be done in order to succeed. That's why persistence is vitally important when it comes to doing well in college. I have learned that you not only have to push yourself to do things to improve, you also have to push yourself to do the "right" things. When you are faced with a difficult assignment or something that seems beyond your ability, you can't just give up or turn in work that is not your best. You have to find it within yourself to overcome procrastination, draw from your inner motivation, and stay positive.

When I'm practicing on the field and my joints begin to hurt and I'm tired and weary, these are the moments when I don't think I can go on. However, when these times arise, I think about "the finish line." I think about winning. I think about doing my very best and before I know it, I'm engaged in the activity and nothing can stop me. Recently, for example, by pushing myself harder and further, I ran my best race ever. I trusted my coach's advice, pressed on, and set a new personal record. There is no greater feeling in the world than overcoming obstacles and achieving your best. This is true of your academic work as well. In college, you'll be required to read more, study more, take more tests, and write more papers, but if you do your best, never give up, and face your challenges with a positive attitude, you will be successful. The information in this chapter can help you learn to develop an attitude of motivation, persistence, and winning.

# SCAN & QUESTION

In the preface of this book (page xix), you read about the **SQ3R Study Method**. Right now, take a few moments, **scan this chapter**, and on page 57, write **five questions** that you think will be important to your mastery of this material. In addition to the two questions below, you will also find five questions from your authors. Use one of your *"On The Test"* stickers to flag this page for easy reference.

**EXAMPLES:**

▶ **What is the difference between internal and external motivation?** (from page 32)

▶ **How can developing a guiding statement help with persistence?** (from page 50)

# THE POWER AND PASSION OF MOTIVATION

## Is Motivation Really That Essential to College Persistence?

Motivation can change your life! *Read that statement again. Motivation can change your life!* Ask any successful businessperson. Ask your favorite athlete or actor. Ask your classmates who pass every exam, project, or paper with an A. It is their burning desire—their aspiration to succeed, to live an exceptional life, and to reach their goals—that changed their lives and got them to where they are today. Motivation is a force that can transform your attitude, alter the course of your performance, intensify your actions, illuminate your future, and, yes, help you stay in college and perform well. Motivation can help you live a life that reflects your true potential, and motivation can also help you through many rough times and harsh adversity.

Have you ever faced adversity and heavy odds when attempting to do something? Almost everyone has. If you are one of the people who has refused to let adversity hold you back, faced your fears, and continued with the project at hand, then you know how it feels to thrive and survive. You know the power of motivation. You know the feeling of winning. You know the value of persistence.

Conversely, have you ever given up on something and regretted it later? Have you ever looked back and asked yourself, "What would my life be like if only I had done this or that?" Have you ever made a decision or acted in a way that cost you dearly? If you have, then you know how difficult it can be to begin new projects or face the future with motivation. You know the feeling of defeat. Understand this, however: Defeat DOES NOT have to be a part of your life. It may be a *part of your journey,* but it *does not have to be a permanent part of your life*.

So, what is *Persistence*, and what does motivation have to do with it? The word *persistence* means that you are going to perservere—that you have found a way to stick it out, found a way to make it work, and found a way *to not give up*. That is what this chapter is all about—finding internal motivation, taking initiative, and not waiting until something goes wrong to seek help.

There are two types of motivation: **external** and **internal**. *External motivation* is the weaker of the two because, as the word "external" suggests, there are *external forces or people* causing you to do something. You do not own the motivation. External motivators may be things or people such as your parents, spouse, or partner pushing you to complete your degree; your supervisor telling you to do "x, y, or z" or you will be fired; or even your professor giving you an exam to make sure you have read Chapter 2. You may do the things asked of you, but your reason for doing them is external. External motivation may involve manipulation, pressure, or maybe even fear. You do not necessarily choose to do these things on your own. External motivation can help with persistence to a certain degree, but internal motivation can and will help you more.

***Internal motivation***, however, is uniquely yours. It is *energy* inside of you—energy that pushes YOU to go after what YOU want. Internal motivation is a strong and driving force because you own it. It comes from deep within your soul. There are no external forces or people telling you that you must do a certain action—this motivation comes from your desire *to be something, to have something, to attain a goal that you truly desire, or to solve a problem.* Successful people live in the world of internal motivation or find ways to **convert** external motivation into internal motivation.

ESSENTIAL CORNERSTONE

**Vision:**
How can having a clear vision of your future and what you want to accomplish help you convert external motivators into internal motivators?

**Social Networking Moment:**
Share your response to this Essential Cornerstone with peers in your social network. Choose two responses from your peers and respond to their postings.

A simple example of needing to make this conversion may be that your current degree requires you to take classes that seem to have no value or purpose. You may ask yourself, *"Why would a theater major have to take two classes in college algebra?"* The class is hard, math is not your thing, the chapters are frustrating and difficult to read, and math has little to do with your interests, career goals, or overall life plan. The challenge for you is to find an internal reason to give this class your best. You need to find a rationale for how math is going to help you, now and in the future. This is called ***internalizing***. Perhaps you want to own your own theater, which is a business and which will require the use of math. Internalizing the content of this math class and its requirements can motivate you because now, you see its potential usefulness to your future.

By converting this external motivation (a requirement for your degree) into internal motivation (something that can help you run your business), the math class will become easier and more relevant because you have found a way to link it to your success, your goals, your money, your health, your family, or your overall life plan. By silencing your negative self-talk about math (*"I hate math," "Math is so stupid," "I'm going to fail this class"*), you are able to internalize the rewards of the class and own the outcome. You have made a conversion. Consider the following exercise:

---

FIGURE

**2.1** *Seeing the Importance*

Think about a class that is required for your degree that seems to have no relevance to you or your career field. (You may have to look at your college catalog to check your degree requirements.) What courses do you think you are going to have to work at to convert? One example is given below. We have also provided space for you to do several conversions of your own.

| MY MAJOR IS THEATER/ACTING | HOW CAN THIS CLASS HELP ME IN MY CHOSEN PROFESSION? |
|---|---|
| Seemingly irrelevant Class #1 HISTORY | ✓ A class in history can help me understand the historical and social context in which the plays I'm studying were written. ✓ A class in history can help me understand more about scene design and period costumes. |
| MY MAJOR IS _____ | HOW CAN THIS CLASS HELP ME IN MY CHOSEN PROFESSION? |
| Seemingly irrelevant Class #1 Seemingly irrelevant Class #2 | |

# What Is the Relationship Between Motivation and Maslow?

One important way to think about motivation is to consider the work of Abraham Maslow, a renowned psychologist who in 1943 introduced ***The Hierarchy of Basic Needs*** in his landmark paper *A Theory of Human Motivation*. His basic premise is that EVERY human being is motivated by a set of basic needs and that we will do whatever it takes to have these things in our lives. The bottom four levels are what he calls deficiency needs, and they include things such as the need for food, air, water, security, family, health, sexual intimacy, self-esteem, achievement, and respect from others. The top level, self-actualization, is called a psychological need and it involves personal growth and fulfillment. See Figure 2.2.

    *Self-actualization* is perhaps the most obscure and abstract need to understand, but it is the most important when it comes to motivation. Maslow suggests that we all have a basic, driving desire to matter; to have a life where we are doing what we were meant to do. Self-actualization can also be described as living at our "peak" as fully engaged people. The renowned psychologist, author, and speaker Dr. Wayne Dyer describes self-actualization as meaning ***"You MUST be what you CAN be."*** By this, he suggests that if you know you are living a life that is "less" than the life you know you are capable of living, true happiness will never be yours.

FIGURE **2.2** *Maslow's Hierarchy of Basic Needs*

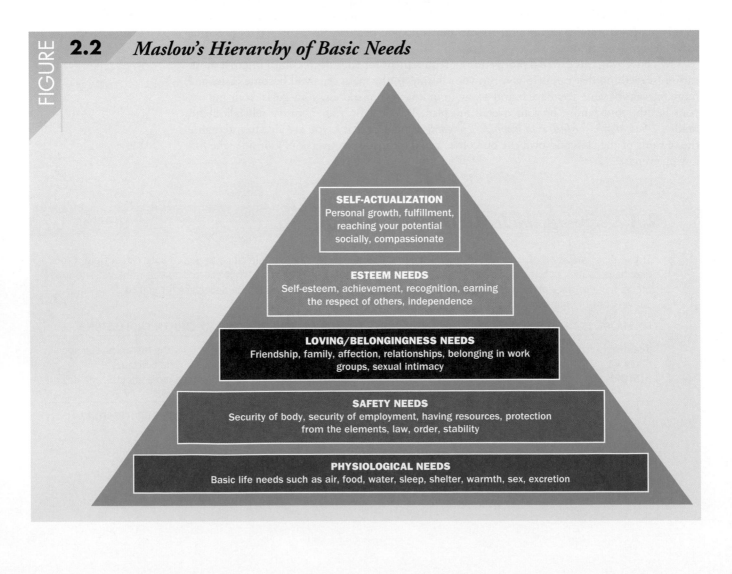

**SELF-ACTUALIZATION**
Personal growth, fulfillment, reaching your potential socially, compassionate

**ESTEEM NEEDS**
Self-esteem, achievement, recognition, earning the respect of others, independence

**LOVING/BELONGINGNESS NEEDS**
Friendship, family, affection, relationships, belonging in work groups, sexual intimacy

**SAFETY NEEDS**
Security of body, security of employment, having resources, protection from the elements, law, order, stability

**PHYSIOLOGICAL NEEDS**
Basic life needs such as air, food, water, sleep, shelter, warmth, sex, excretion

# ACHIEVING YOUR POTENTIAL AND INCREASING YOUR MOTIVATION

## What Is the Ten-Point Plan for Personal and Professional Success?

"I am a winner."
"I fail at everything I do."

"I am a dedicated person."
"I don't really care about anything."

"I can't wait for my day to start."
"I hate getting up in the morning."

As you can see from the two different perspectives above, your attitude and perspective on how you approach life, relationships, problems, and goals can mean the difference between being a motivated, inspired, and successful person and being a weary, frightened, and unsuccessful person.

The reason that we have included this ***Ten-Point Plan for Personal and Professional Success*** is to help you see that by focusing on you—by becoming a person who has a plan and knows where you're going, discovering what you have to offer, and using your college services to assist you—your motivation and passion for learning and growing will flourish. By knowing more about yourself and your institution, you can then establish a clearer vision of your true potential. Take your time and read each point carefully. Consider the questions asked and complete the chapter activities to assist you with your motivation and persistence plan.

*"Watch your thoughts, they become words. Watch your words, they become actions. Watch your actions, they become habits. Watch your habits, they become character. Watch your character, it becomes your destiny."*
—Frank Outlaw

## Point #1

### DEVELOP A NEW ATTITUDE AND STRIVE FOR EXCELLENCE

Your attitude—new or old, good or bad, positive or negative—belongs to you. As you learned in Chapter 1, growing and changing may require a shift in attitude and actions. If your attitude needs changing, no one else can change it for you. Now is the perfect time to begin changing your attitude if it needs an adjustment because small changes in the way you approach life can mean major changes to your success throughout your college career. Your attitude adjustment can also help you make the pursuit of excellence a daily habit.

Just as some people embrace the attitude of ***learned helplessness*** (i.e., letting your past and people in your family or personal community and their failures dictate your future), you can just as easily embrace the attitude of learned optimism and excellence. A ***pessimist*** finds bad news in most situations; he or she lives in a world that has a cloud overhead all the time. ***Optimists***, on the other hand, can handle bad news and difficult challenges because they have a positive way of viewing the world. Optimists learn how to determine why things "went wrong" and can adjust and fix the underlying problem. They know that the road to excellence may not be easy, but they also know that reaching excellence is possible.

People actually create their own success, reach their goals, and become successful by embracing a positive outlook on life. Conversely, a great deal of personal misery and failure is caused by adopting a bad attitude and by embracing negative feelings and ***self-defeating behaviors***. Take the following assessment (Figure 2.3) to determine your current attitudes.

*"NEVER leave well enough alone. If it ain't broke, fix it; take fast and make it faster; take smart and make it smarter; take good and make it great."*
—Cigna advertisement

"Have the courage to say no. Have the courage to face the truth. Do the right thing because it is right. These are the magic keys to living your life with integrity."

—Clement Stone

Basically, ethics is the *accepted* moral code or standard by which we all live, and that code is communicated in many ways, including through our relationships with others. Codes of ethics vary from culture to culture, country to country, college to college, and group to group, but each carries with it certain "rules" and punishments by which members of that culture, country, college, or group are expected to live.

Making professional or personal ethical decisions usually involves three factors or levels, as shown in Figure 2.5. They include: the *law*, *fairness*, and your *conscience* (Anderson and Boldt, 2008). You might also consider adding three other levels: *time*, *pride*, and *publicity*.

If you can respond positively to all six statements, most likely this decision would be in your best interest and the best interests of those around you, but if you have a nagging doubt in the pit of your stomach, you need to rethink your decision.

BLOOM LEVEL 6 QUESTION

Create a list of at least three things you plan to do in your personal life to ensure that you use ethical behavior in your classes and assignments.

1. _____

2. _____

3. _____

FIGURE **2.5**   *Six Levels of Ethical Decision Making*

Is it legal?

Is it fair to me and others?

Can I live with my decision?

Is this decision in my long-term best interest?

Could I tell my mama about it and be proud?

How would I feel if this showed up on the front page of the newspaper tomorrow morning?

**TAKE PRIDE IN YOUR NAME AND PERSONAL CHARACTER** *"My name?"* you may ask. *"What does my name have to do with integrity or ethics?"* The answer: EVERYTHING! At the end of the day, the end of the month, the end of your career, and the end of your life, your name and your character are all that you have. Taking pride in developing your character and protecting your good name can be two powerful, motivational forces. Pride in your name and personal character can also guide you in making ethical decisions regarding your academic work.

Imagine for a moment that you are working with a group of students on a project for your psychology class. The project is to receive a major grade, and you and your group will present your findings to a group of 300 psychology students at a campus forum. Your group works hard and when you present the project, your group receives a standing ovation and earns an A. The name of each individual group member is read aloud as you stand to be recognized. Your name and project are also posted in a showcase. You are proud. Your hard work paid off. Your name now carries weight in the psychology department, with your peers, and among the psychology faculty. It feels good.

Conversely, imagine that your group slacks off; the project is poorly prepared and received by the audience and your professor. Your group earns an F on the project. Your name is associated with this project, and your name and grade are posted with every other group's. Your group is the only one to receive an F. It doesn't feel good.

Basically, it comes down to this: Every time you make a choice, every time you complete a project, every time you encounter another person, your actions define your character and your name. People admire and respect you when you make an honorable and moral choice, especially if it concerns a difficult decision. Both your character and your name are exclusively yours, and you are responsible for their well-being. When you care passionately about your reputation and character, your life is governed by protecting them, and your actions, beliefs, and decisions are all tied to this one credo: "My name and my reputation matter and I will do nothing to bring shame or embarrassment to them."

**WHAT IS THE IMPORTANCE OF PRACTICING ACADEMIC AND PERSONAL INTEGRITY?** As a college student, you will be faced with temptations that require you to make hard choices. You have probably already been forced to make decisions based on ethics. Do I cheat and get a higher grade so that I can compete with top students? Will cheating help me earn higher grades so that I get a better job? Do I copy this paper from the Internet? Who will know? Why shouldn't I buy one of the term papers that is floating around? What if I just copy someone's homework and don't cheat on a test? What if I lie to the instructor and say I was sick so I can get more time for a test for which I am not prepared? What if I let someone look on my paper during a test; I'm not the one cheating, am I? These are all ethical questions that require you to use your personal integrity to make mature decisions. These are the decisions that can and will affect your name, reputation, and character.

**WHAT IS ACADEMIC MISCONDUCT?**
It is important to know what constitutes dishonesty in an academic setting. Following is a partial list of offenses that most colleges consider academic misconduct.

*"Your character is determined by how you treat people who can do you no good and how you treat people who can't fight back."*
—Abigail Van Buren

**Tips for Personal Success**

Assume you are 90 years old and on your deathbed. You are thinking back over your life. Most likely you would think about certain people and events that have transpired. Perhaps you might want people to say or write the following about you:

▶ He was kind to people.
▶ He spent quality time with his children.
▶ He was a wonderful friend.
▶ He was always a giving person.

Now, it is your turn. Create a list of at least three things that you hope to have people say or write about you upon your death.
1. _____
2. _____
3. _____

*"No one will question your integrity if your integrity is not questionable."*
—Nathaniel Bronner, Jr.

**DOES 1 + 1 REALLY = 2? COLLEGE POLICY AND YOUR GPA**
The grade point average (GPA) is the numerical grading system used by almost every college in the nation. GPAs determine whether a student is eligible for continued enrollment, financial aid, and honors. Most colleges operate under a 4.0 system. This means that:

> Each **A** earned is worth **4 quality points**; each **B** is worth **3 points**; each **C** is worth **2 points**; each **D** is worth **1 point**; each **F** is worth **0 points**.

For each course, the number of quality points earned is multiplied by the number of credit hours carried by the course. For example, if you took:

> English 101 for 3 credit hours and earned an A, the formula would be $3 \times 4 = 12$
> Speech 101 for 3 credit hours and earned a C, the formula would be $3 \times 2 = 6$
> History 201 for 3 credit hours and earned a B, the formula would be $3 \times 3 = 9$
> Psychology 101 for 3 credit hours and earned a D, the formula would be $3 \times 1 = 3$
> Spanish 112 for 4 credit hours and earned a B, the formula would be $4 \times 3 = 12$

then you were enrolled for **16 hours of academic credit** and earned **42 quality points**. Examine Figure 2.7 to see an example of this GPA calculation.

You also need to be aware that when transferring, most colleges WILL NOT accept grades below a C (2.0) from another institution. Also, you will find that your future college DOES NOT transfer your grade point average (GPA). When you transfer to your future college, your GPA will start anew. This can be a double-edged sword. If you have a 4.0 at your current college, sadly, your GPA will start over at the future college. However, if you have a 2.0, you get to start again at your future college. Most of your credits will transfer, but your GPA will not.

# Point #5

**WORK HARD TO KNOW AND UNDERSTAND YOUR PROFESSORS AND COUNSELORS**
Are they nutty or nurturing? Friendly or grouchy? Exciting or boring? The answers will certainly vary from instructor to instructor. Regardless, it is important for you to get to know and understand your professors and the responsibilities with which they are charged. The college teaching profession is like no other profession on earth. There are certain rights and privileges that come with this profession that are not granted to any other career; however, there are also demands that no other profession faces. Unlike high school teachers, college professors are charged with much more than just classroom instruction. Many are required to research, write

FIGURE

## 2.7    *Calculating a GPA*

|  | GRADE | SEMESTER CREDIT | | QUALITY POINTS | | TOTAL POINTS |
|---|---|---|---|---|---|---|
| ENG 101 | A | 3 hours | × | 4 | = | 12 points |
| SPC 101 | C | 3 hours | × | 2 | = | 6 points |
| HIS 201 | B | 3 hours | × | 3 | = | 9 points |
| PSY 101 | D | 3 hours | × | 1 | = | 3 points |
| SPN 112 | B | 4 hours | × | 3 | = | 12 points |
|  |  | 16 hours | | | | 42 Total Points |

**42 total points divided by 16 semester hours equals a GPA of 2.62 (or C + average).**

FIGURE

## 2.8    *Give it a Try – Calculating Bennie's GPA*

Using the credit hours and grades provided below, calculate Bennie's GPA.

| | | | | |
|---|---|---|---|---|
| English 101 | 3 credits | Grade = A | Quality Points ____ | Total ____ |
| History 210 | 3 credits | Grade = C | Quality Points ____ | Total ____ |
| Art Lab 100 | 1 credit | Grade = A | Quality Points ____ | Total ____ |
| Math 110 | 4 credits | Grade = B | Quality Points ____ | Total ____ |
| French 101 | 3 credits | Grade = D | Quality Points ____ | Total ____ |
| Speech 101 | 3 credits | Grade = B | Quality Points ____ | Total ____ |
| **Total** | ____ credits | | quality points ____ | Total ____ |

Bennie's Grade Point Average = _____

articles and books, attend and present at academic conferences, advise students, and keep current in their ever-changing fields of study.

### THE FREEDOM TO TEACH AND LEARN

Professors are granted something called **academic freedom**. Most high school teachers do not have this privilege. Academic freedom means that a professor has the right to teach controversial issues, topics, subjects, pieces of literature, scientific theories, religious tenets, and political points of view *without* the threat of termination. However, this does not mean that a faculty member has the right to push a personal agenda. Teaching information that is related to the course is different from spending an hour talking about his or her political or religious agenda.

You may not have been able to read Mart Crowley's *The Boys in the Band The* in your high school drama class because of its homosexual content, but you would be able to study it uncensored in a college literature or drama class. You may have never engaged in a discussion on the "existence of God" in high school, but this may very well be a topic of debate in your logic, religion, sociology, or critical thinking class. This is the right of the college professor—to teach and guide in an unobstructed atmosphere free from parental, administrative, trustee, religious, political, or public pressure.

### I CAN'T BELIEVE MY PROFESSOR GAVE ME AN F

There will be times when you are disappointed with a grade that *you earned* from a professor. And yes, you do **earn** an A or an F; professors *do not give A's or F's*. What do you do? Threaten? Sue? Become argumentative? Those techniques will usually cost you more than they gain for you.

First, remember that the grade assigned by a professor is seldom changeable. If you made a less-than-satisfactory grade, there are several things that you need to do. First, be truthful with yourself and examine the amount of time you spent on the project.

Review the requirements for the assignment. Ask yourself:

▶ Did I miss something or omit some aspect of the project?

▶ Did I take an improper or completely wrong focus?

▶ Did I turn the project in late?

▶ Did I document my sources correctly?

▶ Did I really give it my very best?

Answering these important questions, and the ones listed in Figure 2.9, can help you determine the extent of your personal responsibility and preparation for success.

## 2.9   *Do I Practice Personal Responsibility?*

Think about a grade or project on which you scored lower than you would have liked or expected. Answer these questions truthfully to determine your role in the grading process. Place a check mark beside the questions that truly reflect your effort. If you have not yet turned in a project or taken an exam, consider these questions as a "check list" to success.

☐ I attend class regularly.

☐ I participate in class discussions and group work.

☐ I ask pointed and direct questions in class.

☐ I read my assignments, do my homework, and come to class prepared.

☐ I work with a study group.

☐ I have all of the supplies I need to be successful in this class (text, workbook, calculator, highlighters, etc.).

☐ I visit my professor during office hours to ask questions and seek clarification.

☐ If my professor and I have a disagreement, I approach himor her with a positive attitude.

☐ If my professor and I have a disagreement, I approach himor her first before going to a department chair, dean, or vice president.

☐ I use the academic support services on my campus (tutorial services, math lab, writing centers, communication lab, language lab, science lab, etc.).

☐ I use the library and librarian as resources for greater understanding.

☐ I practice academic integrity and avoid cheating and plagiarizing.

☐ I bring my best to the class every time we meet.

☐ If my professor's first language is not my first language (and he or she is difficult to understand), I work hard to rectify this situation by sitting up front, listening carefully, and asking questions to aid in my understanding.

Being able to answer these personal responsibility questions positively can mean the difference between success and failure with a project, assessment, or class. If you are truly concerned about the grade, talk to the professor about the assignment. Ask the professor to describe the most apparent problem with your assignment, and ask how you might improve your studying or how best to prepare for the *next* assignment.

Being able to answer these Personal Responsibility questions positively can mean the difference between success and failure with a project, an assessment, or a class. If you are truly concerned about the grade, talk to your professor about the assignment. Ask the professor to describe the most apparent problem with your work, and ask how you might improve your studying or how best to prepare for the *next* assignment.

### HOW CAN YOU MAKE THE MOST OF YOUR ADVISOR/ COUNSELOR RELATIONSHIPS?

Your academic advisor can be of enormous assistance to you throughout your college career. An advisor may be assigned to you, although a few colleges will allow you to select your own advisor. Your advisor will help you select courses for the completion of your degree. However, you are the person most responsible for registering for the classes that will count toward graduation. You should know as much as your advisor does about your degree.

If you do not know why you have to take certain courses or in what sequence courses should be taken, don't leave your advisor's office until you find out. Lack of understanding of your course sequence, your college catalog, or the requirements for graduation could mean the difference between a four-year degree, a five-year degree, or no college degree at all.

Academic advisors are usually not psychological counselors. Their job is to assist students in completing their academic programs of study. They may offer advice on personal or career matters, but they may not be trained to assist with psychological and emotional matters. However, if you are having problems not related to your academic studies, your academic advisor may be able to direct you to the professional on campus who can best help you address certain issues and problems. Your academic advisor may thus be the first person to contact in times of crisis.

## Point #6

### USE CAMPUS SUPPORT CENTERS

Most colleges offer assistance for academic, social, cultural, spiritual, and physical enrichment outside the classroom. Your tuition or student activities fee may fund many of the centers on your campus. You've paid for them; you should take full advantage of the services. Some college services are easier to find than others, but most are usually listed in your student handbook, college catalog, or schedule of classes. When in doubt, don't be afraid to ask your professor, advisor, or counselor if a particular service exists. It could save you time, effort, and, in many cases, money. Review the list of common college services (Figure 2.10) and using your catalog or online resources, jot down the location and phone number of each service.

### ON THE GO AND GOING ONLINE—ANOTHER IMPORTANT COLLEGE SERVICE

Distance-learning classes can be great for students who live far from campus, have transportation issues, work full time, or have families and small children. These courses have flexible hours and few, if any, class meetings. Most online classes allow you to work at your own pace, but most still have stringent deadlines for assignment submission. Do not let anyone try to tell you that these courses are easier than regular classroom offerings; they are not. Distance-learning courses are usually more difficult for the average student. You need to be a highly motivated self-starter to complete and do well in these courses. Take the following assessment in Figure 2.11 to determine if an online class is right for you.

If you decide to take an online class, consider the following advice:

▶ If at all possible, review the course material before you register. This may help you in making the decision to enroll. Often, professors' syllabi are accessible online.

▶ Make an appointment to meet the professor as soon as possible. Some colleges will schedule a meeting or orientation for you. If it is not possible to meet, at least phone or e-mail the professor and introduce yourself.

▶ Develop a schedule for completing each assignment and stick to it! Don't let time steal away from you. Time management is the biggest problem with online classes.

▶ Keep a copy of all work mailed, e-mailed, or delivered to the professor.

▶ Always mail, e-mail, or deliver your assignments on time—early if possible.

▶ If you have computer failure, have a backup plan.

▶ Log in EVERY DAY even if you do not have an assignment due.

▶ Alert your professor immediately if you have family, computer, or personal problems that will prevent you from completing an assignment on time.

▶ Find out where to go or who to call on campus should you encounter technical problems with the learning platform or getting online.

Briefly describe why you plan (or do not plan) to take an online class. What is your rationale?

_____

_____

_____

BLOOM LEVEL 1
QUESTION

FIGURE

## 2.10 *Campus/Community Success Centers*

| CAMPUS/COMMUNITY SERVICE | HOW IT CAN HELP YOU | PHONE NUMBER AND LOCATION |
|---|---|---|
| **Academic Advisement Center** | Assist in choosing classes for each semester and offer career assessments and advice on careers. | |
| **Transfer Center** | These centers assist students who plan to transfer to another institution by helping them select classes that meet future degree and residency requirements. | |
| **Computer Lab** | Offer students the use of e-mail, Internet services, and other online applications, usually free of charge. | |
| **Writing Center** | Offer assistance with your writing skills. They will not rewrite your paper for you, but they can give you advice on how to strengthen your project. | |
| **Math Center** | Offer help with math problems, one-on-one or group tutoring, and study sessions. | |
| **Tutoring or Mastery Learning Center** | Offer assistance in almost any subject matter. Many colleges offer this service free of charge (or for a very nominal fee). | |
| **Language Lab** | Offer assistance with international languages or sign language. | |
| **Library** | Your college library can be the hub of your learning experience, from printed materials to Internet usage to computer-assisted tutorials. Your library and librarians are vital to helping you succeed in your classes and to become information literate. | |
| **Veteran Affairs** | Offers assistance to veterans, especially with government paperwork and financial aid. | |
| **Health Services** | Some campuses offer student services for physical and mental health, complete with a nurse or physician's assistant. | |
| **International Student Services** | Assists international students with admissions, housing, cultural adjustment, and language barriers. | |
| **Minority Student Services** | Offers services and programming for minority students on campus. | |
| **Financial Aid Office** | Assists students with federal, state, and local paperwork to apply for financial aid and scholarships. This office is especially helpful in assisting with your Free Appication for Federal Student Aid form each year. | |
| **Student Activities** | Offers a wide variety of programming in social and cultural activities. | |
| **Disabled Student Services** | If you have a documented disability, colleges and universities across the United States are required by law to offer you "reasonable accommodations" to ensure your success (Americans with Disabilities Act, Sec. 504). Some of these accommodations include: handicapped parking, special testing centers, extended time on tests and timed projects, textbook translations and conversions, interpreters, note-taking services, and TTY/TDD services. | |

FIGURE **2.11**  *Distance-Education Readiness Assessment*

Please answer each question truthfully to determine your readiness for online learning.

| | | |
|---|---|---|
| 1. Do you own your own computer? | Yes | No |
| 2. Is your computer relatively new (enough memory, CD-rom, graphics card, wireless internet, etc . . . )? | Yes | No |
| 3. Can you type (NOT text, but type)? | Yes | No |
| 4. Are you comfortable using a computer and web technology? | Yes | No |
| 5. Do you have the technical requirements for online learning (Internet access, Internet browser, Adobe, Word or compatible program, PowerPoint) | Yes | No |
| 6. Are you highly organized? | Yes | No |
| 7. Are you a good manager of time? | Yes | No |
| 8. Are you highly motivated: a self-starter? | Yes | No |
| 9. If you work full or part-time, do you feel you have at least 6-8 hours per week to spend working with each of your online classes? | Yes | No |
| 10. If you have family issues that require a great deal of your time, do you have family support? | Yes | No |
| 11. Do you have "down time" to spend working on your online classes? | Yes | No |
| 12. Can you get to campus if necessary? | Yes | No |
| 13. Do you feel comfortable chatting online with unknown persons? | Yes | No |
| 14. Do you think you can "relate" to others in an online relationship? | Yes | No |
| 15. Do you consider yourself as a good reader with high-level comprehension? | Yes | No |
| 16. Can you concentrate on your work even with online distractions (e-mail, friends, etc . . . .)? | Yes | No |
| 17. Do you feel comfortable calling your professor during his or her office hours if you need to do so? | Yes | No |
| 18. Do you think you will be able to take notes during an online chat or class session? | Yes | No |
| 19. Are you comfortable with online terminology such as URL, listserv, Portal, Streaming Video, Podcasts, Facebook, Twitter, etc . . . . ? | Yes | No |
| 20. Are you excited about taking an online class? | Yes | No |

© Robert M. Sherfield, Ph.D. 2009

If you answered NO to more than five of these questions, you should reconsider taking an online class at this time. To prepare for future classes, you may also want to spend time researching and becoming more familiar with the questions that you marked "NO." You can also speak with your advisor or professor about your possibility for success in his or her course. Your campus probably offers an online orientation from which you might benefit.

# Point #7

## PRACTICE CIVILITY AND ETIQUETTE

Do civility, classroom etiquette, and personal decorum impact success? You may be surprised to read this, but the way you act in (and out) of class can mean as much to your success as what you know. No one can make you do anything or act in any way that you do not want to. The following tips are provided from years of research and actual conversations with thousands of professors teaching across the United States. You have to be the one who chooses whether or not to use this advice.

▶ First, make every effort not to be late for class. If you are late, enter quietly, DO NOT walk in front of the professor, don't let the door slam, don't talk on your way in, and take the seat nearest the door.

▶ Wait for the professor to dismiss class before you begin to pack your bags to leave. You may miss important information or cause someone else to miss important information.

▶ Do not carry on a conversation with another student while the professor or another student is talking.

▶ Don't ask your professor to "break the rules" just for you. The rules in your class syllabus are provided to everyone so that all students will be treated fairly. If you have a true, legitimate reason to ask for an extension or some other exception, talk to your professor *beforehand*.

▶ Do not sleep in class. If you are having problems staying awake, you should consider dropping the class and taking it at another time.

▶ If for any reason you must leave during class, do so quietly and quickly. It is customary to inform the professor before class begins that you will be leaving early.

▶ If you make an appointment with a professor, keep it. If you must cancel, a courtesy call is in order.

▶ If you don't know how to address your professors—that is, by Mr., Mrs., Miss, Ms., or Dr.—ask them which they prefer, or simply call them "Professor ."

▶ Turn off your electronic devices (iPods, phones, etc. . . . ). Even if the device is off, take your earplugs out of your ears. Leaving them in is disrespectful.

▶ Be respectful of other students. Profanity and obscene language may offend some people. You can have strong, conflicting views without being offensive.

▶ Visit professors during office hours. The time before and after class may not be the most appropriate time for you or the professor. Your professor may have back-to-back classes and be unable to assist you.

▶ If you act like an adult (which you are), you'll be treated like one.

Remember that having respect for others will afford you the opportunity to establish relationships that otherwise you might never have had. Respect begets respect.

# Point #8

### IDENTIFY AND CLARIFY WHAT YOU VALUE IN LIFE

Values, self-esteem, motivation, and goal setting are all mixed up together, making it difficult to separate one from another. The things you work to accomplish are directly connected to the things you value. Therefore, your ATTITUDE and ACTIONS are tied to your VALUES. If you value an attitude or belief, your actions will be centered on these ideals. If you love to spend time with your friends and this is valuable to you, you will make the time for this on a regular basis. Why? Because your friendships are a fundamental part of your value system. You like it and get pleasure from it; therefore you do it. It is that simple. Our values influence our actions. This idea is, once again, tied to Maslow's Hierarchy of Basic Needs.

You will find a wide and varied list of items that many people value. Read them over carefully and circle the ones *you truly value*. Be careful and selective. DO NOT just randomly circle words. As a criterion for each word you circle, ask yourself, "Can I defend why I value this in my life?" and "Is this truly something *I value* or something I was told to value and never questioned why?" If you value something and it is not on the list, add it in the spaces at the bottom.

## THINKING for CHANGE: An Activity for Critical Reflection

Your friend Jamal is struggling with staying motivated during his first semester at college. He didn't have to study much in high school and still pulled good grades, but he has been overwhelmed with the amount of work his college professors are assigning. He knows he is not doing his best work, but he can't seem to get motivated to excel. You know he is capable because he participated in your study group several times before he stopped coming.

Lately, Jamal has begun to wake up during the night very stressed out and afraid that he is going to flunk out. His parents will be devastated if this happens because he is a first-generation college student, and they have sacrificed so much to send him to college. His fears gnaw at him all the time.

Sometimes he can see himself going home and telling his parents that he is failing. He visualizes how embarrassed he would be to tell them and his friends that he has failed. One of his professors has told him that he has a bad attitude. He spent a long time this afternoon talking to you about his lack of motivation and thoughts of dropping out.

What advice and motivational tips would you offer Jamal to help him get on the right track?

1. _____

2. _____

| | | | |
|---|---|---|---|
| Honesty | Affection | Punctuality | Respect |
| Frankness | Open-Mindedness | Reliability | Trustworthiness |
| Sincerity | Wit/Humor | Spontaneity | Devotion |
| Frugality | Justice | Creativity | Caring |
| Spirituality | Friendliness | Energy | Intellect |
| Attentiveness | Conversational | Money | Security |
| Fine Dining | Beauty | Devotion | Enthusiasm |
| Positivism | Commitment | Foresightedness | Giving |
| Organization | Learning | Listening | Success |
| Control | Comfort | Knowledge | Courage |
| Athletic Ability | Thoughtfulness | Independence | Partying |
| Safety | Fun | Excitement | Speaking |
| Love | Friendship | Writing | Teamwork |
| Reading | Family | Dependability | Walks |
| Time Alone | Time w/Friends | Phone Calls | Integrity |
| Exercise | Problem Solving | Empowerment | Tolerance |
| Service to Others | Modesty | Strength | Power |
| Imagination | Self-Esteem | Food | Change |
| Winning | Goals | Risk Taking | Optimism |
| Self-Improvement | Forgiveness | Fairness | Direction in Life |
| Successful Career | Motivation | Trust | Mentoring |
| Working | Hobbies | Books | Stability |

_____  _____  _____  _____
_____  _____  _____  _____
_____  _____  _____  _____

Now that you have circled or written what you value, choose the five that you value the most. In other words, if you were allowed to value ONLY five things in life, what five would you list? In the space to the right of each value, rank them from 1 to 5 (1 being the most important to you, your life, your relationships, your actions, your education, and your career).

Take your time and give serious consideration to this activity, as you will need to refer back to this exercise later in this chapter.

**LIST**                                                                                    **RANK**

▶ _____

▶ _____

▶ _____

▶ _____

Now, look at YOUR #1. Where did this value originate?

_____

_____

_____

Defend why this is the one thing you value more in life than anything else.

_____

_____

_____

How does this one value motivate you?

_____

_____

_____

# Point #9

### DEVELOP A STRONG, PERSONAL "GUIDING STATEMENT"

You're wearing a T-shirt to class. It is not your normal, run-of-the-mill T-shirt, however. You designed this T-shirt for everyone to see and read. It is white with bright red letters. On the front of the T-shirt is written your ***personal guiding statement***—the words by which you live. The words govern your life. What does your T-shirt say? Perhaps you used the golden rule, "Do unto others. . . . " It might be an adaptation of the Nike® slogan, "Just Do It," or it might be something more profound, such as, "I live my life to serve others and to try to make others' lives better," or "Be a blessing," or "Live, Love, Laugh."

Whatever your guiding statement, it must be yours. It can't be your parents' or your professor's, or your best friend's statement. It must be based on something you value and it must be strong enough to motivate you in hard, tough times. Your guiding statement must be so powerful that it will literally "guide you" when you are ethically challenged, broke, alone, angry, hurt, sad, or feeling vindictive. It is a statement that will guide you in relationships with family, friends, spouses, partners, or would-be love interests. It is a statement that gives direction to your DAILY actions. Think about how different your life would be if you woke up each morning and LIVED your guiding statement to the fullest.

One of the best ways to start working on your guiding statement is to look back at the words you circled as valuable to you on page 49 of this chapter. If you value something, it might appear in your guiding statement. For example, if you circled the words *Respect*, *Giving*, and *Optimistic* among the things you value, your guiding statement (based on these words) might read:

**"I will live my life as a positive, upbeat, motivated person who respects others and enjoys giving to others on a daily basis."**

If your circled words included *Integrity*, *Truth*, and *Fairness*, your statement might read:
**"My integrity is the most important thing in my life and I will never act in any way that compromises my integrity. I will be truthful, fair, and honest in all my endeavors."**

More simply, your guiding statement may be as simple as:
***"Be reliable,"*** or ***"Live optimistically,"*** or ***"Never give up."***

In the space below, transfer the most important words from the Value List on page 49 and then work to develop your guiding statement.

The most important values were

_____    _____    _____

_____    _____    _____

Draft of my Guiding Statement (Take your time and be sincere. You will need this statement later in the chapter.)

_____

_____

_____

_____

# Point #10

### MAKE A COMMITMENT TO STRENGTHEN YOUR SELF-ESTEEM

If you were asked to name all the areas of your life that are impacted by self-esteem, what would you say? The correct answer is, "Everything." Every area of your life is affected by your self-esteem. Self-esteem and self-understanding are two of the most important components of your personal makeup! To be truly motivated, you have got to know yourself and love yourself! Many people who are in therapy are there simply because they cannot accept the fact that they are OK.

You might think of self-esteem as a photograph of yourself that you keep locked in your mind. It is a collective product—the culmination of everyone with whom you have associated, everywhere you have traveled, and all of the experiences you have had. William James, the first major psychologist to study self-esteem, defined it as *"the sum total of all a person can call their own*: the *Material Me* (all that you have), the *Social Me* (recognition and acceptance from others), and the *Spiritual Me* (your innermost thoughts and desires)."

Stanly Coopersmith, noted psychologist and developer of the most widely used self-esteem inventory in the United States, defined self-esteem as *"a personal judgment of worthiness."* Psychologist and author Nathanial Branden defines self-esteem as *"confidence in our ability to cope with the basic challenges of life."* And finally, psychologist Charles Cooley called it *"the looking glass."* Perhaps in everyday terms, we can define healthy self-esteem as "I know who I am, I accept who I am, I am OK, and I'm going to make it."

Self-esteem has five basic characteristics based on Maslow's Hierarchy of Basic Needs. They are:

▶ A sense of **security** (I am safe and have the basics of life, food, water, etc. . . . )

▶ A sense of **identity** (I know who I am and where I'm going)

▶ A sense of **belonging** (I know how to love and I am loved)

▶ A sense of **purpose** (I know why I'm here and what I am going to do with my life)

▶ A sense of **personal competence** (I have the ability to achieve my goals and grow)

These characteristics are considered key to a person's ability to approach life with motivation, confidence, self-direction, and the desire to achieve outstanding accomplishments.

### TIPS TO ENHANCE YOUR SELF-ESTEEM

**Take control of your own life.** If you let other people rule your life, you will always have unhealthy self-esteem. Get involved in the decisions that shape your life. Seize control—don't let life just happen to you!

# From Ordinary to Extraordinary

## REAL PEOPLE | REAL LIVES | REAL CHANGE

**LYDIA HAUSLER LEBOVIC**
Jewish Holocaust Survivor
Auschwitz Concentration/Extermination Camp.
Auschwitz, Poland, 1944

"Sweet Sixteen." Isn't that the moment of joy for so many female teens today? It is a milestone date when childhood passes and young adulthood arrives. One can legally drive and in many states, "Sweet Sixteen" signifies the age of consent.

My "Sweet Sixteen" was very different. Yes, I was dating, had a somewhat rebellious relationship with my mother, and socialized with friends, but in the countryside around me, World War II raged. In 1944 when I was 16, my family and I were ordered to pack 20 pounds of personal belongings and told that we were being taken to "the Ghetto," a holding area for Jews in my hometown of Uzhorod, Czechoslovakia, now a part of Ukraine. I understood that the situation was not good and that things were changing, but I had no real idea of how my life would forever be altered in the coming weeks, months, and years.

After two weeks in "the Ghetto," my family, friends, neighbors, and I were ordered onto cattle cars—60 to 80 per car—and told that we were be-

> *Little did I know at that point that those shoved to the right would be put to work and those shoved to the left would be dead by the evening.*

ing taken to Hungary to work in the corn and wheat fields. So there, in the darkness of night, our journey began—young, old, weak, strong, nursing mothers, and babies—all in the same cattle car with no water and only two buckets to use for a bathroom.

After two days of travel, the train stopped and the doors of the cattle car opened. My mother recognized that we were not in southern Hungary, but rather on the Hungary/Poland border in the north. She took us aside in the car and told us of her suspicion—that we were being taken to Auschwitz concentration camp. After another two days on the train, we arrived at Auschwitz in the early dawn hours.

The doors of the cattle cars opened and the men were quickly separated from the women and the children from the adults. We were put into lines of five and marched forward. In front of every line was an SS officer. Quickly, I was pushed to the right and my mother and sister were pushed to

the left. Little did I know at that point that those shoved to the right would be put to work and those shoved to the left would be dead by the evening. I never saw my mother or sister again after that moment. I never said goodbye. I was "Sweet Sixteen."

After the separation, my group was taken to a very large building and told to undress. We were completely shaven, sponged from head to toe with a bleach-like substance, showered, and given a uniform. We were then marched to the barracks where we would sleep 12–14 to a bed with 600 to 800 people per barracks. The black and white photo was taken as we marched toward the barracks from the shower facility and now hangs in the National Holocaust Museum in Washington, DC.

Some of the Jewish girls who had been in the camp for a while were considered "foremen." I remember approaching one such female. I asked her, "When do I get to see my mother and my sister?"

She took me by the arm and pointed me toward the billowing chimney of the crematory. *"You see that smoke? You see that ash? You smell that flesh burning? That's your mother. That's your sister."* She walked away. I did not believe her at the time, but she was

# From Ordinary to *Extraordinary*

absolutely right. This realization remains the most distressing of all events in my life—past and present—that my mother and sister died in such a horrific manner. Gassed and cremated.

I remained in Auschwitz until I was shipped to the labor camp, Bergen-Belsen, in Germany. We were liberated on April 15, 1945. Upon liberation, I began working for the British Red Cross. Later that year, I was reunited with a friend of my brother and we were married in November of 1945. We moved to Chile in 1947 and then to Los Angeles, CA, in 1963.

I now travel the nation speaking about the events of my life and delivering the message, "NEVER AGAIN." I write this to essay to you for many reasons, but specifically to let you know this: The Holocaust did not ruin me. They did not destroy me. They did not destroy my belief in love. They did not destroy my faith in people. They did not destroy my religion or values. The events made me a stronger, more compassionate person. I went on to become a loving wife and mother, a successful businesswoman, and eventually a devoted grandmother. *I refused to be ruined.* I encourage you to use the adversity in your life to make you stronger, more compassionate, more caring, and more helpful to mankind.

## EXTRAORDINARY REFLECTION

**Read the following statement and respond in your online journal or class notebook.**

Mrs. Lebovic suffered the death of family members during the Holocaust, but she makes the statement, *"The Holocaust did not ruin me. They did not destroy me. They did not destroy my belief in love. . . . . I refused to be ruined."* How can adversity in your live, like that in Mrs. Lebovic's, make you a stronger and more motivated person?

> *"To every person there comes that special moment when he is tapped on the shoulder to do a very special thing unique to him. What a tragedy if that moment finds him unprepared for the work that would be his finest hour."*
>
> —Winston Churchill

# KNOWLEDGE *in* BLOOM

## Using and Evaluating your Guiding Statement

Each chapter-end assessment is based on *Bloom's Taxonomy of Learning*. See the inside front cover for a quick review.

### UTILIZES LEVELS 3 AND 6 OF THE TAXONOMY

**PROCESS:** Now that you have developed your guiding statement, consider how *it can be used to guide you* in the following situations:

**Guiding Statement** as written on page 53 of this chapter:

_____

_____

_____

### HOW WILL YOUR GUIDING STATEMENT HELP . . .

If you have a disagreement with your supervisor at work. _____

_____

_____

_____

If your class paper or project receives a failing grade from your professor. _____

_____

_____

_____

If you are having a disagreement with someone for whom you care deeply (friend, spouse, partner, parent, work associate, etc. . . . )?

_____

_____

_____

_____

If you see that someone is struggling and having a hard time "making it"? _____

_____

_____

Now that you have had a chance to apply your guiding statement to several simulations, on a scale of 1 to 10 (1 being not effective at all and 10 being very effective), how would you rate its effectiveness to you and to those involved? Why? Discuss. _____

_____

_____

_____

# SQ3R *Mastery* STUDY SHEET

| | | |
|---|---|---|
| **EXAMPLE QUESTION:** *(from page 32)*<br>What is the difference between internal<br>and external motivation? | | **ANSWER:,** |
| **EXAMPLE QUESTION:** *(from page 50)*<br>How can developing a guiding statement<br>help with persistence? | | **ANSWER:** |
| **AUTHOR QUESTION:** *(from page 34)*<br>Explain how self-esteem plays a role<br>in one's motivation. | | **ANSWER:** |
| **AUTHOR QUESTION:** *(from page 36)*<br>Discuss how you can put adversity and past<br>failures into perspective. | | **ANSWER:** |
| **AUTHOR QUESTION:** *(from page 37)*<br>What is academic integrity and how do you<br>practice it? | | **ANSWER:** |
| **AUTHOR QUESTION:** *(from page 39)*<br>Define the word "character" and discuss how it<br>plays a role in your motivation level. | | **ANSWER:** |
| **AUTHOR QUESTION:** *(from page 48)*<br>Why are values important to your motivation<br>and persistence plan? | | **ANSWER:** |
| **YOUR QUESTION:** *(from page ___)* | | **ANSWER:** |
| **YOUR QUESTION:** *(from page ___)* | | **ANSWER:** |
| **YOUR QUESTION:** *(from page ___)* | | **ANSWER:** |
| **YOUR QUESTION:** *(from page ___)* | | **ANSWER:** |
| **YOUR QUESTION:** *(from page ___)* | | **ANSWER:** |

Finally, after answering these questions, recite this chapter's major points in your mind. Consider the
following general questions to help you master this material.

▶ What was it about?
▶ What does it mean?
▶ What was the most important thing I learned? Why?
▶ What were the key points to remember?

# CHAPTER 3
# COMMUNICATE

IMPROVING
PERSONAL
COMMUNICATION,
CULTIVATING
RELATIONSHIPS,
AND MANAGING
CONFLICT

"Words can destroy relationships. What we call each other ultimately becomes what we think about each other, and what we think about each other matters."

—Jeanne S. Kirkpatrick

# WHY READ THIS CHAPTER?

## What's in it for me?

WHY will interpersonal communication be important to my life and career? WHY is it important to understand computer mediated communication? WHY does managing conflict really matter at this point in my life? WHY is it important to understand diverse relationships?

Why? Because people do not live alone. We are constantly communicating and relating to others even when we think we may not be and even when we are not trying to do so. The ability to know yourself and how to communicate with others; to understand them, to work with them, and to manage conflicts that may arise with them are some of THE MOST valuable tools you will ever learn. Effective communication determines so much about the nature and quality of your life, including aspects of your education, your relationships, your romances, your career, your future, your friends, your values, your ethics, and, indeed, your character. Also, these qualities are important because most employers name interpersonal communication skills as one of the top attributes that any potential employee should possess.

*By carefully reading this chapter and taking the information provided seriously, you will be able to:*

1. Identify the elements and power of the communication process.
2. Define the concept of interpersonal communication and learn the associated essential skills.
3. Discuss computer mediated communication as it relates to interpersonal communication.
4. Define and discuss the role of nonverbal communication.
5. Navigate and learn how to manage conflict more effectively.

# CHAPTER 3 / COMMUNICATE

*"I see communication as a huge umbrella that covers and affects all that goes on between human beings."*

—Joseph Adler

# WHY READ THIS CHAPTER?

## . . . FROM MY PERSPECTIVE

**NAME:** Stacy Seals
**INSTITUTION:** Delgado Community College, New Orleans, LA
**MAJOR:** Office Technology Administration
**AGE:** 18

Without communication, we would never get anything accomplished. We would not learn because we would not be able to ask questions. We would not have relationships because we would not know how to approach people. In my chosen major and profession, interpersonal communication is very important, but I can't imagine a profession where it would not be. In the field of Office Technology Administration, communication is a vital part of everyday functions, from making telephone calls to taking minutes in meetings to interacting with colleagues to supervising staff. It would be impossible to function and be successful without having superior interpersonal communication skills.

When I began my degree program at Delgado Community College, I was very shy and withdrawn. Some of this was due to my age (I was only 16) but some of this shyness came from not knowing how to communicate very well with others. I enrolled in a student success class, where we were required to participate, speak up, and work in groups. At first, I was terrified, but as the semester progressed, I learned how to ask questions, comment on different topics, and participate in discussion groups. By learning how to engage in interpersonal communications more effectively, I became a better student. Also, my fears of communicating with, and in front of, others lessened. Learning to communicate better helped me improve in all of my classes as well as my relationships.

Another way that interpersonal communication has helped me is by allowing me to meet and establish friendships and relationships with other people. Once I began meeting other people, I became more open and willing to take chances. I started learning more about people and their backgrounds and families. I even started a study group for one of my classes. By learning to communicate and apply many of the techniques discussed in this chapter, I began to participate more in my own education, I learned more about others, and I began to understand the world more effectively and how to get along in it. Nothing has helped me change more than learning how to communicate with others. Improving your interpersonal communication skills will be a great tool for you, too.

# SCAN & QUESTION

In the preface of this book (page xix), you read about the **SQ3R Study Method.** Right now, take a few moments, **scan this chapter**, and on page 81, write **five questions** that you think will be important to your mastery of this material. In addition to the two questions below, you will also find five questions from your authors. Use one of your "*On The Test*" stickers to flag this page for easy reference.

**EXAMPLES:**

▶ **What are the six elements of the communication process?** (from page 62)

▶ **What is self-disclosure and why is it important for healthy relationships?** (from page 68)

# THE COMMUNICATION PROCESS

## How Does Communication Work?

Communication is not something we do *to people*; rather, it is something that is done *between people*. Communication can take on a variety of forms such as oral speech, the written word, body movements, electronic messages, and even yawns. All of these actions communicate something to another person. As you begin thinking about communication, it is paramount that you know this: If you are in the presence of another person, communication cannot be stopped.

Basically, the communication process involves **SIX ELEMENTS:** the source, the message, the channel, the receiver, barriers, and feedback. Consider Figure 3.1.

**Barriers** (represented by the lines in Figure 3.1) are things that can interfere with the source, the message, the channel, or the receiver. Barriers can occur anywhere within the communication process and can include things like external noise (others talking, cell phones, and traffic), internal noise (self-talk, doubt, and questioning), interference, and poor communication habits. Your emotions, past experiences, social norms, communication expectations, and

**FIGURE 3.1** *Six Elements of Communication*

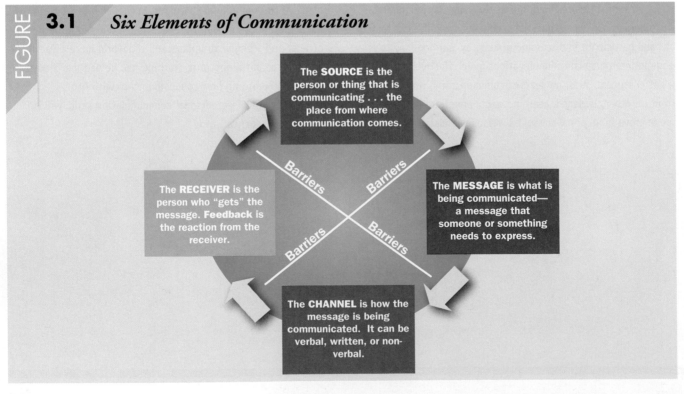

The **SOURCE** is the person or thing that is communicating . . . the place from where communication comes.

The **MESSAGE** is what is being communicated— a message that someone or something needs to express.

The **CHANNEL** is how the message is being communicated. It can be verbal, written, or non-verbal.

The **RECEIVER** is the person who "gets" the message. **Feedback** is the reaction from the receiver.

Barriers

prejudices can also be barriers to effective communication. Think about a time when your feelings for someone interfered with your ability to listen to that person objectively. This would be a perfect example of a barrier. **Feedback** is the verbal and nonverbal responses the receiver gives you.

## What Is the Role of Interpersonal Communication in Everyday Life?

**Interpersonal communication** is a part of the greater communication spectrum. It is "a dynamic form of communication between two (or more) people in which the messages exchanged significantly influence their thoughts, emotions, behaviors, and relationships" (McCornack, 2007). The messages in interpersonal communication are not necessarily static like the words in a book, a written letter, or a text message; they are fluid and constantly changing, potentially causing your relationships to change along with them. Texting and e-mails are components of interpersonal communication as well as computer mediated communication, which we will discuss later in this chapter.

Steven McCornack, in his book *Reflect and Relate* (2007), suggests that there are three Interpersonal Communication Goals, as shown in Figure 3.2. They are: *Self-presentation*, *Instrumental*, and *Relationship Goals*.

Take a moment and identify one way that you could use each of the interpersonal communication goals to help you succeed in college and establish strong relationships.

ESSENTIAL CORNERSTONE

**Communication:**
How can becoming more adept at developing positive relationships help you with your career aspirations?

**Social Networking Moment:**
Share your response to this Essential Cornerstone with peers in your social network. Choose two responses from your peers and respond to their postings.

**Self-Presentation Goal**   I can use this to _____

_____

**Instrumental Goal**   I can use this to _____

_____

**Relationship Goal**   I can use this to _____

_____

BLOOM LEVEL 3 QUESTION

FIGURE

### 3.2   *Interpersonal Communication Goals*

| TYPE OF GOAL | EXPLANATION | EXAMPLE |
|---|---|---|
| Self-Presentation Goals | Goals that help us present ourselves to others in a particular fashion and help others see us as we wish to be seen. | If you want a new acquaintance or love interest to see you as a caring, compassionate person, you will use words and actions that reveal yourself as caring, trustworthy, honest, and compassionate. |
| Instrumental Goals | Goals that help us present information in a way that we get what we want or need from another person; to possibly win approval | If you wanted to borrow your best friends laptop computer, you would remind him or her that you are always careful and respect other's property. |
| Relationship Goals | Goals that help us build meaningful, lasting, effective relationships with other people. | If your friend loaned you her computer, you might write a thank you note or buy a small gift as a token of your appreciation. |

**3.3**   *The Classification of Spatial Zones*

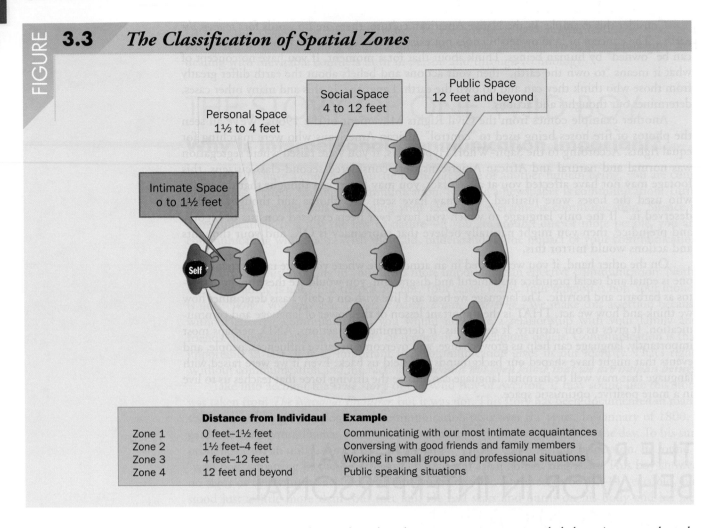

| | Distance from Individaul | Example |
|---|---|---|
| Zone 1 | 0 feet–1½ feet | Communicatinig with our most intimate acquaintances |
| Zone 2 | 1½ feet–4 feet | Conversing with good friends and family members |
| Zone 3 | 4 feet–12 feet | Working in small groups and professional situations |
| Zone 4 | 12 feet and beyond | Public speaking situations |

Consider the spatial zone chart describing more common nonverbal clues. As you study each action and example in Figure 3.4, try to determine what it would mean to YOU based on your thoughts and cultural traditions.

Understanding nonverbal communication and the cultural clues that can accompany it can greatly enhance your ability to establish effective interpersonal relationships and avoid conflicts caused by misunderstanding. As you grow in your ability to communicate effectively, work hard to hear the verbal message and learn to decode the nonverbal clues in conjunction with the verbal message. This will help you establish a rich, rewarding communication environment.

# O M G   U R   O T T (Oh My God, You Are Over The Top)

## Why Is Studying Computer Mediated Communication Important in Today's Society?

Believe it or not, there was a time not too long ago when there was no such term as computer mediated communication (CMC). There were no e-mails, Blackberries, iPhones, text messages, blogs, twittering, Facebook, MySpace, or instant messaging. OMG, YKM! No, we're not kidding you. As a matter of fact, it was not until a few years ago that the study of interpersonal communication even mentioned CMC. It was not considered to be a part of interpersonal communication at all, as it was believed that interpersonal communication had to take place *in person*.

FIGURE **3.4**  *Nonverbal Communication*

| NONVERBAL ACTION | EXAMPLES | WHAT THEY COULD MEAN |
|---|---|---|
| Eye Contact | Looking directly at someone<br>Avoiding eye contact<br>Fixed gaze | _____<br>_____<br>_____ |
| Posture | Slumping<br>Standing very erect<br>Leans forward when seated | _____<br>_____<br>_____ |
| Facial Expressions | Smiling/Frowning<br>Squinted eyes<br>Blank stare | _____<br>_____<br>_____ |
| Clothing/Emblems | Well dressed and pressed<br>Wrinkled and sloppy<br>Smelly | _____<br>_____<br>_____ |
| Artifacts | Jewelry<br>Tattoos<br>Body/Facial piercings | _____<br>_____<br>_____ |
| Gestures | Waving arms<br>Fingers pointed toward person<br>Crossed arms | _____<br>_____<br>_____ |
| Touch | Patting someone on the back<br>Firm handshake<br>Weak handshake | _____<br>_____<br>_____ |

Today, it is widely considered that CMC is a vital subcategory of interpersonal communication studies. "There is some evidence that those wishing to communicate a message to someone, such as a message ending a relationship, may select a less-rich communication message—they may be more likely to send a letter or an e-mail rather than share the bad news face-to-face" (Beebe, 2008). Technology has become an integral part of our communication strategies.

Some may ask, can CMC really be considered "interpersonal" when we are not meeting face-to-face with another person. The answer is yes. Why? Because in today's rich CMC environment, we can *infer or imply emotions* as we send and receive electronic communication. For example, we use symbols such ☺ as to indicate happiness or funny and to indicate sad or upset. We use abbreviations such as LOL (for "laugh out loud"). We even SCREAM AT OTHERS or SPEAK WITH EMPHASIS when we use all capital letters in our communication. Additionally, many people have cameras connected to their computers, allowing the sender and receiver to see each other's facial expressions on the screen. Therefore, emotions can be conveyed through CMC, although there are not as many nonverbal clues to view and interpret as in face-to-face communication (Lane, 2008). Because we cannot see all the nonverbal clues that are associated with face-to-face communications, we are more likely to misunderstand the message when using CMC.

The fact that we are not face-to-face does not seem to negatively affect our communication efforts via technology. Several studies suggest that CMC relationships differ very little from relationships that involve face-to-face

"The information superhighway is clearly not just a road for moving data from one place to another, but a roadside where people can pass each other, occasionally meet, and decide to travel together."
—Beebe, Beebe, and Redmond

### bring the CHANGE

**Tips for Persaonal Success**

Consider the following tips for using CMC (e-mails, text and instant messaging, etc.):

▶ Never send an electronic message that you would not want the public to see. They are not private and quite difficult, if not impossible, to destroy. If you put things in writing that attack or libel other people, you could be sued for damaging someone else's reputation.

▶ When using CMC, choose your words carefully, as you cannot change them once you have pressed the "send" button.

▶ Never send CMC when you are angry, frustrated, or stressed. If you write a message when you're angry, wait at least 24–48 hours before you consider sending it.

Now, it is your turn. Create a list of at least three more tips that you would offer a fellow classmate to assist him or her with using CMC more effectively.

1. _____
2. _____
3. _____

*"Confiding a secret to an unworthy person is like carrying grain in a bag with a hole in it."*

*—Ethiopian proverb*

meetings. Further research also suggests that CMC relationships may even be stronger than face-to-face relationships because people using CMC ask more pointed and direct questions, reveal more about themselves, and communicate more frequently (Tidwell, and Walther, 2002; Walther and Burgoon, 1992). Think about the last time you revealed something online that you may have never revealed to that person face-to-face.

There is a downside to CMC, however. For years, communication experts have worried about the effects of electronic communication on the entire communication process, especially traditional interpersonal communication. In today's technologically advanced world, we do not have to speak to anyone if we don't want to. We purchase gasoline at the pump, pay for groceries at self-checkout, use automated tellers to get money, go to Amazon.com or iTunes to purchase our music and books, search eBay for sale items, and e-mail others rather than pick up the phone or visit them. Social isolation is a major concern, and you have to work hard to guard against becoming a ***technological recluse***.

# SELF-DISCLOSURE AND INTERPERSONAL COMMUNICATION

## Are You Willing to Let Others into Your Life?

**Self-disclosure** is how much you are willing to share with others about your life, your goals, your dreams, your fears, and your setbacks. Often, self-disclosure determines the *quality* of your interpersonal relationships. The level of self-disclosure is up to you, and it can vary from ***insignificant*** facts ("I had dinner at O'Toole's last night" or "I'm a Leo") to ***informational*** facts ("I'm majoring in history" or "I have two children") to ***highly significant*** facts ("I'm fighting ovarian cancer" or "I'm going through a divorce"). True self-disclosure must present new information about the parties involved.

Irwin Altman and Dalmas Taylor (1973) state that self-disclosure is "showing ourselves to others on a conscious and unconscious level." They use the analogy of an onion and suggest that you think of your life as having multiple layers. As you know, an onion has layer after layer, each hidden beneath another layer. The outer layer is different from the inner layers and is only the covering of what lies inside—much like our clothes are a covering for what is inside us. The skin of an onion is easily peeled away. The further you peel into the onion, the smaller it becomes and the more protected those inner layers are. We too have many layers and we can choose to "peel" them away or keep them all intact.

Consider Figure 3.5. What would you be willing to reveal (peel away) about yourself and to whom would you feel comfortable revealing this information?

Everyone has more than three layers, but this figure gives you a good example of how you can peel away layers to let others know you more intimately. By self-disclosing and getting past your outer layers, you can enrich the quality of your relationships with others and also strengthen your own self-concept. You must, however, self-disclose (tell the truth) to yourself before you can ever self-disclose to others. Without personal and interpersonal self-disclosure, you cannot have mature, intimate, well-developed, sincere interpersonal relationships because your inner life will remain hidden.

**FIGURE 3.5** *The Third Layer*

**Outer (public) Layer or Insignificant fact:** What would you be willing to reveal?
_____
_____
_____
To Whom? _____

**Second Layer or Informational fact:** What would you be willing to reveal?
_____
_____
To Whom? _____

**Third Layer or Highly Significant fact:** What would you be willing to reveal?
_____
_____
_____
To Whom? _____

# THE TIES THAT BIND

## How Can You Strengthen Your Relationships with Friends?

Think about your best friend. How did you meet? In class? Through another person? By chance? What was the force that brought you together, and more importantly, what is the "glue" that holds you together? If you compare your relationships with your closest friends, you will probably recognize that honest communication, self-disclosure, and trust are paramount in these relationships. You can't choose your family, but you can, and do, choose your friends.

So, why are friendships important? Friendships can bring a plethora of joys including comfort, understanding, a loyal confidant, and a listening ear. A friend gives you someone to talk with about happiness and sorrow and someone to laugh with when things are funny. You can share your hopes, dreams, and fears with good friends. Take a moment and list the qualities that you like in your close friends. Consider the emotional, intellectual, spiritual, and physical aspects of friendship.

*"The worst solitude is to be destitute of sincere friendship."*
—Francis Bacon

_____
_____
_____

As a new college student, you are in the process of building a community of friends and associates. When making new friends, consider adding people to your life who:

▶ Treat you kindly, fairly, and equally.

▶ Bring new and different ideas and experiences to your life.

▶ May be very different from friends you have had in the past.

▶ Have ambition and courage and are outgoing and adventurous.

▶ Have healthy work habits, strong ethics, and pride in his or her character.

▶ Enjoy college and learning new things.

▶ Have found their goals and mission in life.

origin. These groups may be marked or identified by distinguishing features and physical characteristics. But in some cases, they can be identified by their religion or language even when physical differences do not exist. To others, ethnicity might simply mean national origin. According to Feagin and Feagin (2008), an ethnic group is "a group socially distinguished or set apart, by others or by itself, primarily on the basis of cultural or national-origin characteristics."

## ESSENTIAL CORNERSTONE

### Adaptability:
How can learning about different types of diversity help you become more adaptable in a changing workplace?

### Social Networking Moment:
Share your response to this Essential Cornerstone with peers in your social network. Choose two responses from your peers and respond to their postings.

**SEXUAL ORIENTATION** According to the American Psychological Association, sexual orientation "refers to an enduring pattern of emotional, romantic, and/or sexual attractions to men, women, or both sexes. Sexual orientation also refers to a person's sense of identity based on those attractions, related behaviors, and a membership in a community of others who share those attractions.... There is no consensus among scientists about the exact reasons that an individual develops a heterosexual, bisexual, gay, or lesbian orientation. Some think that both nature and nurture both play complex roles" (2008). The conclusion, however, is that most people experience little or no sense of choice about their sexual orientation: "Most scientific thinking holds that one's sexuality is genetically determined rather than being a matter of choice" (DeVito, 2008).

**SOCIAL CLASS DIVERSITY** Socioeconomic status or social class can be defined using the parameters of a person's income, education level, type of work he or she does, and family heritage. Someone may have social status because his grandfather was a U.S. senator, but that social status doesn't necessarily mean that he has large wealth. When class is discussed in this country, this terminology is generally used: *upper class* (wealthy), *middle class* (people who have jobs requiring a considerable amount of education or who own businesses that afford them a certain level of income), and *lower class* (people who are unemployed or hold very low-level jobs that do not provide them with a good standard of living).

**GENERATIONAL DIVERSITY** While you may have heard of many different types of diversity, you are less likely to have been informed about generational diversity. More than likely, you know that different generations have been labeled with names such as the "Traditionals," "Boomers," "Generation X," and the current generation, which is referred to as the "Millennials." For the first time, four distinctly different generations, each with its own loyalties, priorities, and expectations, are working side by side in the workplace. (Glenn, 2007). Naturally, with such a wide range of ages, there are conflicts over how work should be processed, what constitutes company loyalty, how many hours one should work after closing time, and how best to communicate.

**GEOGRAPHIC REGION DIVERSITY** As strange as it may seem, there are some who are prejudiced against people from certain geographic regions in this country. It is true that there are people in all parts of our country who have very different ideas from those of the masses; however, we should not label an entire section of the country based on the actions of a few. In the case of geographic regions, as in all cases, one should determine the characteristics of an individual rather than assume that that person's characteristics are based on his or her membership in a particular group. You might find that a friend from California could open up all kinds of new ideas and thinking for you, or that a friend from the South could show you beautiful beaches and golf courses, or that a friend from New York could introduce you to Broadway and Central Park. As you expand your personal community of friends, make a special effort to get to know people from other regions of the country and learn to consider their character rather than where they come from.

**PHYSICAL, MENTAL, AND EMOTIONAL DIVERSITY** You will encounter a number of students who deal with physical, mental, and emotional challenges. They could be visually impaired or deaf or confined to a wheelchair. Quite a few college students suffer from depression and others battle bipolar disorders. Research shows that 49.2% of all students experience some kind of learning disability such as dyslexia. We tend to assume that students who are labeled legally blind cannot see, when, in fact, 80% can read large- or regular-print books. They may have a problem in only one eye. Truthfully, these students are just like everyone else except that they have a physical or mental condition that makes life a little more difficult. They have feelings just like the rest of us; they want to be included in social life and activities; and they don't won't to be treated as disabled, different, and unable to participate.

**IDEOLOGICAL DIVERSITY** The fact that we all have different opinions and ideas that are rooted in our family backgrounds, socioeconomic status, religious beliefs, cultural experiences, political beliefs, educational levels, and travel experiences creates great diversity and can cause difficulties between individuals and groups of people. "Individuals tend to come to more extreme views if they deliberate a given issue with like-minded people" (Kallock, 2008). In other words, internal diversity among individuals tends to be squelched by the forces of group polarization. People tend to remain moderate in expressing their beliefs until they are confident that others agree with them, and then they tend to become more extreme in their beliefs. These personal beliefs create diversity in thoughts, reasoning, ideas, and creativity. Political beliefs, for example, can be quite polarizing between individuals and groups. As an educated, enlightened individual, you will need to practice patience and understanding of other people's viewpoints and why they believe them even when you are diabolically opposed to those beliefs.

# CONFLICT IN RELATIONSHIPS IS INEVITABLE

## Why Is It Important to Learn How You Deal with Conflict?

Many people intensely dislike conflict and will go to extreme measures to avoid it. On the other hand, some people seem to thrive on conflict and enjoy creating situations that put people at odds with each other. While in college, you certainly will not be sheltered from conflicts. In fact, on a college campus where a very diverse population lives and learns together, conflict is likely to arise on a regular basis. The simple truth is that conflict is pervasive throughout our culture, and you simply cannot avoid having some confrontations with other people. Therefore, you should not try to avoid conflict; rather, you can use it to create better relationships by exploring workable solutions—hopefully, win-win solutions.

Consider the Chinese symbol for *Conflict* in Figure 3.6. You can see that it is made up of two different symbols: **Danger** and **Hidden Opportunity**. Why? Because when you are engaged in a conflict, you have the potential to enter into *dangerous* territory. Violence, alienation, and irreparable damage could be caused. However, you also have the *hidden opportunity* to grow, learn, and strengthen your relationships. Just because conflict in relationships is inevitable does not mean that it has to be permanent, dangerous, or destructive. Con-

**FIGURE 3.6** *Chinese Figure for Conflict*

危

**Danger**

機

**Hidden Opportunity**

# From Ordinary
## to *Extraordinary*

REAL PEOPLE | REAL LIVES | REAL CHANGE

**VIVIAN WONG**
Founder
Global Trading Consortium, Greenville, SC

In the early 1960s, I was a very young woman and a new wife when my husband began talking about coming to America. We dreamed of living in our own house with a yard rather than a flat as we did in China. We were working as front desk clerks in a Hong Kong hotel when fate intervened in the person of Robert Wilson, who was in China marketing his Barbeque King grills. We told him about our dream, and he decided to help us. Many people would have never followed through but Mr. Wilson gave us $100 and told us to get photos made and to acquire passports. He promised to work on a Visa for us. It took a year for us to finally be granted a Trainee Visa, and we headed to Greenville, SC, to work for Mr. Wilson, leaving our little girl behind with her grandparents.

In South Carolina we trained and learned to sell Barbeque King grills in China. After about ten months, we were very homesick for China so we went home. We realized after we got to Hong Kong that our hearts were really in America because now we were homesick for Greenville. Without even realizing it, Greenville and America had become our home. Mr. Wilson brought us back and this time, we brought our little girl.

In 1967 we were blessed with twin girls, and in 1968 we were given a permanent Visa and U.S. citizenship. I often say, "We spent the first twenty years in America simply trying to earn a meager living and put food on the table." We began to look around to try to figure out what kind of edge we had that we could use to start our

*"We spent the first twenty years in America simply trying to earn a meager living and put food on the table."*

own business in Greenville because we didn't want to work for other people the rest of our lives. In 1970, with Mr. Wilson as a partner, we opened our first business, a Chinese restaurant, but before we opened, my husband had spent two years in Washington, DC, training for restaurant ownership. We opened other restaurants in 1975, 1976, and 1988. By now, I could put food on the table, and I wanted to do something other than sell egg rolls.

I became very interested in commercial real estate and began to learn everything I could and branched out into real estate. Today I own several hotels in America, and I am starting a chain in China with my brother. This chain will be called Hotel Carolina and is aimed at business travelers. We found a niche that had not been tapped—a clean, reasonable, three-star hotel for business travelers who can't afford five-star accommodations. We also own and operate a large business park and foreign trade zone in Greenville, SC. We are part-

# From Ordinary to Extraordinary

REAL PEOPLE | REAL LIVES | REAL CHANGE

ners and franchisees of the Medicine Shoppe, China's first American pharmacy.

I am also a partner in three banks located in Greenville, Atlanta, and Myrtle Beach. People ask me how I know how to own and manage such a disparate collection of businesses. My answer is simple: "I know how to connect the dots; this is what I do best." I also believe strongly in networking and communicating with partners and people who know how to get things done. I have partners all over the world in a great variety of businesses. I have developed the vision, action plans, and good teams to make things happen. I take nothing for granted!

We have been very blessed to live in America and now to open businesses in our native land. In this wonderful country, we have succeeded beyond our wildest dreams! So can you!

## EXTRAORDINARY REFLECTION

**Read the following statement and respond in your online journal or class notebook.**

Mrs. Wong mentions how important it is to establish relationships, communicate, and network with other people. How can communication, networking, and strong relationships help you in your chosen field?

flict can occur in any relationship, whether it is with your parents, your girlfriend or boyfriend, your best friend, a roommate, a spouse or partner, your children, or a total stranger.

Some of the causes of *relationship tensions* include:

| | | |
|---|---|---|
| Jealousy | Honesty | Emotions |
| Dependency | Culture | Sexual orientation |
| Outside commitments | Opinions, values, beliefs | Perceptions |
| Personality traits or flaws | Affiliations | |

**DEALING WITH CONFLICT**  Conflict does not happen in just one form. Conflict can be personal or situational. There are several ways that people deal with issues. They include:

▶ **Blowing your lid**—This involves screaming, uncontrolled anger, hurling insults, and an unwillingness to listen.

▶ **Shunning**—This involves shutting the other person out and being unwilling to engage in any type of communication or resolution.

▶ **Sarcasm**—This involves using stinging remarks to make the other person feel small, unimportant, insignificant, or stupid.

▶ **Mocking** This involves using past experiences or words to "mock" or ridicule the other person; laughing at him or her; or poking fun at him or her or [run up]the situation.

▶ **Civility** This involves sitting down and logically, rationally discussing the issues or problems and trying to come to a win-win solution. (Adapted from Baxter et al., 1993)

**3.7**  *Types of Difficult Behaviors and People*

FIGURE

| Types of Difficult Behaviors by Difficult People | Description | What can you do to effectively deal with them? |
|---|---|---|
| Gossiping | They don't do a lot of work and would rather spread rumors and untruths about others to make themselves feel better. | |
| Manipulating | They constantly try to negotiate every aspect of life. I'll do this for you if you do this for me." | |
| Showing Off | They usually talk more than they work. They know everything about every subject and are not willing to listen to anything or anybody new. | |
| Goofing Off | They usually do very little and what they do is incorrect. They pretend to be involved, but spend more time looking busy more than actually being busy. | |
| Standing By | They do not get involved in anything or any cause but then complain because something did not go their way. | |
| Complaining | They may produce work and be involved, but complains about everything and everybody and seems to exist under a rain cloud. Nothing is ever good enough. | |
| Dooming and Glooming | They are so negative they make death look like a joy ride. They are constantly thinking about the "worst-case" scenario and don't mind voicing it. | |

## THINKING *for* CHANGE: An Activity for Critical Reflection

In a student leadership council meeting, John suggested that the council sponsor a fund raiser to secure funds to send the officers to a leadership retreat. His suggestion included having all members of the council participate in raising the funds even though only the officers would get to attend the retreat. This suggestion set Barry off, and he began to talk very animatedly in a loud, intimidating voice about how this would be unfair to everyone who worked and didn't get to attend the retreat. He stood up and towered over John and continued to use abusive language.

Rather than fuel Barry's argument, John remained calm, and in a very quiet, controlled, but firm voice,

said, "Barry, I understand your feelings, but what you need to realize is that next year you will be an officer, and all of us will be working to send you and your team. Why don't we move on to another agenda item and come back to this one after we have all had time to collect our thoughts."

In your own words, what two suggestions would you give John to help him further control the situation at hand?

1. _____

2. _____

# THE FACES OF CONFLICT

## Uggggg! How Do I Deal with Negative, Nasty, Difficult People?

We've all encountered them from time to time: DIFFICULT people who are negative, angry, unhappy, destructive, argumentative, sad, depressed, and/or judgmental. They are people who seem to walk around with a black cloud above their heads and seem to enjoy causing interpersonal conflict—like the negative people discussed in Chapter 1. They are likely to pop up everywhere—at work, in class, in traffic, in restaurants, and even in places of worship. They cannot be avoided. Figure 3.7 profiles the most common types of negative, difficult people. Perhaps you recognize some of them. Read the descriptions and try to develop at least two or three strategies to effectively deal with each type of difficult person. In developing your strategies, you may have to rely on others in your class for assistance, pull from your past experiences (what worked and what did not), and do some research on your own.

Learning to manage conflict and work with difficult people is a very important step in developing sound communication practices and healthy relationships. If you can learn to stay calm, put yourself in the other person's shoes, and try to find mutually beneficial solutions, you will gain admiration and respect from your friends, family, peers, and colleagues. As you consider conflicts in your life and relationships, take a moment to complete the Conflict Management Assessment (Figure 3.8) to determine your awareness of issues related to conflict and managing conflict.

# STANDARDS FOR DEALING WITH DIFFICULT PEOPLE AND MANAGING CONFLICT

▶ Check your own behavior before doing anything else. Don't become the same type of difficult person as the people with whom you are dealing. Fighting fire with fire will only make the flame hotter. Learn to be the "cool" one.

## DID You KNOW?

**DITH PRAN** was born in 1942 in Cambodia. He learned English and French and worked for the U.S. government as a translator, then for a British film crew, and then as a hotel receptionist. In 1975, after meeting a *New York Times* reporter, he taught himself how to take pictures.

After U.S. forces left Cambodia, he stayed behind to cover the fall of Phnom Penh to the communist Khmer Rouge. Having stayed behind, he was forced to remain in Cambodia while foreign reporters were allowed to leave. From this point, Dith witnessed many atrocities and had to hide the fact that he was educated or knew any Americans. He pretended to be a taxicab driver.

Cambodians were forced to work in labor camps, and Dith was not immune from this. He endured four years of starvation and torture before Vietnam overthrew the Khmer Rouge and he was able to escape the labor camp. He coined the term "the Killing Fields" because of the number of dead bodies he encountered during his escape. He later learned that his three brothers and 50 members of his family had been killed during the genocide.

*"Everything we shut our eyes to, everything we run away from, everything we deny, denigrate or despise, serves to defeat us in the end. What seems nasty, painful, and evil, can become a source of beauty, joy, and strength, if faced with an open mind."*

—Henry Miller

# KNOWLEDGE *in* BLOOM

## Managing Conflict in Interpersonal Relationships

Each chapter-end assessment is based on *Bloom's Taxonomy of Learning.* See the inside front cover for a quick review.

### UTILIZES LEVELS 1–6 ON THE TAXONOMY

**EXPLANATION:** Read the following brief case study. After you have familiarized yourself with the situation, work through each level of Bloom's Taxonomy to discuss, analyze, and solve the conflict.

**CASE:** My (*choose one: boyfriend, girlfriend, husband, wife, partner, best friend*) is a nice person. Most of the time, he or she is very affectionate and passionate toward me. He or she is supportive of my career and most of the time, we get along well. However, it seems that whenever something goes wrong or he or she gets angry or stressed, I am the person who receives the brunt of his or her aggression regardless of the cause. He or she can become very verbally abusive, sometimes yelling, screaming, cursing, and hurling insults. Sometimes, I just get the "silent treatment." On certain occasions, he or she has used personal and private information that I shared with him or her to hurt or insult me. He or she has never physically abused me, but I sometimes worry that the verbal aggression may turn into physical aggression. I'm not sure what to do or what to make of this situation.

**Procedure:** Answer the following questions, from each level of Bloom's Taxonomy, related to the case. Be specific and use the information from this chapter, your own experiences, and outside research to aid in your responses.

| BLOOM LEVEL | QUESTION | RESPONSE |
|---|---|---|
| **LEVEL 1 REMEMBERING** | In your own words, define the conflict(s) and the cause(s). | |
| **LEVEL 2 UNDERSTANDING** | Identify at least three major problems in this interpersonal relationship. | |
| **LEVEL 3 APPLYING** | What solutions would you offer to both parties? | |
| **LEVEL 4 ANALYZING** | Compare and contrast this interpersonal relationship with a "healthier," more mature, productive relationship. | |
| **LEVEL 5 EVALUATING** | Develop a brief argument as to why you think this relationship is more the norm than the unusual. | |
| **LEVEL 6 CREATING** | Develop/design a plan by which you would make this situation better. List at least five positive steps to bring about change. | |

# SQ3R *Mastery* STUDY SHEET

| | |
|---|---|
| **EXAMPLE QUESTION:** *(from page 62)*<br>What are the six elements of the communication process? | **ANSWER:** |
| **EXAMPLE QUESTION:** *(from page 68)*<br>What is self-disclosure and why is it important for healthy relationships? | **ANSWER:** |
| **AUTHOR QUESTION:** *(from page 63)*<br>Why is interpersonal communication important to your professional growth? | **ANSWER:** |
| **AUTHOR QUESTION:** *(from page 66)*<br>What is Computer Mediated Communication (CMC)? | **ANSWER:** |
| **AUTHOR QUESTION:** *(from page 77)*<br>Discuss at least two strategies for managing conflict. | **ANSWER:** |
| **AUTHOR QUESTION:** *(from page 68)*<br>In your own words, define "technological recluse." | **ANSWER:** |
| **AUTHOR QUESTION:** *(from page 71)*<br>Discuss three dimensions of diversity. | **ANSWER:** |
| **YOUR QUESTION:** *(from page ____)* | **ANSWER:** |
| **YOUR QUESTION:** *(from page ____)* | **ANSWER:** |
| **YOUR QUESTION:** *(from page ____)* | **ANSWER:** |
| **YOUR QUESTION:** *(from page ____)* | **ANSWER:** |
| **YOUR QUESTION:** *(from page ____)* | **ANSWER:** |

Finally, after answering these questions, recite this chapter's major points in your mind. Consider the following general questions to help you master this material.

► What was it about?
► What does it mean?
► What was the most important thing I learned? Why?
► What were the key points to remember?

# CHAPTER 4
# THINK

EXPANDING YOUR APTITUDE FOR CRITICAL THINKING, EMOTIONAL INTELLIGENCE, AND INFORMATION LITERACY SKILLS

"Many people think they are thinking when they are merely rearranging their prejudices."

—William James

PART ONE CHANGING YOUR THOUGHTS

# SCAN & QUESTION

In the preface of this book (page xix), you read about the **SQ3R Study Method**. Right now, take a few moments, **scan this chapter**, and on page 110, write **five questions** that you think will be important to your mastery of this material. In addition to the two questions below, you will find five questions from your authors. Use one of your **"On The Test"** stickers to flag this page for easy reference.

**EXAMPLES:**

▶ **Why is emotional intelligence important to critical thinking?** (from page 89)

▶ **What is information literacy?** (from page 94)

# THINKING ABOUT THINKING

## Do You Know *Why* You Think *What* You Think?

Same-sex couples should be able to marry and adopt children. Think about that statement for a moment. You may be saying to yourself, *"I don't have to think about it—I know what my opinions on same-sex marriage and adoption are."* However, do you know WHY you have these opinions? Can you trace your decisions back to certain events or moments in your life? Do you think that your emotions cloud your thoughts on this issue? Is there a right or wrong side to this debate? Does your religion or culture come into play when thinking about this issue? Did someone else influence your thoughts or are they your very own, developed through research and conversations regarding this issue?

What are you thinking right now? More importantly, why are you thinking the way you are right now? What is causing you to believe, feel, or think one way or the other regarding this issue? What are the facts and/or opinions that have led you to your conclusion? At this moment, what are the origins on which you are basing your thoughts about this issue—emotions or facts, fallacies or truths, data or opinions, interviews or hearsay, reason or misjudgment, fear or empathy?

We purposefully chose a "hot topic" issue to open this chapter because understanding why and how we formulate thoughts and ideas is the main objective of this chapter and critical thinking in general. This chapter is about believing and disbelieving, seeking, uncovering, debunking myths, uncovering biases, identifying and solving problems, using information correctly, and proving the impossible possible. It is about proof, logic, evidence, and developing ideas and opinions based on hard-core facts and credible research. This chapter is about seeking truth and expanding your mind to unimaginable limits. This chapter is about the fundamental hallmarks of becoming an educated citizen; it is about human thought and reasoning.

# THE IMPORTANCE OF CRITICAL THINKING

## When Will I Ever Use it?

Have you ever made a decision that turned out to be a mistake? Have you ever said to yourself, *"If only I could go back and . . . "*? Have you ever regretted actions you took toward a person or situation? Have you ever planned a paper or speech that was flawless? Have you ever had to make a hard, painful decision that turned out to be "the best decision of your life"? If the answer to any of these questions is yes, you might be able to trace the consequences back to your *thought process* at the time of the decision. Let's face it, sometimes good and bad things just happen out of luck or circumstance. More often than not, however, many events in our lives are driven by the thought processes involved when we made the initial decision and chose to act on that decision.

Critical thinking can serve us in many areas as students and citizens in a free society. As a student, *critical thinking can help you*:

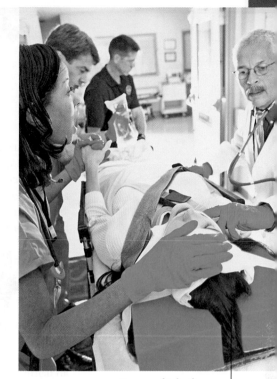

► focus on relevant issues/problems and avoid wasting time on trivia.

► gather relevant, accurate information regarding finances, goals, decision making, relationships, civic responsibility, and environmental issues, to name a few.

► understand and remember facts and organize thoughts logically.

► look more deeply at problems, analyze their causes, and solve them more accurately.

► develop appropriate and meaningful study plans and manage your priorities.

► improve your problem-solving skills.

► control your emotions so that you can make rational judgments and become more open-minded.

► produce new knowledge through research and analysis.

► determine the accuracy of printed and spoken words.

► detect bias and determine the relevance of arguments and persuasion.

Can you think of a professional career where critical thinking will not be required?

# AN EIGHT-POINT PLAN FOR CRITICAL THINKING

## Can You Really Make Critical Thinking Work for You in Everyday Life?

Does critical thinking really matter? Seriously? Can it do anything to improve the quality of your life? The answer is yes. Critical thinking has daily, practical uses, from making sound financial decisions to improving personal relationships to helping you become a better student. You can improve your critical thinking skills by watching your emotional reactions, using solid research and facts to build your examples and thoughts, and practicing open-mindedness.

Conversely, can the lack of critical thinking skills cause real problems? The answer, once again, is yes. Poor critical thinking skills can impair your judgment, lead you to make rash decisions, and even cause you to let your emotions rule (and sometimes ruin) your life. Critical thinking can be hampered by a number of factors including closed-mindedness, unflappable opinions based on rumor instead of facts, cultural and/or religious bias, lack of accurate information, faulty arguments, and negativity.

As you begin to build and expand your critical thinking skills, consider the eight steps in Figure 4.1.

### Step One: Understanding and Using Emotional Intelligence

Emotions play a vital role in our lives. They help us feel compassion, help us help others, help us reach out in times of need, and help us relate to others. On the other hand, emotions can also cause some problems in your critical thinking process. You do not—and should not have to—eliminate emotions from your thoughts, but it is crucial that you know when your emotions are clouding an issue and causing you to act and speak before thinking.

Our emotions originate in the brain. If you have EI skills, your ***thinking mind*** and ***emotional mind*** should function together, making it more likely that you will craft sound, rational decisions. In other words, you will **think** before you **act**. When these two minds do not operate in harmony, you might make highly emotional decisions that can be viewed as irrational.

To become a successful, happy person, interpersonal relationships are important and learning to manage the entire spectrum of your personal emotions from the extreme **negative side** to the extreme **positive side** will be vitally important. This spectrum ranges from the darker side of your emotions (extreme negative pole) to the optimistic side (extreme positive pole).

---

FIGURE **4.3**    *The Amygdala*

Don't let this word or concept frighten you. If you have never heard the word ***"amygdala"*** (pronounced ah-MIG-da-la), you're not alone. Most people have not. But this term and concept are important for you to be able to understand the overall aspects of EI. The amygdala, simply a part of the brain's emotional system, can cause us to go into default behavior based on what we remember from a similar experience. Do I use ***fight*** or ***flight***? Basically, the amygdala is there to protect us when we become afraid or emotionally upset. When influenced by the amygdala, everything becomes ***about us***. We become more judgmental. We don't stop to think about differences or the other person's feelings or the relationship. The amygdala can trigger an emotional response **before** the rest of the brain has had time to understand what is happening, and this situation causes us to have problems with others.

The amygdala remembers frustrations, fears, hurt feelings, and anger from our past. The tension from these past experiences causes the amygdala to go into default behavior—we ***feel*** before we ***think***—and this can create a potentially explosive situation. If you had a bad experience several years ago and are placed in a similar situation, the amygdala will remember and trigger emotions that cause the body to respond. These feelings often cause people to bypass critical thinking (the logical brain) and to respond with angry words or actions (the emotional brain). For example:

▶ They get angry—you get angry.

▶ They curse you—you curse them.

▶ They use physical violence—you use physical violence.

However, if you remain calm and level-headed, you will begin to see that the other person usually begins to calm down, too. He or she will follow your emotional lead, positive or negative, and if you're calm and rational, anger and violence become out of place for most people.

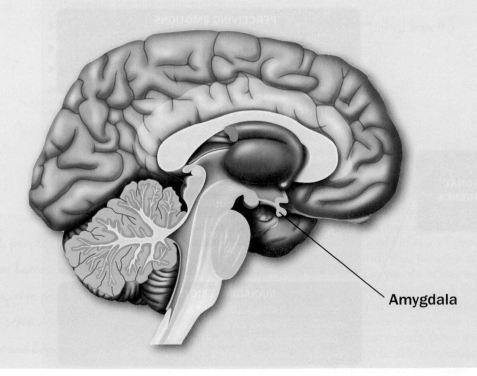

**Amygdala**

Study the spectrum of emotions illustrated in Figure 4.4. Think about which of these emotions you experience frequently and where you are located most of the time on this emotional continuum.

As you can see, the restraint and management of your personal emotional spectrum can impact you and your thinking skills greatly at home, at school, and at work. Today, this relatively new concept is being given a great deal of attention on college campuses and in the workplace. Not only will you find it helpful and necessary to manage your emotions at school, you will also need to be able to apply emotional management techniques at home and with family, friends, and work associates.

Think about one experience you've had in the past where your negative emotions "took over." Perhaps it was anger, fear, sorrow, hatred, or rage.

What was the situation and where were you when it happened? Be specific. _____

_____

_____

What triggered these emotions? _____

_____

_____

What were the negative consequences to you (or someone else) because of your emotions?

_____

_____

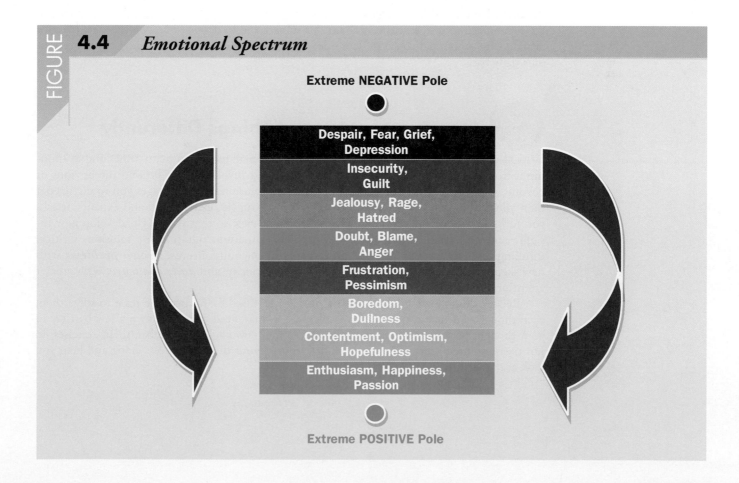

FIGURE 4.4   *Emotional Spectrum*

Extreme NEGATIVE Pole

Despair, Fear, Grief, Depression

Insecurity, Guilt

Jealousy, Rage, Hatred

Doubt, Blame, Anger

Frustration, Pessimism

Boredom, Dullness

Contentment, Optimism, Hopefulness

Enthusiasm, Happiness, Passion

Extreme POSITIVE Pole

FIGURE

**4.5** *Guidelines for Emotional Management at School, Work, and Beyond*

▶ Face each day with an "I feel great, nothing is going to ruin my day" attitude.

▶ Hear all sides of an argument before you say anything, make a decision, or take an action.

▶ Practice a win-win philosophy at all times and work tirelessly to make it happen.

▶ Avoid letting your personal feelings about a person dictate your decisions.

▶ Never, never, never lose control!

▶ Avoid negative stereotyping and typecasting people into negative categories.

▶ Never look at or judge someone through someone else's eyes or experiences.

▶ Learn to keep a tight rein on any emotional "hotspots" such as anger, rage, and jealousy.

▶ Strive to treat people so well that you can always put your head on your pillow and sleep well, knowing that you have not been underhanded, rude, or unfair.

How did these emotions affect your ability to think clearly and critically? _____

_____

_____

_____

Because EI skills and knowledge are so important to your success in all areas of your life, you are encouraged to read extensively about this subject and to design your own personal plan for dealing with emotional concerns. Consider the tips in Figure 4.5 for managing your emotions on a daily basis.

## Step Two: Looking at Things Differently

Critical thinking involves looking at something you may have seen many times and examining it from many different angles and perspectives. It involves going beyond the obvious or beyond "easy" to seek new understanding and rare solutions. It encourages you to dig deeper than you have before, to get below the surface, to struggle, experiment, and expand. It asks you to look at something from an entirely different view so that you might develop new insights and understand more about the problem, situation, question, or solution. Critical thinking involves looking at *common issues* with uncommon eyes, *known problems* with new skepticism, *everyday conflicts* with probing curiosity, and *daily challenges* with greater attention to detail.

Review the following "brain teasers" in Figures 4.6–4.8 and take the time to solve them even though you may not "get" them quickly. You may need to break down a few barriers in your thought process and look at the puzzles from a new angle. Remember, these exercises do not measure intelligence. They are included to prod your thought process along and help you look at things differently.

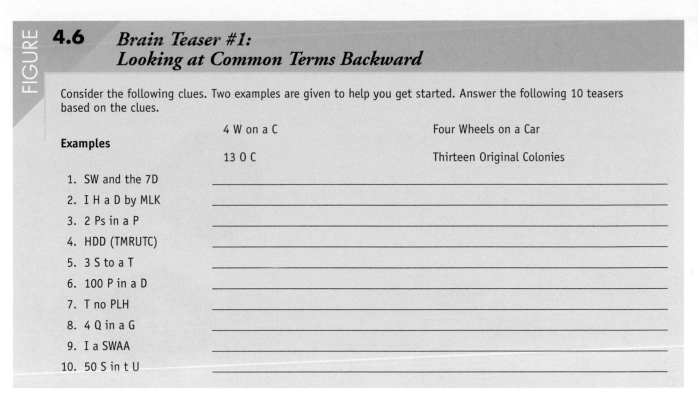

**FIGURE 4.6   Brain Teaser #1:
Looking at Common Terms Backward**

Consider the following clues. Two examples are given to help you get started. Answer the following 10 teasers based on the clues.

**Examples**

| 4 W on a C | Four Wheels on a Car |
| 13 O C | Thirteen Original Colonies |

1. SW and the 7D _____
2. I H a D by MLK _____
3. 2 Ps in a P _____
4. HDD (TMRUTC) _____
5. 3 S to a T _____
6. 100 P in a D _____
7. T no PLH _____
8. 4 Q in a G _____
9. I a SWAA _____
10. 50 S in t U _____

How did you do? Was it hard to look at the situation backward or have to look for clues within a series of letters and numbers? Most of us are not used to that. But part of critical thinking is trying to find **clues or patterns**. Perhaps the easiest teaser above was number two in Figure 4.6. Most people know MLK as Martin Luther King, Jr. When you figure that part out, the name of his most popular speech, *I Have a Dream*, becomes easy to figure out. Often, when trying to solve problems or dealing with unknowns, things become easier when you can find a clue or a pattern and build from WHAT you already know.

Examine the brain teaser in Figure 4.7. This teaser is included to help you look at an issue beyond what is actually given to you and considering what is not given.

Once again, you are given a basic clue, but you must go beyond what is given. You must look at the nine dots, but you must NOT let them confine you. You can't let the nine dots control your thoughts—you must move beyond what is given, beyond what you actually see. When you do this, the answer will come to you.

**FIGURE 4.7   Brain Teaser #2:
Seeing What Is Not Given**

Look at the design below. You will find nine dots. Your mission is to connect all nine dots with four straight lines without removing your pencil or pen from the paper. Do not retrace your lines.

· · ·

· · ·

· · ·

**FIGURE**

**4.8** *Brain Teaser #3:*
*The Penny*

Pretend that all life on earth has ended and all traces of civilization are gone–there are no buildings, no people, no animals, no plants–nothing is left but dirt and one penny. Someone from another planet, who knows our language, comes to earth and finds the penny. List all of the things that could be inferred about our civilization based on this one small penny. You should find at least 10 for each side.

1._____
2._____
3._____
4._____
5._____
6._____
7._____
8._____
9._____
10._____

As you continue to look at common things differently and think beyond the obvious, examine the penny in Figure 4.8

Drawing inferences often takes the ability to look at things differently and take something very common and examine it like you have never examined it before. Just as you looked at the penny, you learned new things about it by studying it with different eyes. Think about how you might solve a common problem that you face every day simply by looking at that problem with different eyes, too.

While these activities may seem somewhat trivial, they are provided to help you begin to think about and consider information from different angles. This is a major step in becoming a critical thinker: looking beyond the obvious, thinking outside the box, examining details, and exploring possibilities—basically, looking BEYOND what is given to you.

## Step Three: Managing Information and Becoming Information Literate

"The sheer abundance of information will not in itself create a more informed citizenry without a complementary cluster of abilities necessary to use information correctly."
—ACRL

Critical thinking involves knowing how to deal with all types of information, and ***information literacy*** refers to the skills a person needs to "recognize when information is needed and the ability to locate, evaluate, and effectively use the needed information" (American Library Association, 1989). *Information literacy* impacts all aspects of your college career and will later play a major role in your success in the workplace. You will use information literacy when you write a paper, read and evaluate an article, listen to presenters and determine if you believe what the speakers are saying, and prepare and make your own presentation.

Quite simply, if you are an information literate person, you have learned how to acquire and use information accurately and effectively. Figure 4.9 demonstrates a system for understanding and applying the concepts of information literacy.

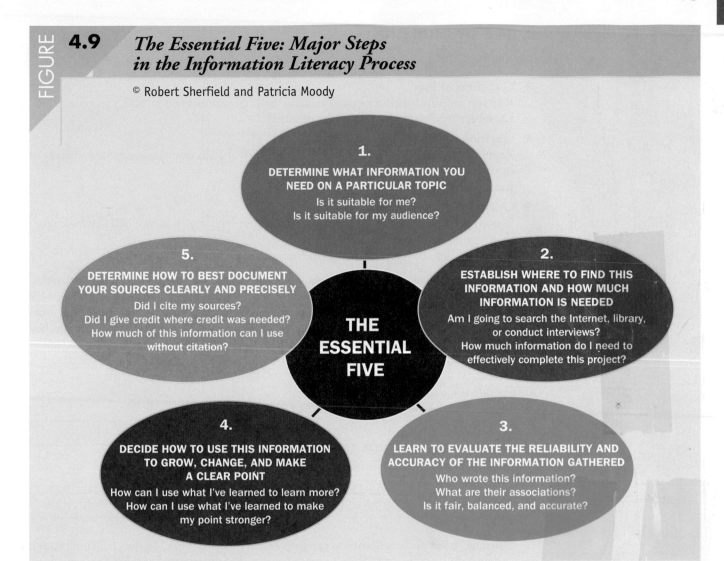

**FIGURE 4.9**  *The Essential Five: Major Steps in the Information Literacy Process*

© Robert Sherfield and Patricia Moody

**THE ESSENTIAL FIVE**

**1.**
DETERMINE WHAT INFORMATION YOU NEED ON A PARTICULAR TOPIC
Is it suitable for me?
Is it suitable for my audience?

**2.**
ESTABLISH WHERE TO FIND THIS INFORMATION AND HOW MUCH INFORMATION IS NEEDED
Am I going to search the Internet, library, or conduct interviews?
How much information do I need to effectively complete this project?

**3.**
LEARN TO EVALUATE THE RELIABILITY AND ACCURACY OF THE INFORMATION GATHERED
Who wrote this information?
What are their associations?
Is it fair, balanced, and accurate?

**4.**
DECIDE HOW TO USE THIS INFORMATION TO GROW, CHANGE, AND MAKE A CLEAR POINT
How can I use what I've learned to learn more?
How can I use what I've learned to make my point stronger?

**5.**
DETERMINE HOW TO BEST DOCUMENT YOUR SOURCES CLEARLY AND PRECISELY
Did I cite my sources?
Did I give credit where credit was needed?
How much of this information can I use without citation?

## Step Four: Asking Questions and Learning to Tolerate Uncertainty

You've asked questions all your life. As a child, you asked your parents, "What's that?" a million times. You probably asked them, "Why do I have to do this?" In later years, you've asked questions of your friends, teachers, strangers, store clerks, and significant others.

Questioning is not new to you, but it may be a new technique to you for exploring, developing, and honing your critical thinking skills. Curiosity may have killed the cat, but it was a smart cat when it died! Your curiosity is one of the most important traits you possess. It helps you grow and learn, and sometimes it may cause you to be uncomfortable. That's OK. This section is provided to assist you in learning how to ask questions to promote knowledge, solve problems, foster strong relationships, and critically analyze difficult situations. It is also included to help you understand the value of knowing how to tolerate uncertainty and avoid jumping to faulty conclusions because uncertainty "got the better of you." It is important to know that sometimes, ***the question is more important than the answer***—especially a faulty answer.

> "It is not possible to become a good thinker and be a poor questioner. Thinking is not driven by answers, but, rather, by questions."
> —Paul and Elder

## Types of Questions

Basically, there are three types of questions, according to Paul and Elder (2006):

▶ **Questions of Fact**
Requires answers based in fact and evidence and have correct and incorrect reponses
**Example:** What is the freezing point of water?

▶ **Questions of Preference**
Requires answers that state a subjective preference and do not necessarily have correct or incorrect responses
**Example:** What is your favorite color?

▶ **Questions of Judgment**
Requires answers based on your judgment based in logic and evidence and can have more than one defensible answer
**Example:** Should Roe vs. Wade be overturned?

Asking questions helps us gain insight where we may have limited knowledge. Answering properly posed questions can also help us expand our knowledge base. For example, if you were assigned to write a paper or give a speech on the topic of *creationism versus evolution*, what five questions would you definitely want that paper or speech to answer when you are finished writing/delivering it? Take some time to think about this issue. Write down at least five questions that you consider essential to the topic of creationism versus evolution.

My five questions are:

1. _____
2. _____
3. _____
4. _____
5. _____

Learning to ask probing questions can help you in everyday situations by challenging you to look beyond the obvious and critically examine everyday situations. **Examine the car advertisement in Figure 4.10.** The car dealership has provided some information, but it is not enough to make a smart, rational decision. What other questions would you ask the dealer to make sure that you are getting a good deal?

What additional questions would you need to ask the dealer to ensure that you are getting a "good" deal?

1. _____
2. _____
3. _____
4. _____
5. _____

## I Am 100% Sure That I Am Not Sure

### CAN YOU TOLERATE UNCERTAINTY?

Asking questions that can be answered is vitally important to critical thinking, but so is learning to tolerate uncertainty and learning to ask questions that may not have an **immediate answer**. Uncertainty causes you to keep going—to not get lazy or give up. If we thought we knew the

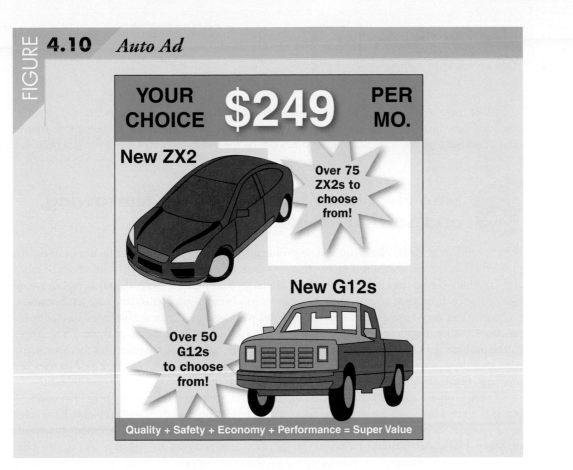

**FIGURE 4.10** *Auto Ad*

answers to everything, we would still be beating rocks together to make fire and we would still be walking everywhere instead of driving or flying. Uncertainty causes humanity to move forward and create new knowledge, to try new things, to consider the impossible. Uncertainty also breeds creative thinking.

Think about all of the uncertainty that can arise in your daily life:

*"Can I be certain that my spouse/partner will not leave me?"* No.
*"Can I be certain that I will remain healthy?"* No.
*"Can I be certain that my children will turn out to be good, caring, loving adults?"* No.
*"Can I be certain what happens to me after I die?"* No.
*"Can I be certain that the plane won't crash or that someone won't crash into my car?"* No.
*"Can I be certain that this will not embarrass me or someone else?"* No.
*"Can I be certain that my investments will grow and I can retire comfortably?"* No.

The inability to tolerate uncertainty can cause stress and anxiety. Sometimes, we just have to "let go" and accept that we do not know the answers. We can work hard to try to find the answers and/or direct our actions so that the answers will be favorable to us, but ultimately, many things in this universe require our tolerance of uncertainty. Sometimes, the best we can hope for is to keep asking questions and seeking the truth.

Think of the good things that initially unanswered questions and uncertainty brought to humanity in many fields of study.

*"Can we send someone to the moon and have them return safely?"*
*"Can we transplant a human heart and have that person live and prosper afterward?"*
*"Can we establish a new country with a new constitution and have it work?"*

*"Can we design and build a skyscraper that is over 140 stories high and have
       it remain safe?"*
*"Can we create an automobile that will get over 50 miles per gallon of fuel?"*
*"Can we help reduce global warming and its effects on the polar ice caps?"*

All of these uncertainties have contributed to the development of new knowledge, new skills,
new jobs, new outlooks, and new ways of living. Therefore, it is important to remember that in
your quest for answers, sometimes uncertainty can be the most important thing you discover.

## Step Five: Identifying, Defining, Narrowing, and Solving Problems

What would your life be like if you had no problems? Most people do not like to face or deal with
problems, but the critical thinker knows that problems exist every day and that they must be faced
and hopefully solved. Some of our problems are larger and more difficult than others, but we all
face problems from time to time. You may have transportation problems. You may have financial
problems. You may have child care problems. You may have academic problems or interpersonal
problems. Many people don't know how to solve problems at school, home, or work. They simply
let the problem go unaddressed until it is too late to reach an amiable solution. But there are many
ways to address and solve problems. In this section, we will discuss how to *identify and narrow* the
problem, *research and develop* alternatives, *evaluate* the alternatives, and *solve* the problem.

Every problem may not have a solution. That can be a hard pill for many people to swallow,
but it is a raw truth and a part of the uncertainty we just discussed. Many problems have solutions, but the solution may not be the one you wanted. It is imperative to remember the words
of Mary Hatwood Futrell, President of the National Education Agency. She states that
*"finding the right answer is important, of course. But more important is developing the ability to see
that many problems have multiple solutions, that getting from X to Y demands basic skills and mental
agility, imagination, persistence, patience."* Consider the problem-solving model in Figure 4.11.

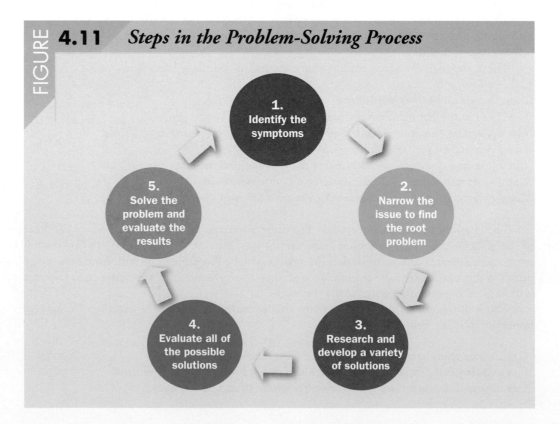

FIGURE **4.11** *Steps in the Problem-Solving Process*

1. Identify the symptoms

2. Narrow the issue to find the root problem

3. Research and develop a variety of solutions

4. Evaluate all of the possible solutions

5. Solve the problem and evaluate the results

## 1. Identify the Symptoms

*Symptoms* and *problems* are not the same thing. Symptoms are PART of the problem, but may not be the problem itself. Think of a problem like you think of your health. For example, you may have aches in your joints, cold chills, and a severe headache. Those seem like problems; but in actuality, they are really symptoms of something larger—perhaps the flu or an infection. You can treat the headache with medicine, and soothe your joint pain with ointment, but until you get at the ROOT of the problem, these symptoms will come back. Problems are much the same way. If you don't move beyond the symptoms, the problem may seem to be solved, but shortly, it will reappear, usually worse than before. Therefore, it is imperative that you identify the symptoms of the **greater problem** before you begin solving anything.

> "When I'm getting ready to reason with a man, I spend one-third of my time thinking about myself and what I am going to say—and two-thirds thinking about him and what he is going to say."
> —Abraham Lincoln

## 2. Narrow the Symptoms to Find the Root Problem

Often, problems keep coming up because we did not deal with the **real problem**—the root problem—but, rather, we dealt with a symptom. Getting to the heart of a problem is hard work that requires a great deal of thought, research, and patience. Begin by putting your symptoms in writing, perhaps on note cards, so that you can lay them out and see them all at once. When doing this, be sure to jot down all of the major and minor symptoms such as:

- ▶ What are the daily challenges that keep coming up?
- ▶ Who is involved?
- ▶ How are the symptoms hindering your overall goals?
- ▶ Who or what is responsible for creating these symptoms?
- ▶ Are the symptoms internal (self-inflicted) or external (other-inflicted)?
- ▶ What obstacles are these symptoms creating?
- ▶ Are the symptoms part of ONE major problem or several problems?

## 3. Research and Develop a Variety of Solutions

It is a mistake to try to solve a problem when you don't have enough information to do so. It may be that you need to conduct interviews, research what others have done who face similar issues, read current data and reports, or even explore historical documents. Paul and Elder (2006) suggest that the type of information you need is determined by the type of problem you have and the question(s) you are trying to answer: "If you have a historical question, you need **historical information**. If you have a biological question, you need **biological information**. If you have an ethical question, you must identify at least one relevant **ethical principle**." Therefore, part of the problem-solving process is to gather your facts—the correct facts—before you try to reach a resolution.

## 4. Evaluate and Analyze All of the Possible Solutions

After you have gathered your research (through formal methods and/or brainstorming), you must now evaluate your solutions to determine which would work best and why. After careful study and deliberation, without emotional interference, analyze the solutions you came up with and determine if they are appropriate or inappropriate. To analyze them, create Columns A and B. Write the possible **solutions in Column A** and an evaluative **comment in Column B**.

## ESSENTIAL CORNERSTONE

**Creativity:**
How can being more creative help you learn to be a better problem solver?

**Social Networking Moment:**
Share your response to this Essential Cornerstone with peers in your social network. Choose two responses from your peers and respond to their postings.

# THINKING FOR CHANGE: An Activity for Critical Reflection

Carson's class was assigned an activity asking them to determine whom they would like to meet if they could meet anyone and which questions they would like to ask them. Some of the class members thought it was a stupid assignment—and Carson was not so sure that she wanted to spend any time on this "weird" activity, either. That evening, she began to think about the question seriously. "Who has been important to the world?" she thought. "Who has done something powerful and extraordinary?" "Who has been awful and caused needless pain?"

She decided that if she could ask anyone anything, she would choose Hitler. She decided that she would ask him these questions: (1) If you had to do it all over again, would you? (2) From where did your hatred come? (3) Why did you have everyone killed who could have revealed your own past? (4) You did not look like the master race you chose to promote. Why did you choose to promote it? (5) Why did you become such a coward in the end and kill yourself?

This interesting project led Carson to use WWII, Hitler, and the German occupation as the basis for her presentation in speech class. She did not just brush off what had seemed to be a "crazy" assignment.

In your own words, what three suggestions would you give to a classmate who thinks an assignment is crazy or useless? Be specific.

1. _____
2. _____
3. _____

**Example** (Using the problem "I don't have enough time to study due to my job"):
With your comments in Column B, you can now begin to eliminate some of the alternatives that are inappropriate at this time.

| A (POSSIBLE SOLUTIONS) | B (COMMENTS) |
|---|---|
| Quit the job. | Very hard to do. I need the money for tuition and car. |
| Cut my hours at work. | Will ask my boss. |
| Find a new job. | Hard to do because of the job market—but will look into it. |
| Get a student loan. | Visit financial aid office tomorrow. |
| Quit school. | No—it is my only chance for a promotion. |

## 5. Solve the Problem and Evaluate the Results

Now that you have a few strong possible solutions, you have some work to do. You will need to talk to your boss, go to the financial aid office, and possibly begin to search for a new job with flexible hours. Basically, you are creating a PLAN to bring this solution to life. After you have researched each possible solution further, you will be able to make a decision based on solid information and facts. You will be able to figure out which solution is the best option for you.

Using the diagram in Figure 4.12 on the next page, work through the following situation and determine the steps that could be taken to solve this problem.

*YOUR TURN: Pretend that your best friend, Nathan, has just come to you with a problem. He tells you that his parents are really coming down hard on him for going to college. It is a strange problem. They believe that Nathan should be working full time and that he is just wasting his time and money, since he did*

FIGURE **4.12** *Solutions in Bloom Diagram*

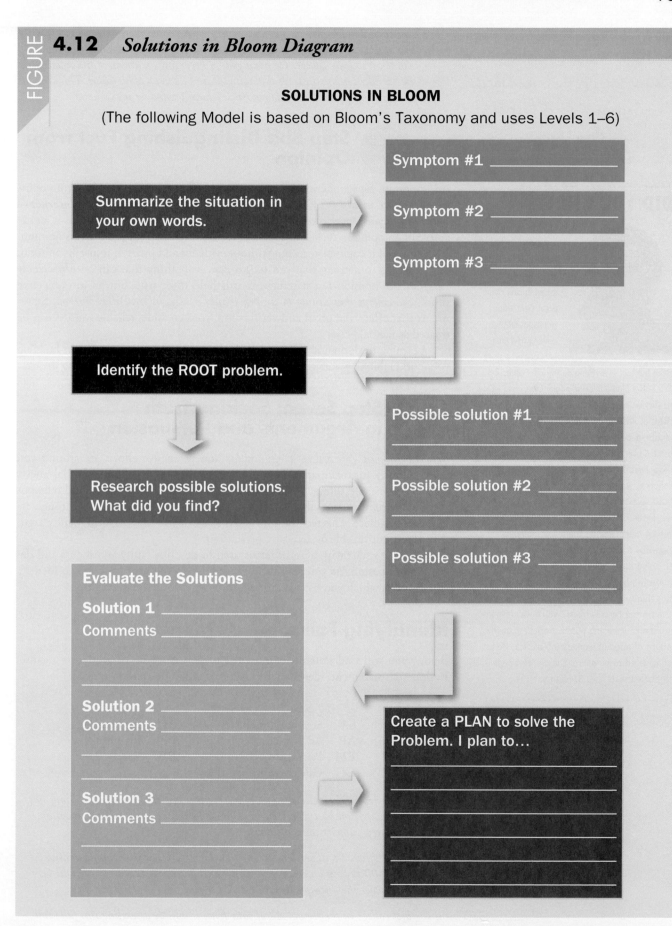

**SOLUTIONS IN BLOOM**
(The following Model is based on Bloom's Taxonomy and uses Levels 1–6)

Summarize the situation in your own words.

Symptom #1 _____

Symptom #2 _____

Symptom #3 _____

Identify the ROOT problem.

Possible solution #1 _____
_____

Research possible solutions. What did you find?

Possible solution #2 _____
_____

Possible solution #3 _____
_____

Evaluate the Solutions

Solution 1 _____
Comments _____
_____
_____

Solution 2 _____
Comments _____
_____
_____

Solution 3 _____
Comments _____
_____
_____

Create a PLAN to solve the Problem. I plan to...
_____
_____
_____
_____
_____
_____

**DID YOU KNOW**

**CESAR CHAVEZ**

was born in 1927 near Yuma, Arizona. He was raised during the Great Depression in unspeakable poverty. His parents owned a small store but lost everything during the Depression. The entire family became migrant workers just to survive. He spent his youth working in the fields of Arizona and California. From the first to eighth grades (when he left school), he attended over 30 schools. Often his family did not have even the basic necessities of water and toilets to survive. They faced not only poverty, but also extreme prejudice and injustice.

Later, Chavez joined the Navy. Upon his return home, seeing the many problems faced by migrant families, he vowed to try to solve the problems and find a way to make life better for his family and the families living in such poverty. He thus founded the United Farm Workers, which was responsible for increasing public awareness of the plight of migrant workers in America. He is considered to be one of the greatest civil rights activists in U.S. history.

not do well in high school. They have threatened to take away his car and kick him out of the house if he does not find a full-time job. Nathan is doing well and does not want to leave college. He has a goal of becoming an architect and knows that he has talent in this area. He is making A's and B's in all of his classes. This does not matter to his parents. They do not value education and see it as a luxury.

## Step Six: Distinguishing Fact from Opinion

An important aspect of critical thinking is the ability to distinguish fact from opinion. ***In most media—TV, radio, newspapers, magazines, and the Internet—opinions surface more often than facts.*** *Reread the previous sentence.* This is an example of an opinion cloaked as a fact. There is no research supporting this opinion. It sounds as if it could be true, but without evidence and proof, it is just an opinion.

A fact is something that can be ***proven***, something that can be ***objectively verified***. An opinion is a statement that is held to be true, but has no objective proof. *Statements that cannot be proven should always be treated as opinion.* Statements that offer valid proof and verification from credible, reliable sources can be treated as factual.

Learning to distinguish fact from opinion can be a paramount step in building your critical thinking skills at work, with family, and especially when analyzing media.

## Step Seven: Seeking Truth in Arguments and Persuasion

Whether or not you realize it, arguments and persuasive efforts are around you daily—hourly, for that matter. They are in newspaper and TV ads, editorials, news commentaries, talk shows, TV magazine shows, political statements, and religious services. It seems at times that almost everyone is trying to persuade us through arguments or advice. This section is included to assist you in recognizing faulty arguments and implausible or deceptive persuasion.

First, let's start with a list of terms used to describe faulty arguments and deceptive persuasion. As you read through the list on the next page, try to identify situations in which you have heard arguments that fit these descriptions.

## Identifying Fallacious Arguments

Below, you will find statements intended to persuade you or argue for a cause. Beside each statement, identify which type of faulty persuasion is used.

| | | | | | |
|---|---|---|---|---|---|
| **AB** | Ad baculum | **SA** | Straw argument | **AH** | Ad hominem |
| **AT** | Appeal to tradition | **AP** | Ad populum | **PF** | Plain folks |
| **AV** | Ad verecundiam | **PM** | Patriotism | **BW** | Bandwagon |
| **ST** | Scare tactic | **GG** | Glittering generalities | | |

_____ 1. *This country has never faltered in the face of adversity. Our strong, united military has seen us through many troubled times, and it will see us through our current situation. This is your country; support your military.*

_____ 2. *If I am elected to office, I will personally lobby for lower taxes, a new comprehensive crime bill, a $2,500 tax cut on every new home, and better education, and I will personally work to lower the unemployment rate.*

_____ 3. *This is the best college in the region. All of your friends will be attending this fall. You don't want to be left out; you should join us, too.*

_____ 4. *If you really listen to Governor Wise's proposal on health care, you will see that there is no way that we can have a national system. You will not be able to select your doctor, you will not be able to go to the hospital of your choice, and you will not be able to get immediate attention. His proposal is not as comprehensive as our proposal.*

_____ 5. *My father went to Honors College, I went to Honors College, and you will go to Honors College. It is the way things have been for the people in this family. There is no need to break with tradition now.*

_____ 6. *The witness's testimony is useless. He is an alcoholic; he is dishonest and corrupt. To make matters worse, he was a member of the Leftist Party.*

_____ 7. *The gentleman on the witness stand is your neighbor, he is your friend, he is just like you. Sure, he may have more money and drive a Mercedes, but his heart never left the Elm Community.*

_____ 8. *John F. Kennedy once said, "Ask not what your country can do for you; ask what you can do for your country." This is the time to act, my fellow citizens. You can give $200 to our cause and you will be fulfilling the wish of President Kennedy.*

_____ 9. *Out of the 7,000 people polled, 72% believe that there is life beyond our planet. Therefore, there must be life beyond earth.*

_____ 10. *Without this new medication, you will die.*

_____ 11. *I don't care what anyone says. If you don't come around to our way of thinking, you'd better start watching your back.*

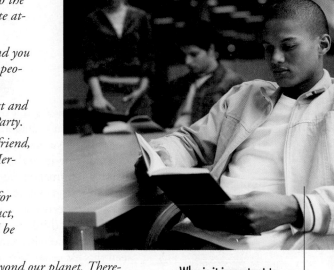

Why is it important to read and research possible solutions before you make decisions?

As you develop your critical thinking skills, you will begin to recognize the illogical nature of many thoughts, the falsehoods of many statements, the deception in some advertisements, and the irrational

## Terminology for Fallacious Arguments

| | |
|---|---|
| Ad baculum | Ad baculum is an argument that tries to persuade based on force. Threats of alienation, disapproval, or even violence may accompany this type of argument. |
| Ad hominem | Ad hominem is when someone initiates a personal attack on someone else rather than listening to and rationally debating the person's ideas. This is also referred to as "slander." |
| Ad populum | An ad populum argument is based on the opinions of the majority of people. It assumes that because the majority says X is right, then Y is not. It uses little logic. |
| Ad verecundiam | This argument uses quotes and phrases from people in authority or popular people to support one's own views. |
| Appeal to tradition | This argument looks only at the past and suggests that because we have always done it "this way," we should continue to do it "this way." |
| Bandwagon | The bandwagon approach tries to convince you to do something just because everyone else is doing it. It is also referred to as "peer pressure." |
| Glittering Generalities | This type of persuasion or argumentation is an appeal to generalities (Bosak, 1976). It suggests that a person, candidate, or professional is for all the "right" things: justice, low taxes, no inflation, rebates, full employment, low crime, free tuition, progress, privacy, and truth. |
| Patriotism | This form of persuasion asks you to ignore reason and logic and support what is right for state A or city B or nation C. |
| Plain folks | This type of persuasion is used to make you feel that the people making the argument are just like you. Usually, they are not; they are only using this appeal to connect with your sense of space and time. |
| Scare tactic | A scare tactic is used as a desperate measure to put fear in your life. If you don't do X, then Y is going to happen to you. |
| Straw argument | The straw argument attacks the opponent's argument to make one's own argument stronger. It does not necessarily make argument A stronger; it simply discounts argument B. |

> *"There is nothing so powerful as truth, and often, nothing so strange."*
> —Daniel Webster

fears used to persuade. You will also begin to understand the depths to which you should delve to achieve objectivity, the thought and care that you should give to your own decisions and statements, and the methods by which you can build logical, truthful arguments.

## Step Eight: Thinking Creatively and Being Resourceful

***Creative thinking*** is a major and important aspect of critical thinking, in that you are producing something that is uniquely yours—introducing something to the world that is new, innovative, and useful. Creative thinking does not mean that you have to be an artist, a musician, or a writer. Creative thinking instead means that you have examined a situation and developed a new way of explaining information, delivering a product, or using an item. It can be as simple as discovering that you can use a small rolling suitcase to carry your books around campus instead of the traditional backpack. Creative thinking means that you have opened your mind to possibilities!

Creative thinking is really about being resourceful—and in today's times, resourcefulness is a powerful tool. Resourcefulness is an ***internal*** quality, not an ***external*** gift. If you have ever seen the TV series *Survivorman* or *Man vs. Wild*, you know that it takes a strong person to eat a slug just carved out of a tree trunk. It takes internal will to drink water with so many bacteria that flies die when they drink it. Yes, both shows are somewhat staged, but they show the basics of creativity, intelligence, imagination, and ***resourcefulness***.

To truly understand resourcefulness, you need look no further than a child playing in the backyard. *"What does a worthless, old stick become?"* Because of a child's inability to see limitations, the stick becomes a medieval sword, Luke Skywalker's laser beam, an old man's cane, a crutch, a magic wand, a baseball bat, a witch's stirring stick, or a marshmallow roaster. An old stick now has limitless possibilities because the child refused to see it only as a stick. His refusal to be boxed into the confines of our adult reality created possibilities. Sometimes, we have to become that child and use every stick we have just to survive.

Think of internal resourcefulness as **renewable energy**. When you have to draw on your wits, creativity, and determination, these qualities multiply. The more you are required by circumstances to use these qualities, the stronger and more plentiful they become. Conversely, if you've always been able to buy anything you want or if all that you need is provided to you by an external force, your internal resourcefulness begins to wither and die like uneaten fruit on the winter vine. You are not forced to use the whole of yourself. Your energy fades. Your harvest dies.

Your inner resourcefulness and creativity also make you more secure and offer more protection from outside forces. When you know how to make ends meet, you can always do it. When you know how to pay the rent on limited income, you can always do it. When you know how to cut firewood to heat your home, you can always do it. When you know how to navigate the public transportation system in your town, you can always do it; even when the time comes that you don't have to "do it" anymore, you could if you had to. The more you know and the more inner strength and resourcefulness you have, the safer you are against the unknown. The more confidence you possess, the greater the likelihood that you can survive anything at any time. The more resourceful you are, the more you understand that this one quality will help you rebuild all that may have been lost. When the world ***HAS*** been handed to you on a silver platter, you cannot be ready for what the world ***CAN*** hand you.

To begin the creative process, consider the items in Figure 4.13. These are some of the characteristics creative thinkers have in common. Using your imaginative and innovative juices, think about how you would *creatively* solve the following problem. Write down at least five possibilities. Come on, make it count!

*Jennifer is a first-year student who does not have enough money to pay her tuition, buy her books, and purchase a few new outfits and shoes to wear to class and her work-study job on campus.*

If you had to use your creativity to "survive" in the wild, could you do it?

*What should she do? Should she pay her tuition and purchase her books, or pay her tuition and buy new clothes and shoes to wear to class and work? What creative, resourceful ideas (solutions) can you give Jennifer?*

MY CREATIVE SOLUTIONS:

1. _____

2. _____

3. _____

4. _____

5. _____

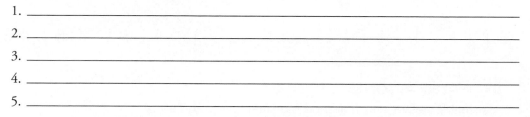

## FIGURE 4.13 *Characteristics of Creative Thinking*

**COMPASSION** — Creative thinkers have a zest for life and genuinely care for the spirit of others.

**Example:** More than 40 years ago, community members who wanted to feed the elderly created Meals on Wheels, now a national organization feeding the elderly.

**COURAGE** — Creative thinkers are unafraid to try new things, to implement new thoughts and actions.

**Example:** An NBC executive moves the *Today Show* out of a closed studio onto the streets of New York, creating the number one morning news show in the United States.

**TRUTH** — Creative thinkers search for the true meaning of things.

**Example:** The astronomer and scientist Copernicus sought to prove that earth was *not* the center of the universe— an unpopular view at the time.

**DREAMS** — Creative thinkers allow themselves time to dream and ponder the unknown. They can see what is possible, not just what is actual.

**Example:** John F. Kennedy dreamed that space exploration was possible. His dream became reality.

**RISK TAKING** — Creative thinkers take positive risks every day. They are not afraid to go against popular opinion.

**Example:** Barack Obama took a risk and ran for President of the United States. He became one of only a few African Americans to ever run for the office and the only African American to be nominated by his party. In November of 2008, he became the first African-American President of the United States.

**INNOVATION** — Creative thinkers find new ways to do old things.

**Example:** Instead of continuing to fill the earth with waste such as aluminum, plastic, metal, and old cars, means were developed to recycle these materials for future productive use.

**COMPETITION** — Creative thinkers strive to be better, to think bolder thoughts, to do what is good and to be the best at any task.

**Example:** Tiger Woods had a several-season slump in golf. Most people thought he was a "has-been" especially after his knee surgery. He came back to win tournament after tournament because he knew that he could and he never gave up. He challenged himself.

**INDIVIDUALITY** — Creative thinkers are not carbon copies of other people. They strive to be true to themselves.

**Example:** A young man decides to take tap dancing instead of playing baseball. He excels and wins a fine arts dancing scholarship to college.

**CURIOSITY** — Creative thinkers are interested in all things; they want to know much about many things.

**Example:** A 65-year-old retired college professor goes back to college to learn more about music appreciation and computer programming to expand her possibilities.

**PERSEVERANCE** — Creative thinkers do not give up. They stick to a project to its logical and reasonable end.

**Example:** Dr. Martin Luther King, Jr., did not give up on his dream in the face of adversity, danger, and death threats.

# From Ordinary to Extraordinary

## REAL PEOPLE | REAL LIVES | REAL CHANGE

**DR. WAYNE A. JONES**
Assistant Professor and Thurgood Marshall Pathways Fellow
Department of Political Science and Public Administration
Virginia State University, Petersburg, VA

I come from a fine family. My mother is a retired social worker, college professor and community activist and my father, a retired Presbyterian minister and college professor. They provided a safe, structured environment and always have encouraged me to do well. Clearly, I had the foundation to do well in school. However I have not always followed my parents' advice. This was especially true for my senior year in high school. The outcome was that I did not graduate. So at 18, I was working, had my own apartment and things were OK. At least, so I thought.

I had always been interested in anything that had wheels on it. If it has wheels, I could drive it —or wanted to! I drove a bus for a few years and then I drove an ambulance. One day, however, I saw our local bookmobile and I wanted to drive it. I applied to do so, but found out that I had to have a high school diploma to be able to drive the bookmobile. At 19, this was my reason for going back to get my GED. Now, I could master driving yet another "thing" with wheels. It was not, however, as exciting as I thought it would be.

My parents begged me to begin my college studies. Reluctantly, at age 21, I enrolled at Virginia Commonwealth University. After only one year, I knew that college was not for me. I dropped out. In 1975, I began working for the Police Department in Chesterfield, VA. I was only the second African American police officer on the force. I held this position for five years.

My desire for wheels was still with me. I left the police department and began working for the Virginia Overland Transportation Company as a safety supervisor. I worked my way up to become supervisor of transportation. With this experience under my belt, I went to work for a transit company in Richmond, VA driving a city transit bus. I left the second bus company after a year to drive for a local construction company. This work, however, turned out to be very "seasonal" and I found myself frequently without income. I asked to be allowed to drive one of their trash trucks so that I could have a steady income and overtime, too. So, there I was in my late twenties, without a college degree,

driving a trash truck. There was not a lot to look forward to.

My late grandmother called me one day and asked me why I didn't go back to college. "You are far from dumb," I remember her telling me. I tried to explain to her that I was making decent money and I could not quit my job. I told her that it would take me at least eight years to get my degree. "I'll be too old by then," I told her. She then said the words that woke me up and changed my life. "Son," she said, "unless you die, you're going to be eight years older in eight years anyway, why not be eight years older with a college degree?"

That was my wake-up call. I found another job with more flexible hours and enrolled at John Tyler Community College with no idea of what I wanted to become. Shortly after I re-enrolled in college, my grandmother died. Her final gift to me was her wonderful words of wisdom.

So, there I was, working full-time, going to college full-time, and barely having enough time to even visit my family who lived nearby. One night, I received another phone call that

# From Ordinary to Extraordinary

## REAL PEOPLE | REAL LIVES | REAL CHANGE

changed my life again. My parents called me and told me that they wanted to talk with me about money. I visited them and to my surprise, they asked me to quit work and concentrate on my studies. "Grandmother had a vision," my mother told me. "She knew that you were going to do great things." They told me that if I quit, they would pay my bills until I finished college. I agreed to take their help.

I transferred from John Tyler Community College and enrolled again at Virginia Commonwealth University. My GPA was not great upon graduation. I took the Graduate Record Exam (GRE) and scored very badly. I was turned down for the graduate program in Public Administration. I was now 35. I met with the director of admissions and said to him, "Just give me a chance, I know I can do this."

> *In just a few short years, I managed to go from driving a trash truck to being a university professor.*

After some conversation, he agreed to give me a chance. I completed my Masters of Public Administration in only 18 months. I applied to the doctoral program in public administration at VCU. The chairman of the doctoral program reviewed my GRE scores and basically told me that based on them, I should not have been able to obtain a master's degree. Then, I applied to George Washington University for their PhD program.

Once again, the admissions office looked at my scores and basically told me that my master's degree was "just a fluke." I was accepted provisionally and only five years later, I graduated with a 3.85. My dissertation won the Outstanding Dissertation of the Year Award in 2000 from the George Washington University chapter of Phi Delta Kappa. I was not a fluke anymore.

I began working as Director of Adult Day Care for a United Way Agency and loved it. It was then that the thought of becoming a college professor came to mind. I saw an ad in the paper for a part-time teaching position working with advanced-placement students. I found the love of my life — teaching. I later applied to become a full-time faculty member at Virginia State University and today, I teach freshman studies and public administration.

## EXTRAORDINARY REFLECTION

**Read the following statement and respond in your online journal or class notebook.**

Dr. Jones was brave enough to take an enormous risk, quit his full-time job, accept help, and reach his goals. Whom do you have in your life that you can depend upon for support (maybe not monetary support, but crucial support of your goals, dreams, and educational plans)? Why?

# CHANGING IDEAS TO *Reality*

Critical thinking, emotional intelligence, and information literacy require a great deal of commitment on your part. They may not be easy for everyone at first, but with practice, dedication, and an understanding of the immense need of all three, everyone can think more critically and logically, evaluate information sources, and use emotional intelligence to best advantage.

Critical thinking and emotional intelligence can affect the way you live your life, from strengthening relationships to purchasing a new car, from solving family problems to investing money, from taking the appropriate classes for graduation to getting a promotion at work. Both are vitally important to your growth and education.

As you continue on in the semester and work toward personal and professional motivation and change, consider the following ideas:

> "The significant problems we face cannot be solved at the same level of thinking we were at when we created them."
> —Albert Einstein

- ▶ Use only *credible* and *reliable* sources.
- ▶ Learn to distinguish *fact* from *opinion*.
- ▶ Be *flexible* in your thinking and *avoid* generalizations.
- ▶ Use emotional intelligence and *restraint*.
- ▶ Avoid *stereotyping* and prejudging and strive for *objectivity* in your thinking.
- ▶ *Reserve* judgment until you have looked at every side.
- ▶ Do *not* assume—do the research and *ask* questions.
- ▶ Work hard to distinguish *symptoms from problems*.

Critical thinking is truly the hallmark of an educated person. It is a hallmark of character and integrity, and a hallmark of successful students. Let it be yours.

# KNOWLEDGE *in* BLOOM

## Developing a Rational, Logical Argument

Each chapter-end assessment is based on *Bloom's Taxonomy of Learning*. See the inside front cover for a quick review.

### UTILIZES LEVEL 3 OF THE TAXONOMY

**EXPLANATION:** Thousands of articles are written every day for magazines, newspapers, online journals, and other print media. Depending on the article or where it is published, it can have a slant. You may have heard this called bias (as in "liberal" or "conservative" bias). One of journalism's objectives should be to present the FACTS of what has happened in an incident or the facts of what is being discussed. Bias should not enter the argument unless it is an editorial.

**PROCESS:** For this activity, you are to find an article (not an editorial) in a mainstream newspaper or magazine (*USA Today, Newsweek, Time, The New York Times, The Washington Post, The National Review*, etc.), read the article, and determine if the article has bias, unsubstantiated opinions, or research that is weak.

The list of questions below will help you evaluate and assess your article.

Name of the article:

_____

Author of the article: _____

His or her affiliation: _____

Publication in which the article was found: _____

Date of publication: _____

Before you read this article, based on the title and subject matter, what five questions do you want to be able to answer once you have read the article?

1. _____
2. _____
3. _____
4. _____
5. _____

After reading the article, what is the author's main reason for writing it?

What is/are the most important fact(s) or information in the article? _____
_____
_____

By writing this article, what is the author implying? _____
_____
_____

By writing this article, what is the author proving? _____
_____
_____
_____

In writing this article, what assumptions were made? _____
_____
_____

What sources does the writer cite to prove his or her point? _____
_____
_____

Is the article fairly presented? In other words, does the author examine both sides of the issue or just one side? Justify your answer. _____
_____
_____

Do you believe and trust the article? Why or why not? Justify your answer. _____
_____
_____

If this article is accurate (or inaccurate, depending on your judgment), what are the implications for society? _____
_____
_____
_____

Answer the five questions you wrote previously in this exercise. _____

1. _____
2. _____
3. _____
4. _____
5. _____

List one way that you can use the information in this article to enhance your creativity and/or resourcefulness. _____
_____
_____

(This project is adapted, in part, from the work of Richard Paul and Linda Elder, 2006.)

# SQ3R *Mastery* STUDY SHEET

| | |
|---|---|
| EXAMPLE QUESTION: *(from page 89)*<br>Why is emotional intelligence important to critical thinking? | ANSWER: |
| EXAMPLE QUESTION: *(from page 94)*<br>What is information literacy? | ANSWER: |
| AUTHOR QUESTION: *(from page 87)*<br>Why is emotional intelligence important? | ANSWER: |
| AUTHOR QUESTION: *(from page 95)*<br>Why is asking questions so important in critical thinking? | ANSWER: |
| AUTHOR QUESTION: *(from page 95)*<br>Discuss the steps in information literacy. | ANSWER: |
| AUTHOR QUESTION: *(from page 102)*<br>Define fact and opinion and give an example of each. | ANSWER: |
| AUTHOR QUESTION: *(from page 103)*<br>Define ad hominem and find an example of this in a recent newspaper or magazine article. | ANSWER: |
| YOUR QUESTION: *(from page ____)* | ANSWER: |
| YOUR QUESTION: *(from page ____)* | ANSWER: |
| YOUR QUESTION: *(from page ____)* | ANSWER: |
| YOUR QUESTION: *(from page ____)* | ANSWER: |
| YOUR QUESTION: *(from page ____)* | ANSWER: |

Finally, after answering these questions, recite this chapter's major points in your mind. Consider the following general questions to help you master this material.

▶ What was it about?
▶ What does it mean?
▶ What was the most important thing I learned? Why?
▶ What were the key points to remember?

**ANSWERS TO TEASERS pp. 93–94**

**Brain Teaser #1, Looking at Common Terms Backwards**

1. Snow White and the Seven Dwarfs

2. I Have a Dream by Martin Luther King, Jr.

3. Two peas in a pod

4. Hickory dickory dock, the mouse ran up the clock

5. Three sides to a triangle

6. One hundred pennies in a dollar

7. There's no place like home

8. Four quarts in a gallon

9. *It's A Small World After All*

10. Fifty states in the Union

**Brain Teaser #2, Seeing What Is Not Given**

(Hint: You have to think "outside the box." Look beyond what is given to you.)

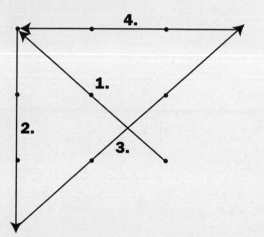

**Brain Teaser #3, The Penny**

Your answers might include things such as:

▶ We had more than one language.

▶ We knew geometry.

▶ We had a calendar system.

▶ We honored people.

▶ We knew metallurgy.

▶ We knew math.

▶ We knew architecture.

▶ We were united.

▶ We valued liberty.

# CHAPTER 5
# PRIORITIZE

PLANNING
YOUR
TIME AND
REDUCING
STRESS

"If you want to make good use of your time, you've got to know what's most important and then give it all you've got."

—Lee Iacocca

# WHY READ THIS CHAPTER?

## What's in it for me?

WHY does time management play a role in my value system and self-discipline? WHY is time management so important to the quality of my life? WHY do I need to know about stress and what causes it? WHY is learning to reduce anxiety and managing stress important to my overall success?

WHY? Because poor time management and stress are partners in crime. Poor time management leads to more stress and more stress leads to poor time management skills. It is a vicious circle. Time, of course, is not the only thing in your life that can cause stress. Stress can be brought on by relationships, work, family issues, and money problems, to name a few. However, by learning to effectively manage your time, you can reduce a major factor that contributes to the stress levels in your life. Have you ever looked at your peers who have children, a full-time job (or two jobs), and outside activities, and yet they still get it all done? *"How do they do that?"* The answer is they have figured out what they value and how to apply their values to their time management plans.

*By carefully reading this chapter and taking the information provided seriously, you will be able to:*

1. Discuss the relationship among time management, your value system, and self-discipline.
2. Beat procrastination and get more done.
3. Evaluate how you spend your time and develop a "to do" list based on your findings.
4. Understand the relationship between poor time management and stress.
5. Identify the major stressors in your life.

# CHAPTER 5 / PRIORITIZE

*"Nothing is a waste of time if you use the experience wisely."*

—Rodin

**NAME:** Eric Despinis
**INSTITUTION:** ITT Technical Institute, Bensalem, PA
**MAJOR:** Computer Network Systems
**AGE:** 31

I am a full-time single parent, work a full-time job, and go to school full time. Having a lot of "free time" has not been a part of my life for years. But that is OK because I have learned how to manage my time so that I can devote enough energy, passion, and enthusiasm to all of the things I value in my life. We tend to spend our time and money on the things that we love and value. Managing my time at work and school is essential so that I can have as much time as possible with my son, who is my number-one priority. However, school is also a major priority because I want to have a career so I can provide a stable future for my son.

There are times when things get rough and everything seems to be crashing down around me. When that happens, I think about my son, my values, and my goals and this pulls me through. I think that the key to time management is having a clear vision of what you want from your future and then dedicating yourself to that vision. When you have a strong set of goals and you value those goals, you find that you do not allow common, everyday things to get in your way. You simply can't!

On the days when things seem overwhelming and out of balance, I step back, remember my overall plan, and play with my son. Creating balance in my life is very important.

I cannot devote every moment of every day to my job or to school because my son's life would suffer. Conversely, after he is settled and happy, my remaining time is devoted to reaching my goals of being a computer system administrator.

I also think it is important to find a strong support network of positive people in your life. My family has always been there for me and so has my advisor at ITT, Al Dornbach. He has helped me understand so much about life and work and family. His wisdom and guidance are paramount in helping me reach my goals. I suggest that you find people who support you and are behind you and this will help you develop a clear vision and a plan to help you succeed. The information in this chapter will be of great assistance to you as you begin to build your own time management plan for the future. Good luck.

# SCAN & QUESTION

In the preface of this book (page xix), you read about the **SQ3R Study Method**. Right now, take a few moments, **scan this chapter,** and on page 143, write **five questions** that you think will be important to your mastery of this material. In addition to the two questions below, you will find five questions from your authors. Use one of your **"On The Test"** stickers to flag this page for easy reference.

**EXAMPLES:**

▶ **How can I simplify my life and get more done?** (from page 122)

▶ **What are the components of self-discipline?** (from page 118)

# TIME—YOU HAVE ALL THERE IS

## Can You Take Control of Your Life and Make the Most of Your Time?

You can definitely say four things about time: *It is fair. It does not discriminate. It treats everyone the same. Everyone has all there is.* No person has any more or fewer hours in a day than the next person. It may seem that Gary or Tamisha has more time that you do, but they do not. In a 24-hour

span we all have 1,440 minutes. No more. No less. There is one more thing you can definitely say about time, too: *It can be cruel and unrelenting.* It is one of the few things in our lives that we cannot stop. There are no time-out periods, no breaks, and try as we might, we can't turn it back, shut it down, or stop it. The good news, however, is that by learning how to manage our time more effectively, we don't need to slow it down or stop it. We can learn how to get things done and have more time for joy and fun.

So, how do you spend your time? Some people are very productive, while others scramble to find a few moments to enjoy life and have quality relationships. According to time management and personal productivity expert Donald Wetmore (2008), "The average working person spends less than two minutes per day in *meaningful* communication with their spouse or significant other and less than 30 seconds per day in *meaningful* communication with their children." Think about that for a moment. THIRTY seconds. If you think that is amazing, consider the following list. As strange as it may seem, these figures are taken from the Bureau of Labor Statistics of the U.S. Department of the Census (2006). During your *working years* (age 20 to 65, a 45-year span), you spend an average of:

Do the figures regarding how we spend our time surprise you?

Where do you think most of your "free" time goes?

▶ 16 years sleeping.

▶ 2.3 years eating.

▶ 3.1 years doing housework.

▶ 6 years watching TV.

▶ 1.3 years on the telephone.

This totals *28.7 years of your working life* doing things that you may not even consider in your time management plan. What happens to the remaining 16.3 years? Well, you will spend *14 of those years working*, which leaves you with 2.3 years, or only 20,000 hours, during your working life to embrace joy, spend time with your family, educate yourself, travel, and experience a host of other life-fulfilling activities. Dismal? Scary? It does not have to be. By learning how to manage your time, harness your energy and passion, and take control of your day-to-day activities, 2.3 years can be a long, exciting, productive time.

Why is it that some people seem to get so much more done than other people? They appear to always be calm and collected and have it together. Many people from this group work long hours in addition to going to school. They never appear to be stressed out, and they seem to be able to do it all with grace and charm. Uggh!

You are probably aware of others who are always late with assignments, never finish their projects on time, rarely seem to have time to study, and appear to have no concrete goals for their lives. Sometimes, we get the idea that the first group accomplishes more because they have more time or because they don't have to work or they don't have children or they are smarter or have more help. Actually, some of these reasons may be true, but in reality, many of the people in the first group have learned how to overcome and beat procrastination, tie their value systems to their time management plans, and use their personal energy and passion to accomplish more.

*"I can't do any more than I am doing right now,"* you may say to yourself. But is that really true? One of the keys to managing your time is to consider your values. We discussed your value system in Chapter 2. What you value, enjoy, and love, you tend to put more passion, energy, and time toward. Do you value your family? If so, you make time for them. Do you value your friends? If so, you make time for them. Now you have to ask yourself, **how much do I value my education**? How important is it that I succeed in college and get my degree? If you make succeeding in college a high value for your life and your future, you will find that you make more time for your studies, your classes, and your projects. **We spend time on what we value!**

# TIME MANAGEMENT AND SELF-DISCIPLINE

## Do You Have What It Takes to Get It Done?

Time management is actually about managing you! It is about taking control and assuming responsibility for the time you are given on this earth. The sooner you understand this and take control of how you use your time, the quicker you will be on your way to becoming successful in college and many other activities. Learning to manage your time is a lesson that you will use throughout your studies and beyond. No, **you can't control time**, but you can control yourself. Time management is basically self-discipline—and self-discipline involves self-motivation. Time management is paying attention to how you are spending your most valuable resource—time—and then devising a plan to use it more effectively. This is one of the goals of this chapter.

The word "discipline" comes from a Latin word meaning "to teach." Therefore, **self-discipline** is really about "teaching ourselves" (Waitley, 1997). Self-discipline implies that you have the ability to teach yourself how to get more done when things are going well and when they are not going so well. If you have self-discipline, you have learned how to hold it all together when things get tough, when you feel beaten, and when defeat seems just around the corner. It also means that when you have important tasks to complete, you can temporarily pull yourself away from enjoyable situations and fun times until those tasks are completed. Consider the chart in Figure 5.1 regarding self-discipline. **Self-discipline is really about four things.**

*"Self-discipline is teaching ourselves to do the things necessary to reach our goals without becoming sidetracked by bad habits."*

*—Denis Waitley*

Once you have made the **choice** to engage in your education, stop procrastinating, and manage your time more effectively, you have to make the **changes** in your thoughts and behaviors to bring those choices to fruition. Then, you have to **accept responsibility** for your actions and take control of your life. You have to call upon your **inner strength** or **willpower**—and you DO have willpower; it may just be hidden or forgotten, but you do have it. You have the ability to empower yourself to get things done. No one can do this for you. You are responsible for your life, your actions, and your willpower. Self-discipline and willpower help you move in the direction of your dreams. Even in the face of fear, anxiety, stress, defeat, and darkness, self-discipline will help you find your way.

Willpower and self-discipline are all about **retraining your mind** to do what YOU want it to do and not what IT wants to do. It is about eliminating the negative self-talk that so often derails us and causes us to procrastinate and get stressed out. By retraining your mind and resisting the urge to simply "obey" your subconscious, you are basically retraining your life. Consider the following situations:

▶ You come home after three classes and are tired and weary. Your subconscious mind tells you to sit down, put your feet up, and watch TV for a while. But you have to tell your mind, *"NO! I am going to take a short walk around the block to get my adrenaline flowing and then I'm going to read my chapter for homework."*

## 5.2 *Time Management Types*

| TYPE | EXPLANATION | Do YOU have any of these tendencies? | WHAT actions make you like this type of person? | What can YOU DO to begin eliminating this type of behavior? |
|------|-------------|--------------------------------------|------------------------------------------------|-------------------------------------------------------------|
| THE CIRCLER | Doing the same things over and over again and again and hoping for a different result; basically, going around in circles. | YES / NO | | |
| THE DOODLER | Not paying attention to details, doing things that do not really matter to the completion of your project. | YES / NO | | |
| THE SQUANDERER | Wasting too much time trying to "get ready" to study or work and never really getting anything done; then it is too late to do a good job. | YES / NO | | |
| THE BEGGAR | Expecting time to "stop" for you after you've wasted time doing nothing or going in circles. Then, becoming frustrated when you don't have enough time. | YES / NO | | |
| THE PLANNER | Planning out your project so carefully and meticulously that by the time you have everything you think you need, there is no time to really do the project. | YES / NO | | |
| THE HUN | Waiting too late to plan or get things done and then stomping on anyone or anything to get the project done with no regard for others' feelings, time, or relationships. | YES / NO | | |
| THE PASSIVIST | Convincing yourself that you'll never get it all done and that there is no use to try anyway. | YES / NO | | |

**Steps to Learning to Say No—It's as Simple as NOT Saying Yes:**

▶ Think before you answer out loud with an insincere or untrue "Yes."

▶ Make sure you understand exactly what is being asked of you and what the project involves before you give a "Yes" or "No" answer.

▶ Review your schedule to see if you really have the time to do a quality job. ("If you have to have an answer immediately, it is 'No.' If you can wait a few days for me to finish project X, and review my schedule, the answer may be 'Yes.'")

▶ Learn the difference between assertiveness (politely declining) and rudeness (responding, "Have you lost your mind?").

▶ Say "No" at the right times (i.e., to the wrong things) so that you can say "Yes" at the appropriate times (i.e., to the right things).

- ▶ Learn how to put yourself and your future first (for a change). By doing this, you can say "Yes" more often later on.

- ▶ Inform others of your time management schedule so that they will have a better understanding of why you say "No."

- ▶ If you must say "Yes" to an unwanted project (something at work, for example), try to negotiate a deadline that works for everyone—you first!

- ▶ Keep your "No" short. If you have to offer an explanation, be brief so that you don't talk yourself into doing something you can't do and so that you avoid giving false hope to the other person. If the answer is "No" right now and it will be "No" in the future, say "No" now.

- ▶ Offer suggestions to the other person as to who may be able to help him or her or when you might be available (if it is in your best interest to accept this request at any time).

- ▶ If you feel you simply have to say yes, try to trade off with the other person and ask him or her to do something on your list.

- ▶ Put a time limit on your "Yes." For example, you might agree to help someone, but you could say, "I can give you 30 minutes and then I have to leave."

## Your Turn

You are taking four classes and the reading and homework are mounting day by day. Your family needs you, your friends think you've abandoned them, and you want to continue to do a good job at work. Your schedule is tight and you have things planned down to the hour in order to be able to get it all done and done well. Suddenly, you are asked to help with a project for disadvantaged children that seems very worthy and timely. You know that your schedule is full but your conscience begins to gnaw at you and you really do want to help.

Applying the tips from the list above, predict how you might be able to address this situation.

_____

_____

_____

_____

Do you think saying "no" is rude or necessary?

BLOOM LEVEL 3 QUESTION

# BEGINNING YOUR DAY WITH PEACE

## Can You Start Your Day as a Blank Page and Simplify Your Life?

Imagine a day with nothing to do! That may be difficult, if not impossible, for you to conceive right now. But as an exercise in building your own day from scratch and simplifying your life, think about having a day where YOU build your schedule and where you do not have to be constrained by activities and projects that others have thrust upon you. Think about a day where you are in charge. Crazy? Impossible? Outrageous? Maybe not as much as you think.

Yes, you will need to plot activities such as work, class, and family duties into your daily calendar, but you also need to learn how to schedule time for fun activities, time for silence and peace,

# THINKING for CHANGE: An Activity for Critical Reflection

Darius is a single father of two young daughters. He and his wife divorced several years ago and he was granted custody of Alice and Marianne. Shortly after the divorce, Darius was laid off from his job as a construction foreman. He had been making a very good living, but now it was hard to make ends meet. He could not find another job that paid well enough to support the three of them.

Therefore, he decided to go back to school to pursue his dream of becoming a draftsman. His classes, along with his new part-time job, demand much of his time. He has found that he is spending much less time with his daughters than he had in the past—and he does not like this at all.

His daughters were cast in the school play and the performance is scheduled for Friday night—the same night as one of his drafting classes. He knows that he has a conflict on his hands. He knows that class is very important, but so is supporting his daughters. In your own words, what would you suggest that Darius do at this point? List at least three things that he could do handle this situation, manage his time to meet all of his obligations, and maintain his sanity.

1. _____

2. _____

3. _____

and time to be alone with your thoughts. By learning how to build your schedule each evening from scratch, you will have the opportunity to plan a day where you simplify your life. There is an old quote that states, "If you want to know what you value in your life, look at your checkbook and your calendar." Basically, this suggests that we spend our money and time on things we value.

**12 Ways to Simplify Your Life:**

> Do you find it difficult or easy to simplify and de-clutter your life? Why?

▶ Know what you value, and work hard to eliminate activities that are not in conjunction with your core value system. This can be whittled down to one statement: ***"Identify what is important to you. Eliminate everything else."***

▶ Get away from technology for a few hours a day. Turn off your computer, cell phone, iPod, and other devices that can take time away from doing what you value.

▶ Learn to delegate to others. You may say to yourself, "My family does not know how to use the washing machine." Guess what? When all of their underwear is dirty, they'll learn how to use it. Don't enable others to avoid activities that complicate your life.

▶ Make a list of everything you are doing. Prioritize this list into what you enjoy doing and what fits into your value system. If you can feasibly do only three or four of these activities per day, draw a line after number four and eliminate the rest of the list.

▶ Do what is essential for the well-being of you and your family and eliminate everything else.

▶ Don't waste time saving money. Spend money to save time. In other words, don't drive across town to save 3 cents per gallon on fuel or 10 cents for a gallon of milk. Pay the extra money and have more time to do what you like.

▶ Clean your home of clutter and mess. Work from cleanliness. Declutter and organize. Make sure everything has a place.

## FIGURE 5.3    *Ways to Simplify Your Life*

| | |
|---|---|
| **Two things I can do to simplify my life at home** | |
| **Two things I can do to simplify my life at work** | |
| **Two things I can do to simplify my life at school** | |
| **Two things I can do to simplify my life with my children** | |
| **Two things I can do to simplify my life with my spouse/partner/loved one** | |
| **Two things I can do to simplify my economics (financial matters)** | |

▶ Donate everything you don't need or use to charity. Simplifying your life may also mean simplifying your closets, drawers, cabinets, and garage.

▶ Go through your home or apartment and eliminate everything that does not bring you joy or have sentimental value. If you don't love it, ditch it.

▶ Clean up the files on your computer. Erase everything that you don't need or want so that you can find material more easily. If you have not used the file in a month, put it on a flash drive for later use.

▶ Live in the moment. Yes, it is important to plan for the future, but if you ignore "the moment," your future will not be as bright.

▶ Spend a few moments each morning and afternoon reflecting on all of the abundance in your life. Learn to give thanks and learn to do nothing.

(Adapted from *Zen Habits,* 2008, and *Get More Done,* 2008)

In the space in Figure 5.3, compile a list that can help you simplify your life in each category. Add ONLY those things to the list that you can actually DO on a daily basis.

BLOOM LEVEL 6
QUESTION

# THE DREADED "P" WORD

## Why Is Procrastination So Easy to Do and How Can You Beat It Once and for All?

It's not just you! Almost everyone procrastinates, and then we worry and tell ourselves, "I'll never do it again if I can just get through this one project." We say things to ourselves like, "If I can just live through this paper, I will never wait until the last minute again." But then someone comes along with a great idea for fun, and off we go. Or there is a great movie on TV, the kids want to play a game of catch, you go to the refrigerator for a snack, and before you know it, you are rewarding yourself *with FREE time* before you have done your work.

The truth is simple: We tend to avoid the hard jobs in favor of the easy ones. Even many of the list makers fool themselves. They mark off a long list of easy tasks while the big ones still loom in front of them. Many of us put off unpleasant tasks until our backs are against the wall. So why do we procrastinate when we all know how unpleasant the results can be? Why aren't we disciplined and organized and controlled so that we can reap the rewards that come from being prepared? Why do we put ourselves through so much stress by putting things off?

"If you have to eat two frogs, eat the ugliest one first."
—Brian Tracy

The biggest problem with procrastination, even beyond not getting the job, task, or paper completed on time, *is doing it poorly* and then suffering the stress caused by having put it off or turning in a subpar project. By putting the project off, you have cheated yourself out of the time needed to bring your best to the table and, most likely, you are going to hand over a project, with your name on it, that is not even close to your potential. And to top it off, more stress is created by this vicious cycle of "I'll do it tomorrow—or this weekend."

*What has procrastination cost you?* This is perhaps one of the most important questions that you can ask and answer with regard to managing your time more effectively. Did it cost you a good grade? Did it cost you money? Did it cost you your reputation? Did it cost you your dignity? Did it cost you your ability to do your best? *Procrastination is not free.* Every time you do it, it costs you something. You need to determine what it is worth.

In order to beat procrastination, you will also need to consider *what type* of procrastinator you are (Figure 5.4). Each type requires a different strategy and different energy to overcome, but make no doubt about it, success requires overcoming all degrees and types of procrastination. Before you complete the Time Management Assessment, examine figure 5.4 to determine if any of these procrastination types fit you.

Take a moment to complete the following *Time Management Assessment.* Be honest and truthful in your responses. The results of your score are located after the assessment.

Procrastination is quite simply a bad habit formed after many years of practice. There are reasons, however, that cause us to keep doing this to ourselves. Often, we let our negative self-talk cause us to procrastinate. We allow our negative attitude to override what we know is best for us. An attitude adjustment may be just the thing you need to overcome and beat the trap of procrastination.

FIGURE **5.4** *Procrastinator Types*

**CHRONIC Procrastinator**
You procrastinate all of the time on most everything in most aspects of your life including social situations, financial affairs, career decisions, personal responsibility, and academic projects. Usually, you do not meet any deadlines if you complete the project at all. It is going to take a great deal of thought, planning, and energy to overcome this type of procrastination.

**MODERATE Procrastinator**
You procrastinate much of the time. You usually get things done, but it is not your best work and you create a great deal of stress in your own life. It is going to take a fair amount of planning and energy to overcome this type of procrastination. With some planning, your projects could be much more effective and you could eliminate much stress and guilt.

**OCCASIONAL Procrastinator**
You occasionally put things off. You do not do this often, but when you do, you feel guilty and rush to get the project completed. Sometimes, you turn in work that is not your best. You are good at planning most things, but you do need to concentrate on sticking to your plan and not letting unscheduled events obstruct your success.

FIGURE

## 5.5   *Time Management Assessment*

Answer the following questions with the following scale:

1 = Not at all     2 = Rarely     3 = Sometimes     4 = Often     5 = Very often

| | |
|---|---|
| 1. I prioritize my tasks every day and work from my priority list. | 1  2  ③  4  5 |
| 2. I work hard to complete tasks on time and not put them off until the last minute. | 1  2  ③  4  5 |
| 3. I take time to plan and schedule the next day's activities the night before. | 1  2  ③  4  5 |
| 4. I have made time during my daily schedule to study and get my projects completed so that I can have more quality time at home. | 1  ②  3  4  5 |
| 5. I study and get my work done before I take fun breaks. | 1  ②  3  4  5 |
| 6. I analyze my assignments to determine which ones are going to take the most time and then work on them first and most often. | 1  2  ③  4  5 |
| 7. I have analyzed my daily activities and determined where I actually spend my time. | 1  ②  3  4  5 |
| 8. I know how to say no and do so frequently. | 1  2  3  ④  5 |
| 9. I know how to avoid distractions and how to work through unexpected interruptions. | 1  ②  3  4  5 |
| 10. I do not let "fear of the unknown" keep me from working on a project. | 1  2  3  ④  5 |
| 11. I know how to overcome apathy toward a project. | 1  2  ③  4  5 |
| 12. I know how to fight and overcome my own laziness. | 1  2  ③  4  5 |
| 13. I know how to reframe a project that may not interest me so that I can see the benefits from it and learn from it. | 1  2  3  ④  5 |
| 14. I know how to break down a major, complex, or overwhelming task to get it done in pieces and then put it all together. | 1  2  3  ④  5 |
| 15. I build time into my schedule on a daily or weekly basis to deal with "unexpected" interruptions or distractions. | 1  ②  3  4  5 |

YOUR TOTAL SCORE:                                                                    42

| RESULTS: | 60-75 | You manage your time well and you know how to build a schedule to get things done. Your productivity is high. You don't let procrastination rule your life. |
|---|---|---|
| | 45-59 | You are good at doing some things on time, but you tend to procrastinate too much. Learning how to build and work from a priority list may help you manage your time more effectively. |
| | 30-44 | You need to work hard to change your time management skills and learn how to set realistic goals. Procrastination is probably a major issue for you, causing you much stress and worry. Working from a priority list can help you greatly. |
| | 29-below | Your time management skills are very weak and without change and improvement, your success plan could be in jeopardy. You could benefit from learning to set realistic goals, working from a priority list, and reframing your thought process toward tasks. |

Consider the following negative statements. On the right-hand side, rewrite each statement to make it a positive, procrastination-beating statement.

| NEGATIVE STATEMENT | POSITIVE STATEMENT |
|---|---|
| I'll do it at 9:30 when this TV show is off. | _____ _____ |
| I'm tired. | _____ _____ |
| I can't concentrate. | _____ _____ |
| This is too hard. | _____ _____ |

This is boring.

_____

_____

I don't know why anyone would ask me to
do this crazy stuff.

_____

_____

Learning to apply this type of positive thinking can help you beat the Procrastination Trap and
manage your time and life more effectively.

# GETTING THE MOST OUT OF THIS MOMENT

## Do You Know the Causes of and Cures for Procrastination?

Below, you will find a list of the 10 most COMMON CAUSES of procrastination and some
simple, doable, everyday strategies that you can employ to overcome each cause. We have provided three strategies for each cause. Add at least two of your own strategies to overcome this
type of procrastination.

## ESSENTIAL CORNERSTONE

**Accountability:**

How can being a more
responsible and accountable
person help you overcome
procrastination and "make the
most of now"?

**Social Networking Moment:**

Share your response to this Essential Cornerstone
with peers in your social network. Choose two
responses from your peers and respond to their
postings.

▶ **Superhuman expectations and trying to be a perfectionist**
  ▶ Allow yourself **more time than you think you need** to com-
    plete a project.
  ▶ Realize that no one, including you, is (or ever will be) perfect.
    Perfection does not exist.
  ▶ **Allow enough time to do your very best** and let that be that.
    If you plan and allow time for excellence, you can't do more.
  ▶ _____
  ▶ _____

▶ **Fear of not knowing how to do the task**
  ▶ **Ask for clarification** from whoever asked you to do the project.
  ▶ **Read** as much as you can about the task at hand and **ask for help**.
  ▶ Break up big tasks into **small ones**.
  ▶ _____
  ▶ _____

▶ **Lack of motivation and the inability to find internal motivation**
  ▶ **Reframe your attitude** to find the good and beneficial in any task.
  ▶ Consider how this task will help you **reach your overall goals and dreams**.
  ▶ Take time to do the **things you love**, which will create a healthy balance in your life.
  ▶ _____
  ▶ _____

▶ **Fear of failing or fear of the task being too hard**
  ▶ Start the project with **positive, optimistic thoughts**.
  ▶ **Face your fears**; look them right in the face and make a decision to defeat them.
  ▶ **Visualize your successful completion** of the project.
  ▶ _____
  ▶ _____

► **No real plan or goal for getting the task done**

  ► Set reasonable, concrete goals that you can reach in about **20–25 minutes**.

  ► **Draw up an action plan** the night before you begin the project.

  ► Look at completing the project in terms of your **long-range goals** and your overall life plan.

  ► _____

  ► _____

► **Considering the task too unpleasant or uninteresting**

  ► **Realize** that most tasks are not as unpleasant as we've made them out to be.

  ► **Do the hardest tasks first** and save the easiest for last.

  ► Schedule tasks that you consider unpleasant to be done **during your peak hours**.

  ► _____

  ► _____

► **Utter laziness and/or apathy**

  ► **Concentrate on the rewards** of managing yourself and your time more effectively.

  ► Give yourself a **time limit** to accomplish a task.

  ► Set a regular, realistic time for study, and **stick to it**.

  ► _____

  ► _____

Is there a difference among laziness, procrastination, and resting?

► **Distractions and/or lack of focus**

  ► **Ask for help** from your professors, advisor, counselor, or other professionals.

  ► Start on the difficult, **most boring tasks first**.

  ► Weed out your personal belongings and living space. Organization helps you manage your time and **get to work**.

  ► _____

  ► _____

► **Choosing "fun" before responsibility**

  ► Actually **reward yourself** when you have accomplished an important body of work.

  ► **Don't get involved** in too many organizations, accept too many commitments, or overextend yourself so that you can concentrate on what needs to be done.

  ► **Consider the consequences** of not doing what you're responsible for doing.

  ► _____

  ► _____

► **Waiting for the "right" mood**

  ► **Avoid whining and complaining** and realize that you can create the right mood at any time.

  ► **Just do it!** Force yourself to jump into the task.

  ► Work during your **peak hours of the day**.

  ► _____

  ► _____

# From Ordinary to *Extraordinary*

**MAUREEN RIOPELLE**
President & Founder
Mary's Circle of Hope—The Mary Maguire Foundation
Milford, OH

Things could not have been going better! I was a star basketball player recruited by hundreds of colleges and was a top pick by the University of Iowa. My dream of going to college, becoming an Olympic athlete, and later a sportscaster was so close I could see it all happening. But, life has a funny way of turning on a dime.

I had suffered knee problems for many years and most doctors attributed it to "growing pains." I continued to play sports in high school despite the pain. By the time I got to the University of Iowa, at the urging of my coaches I finally saw a few specialists but the diagnosis was inconclusive. They knew my knee was in serious disrepair and that I had lost over 35% of the range of motion. They just couldn't figure out why.

After surgery, my knees actually began to worsen. The doctors feared a massive infection and after more tests, another surgery was scheduled. It was then determined that the plica in my knees had hardened and formed so much scar tissue that it seemed to almost form another "bone" in my leg. I was told that I would probably have to have surgery every two years to repair the damage and that I only had a 50/50 chance of ever walking again.

In a relatively brief period of time, I went from a college basketball standout and Olympic hopeful to losing my scholarship, dropping out of college, and potentially facing the rest of my life on crutches or in a wheelchair. I had five surgeries in seven months and I spent that summer in a wheelchair and on crutches, but within a year, I was walking on my own again. Within a year and half I walked my first 5K.

I attribute my recovery to my drive and determination. When necessary, I am the most stubborn person you'll ever meet. When I was told that I would not walk, run, or play basketball again, I took it as a *personal challenge* to prove everyone wrong—*"I'll show you."* I eventually went back to college, graduating with a 4.0 GPA. After graduation, I began working, and life was moving along. Little did I know that within a few short years, I would have to call upon that teenager who years earlier had told herself, *"I'll show you."*

One morning I found a lump in my breast and immediately met with my doctor, who scheduled a mammo-

> *In a relatively brief period of time, I went from a college basketball standout and Olympic hopeful to losing my scholarship, dropping out of college, and potentially facing the rest of my life on crutches or in a wheelchair.*

# From Ordinary to Extraordinary

## REAL PEOPLE | REAL LIVES | REAL CHANGE

gram. After the test, I was told that everything was fine. But there was a little voice in my head that said, "You need to ask someone else. Get a second opinion." This little voice saved my life. I did, indeed, have breast cancer and it had even spread to my lymph nodes. My determination and strong will to live and beat the odds became my salvation once again. After surgery and treatment, there are no signs of cancer.

Both of these experiences, while trying and frightening, led me to my real calling in life—founding Mary's Circle of Hope—The Mary Maguire Foundation, a nonprofit organization dedicated to the support of women cancer survivors. We help provide financial assistance; health, fitness, and nutritional assistance; empowerment retreats and workshops; and additional services that help the women go from surviving to thriving. Being able to help others thrive in the face of adversity has become my passion and focus in life. Visit us at www.marymaguirefoundation.org.

## EXTRAORDINARY REFLECTION

**Read the following statement and respond in your online journal or class notebook.**

Ms. Riopelle suffered a major setback with her health, causing her to lose her scholarship and drop out of college for a time. What advice regarding persistence, internal motivation, positive thinking, and determination would you give to someone who is facing a life-threatening health problem?

# EVALUATING HOW YOU SPEND YOUR TIME

## Do You Know Where Your Time Goes?

So, how do you find out where your time goes? The same way that you find out where your money goes—you track it. Every 15 minutes for one week, record exactly how you spent that time. This exercise may seem a little tedious at first, but if you complete the process over a period of a week, you will have a much better concept of where your time is being used. Yes, that's right—for a week, you need to keep a written record of how much time you spend sleeping, studying, eating, working, getting to class and back, cooking, caring for children, watching television, doing yard work, going to movies, attending athletic events, hanging out, doing laundry, whatever.

Take your plan with you and keep track of your activities during the day. To make things simple, round off tasks to 15-minute intervals. For example, if you start walking to the cafeteria at 7:08, you might want to mark off the time block that begins with 7:00. If you finish eating and return to your dorm at 7:49, you can mark off the next two blocks. You will also want to note the activity so that you can later evaluate how you spent your time. Study the example that is provided for you in Figure 5.6.

In Figure 5.7 on pages 131–132, you will find a daily time log that you can use for this exercise. Remember to take these pages with you and record how you are spending your time during the day. As you progress through the week, try to improve the use of your time. When you finish this exercise, review how you spent your time.

**FIGURE 5.6** *How You Really Spend Your Time*

FIGURE

## 5.7    *Daily Time Sheet*

| Monday | | Tuesday | | Wednesday | |
|---|---|---|---|---|---|
| 6:00 | 6:00 | 6:00 | 6:00 | 6:00 | 6:00 |
| | 6:15 | | 6:15 | | 6:15 |
| | 6:30 | | 6:30 | | 6:30 |
| | 6:45 | | 6:45 | | 6:45 |
| 7:00 | 7:00 | 7:00 | 7:00 | 7:00 | 7:00 |
| | 7:15 | | 7:15 | | 7:15 |
| | 7:30 | | 7:30 | | 7:30 |
| | 7:45 | | 7:45 | | 7:45 |
| 8:00 | 8:00 | 8:00 | 8:00 | 8:00 | 8:00 |
| | 8:15 | | 8:15 | | 8:15 |
| | 8:30 | | 8:30 | | 8:30 |
| | 8:45 | | 8:45 | | 8:45 |
| 9:00 | 9:00 | 9:00 | 9:00 | 9:00 | 9:00 |
| | 9:15 | | 9:15 | | 9:15 |
| | 9:30 | | 9:30 | | 9:30 |
| | 9:45 | | 9:45 | | 9:45 |
| 10:00 | 10:00 | 10:00 | 10:00 | 10:00 | 10:00 |
| | 10:15 | | 10:15 | | 10:15 |
| | 10:30 | | 10:30 | | 10:30 |
| | 10:45 | | 10:45 | | 10:45 |
| 11:00 | 11:00 | 11:00 | 11:00 | 11:00 | 11:00 |
| | 11:15 | | 11:15 | | 11:15 |
| | 11:30 | | 11:30 | | 11:30 |
| | 11:45 | | 11:45 | | 11:45 |
| 12:00 | 12:00 | 12:00 | 12:00 | 12:00 | 12:00 |
| | 12:15 | | 12:15 | | 12:15 |
| | 12:30 | | 12:30 | | 12:30 |
| | 12:45 | | 12:45 | | 12:45 |
| 1:00 | 1:00 | 1:00 | 1:00 | 1:00 | 1:00 |
| | 1:15 | | 1:15 | | 1:15 |
| | 1:30 | | 1:30 | | 1:30 |
| | 1:45 | | 1:45 | | 1:45 |
| 2:00 | 2:00 | 2:00 | 2:00 | 2:00 | 2:00 |
| | 2:15 | | 2:15 | | 2:15 |
| | 2:30 | | 2:30 | | 2:30 |
| | 2:45 | | 2:45 | | 2:45 |
| 3:00 | 3:00 | 3:00 | 3:00 | 3:00 | 3:00 |
| | 3:15 | | 3:15 | | 3:15 |
| | 3:30 | | 3:30 | | 3:30 |
| | 3:45 | | 3:45 | | 3:45 |
| 4:00 | 4:00 | 4:00 | 4:00 | 4:00 | 4:00 |
| | 4:15 | | 4:15 | | 4:15 |
| | 4:30 | | 4:30 | | 4:30 |
| | 4:45 | | 4:45 | | 4:45 |
| 5:00 | 5:00 | 5:00 | 5:00 | 5:00 | 5:00 |
| | 5:15 | | 5:15 | | 5:15 |
| | 5:30 | | 5:30 | | 5:30 |
| | 5:45 | | 5:45 | | 5:45 |
| 6:00 | 6:00 | 6:00 | 6:00 | 6:00 | 6:00 |
| | 6:15 | | 6:15 | | 6:15 |
| | 6:30 | | 6:30 | | 6:30 |
| | 6:45 | | 6:45 | | 6:45 |
| 7:00 | 7:00 | 7:00 | 7:00 | 7:00 | 7:00 |
| | 7:15 | | 7:15 | | 7:15 |
| | 7:30 | | 7:30 | | 7:30 |
| | 7:45 | | 7:45 | | 7:45 |
| 8:00 | 8:00 | 8:00 | 8:00 | 8:00 | 8:00 |
| | 8:15 | | 8:15 | | 8:15 |
| | 8:30 | | 8:30 | | 8:30 |
| | 8:45 | | 8:45 | | 8:45 |
| 9:00 | 9:00 | 9:00 | 9:00 | 9:00 | 9:00 |
| | 9:15 | | 9:15 | | 9:15 |
| | 9:30 | | 9:30 | | 9:30 |
| | 9:45 | | 9:45 | | 9:45 |
| 10:00 | 10:00 | 10:00 | 10:00 | 10:00 | 10:00 |
| | 10:15 | | 10:15 | | 10:15 |
| | 10:30 | | 10:30 | | 10:30 |
| | 10:45 | | 10:45 | | 10:45 |
| 11:00 | 11:00 | 11:00 | 11:00 | 11:00 | 11:00 |
| | 11:15 | | 11:15 | | 11:15 |
| | 11:30 | | 11:30 | | 11:30 |
| | 11:45 | | 11:45 | | 11:45 |
| 12:00 | 12:00 | 12:00 | 12:00 | 12:00 | 12:00 |

FIGURE **5.7** *Daily Time Sheet (continued)*

| Thursday | Friday |  | Saturday |  | Sunday |  |  |
|---|---|---|---|---|---|---|---|
| 6:00 | 6:00 | 6:00 | 6:00 | 6:00 | 6:00 | 6:00 | 6:00 |
|  | 6:15 |  | 6:15 |  | 6:15 |  | 6:15 |
|  | 6:30 |  | 6:30 |  | 6:30 |  | 6:30 |
|  | 6:45 |  | 6:45 |  | 6:45 |  | 6:45 |
| 7:00 | 7:00 | 7:00 | 7:00 | 7:00 | 7:00 | 7:00 | 7:00 |
|  | 7:15 |  | 7:15 |  | 7:15 |  | 7:15 |
|  | 7:30 |  | 7:30 |  | 7:30 |  | 7:30 |
|  | 7:45 |  | 7:45 |  | 7:45 |  | 7:45 |
| 8:00 | 8:00 | 8:00 | 8:00 | 8:00 | 8:00 | 8:00 | 8:00 |
|  | 8:15 |  | 8:15 |  | 8:15 |  | 8:15 |
|  | 8:30 |  | 8:30 |  | 8:30 |  | 8:30 |
|  | 8:45 |  | 8:45 |  | 8:45 |  | 8:45 |
| 9:00 | 9:00 | 9:00 | 9:00 | 9:00 | 9:00 | 9:00 | 9:00 |
|  | 9:15 |  | 9:15 |  | 9:15 |  | 9:15 |
|  | 9:30 |  | 9:30 |  | 9:30 |  | 9:30 |
|  | 9:45 |  | 9:45 |  | 9:45 |  | 9:45 |
| 10:00 | 10:00 | 10:00 | 10:00 | 10:00 | 10:00 | 10:00 | 10:00 |
|  | 10:15 |  | 10:15 |  | 10:15 |  | 10:15 |
|  | 10:30 |  | 10:30 |  | 10:30 |  | 10:30 |
|  | 10:45 |  | 10:45 |  | 10:45 |  | 10:45 |
| 11:00 | 11:00 | 11:00 | 11:00 | 11:00 | 11:00 | 11:00 | 11:00 |
|  | 11:15 |  | 11:15 |  | 11:15 |  | 11:15 |
|  | 11:30 |  | 11:30 |  | 11:30 |  | 11:30 |
|  | 11:45 |  | 11:45 |  | 11:45 |  | 11:45 |
| 12:00 | 12:00 | 12:00 | 12:00 | 12:00 | 12:00 | 12:00 | 12:00 |
|  | 12:15 |  | 12:15 |  | 12:15 |  | 12:15 |
|  | 12:30 |  | 12:30 |  | 12:30 |  | 12:30 |
|  | 12:45 |  | 12:45 |  | 12:45 |  | 12:45 |
| 1:00 | 1:00 | 1:00 | 1:00 | 1:00 | 1:00 | 1:00 | 1:00 |
|  | 1:15 |  | 1:15 |  | 1:15 |  | 1:15 |
|  | 1:30 |  | 1:30 |  | 1:30 |  | 1:30 |
|  | 1:45 |  | 1:45 |  | 1:45 |  | 1:45 |
| 2:00 | 2:00 | 2:00 | 2:00 | 2:00 | 2:00 | 2:00 | 2:00 |
|  | 2:15 |  | 2:15 |  | 2:15 |  | 2:15 |
|  | 2:30 |  | 2:30 |  | 2:30 |  | 2:30 |
|  | 2:45 |  | 2:45 |  | 2:45 |  | 2:45 |
| 3:00 | 3:00 | 3:00 | 3:00 | 3:00 | 3:00 | 3:00 | 3:00 |
|  | 3:15 |  | 3:15 |  | 3:15 |  | 3:15 |
|  | 3:30 |  | 3:30 |  | 3:30 |  | 3:30 |
|  | 3:45 |  | 3:45 |  | 3:45 |  | 3:45 |
| 4:00 | 4:00 | 4:00 | 4:00 | 4:00 | 4:00 | 4:00 | 4:00 |
|  | 4:15 |  | 4:15 |  | 4:15 |  | 4:15 |
|  | 4:30 |  | 4:30 |  | 4:30 |  | 4:30 |
|  | 4:45 |  | 4:45 |  | 4:45 |  | 4:45 |
| 5:00 | 5:00 | 5:00 | 5:00 | 5:00 | 5:00 | 5:00 | 5:00 |
|  | 5:15 |  | 5:15 |  | 5:15 |  | 5:15 |
|  | 5:30 |  | 5:30 |  | 5:30 |  | 5:30 |
|  | 5:45 |  | 5:45 |  | 5:45 |  | 5:45 |
| 6:00 | 6:00 | 6:00 | 6:00 | 6:00 | 6:00 | 6:00 | 6:00 |
|  | 6:15 |  | 6:15 |  | 6:15 |  | 6:15 |
|  | 6:30 |  | 6:30 |  | 6:30 |  | 6:30 |
|  | 6:45 |  | 6:45 |  | 6:45 |  | 6:45 |
| 7:00 | 7:00 | 7:00 | 7:00 | 7:00 | 7:00 | 7:00 | 7:00 |
|  | 7:15 |  | 7:15 |  | 7:15 |  | 7:15 |
|  | 7:30 |  | 7:30 |  | 7:30 |  | 7:30 |
|  | 7:45 |  | 7:45 |  | 7:45 |  | 7:45 |
| 8:00 | 8:00 | 8:00 | 8:00 | 8:00 | 8:00 | 8:00 | 8:00 |
|  | 8:15 |  | 8:15 |  | 8:15 |  | 8:15 |
|  | 8:30 |  | 8:30 |  | 8:30 |  | 8:30 |
|  | 8:45 |  | 8:45 |  | 8:45 |  | 8:45 |
| 9:00 | 9:00 | 9:00 | 9:00 | 9:00 | 9:00 | 9:00 | 9:00 |
|  | 9:15 |  | 9:15 |  | 9:15 |  | 9:15 |
|  | 9:30 |  | 9:30 |  | 9:30 |  | 9:30 |
|  | 9:45 |  | 9:45 |  | 9:45 |  | 9:45 |
| 10:00 | 10:00 | 10:00 | 10:00 | 10:00 | 10:00 | 10:00 | 10:00 |
|  | 10:15 |  | 10:15 |  | 10:15 |  | 10:15 |
|  | 10:30 |  | 10:30 |  | 10:30 |  | 10:30 |
|  | 10:45 |  | 10:45 |  | 10:45 |  | 10:45 |
| 11:00 | 11:00 | 11:00 | 11:00 | 11:00 | 11:00 | 11:00 | 11:00 |
|  | 11:15 |  | 11:15 |  | 11:15 |  | 11:15 |
|  | 11:30 |  | 11:30 |  | 11:30 |  | 11:30 |
|  | 11:45 |  | 11:45 |  | 11:45 |  | 11:45 |
| 12:00 | 12:00 | 12:00 | 12:00 | 12:00 | 12:00 | 12:00 | 12:00 |

# FOCUSING ON AND ELIMINATING DISTRACTIONS AND INTERRUPTIONS

## When Is Enough Really Enough?

If you were diligent and kept an accurate account of all of your time, your evaluation probably reveals that much of your time is spent dealing with distractions, getting side-tracked, and handling interruptions. These three things account for much of the time wasted within a 24-hour period. Below, in Figure 5.8 you will find a list of some of the most common distractions faced by college students. Consider how you might deal with these distractions in an effective, assertive manner.

# PLANNING AND PREPARING

## Is There a Secret to Time Management?

In the past, you may have said to yourself, *"I don't have time to plan." "I don't like to be fenced in and tied to a rigid schedule." "I have so many duties that planning never works."* Scheduling does not have to be a tedious chore or something you dread. Scheduling can be your lifeline to more free time. After all, if YOU build your own schedule, it is yours! As much as you are able, build your schedule the way you want and need it.

FIGURE **5.8** *Common Distractions*

| COMMON DISTRACTIONS | MY PLAN TO OVERCOME THESE DISTRACTIONS |
|---|---|
| Friends / family dropping by unexpectedly | |
| Technology (playing on YouTube, FaceBook, iTunes, Google, etc. . . . ) | |
| Constant phone calls that do not pertain to anything in particular or of importance | |
| Not setting aside any time during the day to deal with "the unexpected" | |
| Friends / family demanding things of you because they do not understand your schedule or commitments | |
| Not blocking private time in your daily schedule | |
| Being unorganized and spending hours upon hours dawdling and calling it "work" | |
| Playing with your children or pets before your tasks are complete (and not scheduling time to be with them in the first place) | |
| Saying "Yes" when you need to say "NO" | |
| Other distractions faced by you . . . | |

To manage your time successfully, you need to spend some time planning. To plan successfully, you need a calendar that has at least a week-at-a-glance or a month-at-a-glance section as well as sections for daily notes and appointments. If you have not bought a calendar, you can download one from the Internet or create one using Word or another computer program.

## Planning and Organizing for School

Each evening, you should take a few minutes (and literally, that is all it will take) and sit in a quiet place and make a list of all that needs to be done tomorrow. Successful time management comes from **planning the NIGHT BEFORE!** Let's say your list includes

| | |
|---|---|
| Research speech project | Exercise |
| Study, finance test on Friday | Buy birthday card for Mom |
| Read Chapter 13 for chemistry | Wash the car |
| Meet with chemistry study group | Take shirts to dry cleaner |
| Attend English class at 8:00 a.m. | Buy groceries |
| Attend mgt. class at 10:00 a.m. | Call Janice about weekend |
| Work from 2:00 to 6:00 p.m. | |

Now you have created a list of tasks that you will face tomorrow. Next, separate this list into three categories:

| MUST DO | NEED TO DO | WOULD LIKE TO DO |
|---|---|---|
| Read Ch. 13 for chem. | Research speech project | Wash the car |
| Study for finance test on Fri. | Buy birthday card for Mom | Call Janice @ w/end |
| Exercise | Shirts to cleaner | |
| English class @ 8:00 | Buy groceries | |
| Mgt. class @ 10:00 | | |
| Meet w/chem study gp. | | |
| Work 2:00–6:00 p.m. | | |

Don't get too excited yet! Your time management plan is *NOT finished*. The most important part is still ahead of you. Now you will need to rank the items in order of their importance. You will put a 1 by the most important tasks, a 2 by the next most important tasks, etc., in each category.

| MUST DO | NEED TO DO | WOULD LIKE TO DO |
|---|---|---|
| 1 Read Ch. 13 for chem. | 1 Research speech project | 2 Wash the car |
| 2 Study for finance test on Fri. | 2 Buy birthday card for Mom | 1 Janice @ w/end |
| 3 Exercise | 3 Shirts to cleaner | |
| 1 English class @ 8:00 | 2 Buy groceries | |
| 1 Mgt. class @ 10:00 | | |
| 2 Meet w/ chem study gp. | | |
| 1 Work 2:00–6:00 p.m. | | |

Now you have created a PLAN to actually get these tasks done! Not only have you created your list, but you have also divided them into important categories, ranked them, and made a written commitment to these tasks.

FIGURE

**5.9**  *Daily Calendar*

| DAY | Monday | Priority | Complete? |
|-----|--------|----------|-----------|
| **Time** | **Task** | | |
| 6:00 | | | ___ Yes ___ No |
| 6:30 | | | ___ Yes ___ No |
| 7:00 | Study for finance | | ___ Yes ___ No |
| 7:30 | ↓ | | ___ Yes ___ No |
| 8:00 | English 101 | | ___ Yes ___ No |
| 8:30 | ↓ | | ___ Yes ___ No |
| 9:00 | ↓ | | ___ Yes ___ No |
| 9:30 | Read Pg. 1–10 of Chem. Chapter | | ___ Yes ___ No |
| 10:00 | Management 210 | | ___ Yes ___ No |
| 10:30 | | | ___ Yes ___ No |
| 11:00 | ↓ | | ___ Yes ___ No |
| 11:30 | Finish Reading Chem. Chapter | | ___ Yes ___ No |
| 12:00 | | | ___ Yes ___ No |
| 12:30 | ↓ | | ___ Yes ___ No |
| 1:00 | Meet w/Chemistry group (take lunch) | | ___ Yes ___ No |
| 1:30 | ↓ | | ___ Yes ___ No |
| 2:00 | Work | | ___ Yes ___ No |
| 2:30 | | | ___ Yes ___ No |
| 3:00 | | | ___ Yes ___ No |
| 3:30 | | | ___ Yes ___ No |
| 4:00 | | | ___ Yes ___ No |
| 4:30 | | | ___ Yes ___ No |
| 5:00 | | | ___ Yes ___ No |
| 5:30 | | | ___ Yes ___ No |
| 6:00 | ↓ | | ___ Yes ___ No |
| 6:30 | Dinner/run by grocery store | | ___ Yes ___ No |
| 7:00 | ↓ | | ___ Yes ___ No |
| 7:30 | Internet Research for speech | | ___ Yes ___ No |
| 8:00 | | | ___ Yes ___ No |
| 8:30 | ↓ | | ___ Yes ___ No |
| 9:00 | call Janice @ w/end | | ___ Yes ___ No |
| 9:30 | | | ___ Yes ___ No |
| | | | ___ Yes ___ No |

Now, take these tasks and write them into your daily calendar (see Figure 5.9). You would schedule category 1 (MUST DO) first, category 2 (NEED TO DO) next, and category 3 (WOULD LIKE TO DO) next. Remember, NEVER keep more than one calendar. Always carry it with you and always schedule your tasks immediately so that you won't forget them.

# STRESS? I DON'T HAVE ENOUGH TIME FOR STRESS!

## Do You Feel Like You're Going to Explode?

The word *stress* is derived from the Latin word *strictus,* meaning "to draw tight." Stress is your body's response to people and events in your life; it is the mental and physical wear and tear on your body as a result of everyday life and all that you have to accomplish. Stress is inevitable,

## ESSENTIAL CORNERSTONE

**Creativity:**
How can managing your time more effectively, thus reducing stress, help you become a more creative person?

**Social Networking Moment:**
Share your response to this Essential Cornerstone with peers in your social network. Choose two responses from your peers and respond to their postings.

but it is not in itself bad. It is your response to stress that determines whether it is good stress (*eustress*) or bad stress (*distress*). The same event can provoke eustress or distress, depending on the person experiencing the event; just as "one person's trash is another's treasure," so one person's eustress may be another person's distress.

The primary difference between eustress and distress is your body's response. It is impossible to exist in a totally stress-free environment; in fact, some stress is important to your health and well-being. Good stress can help you become more motivated and even more productive. It helps your energy level, too. It is only when stress gets out of hand that your body becomes distressed.

FIGURE

## 5.10 *Test Your Stress*

Take the following **Stress Assessment** to determine the level of distress you are currently experiencing in your life. Check the items that reflect your behavior at home, work, or school, or in a social setting.

☐ 1. Your stomach tightens when you think about your schoolwork and all that you have to do.
☐ 2. You are not able to sleep at night.
☐ 3. You race from place to place trying to get everything done that is required of you.
☐ 4. Small things make you angry.
☐ 5. At the end of the day, you are frustrated that you did not accomplish all that you needed to do.
☐ 6. You get tired throughout the day.
☐ 7. You need some type of drug, alcohol, or tobacco to get through the day.
☐ 8. You often find it hard to be around people.
☐ 9. You don't take care of yourself physically or mentally.
☐ 10. You tend to keep everything inside.
☐ 11. You overreact.
☐ 12. You fail to find the humor in many situations others see as funny.
☐ 13. You do not eat properly.
☐ 14. Everything upsets you.
☐ 15. You are impatient and get angry when you have to wait for things.
☐ 16. You don't trust others.
☐ 17. You feel that most people move too slowly for you.
☐ 18. You feel guilty when you take time for yourself or your friends.
☐ 19. You interrupt people so that you can tell them your side of the story.
☐ 20. You experience memory loss.

**Total Number of Check Marks**

0–5 = Low, manageable stress

6–10 = Moderate stress

11+ = High stress, could cause medical or emotional problems

Some physical signs of distress are:

| | | |
|---|---|---|
| Headaches | Muscular tension and pain | Fatigue |
| Coughs | Abdominal pain and diarrhea | Mental disorders |
| Dry mouth | Hypertension and chest pain | Insomnia |
| Impotence | Heartburn and indigestion | Suicidal tendencies |
| Twitching/Trembling | Abdominal pain | Apprehension |
| Jitters | Diminished performance | Decreased coping ability |

If you begin to experience any of these reactions for an extended period of time, you know that your body and mind are probably suffering from undue stress, anxiety, and pressure. This can lead to a very unhealthy situation. You may even require medical attention for hypertension.

# I DON'T THINK I FEEL SO WELL

## What Is the Relationship Among Poor Time Management, Monumental Stress, and Your Health?

There are probably as many stressors in this world as there are people alive. For some people, loud music causes stress. For others, a hectic day at the office, with people demanding things and equipment breaking down, causes stress. For others, that loud music and busy day at the office are just what the doctor ordered—they love it and thrive off of the energy and demands. For some people, being idle and sitting around reading a book cause stress, while others long for a moment of peace walking on the beach or just sitting out in the backyard with a good book. One thing is for sure: Poor planning and "running out of time" are on most people's lists of major stressors.

Most stress does not "just happen" to us. We allow it to happen by not planning our day or week. We allow our "to do" list to get out of hand (or we do not create a to-do list), and before we know it, our lives are out of control because of all the activities we are required to accomplish or because of all the things we agreed to by saying "Yes." Because of poor planning and procrastination, we become anxious and nervous about not getting it all done. By planning, prioritizing, and developing an action strategy, we can actually lower our stress level and improve our general, overall health and our memory.

Medical research has shown that exposure to stress over a long period of time can be damaging to one's body. Many of the physical and mental symptoms of stress are previously mentioned, but consider these effects as well: Stress can also have an effect on *memory*. When you are stressed, your brain releases *cortisol*, which has effects on the neurons in your brain. Over time, cortisol can be toxic and damage parts of the hippocampus—the part of the brain that deals with memory and learning. Therefore, learning to control stress through managing your time more effectively can be a key to better memory. In Chapter 4, "Think," we discussed the amygdala (the part of the brain that causes "fight or flight"). The amygdala is also affected negatively by prolonged stress, causing you to say and do things you regret later.

Other physical symptoms include *exhaustion,* where one part of the body weakens and shifts its responsibility to another part and causes complete failure of key organ functions.

Have you ever allowed procrastination to stress you out? What was the result?

**Tips for Personal Success**

Consider the following tips for dealing with and reducing stress in your life:

▶ Use relaxation techniques such as visualization, listening to music, and practicing yoga.

▶ Let minor hassles and annoyances go. Ask yourself, *"Is this situation worth a heart attack, stroke, or high blood pressure?"*

▶ Don't be afraid to take a break. Managing your time can help you take more relaxation breaks.

Now, it is your turn. Create a list of at least two more tips that you would offer a fellow classmate to assist him or her with reducing unhealthy stress in his or her life.

1. _____
2. _____

*Chronic muscle pain* and malfunction are also caused by unchecked stress. "Chronically tense muscles also result in numerous stress-related disorders including headaches, backaches, spasms of the esophagus and colon (causing diarrhea and constipation), posture problems, asthma, tightness in the throat and chest cavity, some eye problems, lockjaw, muscle tears and pulls, and perhaps rheumatoid arthritis" (Girdano et al., 2009).

As you can see from this medical research, stress is not something that you can just ignore and hope it will go away. It is not something that is overblown and insignificant. It is a real, bona fide condition that can cause many physical and mental problems from simple exhaustion to death. By learning how to recognize the signs of stress, what causes you to be "stressed out," and effectively dealing with your stress, you can actually control many of the negative physical and emotional side effects caused by prolonged stress. Examine Figure 5.11.

FIGURE

## 5.11 *Three Types of Major Stressors in Life*

| TYPE | CAUSE | WHAT YOU CAN DO TO REDUCE STRESS |
|---|---|---|
| **SITUATIONAL** | | |
| | Change in physical environment | ▶ If at all possible, change your residence or physical environment to better suit your needs. If you can't change it, talk to the people involved and explain your feelings. |
| | Change in social environment | ▶ Work hard to meet new friends who support you and upon whom you can rely in times of need.<br>▶ Get involved in some type of school activity.<br>▶ Enroll in classes with friends and find a campus support group. |
| | Daily hassles | ▶ Try to keep things in perspective and work to reduce the things that you allow to stress you out.<br>▶ Allow time in your schedule for unexpected events.<br>▶ Find a quiet place to relax and study. |
| | Poor time management | ▶ Work out a time management plan that allows time to get your projects complete while allowing time for rest and joy, too.<br>▶ Create "to do" lists. |

**FIGURE**

**5.11**    *Three Types of Major Stressors in Life (continued)*

| TYPE | CAUSE | WHAT YOU CAN DO TO REDUCE STRESS |
|---|---|---|
| **SITUATIONAL** | | |
| | Conflicts at work, home, and school | ▶ Read about conflict management (Chapter 3 in this text) and realize that conflict can be managed. |
| | | ▶ Avoid "hot" topics such as religion or politics if you feel this causes you to engage in conflicts. |
| | | ▶ Be assertive, not aggressive or rude. |
| | People | ▶ Try to avoid people who stress you out. |
| | | ▶ Put people into perspective and realize that we're all different with different needs, wants, and desires. |
| | | ▶ Realize that everyone is not going to be like you. |
| | Relationships | ▶ Work hard to develop healthy, positive relationships. |
| | | ▶ Move away from toxic, unhealthy relationships and people who bring you down. |
| | | ▶ Understand that you can NEVER change the way another person feels, acts, or thinks. |
| | Death of a loved one | ▶ Try to focus on the good times you shared and what they meant to your life. |
| | | ▶ Remember that death is as much a part of life as living. |
| | | ▶ Talk about the person with your friends and family—share your memories. |
| | | ▶ Consider what the deceased person would have wanted you to do. |
| | Financial problems | ▶ Cut back on your spending. Seek the help of a financial planner. |
| | | ▶ Determine why your financial planning or spending patterns are causing you problems. |
| | | ▶ Apply for financial assistance. |
| **PSYCHOLOGICAL** | | |
| | Unrealistic expectations | ▶ Surround yourself with positive people and work hard to set realistic goals with doable timelines and results. |
| | | ▶ Expect and anticipate less. |
| | Homesickness | ▶ Surround yourself with people who support you. |
| | | ▶ Call or visit home as often as you can until you get more comfortable. |
| | | ▶ Meet new friends on campus through organizations and clubs. |

*(continued)*

FIGURE

## 5.11   *Three Types of Major Stressors in Life (continued)*

| TYPE | CAUSE | WHAT YOU CAN DO TO REDUCE STRESS |
|---|---|---|
| **PSYCHOLOGICAL** | | |
| | Fear | ▶ Talk to professors, counselors, family, and friends about your fears. Put them into perspective.<br>▶ Visualize success and not failure.<br>▶ Do one thing every day that scares you to expand your comfort zone. |
| | Anxiety over your future and what is going to happen | ▶ Put things into perspective and work hard to plan and prepare, but accept that life is about constant change.<br>▶ Talk to a counselor or advisor about your future plans and develop a strategy to meet your goals.<br>▶ Don't try to control the uncontrollable. |
| | Anxiety over your past | ▶ Try to see the big picture and how "the puzzle" is going to come together.<br>▶ Work hard to overcome past challenges and remember that your past does not have to dictate your future.<br>▶ Learn to forgive.<br>▶ Focus on your future and what you really want to accomplish. |
| **BIOLOGICAL** | | |
| | Insomnia | ▶ Watch your caffeine intake.<br>▶ Avoid naps.<br>▶ Do not exercise two hours prior to your normal bedtime.<br>▶ Complete all of your activities before going to bed (studying, watching TV, e-mailing, texting, etc.) Your bed is for sleeping. |
| | Anxiety | ▶ Laugh more. Share a joke.<br>▶ Enjoy your friends and family.<br>▶ Practice breathing exercises.<br>▶ Talk it out with friends.<br>▶ Learn to say "No" and then do it.<br>▶ Turn off the TV if the news makes you anxious or nervous. |
| | Weight loss/gain | ▶ Develop an exercise and healthy eating plan.<br>▶ Meet with a nutrition specialist on campus or in the community.<br>▶ Join a health-related club or group. |

FIGURE

## 5.11 *Three Types of Major Stressors in Life (continued)*

| TYPE | CAUSE | WHAT YOU CAN DO TO REDUCE STRESS |
|------|-------|----------------------------------|
| **BIOLOGICAL** | | |
| | Reduced physical activities | ▶ Increase your daily activity. <br> ▶ If possible, walk to class instead of drive. <br> ▶ Take the stairs instead of the elevator. |
| | Sexual difficulties/ dysfunction | ▶ Seek medical help in case something is physically wrong. <br> ▶ Determine if your actions are in contradiction with you value system. |

CHANGING IDEAS TO *Reality*

**REFLECTIONS ON TIME AND STRESS MANAGEMENT**

Managing your time and reducing your levels of stress are two skills that you will need for the rest of your life. By learning to avoid procrastinating and taking the time to enhance the quality of your life, you are actually increasing your staying power as a college student. Further, as you enter the world of work, both of these skills will be necessary for your success. Technological advances, fewer people doing more work, and pressure to perform at unprecedented levels can put your life in a tailspin, but with the ability to plan your time and reduce your own stress level, you are making a contribution to your own success.

As you continue this term in college and work toward managing your time and stress levels, consider the following ideas:

▶ Make a to-do list every evening to plan for the next day.

▶ Always include time for friends, joy, and adventure in your schedule.

▶ Avoid procrastination by practicing the "Just Do It" mentality.

▶ Work hard to lose the "Superhuman" and perfectionist attitudes.

▶ Delegate everything that you can.

▶ Plan your day and week to avoid becoming too stressed.

▶ To reduce stress, take a few moments to relax in private.

▶ When stress is overwhelming, take time to decompress.

Good luck to you as you develop your plan for managing your time and stress.

*"I wanted a perfect ending. Now I've learned, the hard way, that some poems don't rhyme, and some stories don't have a clear beginning, middle and end. Life is about knowing, having to change, taking the moment and making the best of it without knowing what is going to happen next."*

*—Gilda Radner*

# KNOWLEDGE in BLOOM

**Reducing Stress In Your Everyday Life**

Each chapter-end assessment is based on *Bloom's Taxonomy of Learning*. See the inside front cover for a quick review.

## UTILIZES LEVELS 4, 5, AND 6 OF THE TAXONOMY

Take a moment and examine your academic and personal life right now. You probably have many things going on and may feel as if you're torn in many directions.

If you had to list the one major stress in your life at this moment, what would it be?

_____

_____

Why is this a major cause of stress in your life? _____

_____

_____

Are there other people or things contributing to this stress? In other words, is someone or something making the matter worse? If so, who or what?

_____

_____

In Chapter 1, you learned to write a narrative statement. This is the statement that "paints a verbal picture" of how your life is going to look once a goal is reached. Reflect for a moment and then write a paragraph predicting how your life would change if this major source of stress was gone from your life. Be realistic and optimistic.

_____

_____

_____

_____

_____

_____

_____

_____

_____

As you know, accomplishing anything requires action. Now that you have a picture of how your life would look if this stress was gone, develop a plan from beginning to end to eliminate this stressor from your life.

Step 1 _____

_____

Step 2 _____

_____

Step 3 _____

_____

Step 4 _____

_____

Step 5 _____

_____

# CHAPTER 6
# LEARN

USING YOUR
DOMINANT
INTELLIGENCE,
PREFERRED
LEARNING
STYLE, AND
UNIQUE
PERSONALITY
TYPE TO
BECOME AN
ACTIVE
LEARNER

# SQ3R *Mastery* STUDY SHEET

| | |
|---|---|
| **EXAMPLE QUESTION** *(from page 122)*<br>How can I simplify my life and get more done? | **ANSWER:** |
| **EXAMPLE QUESTION** *(from page 118)*<br>What are the components of self-discipline? | **ANSWER:** |
| **AUTHOR QUESTION** *(from page 117)*<br>What is self-discipline and how is it related to time management? | **ANSWER:** |
| **AUTHOR QUESTION** *(from page 119)*<br>What are the benefits of learning how to say no? | **ANSWER:** |
| **AUTHOR QUESTION** *(from page 126)*<br>What are three strategies to effective time management and planning? | **ANSWER:** |
| **AUTHOR QUESTION** *(from page 136)*<br>How does good stress differ from bad stress? | **ANSWER:** |
| **AUTHOR QUESTION** *(from page 137)*<br>What are some of the physical and mental symptoms of stress? | **ANSWER:** |
| **YOUR QUESTION** *(from page ____)* | **ANSWER:** |
| **YOUR QUESTION** *(from page ____)* | **ANSWER:** |
| **YOUR QUESTION** *(from page ____)* | **ANSWER:** |
| **YOUR QUESTION** *(from page ____)* | **ANSWER:** |
| **YOUR QUESTION** *(from page ____)* | **ANSWER:** |

Finally, after answering these questions, recite this chapter's major points in your mind. Consider the following general questions to help you master this material.

- ▶ What was it about?
- ▶ What does it mean?
- ▶ What was the most important thing I learned? Why?
- ▶ What were the key points to remember?

"We are led to truth by our weaknesses as well as our strengths."

—Parker Palmer

# WHY READ THIS CHAPTER?

## What's in it for me?

WHY is it important to understand what some old guy said about learning theory? WHY do I need to know my personality type? WHY will a chapter on discovering my learning style and dominant intelligence help me study better? WHY is it important to know the difference between my learning style and a learning strategy?

Why? Because discovering how "*TO* LEARN" and discovering how "*YOU* LEARN" are two of the most important things you will ever do for yourself as a college student. Learning ***how TO learn*** means that you know where to find information, how to store information in your brain so that it is easily retrievable, and how to make connections between one thing and another. Learning ***how you learn*** means that you know your own learning style, your primary intelligence, and your personality type and understand how to apply these characteristics to various learning situations. Knowing how you learn also affects the way you approach the task of mastering content. It is a dynamic discovery that will help you change your academic performance.

*By carefully reading this chapter and taking the information provided seriously, you will be able to:*

1. Define learning and discuss several historical learning theories.
2. Identify and discuss the steps in the learning process.
3. Identify and use your learning style to increase active and authentic learning.
4. Identify and use your primary intelligence to increase active and authentic learning.
5. Identify and use your personality type to increase active and authentic learning.

## CHAPTER 6 / LEARN

"*Learn everything you can, anytime you can, from anyone you can—there will always come a time when you will be grateful you did.*"

—Sarah Caldwell

**NAME:** Sakinah Pendergrass
**INSTITUTION:** The Art Institute of Philadelphia, Philadelphia, PA
**MAJOR:** Hospitality—Culinary Arts
**AGE:** 27

There were times when I thought I might not make it. I struggled with some of my classes and had a few problems that almost sidetracked me, but I was determined to be a success and after my first term, I was determined to do whatever was necessary to learn how to study, how to process information, and how to make that information "stick." I had not had much success with this in the past and I quickly learned that it was because I did not know how I learned best.

I quickly found that learning *how I learn* was very important to every aspect of my academic life. When you're going to college, working, studying, and trying to have a life, your time is limited and valuable. Learning how to learn and learning how to use your memory correctly are two very important aspects of success. I found that I am a tactile and visual learner and this has helped me greatly. I know that classes where I do not have the opportunity to have a "hands-on approach" will require me to work harder. I learned that it also takes me longer to process information when the lecture is all I have to go on. The student success class I took showed me how to make the best of this situation by creating charts and pictures in my notes. I also found that using color is important to my retention as well.

I have found that for me, my classes in culinary arts are easiest—certainly because this is my major and I enjoy them, but also because these classes are very tactile. We don't just listen to a lecture, we actually "do" things. The more I can do and see, the better I learn. Whatever your learning style, discover it, use it to your best advantage, and work hard to develop skills to get you through the classes that do not match your learning or memory style. By keeping this in mind, I am constantly working hard to overcome any barriers where my learning style and the professor's teaching style do not match.

This chapter will give you the opportunity to discover your learning style, dominant intelligence, and personality type. When you discover which style and type you are, things will begin to change for you and you will have the tools necessary to make some important decisions about learning.

## SCAN & QUESTION

In the preface of this book (page xix), you read about the **SQ3R Study Method.** Right now, take a few moments, **scan this chapter**, and on page 171 write **five questions** that you think will be important to your mastery of this material. In addition to the two questions below, you will find five questions from your authors. Use one of your **"On The Test"** stickers to flag this page for easy reference.

**EXAMPLES:**

▶ **What is the difference between a learning style and a learning strategy?** (from page 156)

▶ **What is the definition of tactile learning and how do you use it?** (from page 157)

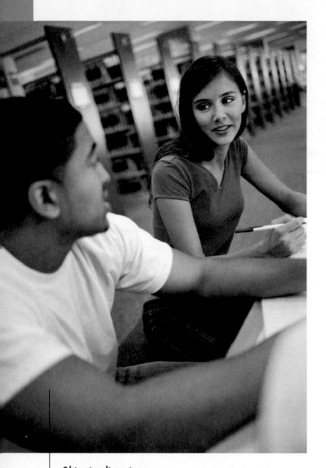

# WE HOPE YOU LEARNED YOUR LESSON!

## What Is This Thing Called Learning, Anyway?

In its purest and simplest form, learning is a *cognitive mental action* in which new information is acquired or in which you learn to use old information in a new way. Learning can be *conscious* and/or *unconscious*. Do you remember the very day you learned how to walk or talk? Probably not. This learning was more of an unconscious nature. However, you probably do remember learning about the 50 states or subtraction or reading an Edgar Allan Poe poem for the first time. This learning was more conscious in nature. Learning can also be *formal* (schooling) or *informal* ("street knowledge"). Learning can happen in many ways such as through play, trial and error, mistakes, successes, repetition, environmental conditioning, parental discipline, social interactions, media, observation, and, yes, through formal study methods.

Learning is what you do *FOR* yourself; it is not done *TO* you. Parents may discipline you time and time and time again, but try as they might, until YOU learn the lesson trying to be taught, it will NOT be learned. Teachers can preach and talk until they are blue in the face about the 13 original colonies, but until you learn them and commit them to memory, they will NOT be learned. That is what this chapter is all about—helping you discover how you learn, why you learn, and assisting you in finding the best way to learn so that you can DO the learning for yourself on a more effective level.

Objective listening can be a difficult skill to learn. Have you encountered people with views radically different from your own? How do you respond?

## What Do the Experts Say?

The question still begs: *HOW do we really learn?* By studying a textbook? By reading a newspaper? By looking at pictures? By interviewing someone about a topic? By watching a movie? By trying something to see if it works? Yes, but the process is much more complex than this. Around 300 BC, the great Greek philosopher Socrates introduced his theory of learning. He believed that we learn by asking questions. This is called the Socratic Method. His student, Plato, expanded on this theory, believing that we learn best by dialogue, called the Dialectic Method, which involves "the searcher" beginning a conversation on a topic and having a dialogue with "an expert" on the other side. He believed that through this back-and-forth conversation, knowledge could be acquired.

In the 5th century BC, the Chinese philosopher Lao-Tse wrote, *"If you tell me, I will listen. If you show me, I will see. But if you let me experience, I will learn."* He was one of the first to proclaim that active, involved learning was a viable form of acquiring information. Kung Fu-tse (Confucius) first introduced the case study, which includes telling stories or parables and then having people discuss the issues or the case to learn and acquire knowledge. In 1690, the English philosopher John Locke introduced the theory of "the blank slate." He believed that all humans were born with empty minds and that we learn information about the world through what our senses bring to us (sensory learning). He felt that learning was like a pyramid—we learn the basics and then build on those simple principles until we can master complex ideas.

In the 1760s, the French philosopher Jean-Jacques Rousseau expanded on a theory that suggested that people learn best by experiencing rather

*"The mind is not a vessel to be filled, but rather a fire to be kindled."*
—Plutarch

than by authority. In other words, we learn best by doing something rather than being told how someone else did it. He was the first to thoroughly introduce the concept of individual learning styles, believing that learning should be natural to us and follow our basic instincts and feelings. In the early 1900s, the American psychologist J. B. Watson developed the theory of behaviorism, believing that we learn best by conditioning. His theory was based on that of Pavlov (and his dog) and held the tenant that we act and learn in certain ways because we have been conditioned to do so. If a dog (or a person) is fed when it rings a bell, the dog (or the person) quickly learns to ring the bell when it *wants* to be fed.

In the mid 1900s, Swiss psychologist Jean Piaget introduced the groundbreaking theory of holistic learning. This theory is widely held today as one of the most important breakthroughs in educational psychology. Piaget believed that we learn best by experiencing a wide variety of stimuli such as reading, listening, experimenting, exploring, and questioning. In 1956, Benjamin Bloom introduced his taxonomy (modeled and discussed in this text on page 25). Bloom believed in a mastery approach to learning. This theory suggests that we learn simple information and then transform that information into more complex ideas, solutions, and creations. His was an idea of learning how to process and actually use information in a meaningful way.

As you can see from these historical experts in the fields of learning, educational psychology, and philosophy, there are many theories on just HOW we learn best. Perhaps the most important thing to take from these examples is tied into Jean Piaget's theory of holistic learning—that as individuals with diverse and varied needs, backgrounds, and experiences, we require a variety of stimuli to help us learn and that we all learn differently at different stages in our lives.

> "Many things in life cannot be transmitted well by words, concepts, or books. Colors that we see cannot be described to a person born blind. Only a swimmer knows how swimming feels; the non-swimmer can get only the faintest idea of it with all the words and books in the world. And so it goes. Perhaps it is better to say that all of life must first be known experientially. There is no substitute for experience, none at all."
> —Abraham H. Maslow

# GIVE YOUR BRAIN A WORKOUT
## Can I Really Learn All This Stuff?

YES! YES! YES! YOU CAN LEARN! Think about all that you have already learned in your lifetime. You learned how to eat, walk, talk, play, make decisions, dress yourself, have a conversation, tie your shoes, make your bed, ride a bicycle, play a sport, drive a car, protect yourself, make associations based on observations, use a cell phone, play a video game, ask questions, and countless other simple and highly complex skills. The *proof* that you **CAN learn** is that you **HAVE learned** in the past. The old excuse of *"I can't learn this stuff"* is simply hogwash! You have the capacity to know more, do more, experience more, and acquire more knowledge. Your brain is a natural learning machine just as your heart is a natural pumping machine. It is in our nature to learn every single day. You just have to understand how this process works in order to make the most of your brain's natural learning power. And you have to **devote the time necessary to learn** the basics of something new and then build on that knowledge base. Time and effort are very important aspects of the learning process.

You also have to give your brain a "workout" to make sure it stays in shape. Just as your body needs exercise and activities to stay in shape, your brain does too. When you "work out" your brain and use it to learn new material, your brain releases a chemical called **cypin** (SIGH-pin). Cypin is found throughout the body, but in the brain, it helps build new branches, like a tree sprouting new growth. In a nutshell, when you exercise your brain, your brain rewards you with new learning patterns and new learning receptors. This is sometimes referred to as **neuroplasticity** (new-ro-plas-TIS-i-ty), or the brain's ability to change with new knowledge.

# THE LEARNING PROCESS

## What Are the Steps to Active, Authentic Learning?

"Human beings have an innate learning process, which includes a motivation to learn" (Smilkstein, 2003). You may be saying to yourself, *"If I have a natural, innate ability to learn, then why is chemistry so difficult for me to master?"* or *"Why is English such a crazy language with so many rules?"* The answer to both could rest in the notion that you are going AGAINST your natural, neurological learning pattern—that you are being taught, or are trying to learn by yourself, in a way that is unnatural to you, and your brain simply is having trouble adapting to this unnatural process.

If you learn best by doing and touching, *you need to do and touch*. If you learn best by listening and questioning, you need to *listen and question*. If you learn best by reading and studying in a quiet place, you need to *find a quiet place to read and study*. Basically, you must figure out your natural inclination for learning and build on it. You will also need to understand that learning takes time and that people need different amounts of time to master material. Janet may learn Concept X in a few hours, but it may take William three days of constant practice to learn the same concept. One thing is true for everyone: The more INVOLVED you are with the information you are trying to learn, the more you will retain.

In Figure 6.1 and the exercise shown in Figure 6.2, we have tried to simplify thousands of years of educational study on the topic of learning. Basically, learning something new can happen in the six steps outlined in Figure 6.1.

If you are trying to learn new facts, concepts, procedures, principles, systems, solutions, or processes, you could achieve this goal by using these six steps. Take a moment and carefully review them now.

**BLOOM LEVEL 2 QUESTION**

As a practice activity, research one of the following topics (all of which we purposefully chose because of their uniqueness . . . OK, weirdness) using the six steps in the Learning Process chart (Figure 6.1). You can do this in your notebook or online journal. Remember, however, that you will need to devote some time to this activity. Learning new information does not happen instantaneously. You will also need to use a variety of sources. Do not depend solely on Wikipedia! Yes, there are other sources out there!

Possible topics:

▶ What was The Night of Long Knives?

▶ What is the mystery of the pyramid at Cheops?

▶ Why and how long can a cockroach live without a head?

▶ Who invented the electric chair and why?

▶ What is Sanskrit?

▶ How is paper made?

▶ Who invented the zero and what is its duel function?

▶ Who was Vlad the Impaler? What famous character did his life inspire?

# UNDERSTANDING YOUR STRENGTHS

## What Are the Advantages of Discovering and Polishing Your Talents?

On the next few pages, you will have the opportunity to complete three inventories: one to identify your **learning style**, one to identify your **personality type**, and one to identify your **dominant in-**

FIGURE

**6.1** *The Learning Process*

**1. Motivation to learn the material** is the first step in the learning process. You have to possess the internal motivation and passion to WANT to learn what is being presented or what you are studying. You must also be motivated enough to devote the time to learning something new. Deep, purposeful learning does not happen in an instant; it takes work, patience and yes, motivation.

**2. Understand the material** through ambitious curiousity, keen observations, purposeful questioning, intense studying, eager determination, robust effort, and time devoted to task. You must answer questions such as: Who is involved? What happened? When did it happen? Where did it happen? How did it happen? How could it have happened? What does it all mean? Why is it important? What is the relationship between x and y? You should be able to describe it, discuss it, give examples, put the information into your own words, and tell others about it clearly.

**3. Internalizie the material by asking:** How can this information affect my life, my career, my studies, and my future? Why does this information matter? How can I control my emotions regarding the value of this information? If I think this information is useless, how can I change this perception?

**4. Apply the material by asking:** How can I use this information to improve? How can I use this information to work with others, to develop new ideas, or to build meaningful conclusions? Can I demonstrate it? Can I share this information with, or teach this information to, others intelligently? Is it possible to practice what I have learned?

**5. Evaluate the material** by determining the value of what I just learned. Do I trust my research and sources? Have I consulted others about their findings and knowledge? What did they learn? What can I learn from them? Have I asked for feedback? Can I debate this information with others?

**6. Use the material** to grow and change. How could I take this information (or the process of learning this information) and change my life, attitudes, or emotions? How could this information help me grow? What can I create out of this new information? How can I expand on this knowledge to learn more?

**telligence**. At the end of the chapter, you will have the opportunity to pull all of this information together to help you understand your learning patterns and to formulate a learning plan for the future.

These assessments are in no way intended to "label you." They are not a measure of how smart you are. They do not measure your worth or your capacities as a student or a citizen. The three assessments are included so that you might gain a better understanding of your dominant intelligence, identify your learning style, and discover your strongest personality type.

There are no right or wrong answers and there is no one best way to learn. We hope that by the end of this chapter, you will have experienced a "Wow" or "Ah-ha!" moment as you explore and discover new and exciting components of your education. We also hope that by the end of this chapter, you will have the skills you need to more effectively use your dominant traits and improve your less dominant characteristics.

FIGURE

## 6.2 *Take the MIS*

### The Multiple Intelligences Survey
© *Robert M. Sherfield, Ph.D.*

**Directions:** Read each statement carefully and thoroughly. After reading the statement, rate your response using the scale below. There are no right or wrong answers. This is not a timed survey. The MIS is based, in part, on *Frames of Mind* by Howard Gardner, 1983.

**3 = Often Applies**

**2 = Sometimes Applies**

**1 = Never or Almost Never Applies**

_____ 1. When someone gives me directions, I have to visualize them in my mind in order to understand them.

_____ 2. I enjoy crossword puzzles and word games like Scrabble.

_____ 3. I enjoy dancing and can keep up with the beat of music.

_____ 4. I have little or no trouble conceptualizing information or facts.

_____ 5. I like to repair things that are broken such as toasters, small engines, bicycles, and cars.

_____ 6. I enjoy leadership activities on campus and in the community.

_____ 7. I have the ability to get others to listen to me.

_____ 8. I enjoy working with nature, animals, and plants.

_____ 9. I know where everything is in my home such as supplies, gloves, flashlights, camera, and compact discs.

_____10. I am a good speller.

_____11. I often sing or hum to myself in the shower or car or while walking or just sitting.

_____12. I am a very logical, orderly thinker.

_____13. I use a lot of gestures when I talk to people.

_____14. I can recognize and empathize with people's attitudes and emotions.

_____15. I prefer to study alone.

_____16. I can name many different things in the environment such as clouds, rocks, and plant types.

_____17. I like to draw pictures, graphs, or charts to better understand information.

_____18. I have a good memory for names and dates.

_____19. When I hear music, I "get into it" by moving, humming, tapping, or even singing.

_____20. I learn better by asking a lot of questions.

_____21. I enjoy playing competitive sports.

_____22. I communicate very well with other people.

_____23. I know what I want and I set goals to accomplish it.

_____24. I have some interest in herbal remedies and natural medicine.

_____25. I enjoy working puzzles or mazes.

_____26. I am a good storyteller.

_____27. I can easily remember the words and melodies of songs.

_____28. I enjoy solving problems in math and chemistry and working with computer programming problems.

_____29. I usually touch people or pat them on the back when I talk to them.

_____30. I understand my family and friends better than most other people do.

_____31. I don't always talk about my accomplishments with others.

_____32. I would rather work outside around nature than inside around people and equipment.

_____33. I enjoy and learn more when seeing movies, slides, or videos in class.

_____34. I am a very good listener and I enjoy listening to others' stories.

_____35. I need to study with music.

_____36. I enjoy games like Clue, Battleship, chess, and Rubik's Cube.

FIGURE

### 6.2    *Take the MIS (continued)*

_____37.  I enjoy physical activities such as bicycling, jogging, dancing, snowboarding, skateboarding, or swimming.

_____38.  I am good at solving people's problems and conflicts.

_____39.  I have to have time alone to think about new information in order to remember it.

_____40.  I enjoy sorting and organizing information, objects, and collectibles.

Refer to your score on each individual question. Place that score beside the appropriate question number below. Then, tally each line at the side.

| Score | | | | | Total Across | Code |
|---|---|---|---|---|---|---|
| 1___ | 9___ | 17___ | 25___ | 33___ | ___ | Visual/Spatial |
| 2___ | 10___ | 18___ | 26___ | 34___ | ___ | Verbal/Linguistic |
| 3___ | 11___ | 19___ | 27___ | 35___ | ___ | Musical/Rhythm |
| 4___ | 12___ | 20___ | 28___ | 36___ | ___ | Logic/Math |
| 5___ | 13___ | 21___ | 29___ | 37___ | ___ | Body/Kinesthetic |
| 6___ | 14___ | 22___ | 30___ | 38___ | ___ | Interpersonal |
| 7___ | 15___ | 23___ | 31___ | 39___ | ___ | Intrapersonal |
| 8___ | 16___ | 24___ | 32___ | 40___ | ___ | Naturalistic |

**MIS Tally**

Multiple Intelligences

Look at the scores on the MIS. What are your top three scores? Write them in the spaces below.

|  |  |  |  |
|---|---|---|---|
| Top Score | _____ | Code | _____ |
| Second Score | _____ | Code | _____ |
| Third Score | _____ | Code | _____ |

This tally can help you understand where some of your strengths may be. Again, this is not a measure of your worth or capacities, nor is it an indicator of your future successes. Read the following section to better understand multiple intelligences.

# UNDERSTANDING MULTIPLE INTELLIGENCES

## Why Is It Important to Discover New Ways of Looking at Yourself?

In 1983, Howard Gardner, a Harvard University professor, developed a theory called Multiple Intelligences. In his book *Frames of Mind,* he outlines seven intelligences that he feels are possessed by everyone: visual/spatial, verbal/linguistic, musical/rhythm, logic/math, body/kinesthetic, interpersonal, and intrapersonal. In 1996, he added an eighth intelligence: naturalistic. In short, if you have ever done things that came easily for you, you were probably drawing on one of your well-developed intelligences. On the other hand, if you have tried to do things that are very difficult to master or understand, you may be dealing with material that calls on one of your less developed intelligences. If playing the piano by ear comes easily to you, your musical/rhythm intelligence may be very strong. If you have trouble writing or understanding poetry, your verbal/linguistic intelligence may not be as well developed. This does not mean that you will never be able to write poetry; it simply means that this is not your dominant intelligence and you may need to spend more time on this activity.

### DID YOU KNOW

**PABLO PICASSO,** the world-renowned, trend-setting artist, was born in Spain. He had a hard time in school and is said to have had a very difficult time with reading. He was diagnosed with a learning disability and his formal education never really benefited him. He left his college-level courses at the Academy of Arts in Madrid after less than a year of study. However, because of his immense artistic talent and his cubist interpretation of the universe, he changed the way the world looks at art. He is listed in the *Guinness Book of World Records* as THE most prolific painter in history, having completed nearly 14,000 paintings.

**6.3** *The Eight Intelligences*

**VISUAL/SPATIAL**
- Picture Smart
- Thinks in pictures; knows where things are in the house; loves to create images and work with graphs, charts, pictures, and maps.

**VERBAL/LINGUISTIC**
- Word Smart
- Communicates well through language, likes to write, is good at spelling, great at telling stories, loves to read books.

**MUSICAL/RHYTHM**
- Music Smart
- Loves to sing, hum, and whistle; comprehends music; responds to music immediately; performs music.

**LOGICAL/MATHEMATICAL**
- Number Smart
- Can easily conceptualize and reason, uses logic, has good problem-solving skills, enjoys math and science.

**BODY/KINESTHETIC**
- Body Smart
- Learns through body sensation, moves around a lot, enjoys work involving the hands, is graced with some athletic ability.

**INTERPERSONAL**
- People Smart
- Loves to communicate with other people, possesses great leadership skills, has lots of friends, is involved in extracurricular activities.

**INTRAPERSONAL**
- Self Smart
- Has a deep awareness of own feelings, is very reflective, requires time to be alone, does not get involved with group activities.

**NATURALISTIC**
- Environment Smart
- Has interest in the environment and in nature; can easily recognize plants, animals, rocks, and cloud formations; may like hiking, camping, and fishing.

# USING MULTIPLE INTELLIGENCES TO ENHANCE STUDYING AND LEARNING

## Can You Make Them Work for You?

In Figure 6.4, you will find some helpful tips to assist you in creating a study environment and study habits using your multiple intelligences. Read each category because you may need to improve your less dominant intelligence in some of the classes you take. This list can help you build on your strengths and develop your less dominant areas.

FIGURE **6.4**   *Using the Multiple Intelligences*

**VISUAL/SPATIAL**
- Use visuals in your notes such as timelines, charts, graphs, and geometric shapes.
- Work to create a mental or visual picture of the information at hand.
- Use colored markers to make associations or to group items together.
- Use mapping or webbing so that your main points are easily recognized.
- When taking notes, draw pictures in the margins to illustrate the main points.
- Visualize the information in your mind.

**VERBAL/LINGUISTIC**
- Establish study groups so that you will have the opportunity to talk about the information.
- Using the information you studied, create a story or a skit.
- Read as much information about related areas as possible.
- As you read chapters, outline them in your own words.
- Summarize and recite your notes aloud.

**MUSICAL/RHYTHM**
- Listen to music while studying (if it does not distract you).
- Write a song, jingle, or rap about the chapter or information.
- Take short breaks from studying to listen to music.
- Associate the information being studied to the music from your favorite song.

**LOGICAL/MATHEMATICAL**
- Strive to make logical connections between subjects.
- Don't just memorize the facts; apply them to real-life situations.
- As you study the information, think of problems in society and how this information could solve those problems.
- Create analyzing charts. Draw a line down the center of the page, put the information at hand in the left column and analyze, discuss, relate, and synthesize it in the right column.
- Allow youself some time to reflect after studying.

*(continued)*

## 6.4 *Using the Multiple Intelligences (continued)*

| | |
|---|---|
| **BODY/KINESTHETIC** | • Don't confine your study area to a desk or chair; move around, explore, go outside.<br>• Act out the information.<br>• Study in a group of people and change groups often.<br>• Use charts, posters, flash cards, and chalkboards to study.<br>• When appropriate or possible, build models using the information studied.<br>• Verbalize the information to others.<br>• Use games such as chess, Monopoly, Twister, or Clue when studying.<br>• Trace words as you study them.<br>• Use repetition to learn facts; write them many times.<br>• Make study sheets. |
| **INTERPERSONAL** | • Study in groups.<br>• Share the information with other people.<br>• Teach the information to others.<br>• Interview outside sources to learn more about the material at hand.<br>• Have a debate with others about the information. |
| **INTRAPERSONAL** | • Study in a quiet area.<br>• Study by youself.<br>• Allow time for reflection and meditation about the subject matter.<br>• Study in short time blocks and then spend some time absorbing the information.<br>• Work at your own pace. |
| **NATURALISTIC** | • Study outside whenever possible.<br>• Relate the information to the effect on the environment whenever possible.<br>• When given the opportunity to choose your own topics or research projects, choose something related to nature.<br>• Collect your own study data and resources.<br>• Organize and label your information.<br>• Keep separate notebooks on individual topics so that you can add new information to each topic as it becomes available to you. |

# UNDERSTANDING LEARNING STYLES THEORY

## Why Is It Important to Know HOW I Learn?

A learning style is "the way in which each learner begins to concentrate on, process, and retain new and difficult information" (Dunn and Griggs, 2000). There is a difference between a ***learning style*** and a ***learning strategy***. A learning ***style*** is innate and involves your five senses. It is how you best process information that comes to you. A learning *strategy* is how you might choose to learn or study, such as by using note cards, flip charts, color slides, or cooperative learning groups. Your learning strategy also involves where you study (such as at a desk, in bed, at the library, in a quiet place, with music, etc.), how long you study, and what techniques you use to help you study (such as mnemonics, cooperative learning teams, or SQ3R).

If you learn best by *seeing* information, you have a more dominant *visual learning style*. If you learn best by *hearing* information, you have a more dominant *auditory learning style*. If you learn best by *touching or doing*, you have a more dominant *tactile learning style*. You may also hear the tactile learning style referred to as kinesthetic or hands-on.

---

**FIGURE**

## 6.5    *Take the Lead*

**The Learning Evaluation and Assessment Directory**

© *Robert M. Sherfield, Ph.D.*

**Directions:** Read each statement carefully and thoroughly. After reading the statement, rate your response using the scale below. There are no right or wrong answers. This is not a timed survey. The LEAD is based, in part, on research conducted by Rita Dunn.

**3 = Often Applies**

**2 = Sometimes Applies**

**1 = Never or Almost Never Applies**

1. I remember information better if I write it down or draw a picture of it.
2. I remember things better when I hear them instead of just reading or seeing them.
3. When I get something that has to be assembled, I just start doing it. I don't read the directions.
4. If I am taking a test, I can "see" the page of the text or lecture notes where the answer is located.
5. I would rather the professor explain a graph, chart, or diagram than just show it to me.
6. When learning new things, I want to "do it" rather than hear about it.
7. I would rather the instructor write the information on the board or overhead instead of just lecturing.
8. I would rather listen to a book on tape than read it.
9. I enjoy making things, putting things together, and working with my hands.
10. I am able to quickly conceptualize and visualize information.
11. I learn best by hearing words.
12. I have been called hyperactive by my parents, spouse, partner, or professor.
13. I have no trouble reading maps, charts, or diagrams.
14. I can usually pick up on small sounds like bells, crickets, or frogs, or distant sounds like train whistles.
15. I use my hands and gesture a lot when I speak to others.

Refer to your score on each individual question. Place that score beside the appropriate question number below. Then, tally each line at the side.

| Score | | | | | Total Across | Code |
|---|---|---|---|---|---|---|
| 1 | 4 | 7 | 10 | 13 | | Visual |
| 2 | 5 | 8 | 11 | 14 | | Auditory |
| 3 | 6 | 9 | 12 | 15 | | Tactile |

**LEAD (Learning Styles) SCORE**

Look at the scores on the LEAD. What is your top score?

Top Score _____

Code _____

# From Ordinary to Extraordinary

## REAL PEOPLE | REAL LIVES | REAL CHANGE

**CHEF ODETTE SMITH-RANSOME**
Hospitality Instructor
The Art Institute of Pittsburgh, Pittsburgh, PA

At the age of 15, I found myself constantly in conflict with my mother, until one day I stood before her as she held a gun to my head. It was at that moment I knew I had to leave my parents' home, not just for my emotional well-being, but for my actual life and survival. My father was a good man, but he did not understand the entire situation with my mother's alcohol and diet pill addiction and he could do little to smooth out the situation between my mother and me. To complicate matters even more, my brother had just returned home from fighting in Vietnam and everyone was trying to adjust. It was a horrible time in the house where my ancestors had lived for over 100 years. So, I packed my clothes, dropped out of the 10th grade, and ran away over 1,000 miles to Charleston, South Carolina.

> So, I packed my clothes, dropped out of the 10th grade, and ran away over 1,000 miles to Charleston, South Carolina.

My first job was as a waitress. I worked in that job for over three years, realizing more every day that I was not using my talents and that without an education, I was doomed to work for minimum wage for the rest of my life. During this time, I met a friend in Charleston who was in the Navy. When he was released, he offered to take me back to Pittsburgh. I agreed and upon my return, I went to work in the kitchen of a family-owned restaurant. They began to take an interest in me and made me feel proud of my work. I then decided to get my GED and determine what road to take that would allow me to use my culinary talents and help others at the same time.

I began my associate's degree, which required that students complete an apprenticeship. We worked 40 hours per week, Monday through Thursday, under the direction of a master chef and we were in class 8 hours a day on Friday. My apprenticeship was at the Hyatt Regency in Pittsburgh. In order to obtain your degree, you had to pass the apprenticeship, all of the classes, and a bank of tests that proved your profi-

# From Ordinary to Extraordinary

## REAL PEOPLE | REAL LIVES | REAL CHANGE

ciency in a variety of areas. If you failed one part of the tests, you could not get your degree. Proudly, I passed every test, every class, and my apprenticeship.

My first professional job came to me upon the recommendation of a friend. I interviewed for and was hired to become the Private Chef for the Chancellor of the University of Pittsburgh. I loved the job and it afforded me the opportunity to get my bachelor's degree. So, I juggled a full-time job, a two-year-old child, and a full load of classes. As I neared the end of my degree, I was offered a fellowship at the University of Pittsburgh that trained people to teach students with special needs. I graduated Cum Laude and began teaching and working with people who had cerebral palsy at Con-

nelley Academy. I loved the work, and the position solidified my desire to work with adults.

From there I taught at the Good Will Training Center and later at the Pittsburgh Job Corps, where my culinary team won a major national competition. Today, I am an Instructor at The Art Institute® of Pittsburgh, helping others reach their dreams of working in the hospitality industry. In 2005, I was named *Culinary Educator of the Year* by the American Culinary Federation®. I try to let my life and my struggles serve as a light for students who have faced adversity and may have felt that their past was going to determine their future. My advice to my students—and to you—is this: NEVER let anyone tell you that you can't do it, that you're not able to do it,

that you don't have the means to do it, or that you'll never succeed. YOU set your own course in life and you determine the direction of your future.

## EXTRAORDINARY REFLECTION

**Read the following statement and respond in your online journal or class notebook.**

Chef Smith-Ransome had to literally leave her family to protect her life. Think about your family situation at the moment. Are your family members supportive of your efforts? Do they offer you support? Are they working with you to help you achieve your goals? If so, how does this make you stronger? Do they offer you guidance?

## THINKING for CHANGE: An Activity for Critical Reflection

Kristin knew that her most powerful learning style was visual. She knew that she had always learned best when she could "see" the information in pictures, charts, graphs, PowerPoint® slides, videos, or other powerful visuals. Kristin also knew that when she was able to get involved with the information, she seemed to retain it better. She did not at first know what this was called, but later learned that she was also a tactile or "hands-on" learner.

When she discovered that different people have different ways of learning and instructors have different ways of teaching, things began to make more sense to her. She had wondered why she had always done poorly in classes that were all lecture—like her history class. This semester, she was becoming increasingly worried about her performance in her literature class. It, too, was all lecture—information about poems, plays, and sonnets. She decided to go to the Tutoring Center to find out what she could do to retain the information

more effectively. Her tutor showed her how to make the terms and ideas more "visual" by drawing pictures beside each one, using colors in her notes, creating small story boards, and creating a visual image of what was being discussed.

In your own words, what would you suggest that a classmate do if he or she is having trouble understanding, interpreting, or remembering information from a class where there is very little discussion or lecture and he or she is a very strong auditory learner? List at least three things that your classmate could do to strengthen his or her less dominant intelligence or learning style. Think about what services are offered on your campus and what people might be of assistance to him or her.

1. _____

2. _____

3. _____

Some of the most successful students master information and techniques by using all three styles. If you were learning how to skateboard, you might learn best by *hearing someone talk* about the different styles or techniques. Others might learn best by *watching a video* in which someone demonstrates the techniques. Still others would learn best by actually getting on the board and *trying it out.* Those who engage all of their senses gain the most.

After taking the LEAD and reading more about learning styles (Figure 6.6) list at least three concrete strategies that you can employ to enhance your learning strategies for each of the three areas.

# WANTED: A VISUAL LEARNER WITH TACTILE SKILLS

## Do You Know the Differences Between Your Primary Learning Style and Your Dominant Intelligence?

As discussed previously, a **learning style** and a **learning strategy** are different. A learning style and a **dominant intelligence** are also quite different. When you read over the descriptions of multiple intelligences theory and learning styles theory, you probably noticed several common elements. Both theories deal with the visual, auditory, and tactile (or kinesthetic). There are also similarities between the two theories, but the differences are great and important.

FIGURE

### 6.6 *Learning Styles*

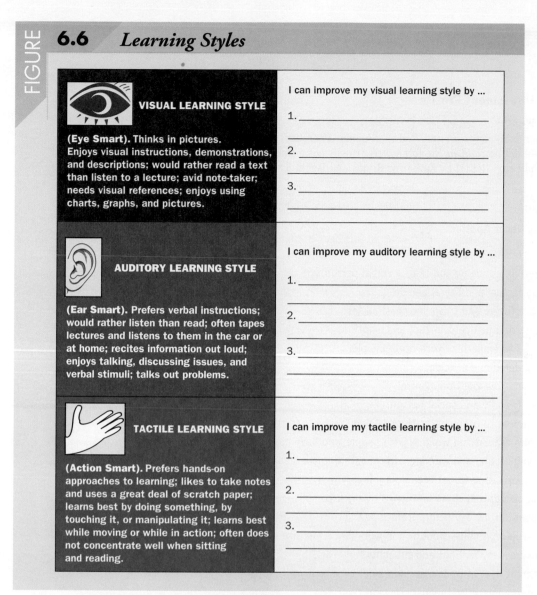

**VISUAL LEARNING STYLE**

**(Eye Smart).** Thinks in pictures. Enjoys visual instructions, demonstrations, and descriptions; would rather read a text than listen to a lecture; avid note-taker; needs visual references; enjoys using charts, graphs, and pictures.

I can improve my visual learning style by ...

1. _____
   _____
2. _____
   _____
3. _____
   _____

**AUDITORY LEARNING STYLE**

**(Ear Smart).** Prefers verbal instructions; would rather listen than read; often tapes lectures and listens to them in the car or at home; recites information out loud; enjoys talking, discussing issues, and verbal stimuli; talks out problems.

I can improve my auditory learning style by ...

1. _____
   _____
2. _____
   _____
3. _____
   _____

**TACTILE LEARNING STYLE**

**(Action Smart).** Prefers hands-on approaches to learning; likes to take notes and uses a great deal of scratch paper; learns best by doing something, by touching it, or manipulating it; learns best while moving or while in action; often does not concentrate well when sitting and reading.

I can improve my tactile learning style by ...

1. _____
   _____
2. _____
   _____
3. _____
   _____

Simply stated, you can have a visual learning style and yet ***not have*** visual/spatial as your dominant intelligence. "*How can this be possible?*" you may be asking. It may be that you **learn best** how to paint a picture by watching someone paint a picture—watching his or her brush-strokes, his or her method of mixing paints, and his or her spatial layout (this is your dominant visual learning style). However, you may not be as engaged or as talented at actually painting as the person you watched. Your painting may lack feeling, depth, and expression. You may find it hard to paint anything that is not copied from something else. You can't visualize a landscape in your mind because your visual/spatial intelligence is not very strong. In other words, you are not an innate artist at heart. This is an example of how your ***visual learning style*** can be a strong way for you to learn, but your visual/spatial intelligence may not be your dominant intelligence.

In your own words, compare and contrast YOUR primary learning style with your dominant intelligences. Give one example.

_____

_____

_____

_____

BLOOM LEVEL 2
QUESTION

## 6.7    *What Can You Learn about Personality?*

**TAKE THE P.A.P.**

**The Personality Assessment Profile**

© *Robert M. Sherfield, Ph.D.*

**Directions:** Read each statement carefully and thoroughly. After reading the statement, rate your response using the scale below. There are no right or wrong answers. This is not a timed survey. The PAP is based, in part, on the Myers-Briggs Type Indicator®(MBTI) by Katharine Briggs and Isabel Briggs-Myers.

**3 = Often Applies**

**2 = Sometimes Applies**

**1 = Never or Almost Never Applies**

_____ 1a.  I am a very talkative person.

_____ 1b.  I am a more reflective person than a verbal person.

_____ 2a.  I am a very factual and literal person.

_____ 2b.  I look to the future and I can see possibilities.

_____ 3a.  I value truth and justice over tact and emotion.

_____ 3b.  I find it easy to empathize with other people.

_____ 4a.  I am very ordered and efficient.

_____ 4b.  I enjoy having freedom from control.

_____ 5a.  I am a very friendly and social person.

_____ 5b.  I enjoy listening to others more than talking.

_____ 6a.  I enjoy being around and working with people who have a great deal of common sense.

_____ 6b.  I enjoy being around and working with people who are dreamers and have a great deal of imagination.

_____ 7a.  One of my motivating forces is to do a job very well.

_____ 7b.  I like to be recognized. I am motivated by my accomplishments and awards.

_____ 8a.  I like to plan out my day before I go to bed.

_____ 8b.  When I get up on a non-school or non-work day, I just like to let the day "plan itself."

_____ 9a.  I like to express my feelings and thoughts.

_____ 9b.  I enjoy a great deal of tranquility and quiet time to myself.

_____10a.  I am a very pragmatic and realistic person.

_____10b.  I like to create new ideas, methods, or ways of doing things.

_____11a.  I make decisions with my brain.

_____11b.  I make decisions with my heart.

_____12a.  I am a very disciplined and orderly person.

_____12b.  I don't make a lot of plans.

_____13a.  I like to work with a group of people.

_____13b.  I would rather work independently.

_____14a.  I learn best if I can see it, touch it, smell it, taste it, or hear it.

_____14b.  I learn best by relying on my gut feelings or intuition.

_____15a.  I am quick to criticize others.

_____15b.  I compliment others very easily and quickly.

_____16a.  My life is systematic and organized.

_____16b.  I don't really pay attention to deadlines.

_____17a.  I can be myself when I am around others.

_____17b.  I can be myself when I am alone.

_____18a.  I live in the here and now, in the present.

*(continued)*

FIGURE **6.7**   *What Can You Learn about Personality? (continued)*

_____18b. I live in the future, planning and dreaming.

_____19a. I think that if someone breaks the rules, the person should be punished.

_____19b. I think that if someone breaks the rules, we should look at the person who broke the rules, examine the rules, and look at the situation at hand before a decision is made.

_____20a. I do my work, then I play.

_____20b. I play, then do my work.

Refer to your score on each individual question. Place that score beside the appropriate question number below. Then, tally each line at the side.

| Score | | | | | Total Across | Code |
|---|---|---|---|---|---|---|
| 1a _____ | 5a _____ | 9a _____ | 13a _____ | 17a _____ | _____ | E Extrovert |
| 1b _____ | 5b _____ | 9b _____ | 13b _____ | 17b _____ | _____ | I Introvert |
| 2a _____ | 6a _____ | 10a _____ | 14a _____ | 18a _____ | _____ | S Sensing |
| 2b _____ | 6b _____ | 10b _____ | 14b _____ | 18b _____ | _____ | N Intuition |
| 3a _____ | 7a _____ | 11a _____ | 15a _____ | 19a _____ | _____ | T Thinking |
| 3b _____ | 7b _____ | 11b _____ | 15b _____ | 19b _____ | _____ | F Feeling |
| 4a _____ | 8a _____ | 12a _____ | 16a _____ | 20a _____ | _____ | J Judging |
| 4b _____ | 8b _____ | 12b _____ | 16b _____ | 20b _____ | _____ | P Perceiving |

**PAP Scores**

Personality Indicator

Look at the scores on your PAP. Is your score higher in the *E or the I* line? Is your score higher in the *S or the N* line? Is your score higher in the *T or the F* line? Is your score higher in the *J or the P* line? Write the code to the side of each section below.

Is your higher score   **E or I**   Code _____

Is your higher score   **S or N**   Code _____

Is your higher score   **T or F**   Code _____

Is your higher score   **J or P**   Code _____

# UNDERSTANDING PERSONALITY TYPE

## Are You ENFJ, ISTP, or ENTJ, and Why Does It Matter?

In 1921, Swiss psychologist **Carl Jung** (1875–1961) published his work *Psychological Types*. In this book, Jung suggested that human behavior is not random. He felt that behavior follows patterns and that these patterns are caused by differences in the way people use their minds. In 1942, Isabel Briggs-Myers and her mother, Katharine Briggs, began to put Jung's theory into practice. They developed the Myers-Briggs Type Indicator®, which after more than 50 years of research and refinement, has become the most widely used instrument for identifying and studying personality.

Personality typing can "help us discover what best motivates and energizes each of us as individuals" (Tieger and Barron-Tieger, 2007). The questions on the PAP helped you discover whether you are an **E** or an **I** (**E**xtroverted or **I**ntroverted), an **S** or an **N**

## ESSENTIAL CORNERSTONE

**Communication:**

How can learning more about your personality, and the personalities of those around you, help you enhance your communication skills?

**Social Networking Moment:**

Share your response to this Essential Cornerstone with peers in your social network. Choose two responses from your peers and respond to their postings.

(**S**ensing or i**N**tuitive), a **T** or an **F** (Thinking or Feeling), and a **J** or a **P** (Judging or Perceiving). When all of the combinations of E/I, S/N, T/F, and J/P are combined, there are 16 personality types. Everyone will fit into **ONE** of the following categories:

| | | | |
|---|---|---|---|
| ISTJ | ISFJ | INFJ | INTJ |
| ISTP | ISFP | INFP | INTP |
| ESTP | ESFP | ENFP | ENTP |
| ESTJ | ESFJ | ENFJ | ENTJ |

Let's take a look at the four major categories of typing. Notice that the higher your score in one area, the stronger your personality type is for that area. For instance, if you scored 15 on the E (extroversion) questions, this means that you are a strong extrovert. If you scored 15 on the I (introversion) questions, this means that you are a strong introvert. However, if you scored 7 on the E questions and 8 on the I questions, your score indicates that you possess almost the same amount of extroverted and introverted qualities. The same is true for every other category of the PAP.

## E versus I (Extroversion/Introversion)

This category deals with the way we *interact with others and the world around us; how we draw our energy*.

*Extroverts* prefer to live in the outside world, drawing their strength from other people. They are outgoing and love interaction. They usually make decisions with others in mind. They enjoy being the center of attention. There are usually few secrets about extroverts.

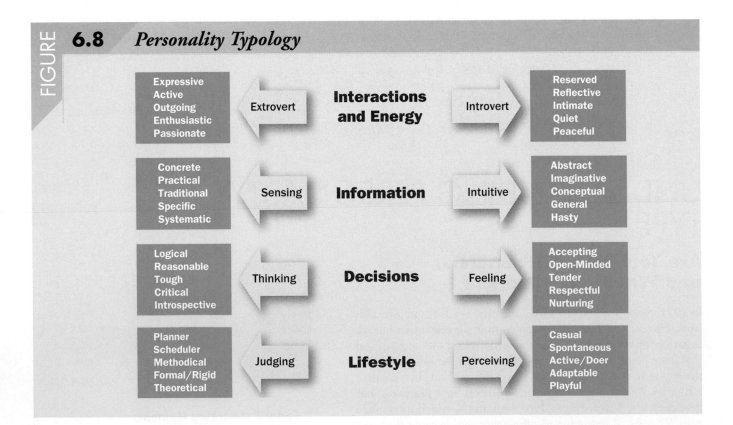

FIGURE **6.8** *Personality Typology*

| Expressive Active Outgoing Enthusiastic Passionate | Extrovert | **Interactions and Energy** | Introvert | Reserved Reflective Intimate Quiet Peaceful |
|---|---|---|---|---|
| Concrete Practical Traditional Specific Systematic | Sensing | **Information** | Intuitive | Abstract Imaginative Conceptual General Hasty |
| Logical Reasonable Tough Critical Introspective | Thinking | **Decisions** | Feeling | Accepting Open-Minded Tender Respectful Nurturing |
| Planner Scheduler Methodical Formal/Rigid Theoretical | Judging | **Lifestyle** | Perceiving | Casual Spontaneous Active/Doer Adaptable Playful |

*Introverts* draw their strength from the inner world. They need to spend time alone to think and ponder. They are usually quiet and reflective. They usually make decisions by themselves. They do not like being the center of attention. They are private

## S versus N (Sensing/iNtuition)

This category deals with the way we *learn and deal with information*.

*Sensing* types gather information through their five senses. They have a hard time believing something if it cannot be seen, touched, smelled, tasted, or heard. They like concrete facts and details. They do not rely on intuition or gut feelings. They usually have a great deal of common sense.

*Intuitive* types are not very detail-oriented. They can see possibilities, and they rely on their gut feelings. Usually, they are very innovative people. They tend to live in the future and often get bored once they have mastered a task.

## T versus F (Thinking/Feeling)

This category deals with the way we *make decisions*.

*Thinkers* are very logical people. They do not make decisions based on feelings or emotions. They are analytical and sometimes do not take others' values into consideration when making decisions. They can easily identify the flaws of others. They can sometimes be seen as insensitive and lacking compassion.

*Feelers* make decisions based on what they feel is right and just. They like to have harmony, and they value others' opinions and feelings. They are usually very tactful people who like to please others. They are very warm people.

### Tips for Personal Success

Consider the following tips for making the most of your learning style, personality type, and dominant intelligence.

► Improve your weaker learning styles by incorporating at least one aspect of those learning styles into your daily study plans.

► If your personality type clashes with your professor's personality type, try to make adjustments that enable you to get through the class successfully.

► Adjust your learning style to match your professor's teaching style if possible.

► Use your primary intelligence to help you decide on your life's vocation.

Now, it is your turn. Create a list of at least three more tips that you would offer a fellow classmate to assist him or her in making the most of his or her learning style, intelligence, and personality type. Develop one strategy for each category.

**1.** Learning Style Tip _____

**2.** Multiple Intelligence Tip _____

**3.** Personality Type Tip _____

## J versus P (Judging/Perceiving)

This category deals with the way we *live and our overall lifestyle*.

*Judgers* are very orderly people. They must have a great deal of structure in their lives. They are good at setting goals and sticking to them. They are the type of people who would seldom, if ever, play before their work was completed.

*Perceivers* are just the opposite. They are less structured and more spontaneous. They do not like timelines. Unlike the judgers, they will play before their work is done. They will take every chance to delay a decision or judgment. Sometimes, they can become involved in too many things at one time.

After you have studied the the Personality Type Chart (Figure 6.9) and other information in the chapter regarding your personality type, you can make some decisions about your study habits and even your career choices. For instance, if you scored very high in the extroversion section, it may not serve you well to pursue a career where you would be forced to work alone. It would probably also be unwise to try to spend all of your time studying alone. If you are a strong extrovert, you would want to work and study around people.

**EXAMPLE:** If Mike's dominant intelligence is **interpersonal**, his learning style is **verbal**, and his personality type is **ENFJ**, *connecting the dots* may suggest that he is the type of person who loves to be around other people and is an extrovert who learns best by listening to other people or explaining how something is done. He is a person who would probably speak up in class, be more of a leader than a follower, and start a study group if one did not exist because he is outgoing, organized, and very much a goal setter. Mike is the type of person who values relationships and listens to what others are saying. He is a person who shares and does not mind taking the time to explain things to others. He could easily become a good friend.

Some of the challenges that Mike could encounter might involve taking a class where discussions are rare, having to sit and never being able to share ideas or views, or having a professor who is not very organized and skips around. He would not deal very well with peers who are disrespectful and do not pull their own weight in the study group. He might also have a hard time with group members or classmates who are very quiet and prefer to observe rather than contribute. He would have trouble being around people who have no goals or direction in life. He might also run into some trouble because he is a very social person and loves to be around others in social settings. He may thus overcommit himself to groups and clubs and, on occasion, socialize more than study.

As you can see, by connecting the dots, Mike's **Personal Life Profile** tells us a great deal about his strengths and challenges. It also gives him an understanding of how to approach many different situations, capitalize on his strengths, and work to improve his weaker areas.

## Now, it is your turn.

Take your time and refer to the chapter for any information you may need. Examine your assessments and create your own profile in the four areas listed below. Discuss your strengths and challenges for each area.

THE PERSONAL LIFE PROFILE OF _____

**Academic** Strengths: I found that I . . .

_____
_____
_____
_____
_____
_____
_____
_____
_____
_____

**Academic** Challenges: I found that I . . .

_____
_____
_____
_____
_____
_____
_____
_____
_____
_____
_____

**Communication** Strengths: I found that I . . .

_____
_____
_____
_____
_____
_____
_____
_____

**Communication** Challenges: I found that I . . .

_____
_____
_____
_____
_____
_____
_____
_____
_____

**Relationship** Strengths: I found that I . . .

_____
_____
_____
_____
_____
_____
_____
_____

**Relationship** Challenges: I found that I . . .

_____

_____

_____

_____

_____

_____

_____

**Career** Strengths: I found that I . . .

_____

_____

_____

_____

_____

_____

_____

_____

**Career** Challenges: I found that I . . .

_____

_____

_____

_____

_____

_____

_____

_____

Looking at all of this together, write an extensive paragraph about what all of this means about you. Include thoughts on your learning style, your personality, your study habits, your communication skills, and your overall success strategy.

_____

_____

_____

_____

_____

_____

# SQ3R *Mastery* Study Sheet

| EXAMPLE QUESTION: *(from page 156)* What is the difference between a learning style and a learning strategy? | ANSWER: |
|---|---|
| EXAMPLE QUESTION: *(from page 157)* What is the definition of tactile and how do you use it? | ANSWER: |
| AUTHOR QUESTION: *(from page 152)* Discuss at least three theories of learning from the historical figures discussed. | ANSWER: |
| AUTHOR QUESTION: *(from page 153)* Who is Howard Gardner and why is his work important? | ANSWER: |
| AUTHOR QUESTION: *(from page 160)* Explain the difference between your learning style and your dominant intelligence. | ANSWER: |
| AUTHOR QUESTION: *(from page 161)* What is the difference between a visual learning style and visual intelligence? | ANSWER: |
| AUTHOR QUESTION: *(from page 163)* How can your personality type affect your study time? | ANSWER: |
| YOUR QUESTION: *(from page ____)* | ANSWER: |
| YOUR QUESTION: *(from page ____)* | ANSWER: |
| YOUR QUESTION: *(from page ____)* | ANSWER: |
| YOUR QUESTION: *(from page ____)* | ANSWER: |
| YOUR QUESTION: *(from page ____)* | ANSWER: |

Finally, after answering these questions, recite this chapter's major points in your mind. Consider the following general questions to help you master this material.

► What was it about?
► What does it mean?
► What was the most important thing I learned? Why?
► What were the key points to remember?

# READ

## BUILDING YOUR READING AND COMPREHENSION SKILLS

"The difference between the right word and the almost right word is the difference between lightning and the lightning bug."

—Mark Twain

# WHY READ THIS CHAPTER?

## What's in it for me?

*WHY* is it important to know my reading speed? *WHY* will a chapter on reading and comprehension help me study better? *WHY* do I need to know how to identify a main point? *WHY*, since I'm already in college, is learning how to read more effectively such a big deal?

WHY? Because there is a monumental difference between recognizing and pronouncing the words on a page and being able to comprehend, interpret, analyze, evaluate, and remember those written words. Your having hands does not make you a mechanic. Having a voice does not make you a singer, and being able to read words does not mean that you comprehend what the author intended. Reading makes you smarter and more knowledgeable about many subjects. You can sit in your easy chair and read all about the Renaissance, the painting of Mona Lisa, the statue of David, the Gold Coast of Australia, Alexander the Great, or the priceless antiquities of China. You might one day learn to do your job better by reading professional journals. Reading covers many terrains, from history to human-interest stories to cutting-edge ideas to scholars' research results. If you really want to learn, reading is the key. No other single skill comes close to offering you the benefits of knowing how to effectively read and comprehend information.

*By carefully reading this chapter and taking the information provided seriously, you will be able to:*

1. Understand the value of reading and identify whether you are an active or a passive reader.
2. Calculate and understand your reading speed and how it affects your study time.
3. Apply strategies to increase your reading comprehension.
4. Understand the skills associated with effective reading, including dictionary usage, fixation and locating main ideas.
5. Understand and use the SQ3R method of reading.

## CHAPTER 7 / READ

*"It is impossible for people to learn what they think they already know."*

—Epictetus

## . . . FROM MY PERSPECTIVE

**NAME:** Thomas Paddock
**INSTITUTION:** Louisville Technical Institute, Louisville, KY
**MAJOR:** Computer Networking Administration
**AGE:** 21

For me, reading was an elusive subject in high school. While students were strongly encouraged to read, most of us didn't have any free time to read, and those who did have free time were busy with other activities. While I was lucky enough to be in an AP English class for two years, I still didn't read as much as I should have. We were exposed to several great works of literature, but even more so, we were exposed to several chances for developing reading skills that I really wish I had honed before I arrived at college. It used to be, "Read Chapters 1–5 by Friday." Now it's, "Read Chapters 1–5 by tomorrow, and be prepared for a quiz."

Fortunately, I was able to recover from the shock of college rush, and I've adapted rather quickly. My career field requires me to read books that are on the level of technical manuals, and whether or not I can even get a job will depend on this knowledge. Every little detail mentioned counts, and oftentimes I've found that what may have seemed to be an obscure or unimportant detail has come back to haunt me later on certification exams, which is why it's important to be able to soak in as much information as possible. Even a small blurb or tip in a textbook may reveal a com-

mon network problem that can lead to a world of trouble if ignored.

Proper reading skills and techniques are some of the most important tools I've developed in college—and this will be true for you, too. There is so much information in our textbooks that it's impossible to cover all of it in class, so being able to actually understand that information without the aid of a teacher is a great benefit. Reading is something that I'm definitely not going to have a lack of, whether in the present or the future, and I can't see myself living or working without highly efficient reading skills. This chapter can help you become a more active reader and it can help you increase your comprehension, too.

## SCAN & QUESTION

In the preface of this book (page xix), you read about the **SQ3R Study Method.** Right now, take a few moments, **scan this chapter**, and on page 197, write **five questions** that you think will be important to your mastery of this material. In addition to the two questions below, you will find five questions from your authors. Use one of your *"On The Test"* stickers to flag this page for easy reference.

**EXAMPLES:**

▶ **Describe the process of fixation.** (from page 182)

▶ **Why is comprehension more important than speed?** (from page 180)

# IS READING *FUNDAMENTAL* OR JUST PURE TORTURE?

## The Answer Can Change Your Life

Quick question: "What are the top two academic problems among college students today?" According to faculty members, assessments, national tests, and yes, even your peers around the nation, the two greatest problems students face today are college math classes and reading comprehension—and some of the math problems can even be attributed to poor reading skills.

**FIGURE 7.1** *A Six Pack that Can Help You with Effective Reading.*

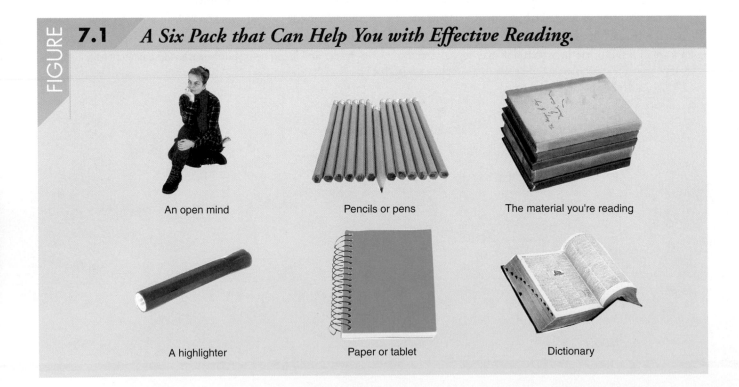

An open mind

Pencils or pens

The material you're reading

A highlighter

Paper or tablet

Dictionary

How many times have you read to the bottom of a page or completed a section in a textbook and said to yourself, *"I don't remember a thing I just read."* In actuality, all of us have experienced this at one time or another. The strategies outlined in this chapter will help you eliminate this common occurrence from your study time. By applying the strategies discussed herein, you will be able to read a page, a section, or an entire chapter so that when you reach the end, you will *comprehend and remember* what you just read.

It may seem elementary, but without the proper tools, you can't improve your reading comprehension, analysis, or speed. Enough said!

# DISCOVERING YOUR READING STYLE

## Are You Active or Passive?

Take a few moments and circle TRUE or FALSE for each of the statements in Figure 7.2 to determine whether you are more of an active or a passive reader.

Active reading is really nothing more than a mind-set. It is the attitude you have as you begin the reading process. For the next few days, try approaching your reading assignments with a positive, open-minded approach and notice the difference in your own satisfaction, understanding, and overall comprehension. Instead of saying things like, "I hate reading" or "This stuff is worthless," reframe your self-talk into statements such as "I'm going to learn from this" and "I think I can apply this to my life now."

---

**FIGURE**

### 7.2   *Discovering Your Reading Style*

Take a few moments and circle true or false for each of the following statements to determine if you are more of an active or passive reader.

**DISCOVERING YOUR READING STYLE**

| | | |
|---|---|---|
| 1. I enjoy reading for pleasure. | TRUE | FALSE |
| 2. College textbooks have little connection to my real life. | TRUE | FALSE |
| 3. I look for the deeper meaning in words and phrases. | TRUE | FALSE |
| 4. I seldom visualize what I am reading. | TRUE | FALSE |
| 5. I look up words that I do not understand. | TRUE | FALSE |
| 6. I read only what I have to read, and that is a stretch for me. | TRUE | FALSE |
| 7. I stop reading to ponder what something means. | TRUE | FALSE |
| 8. I never take notes when reading. | TRUE | FALSE |
| 9. Reading brings me great joy. | TRUE | FALSE |
| 10. My mind wanders constantly when I read. | TRUE | FALSE |
| 11. I make time for reading even when I am not required to read. | TRUE | FALSE |
| 12. Words are just words—they add no real meaning to my life or work. | TRUE | FALSE |
| 13. I get excited about reading something new because I know I will learn something new and useful. | TRUE | FALSE |
| 14. When reading, I just want to get it over with. | TRUE | FALSE |
| 15. I usually have no trouble concentrating when reading. | TRUE | FALSE |
| 16. I never look up words; I just read on. | TRUE | FALSE |

**Total of even-numbered TRUE responses** _____

**Total of odd-numbered TRUE responses** _____

If you answered TRUE to more even numbers, you tend to be a more passive reader.
If you answered TRUE to more odd numbers, you tend to be a more active reader.

Have you ever timed yourself to determine how long it takes you to read a complete chapter?

# I FEEL THE NEED . . . THE NEED FOR SPEED!

## Do You Know Your Personal Reading Rate?

You've heard the advertisements: "Breeze through a novel on your lunch hour," "Read an entire computer instruction book over dinner," or "Read *The New York Times* in 10 minutes." Sure, there are people who have an incredible gift for speed reading and a photographic memory, but those people are not the norm.

This section is included in your text to give you some idea about how long it will take to read a chapter so that you can *plan your reading time* more effectively. There is an average of 450 words on a college textbook page. If you read at 150 words per minute, each page may take you an average of three minutes to read.

---

**FIGURE**

## 7.3   *Calculating Your Reading Rate*

Start Time _____  _____                              Minutes _____  Seconds _____

BINGE DRINKING

Binge drinking is classified as having more than five drinks at one time. Many people say, "I only drink once a week." However, if that one drinking spell includes drink after drink after drink, it can be extremely detrimental to your liver, your memory, your digestive system, and your overall health.

Most college students report that they do not mean to binge drink, but it is caused by the situation, such as a ballgame, a party, a campus event, or special occasions. Researchers at Michigan State University found that only 5 percent of students surveyed say they party to "get drunk" (Warner, 2002).

In their breakthrough work, *Dying to Drink*, Harvard researcher Henry Wechsler and science writer Bernice Wuethrich explore the problem of binge drinking. They suggest, "two out of every five college students regularly binge drink, resulting in approximately 1,400 student deaths, a distressing number of assaults and rapes, a shameful amount of vandalism, and countless cases of academic suicide" (Wechsler and Wuethrich, 2002).

It is a situation reminiscent of the old saying, "Letting the fox guard the henhouse." After a few drinks, it is hard to "self-police," meaning that you may not be able to control your actions once the drinking starts.

Perhaps the greatest tragedy of drug and alcohol abuse is the residual damage of pregnancy, sexually transmitted diseases, traffic fatalities, verbal/physical abuse, and accidental death. You know that drugs and alcohol lower your resistance and can cause you to do things that you would not normally do, such as drive drunk or have unprotected sex. Surveys and research results suggest that students who participate in heavy episodic (HE) or binge drinking are more likely to participate in unprotected sex with multiple sex partners. One survey found that 61 percent of men who do binge drink participated in unprotected sex as compared to 23 percent of men who do not binge drink. The survey also found that 48 percent of women who do binge drink participated in unprotected sex as compared to only 8 percent of women who do not binge drink (Cooper, 2002).

These staggering statistics suggest one thing: alcohol consumption can cause people to act in ways in which they may never have acted without alcohol—and those actions can result in personal damage from which recovery may be impossible.
(387 words)

**Finishing Time** _____                              _____ Minutes _____ Seconds _____
Reading time in SECONDS = _____
Words per MINUTE (use the following chart) = _____

*(continued)*

FIGURE

## 7.3   *Calculating Your Reading Rate (continued)*

**Example:** If you read this passage in 2 minutes and 38 seconds, your reading time in seconds would be 158. Using the Rate Calculator Chart, your reading rate would be about 146 words per minute.

RATE CALCULATOR FOR RELATIVELY EASY PASSAGES

| Time in Seconds and Minutes | Words Per Minute |
| --- | --- |
| 40 | 581 |
| 50 | 464 |
| 60 (1 minute) | 387 |
| 120 (2 minute) | 194 |
| 130 | 179 |
| 140 | 165 |
| 150 | 155 |
| 160 | 145 |
| 170 | 137 |
| 180 (3 minute) | 129 |
| 190 | 122 |
| 200 | 116 |
| 210 | 110 |
| 220 | 106 |
| 230 | 101 |

*Source:* B. Smith, *Breaking Through*, 8th ed. (2007).

Test Your Comprehension Skills

**Answer the following questions with T (true) or F (false) without looking back over the material.**

_____ 1. Binge drinking has resulted in the deaths of students.
_____ 2. Men who binge drink have unprotected sex more often than men who do not binge drink.
_____ 3. Women who binge drink have unprotected sex no more often than women who do not binge drink.
_____ 4. "Self-policing" means that you are able to look out for yourself.
_____ 5. Binge drinking is classified as having more than three drinks at one time.

Each question is worth 20%.        Comprehension = _____%

**Example:** If you answered two correctly, your comprehension rate would be 40% (2 × 20%). If you answered four correctly, your comprehension rate would be 80% (4 × 20%).

**Test Your Comprehension Skills Answers:** 1 = T, 2 = T, 3 = F, 4 = T, 5 = F.

This is a ***raw number*** for basic reading. It DOES NOT allow for marking, highlighting, taking notes, looking up words, reflecting, or comprehending. When these necessary skills are coupled with basic reading, they can sometimes triple the amount of reading time required. So, that page that you estimated would take you 3 minutes to read may actually take you 9 to 10 minutes to read.

In the reading activity (Figure 7.3), you will find a passage about binge drinking. Read the section at your normal pace. Use a stopwatch or a watch with a second hand to accurately record your time, and then calculate your rate and comprehension level using the directions provided.

## ESSENTIAL CORNERSTONE

**Passion:**

How can learning to read more effectively and frequently increase your passion for learning?

**Social Networking Moment:**

Share your response to this Essential Cornerstone with peers in your social network. Choose two responses from your peers and respond to their postings.

# SPEED AND COMPREHENSION

## Why Does It Matter So Much and How Does It Impact My Education?

According to Brenda D. Smith (2007), professor and reading expert, "rate calculators vary according to the difficulty of the material. Research indicates, however, that on relatively easy material, the average adult reading speed is approximately 250 words per minute at 70% comprehension. For college students, the rate is sometimes estimated at closer to 300 words per minute." The passage that you just read would be classified as relatively easy.

If you are reading below the average, 250-words-per-minute rate, several factors could be contributing to this situation. They include:

▶ Not concentrating on the passage.

▶ Vocabulary words with which you are not familiar.

▶ Stopping too long on any given single word (called fixations; discussed later).

▶ Not reading often enough to build your speed.

The remainder of this chapter is intended to assist you with improving your reading speed AND comprehension.

# YOU DON'T HAVE TO BE A LOGODAEDALIAN TO ENJOY WORDS

## Can a Powerful Vocabulary Really Be Developed?

Thankfully, it is not every day that you run across words like *logodaedalian*. (A logodaedalian is a person who has a great passion for unique, sly, and clever words and phrases.) Perhaps the best way to develop a dynamic vocabulary is by reading. While reading, you may come across words with which you are not familiar. You may be exposed to aspects of language that you have not experienced with your family, friends, or geographic location. These unfamiliar words will not become a part of your **vernacular** unless you STOP and look them up. This is the way to begin building a masterful vocabulary.

Let's start by looking up the word *vernacular*. Take a moment and jot down the definition.

*Vernacular* means: _____

_____

_____

_____

See how simple that was? Now you have a new word in your vocabulary—actually, you have two new words from just a few paragraphs: *vernacular* and *logodaedalian*. You have taken a step toward becoming a logophile!

# IT'S NOT JUST A DOORSTOP

## How Can a Dictionary Aid in Reading Comprehension?

Your dictionary will become a good friend to you in college. There may be many words and phrases that you do not understand when reading your college textbooks. This is somewhat common, as many college texts are written on the 13th- and 14th-grade levels. You will need to stop and look up the words you don't understand. When you look up a word in the dictionary, you are given more than just a definition (see Figure 7.4). You are also given the phonetic pronunciation, the spelling, the meaning, the part of speech in which the word can be used, the origin of the word, and usually several definitions. You may have to choose the definition that best suits the context of the sentence. It can be beneficial to you to jot down definitions in the margins of your text.

Using the definition for *magnitude,* determine which definition would be best suited to this sentence: ***The magnitude of the power she had over him was truly amazing.***

**FIGURE**

### 7.4  *Annotated Dictionary Entry*

# LEARNING TO READ FASTER AND SMARTER

## Can Speed and Comprehension Be Improved?

As you begin to practice your reading comprehension, review the following tips for helping you read the material more quickly and understand it more clearly. Whenever you are faced with having to choose between comprehension and speed, choose comprehension every time.

## Concentration

Speed and comprehension both require deep, mindful concentration. Neither can be achieved without it. Your body needs to be ready to concentrate. It will be nearly impossible to concentrate if you are tired and hungry. To increase your concentration for active reading, consider the following:

▶ Reduce outside distractions such as people talking, rooms that are too hot or cold, cell phones ringing, etc.

▶ Reduce internal distractions such as fatigue, self-talk, daydreaming, hunger, and emotions that cause you to think of other things.

▶ Set a goal of reading a certain amount of material in an allotted time. This goal can help you focus.

▶ Take a short break every 20 minutes. Don't get distracted and go off and do something else; come back to your reading in 3–5 minutes.

▶ Take notes as you read. This helps reading become an active process.

## Vocabulary

Building a strong vocabulary may not be the easiest thing to do, and you will not build it overnight. However, it is important that you work on this aspect of reading as often as possible. If you do not know a word, you must stop and look it up. Having to stop and look up a word that you do not know may slow you down and cause you to lose concentration; however, the more words you have in your vocabulary, the fewer times you will need to stop and look up a word. It is difficult and nearly impossible to read, comprehend, and remember a passage when you do not know or understand one or more words.

## Fixation

*Fixation* is when your eyes stop on a single word to read it. Your eyes stop for only a fraction of a second, but those fractions add up over the course of a section or chapter. Your mind sees the words something like this:

**Nutrition    is    important    to    good    health.**

As you read this, you probably had six fixations because the words are spaced out. However, even if they were not spaced out, many people would still have six fixations. To increase your speed, try to see two or three words with one fixation; this will cut your reading time nearly in half. Try to see the sentence like this:

**Nutrition is important        to good health.**

Smith (2007) states: "research has shown that the average reader can see approximately 2.5 words per fixation."

To reduce your fixation time for active reading, consider the following:

▶ Practice seeing two or more words with one fixation.

▶ As you practice, try to read in phrases like the example below:

*Nutrition is important     to good health. Therefore,     you should     work hard to eat     proper meals     every day.     By doing this     you can maintain good health.*

**Read the following passage using the fixation procedure:**

Motivation is an important asset to all students, and it must come from within. No one—not your professors, your parents, or your friends—can motivate you unless you want to be motivated. You will be motivated by one of two things—fear or desire. Fear will cause you to be afraid and not take risks, while desire will make you take a chance on yourself and move out of your comfort zone.

How did you do? Was this easy or difficult? Why?

_____

_____

_____

BLOOM LEVEL 5 QUESTION

# FINDING THE TOPIC AND MAIN IDEAS IN PARAGRAPHS AND SECTIONS

## Can You Get to the Main Point?

Typically, each paragraph has a main idea. You're no doubt familiar with this from your English classes. It is usually called a topic sentence. The topic statement is what the paragraph is about. Identifying the main idea of a paragraph can greatly aid your comprehension of that paragraph and eventually the entire section or chapter.

**Read the following paragraph and determine the main idea—the point.**

*Without exception, the conclusion should be one of the most carefully crafted components of your paper or speech. Long after your reader has finished reading or your listener has finished listening, the last part of your work is more than likely going to be the part they remember the most. Some writers and speakers suggest that you write your conclusion first, so that your paper or speech is directed toward a specific end result. That decision, of course, is up to you. However, a great piece of advice from writing experts tells us that captivating writers always know how their stories will end long before they begin writing them.*

**From *Cornerstone: Building on Your Best*, 5th edition**

Can you determine what the above paragraph is about? We know that the opening statement talks about writing the conclusion of a paper or speech. But it also talks about the importance

ESSENTIAL CORNERSTONE

**Resourcefulness:**
How can reading help you find creative ways to solve old and new problems?

**Social Networking Moment:**
Share your response to this Essential Cornerstone with peers in your social network. Choose two responses from your peers and respond to their postings.

# From Ordinary to Extraordinary

## REAL PEOPLE | REAL LIVES | REAL CHANGE

**SYLVIA EBERHARDT**
Fashion Model, Abercrombie and Fitch, *Hollister Magazine,*
and Other Top Agencies
Honors Graduate, Fairfax High School, Fairfax, VA
Honors Student—Howard University, Washington, D.C.

If you read my resume and looked at my professional credits, you might think I had it made—that the world had been handed to me on a silver platter and that I never wanted for anything. Nothing could be further from the truth. Although I am an honors student at Howard University and a fashion model who has worked with some of the top stores and magazines in the nation, my beginnings were anything but easy and beautiful.

I was born into a crack-infested, gang-ridden, one-bedroom house in inner-city Washington, D.C. I was raised a few doors down from a major crack house, where I saw junkies, prostitutes, and pimps on a daily basis. It was simply a way of life. Poverty surrounded me and my two siblings at every turn. Unemployment was rampant and the streets were filled with trash and used needles. I slept in a bunk bed where nightly I could hear drug deals being made outside my window. The iron bars on the windows were the only things that separated me from the ugliness of the world outside my home.

My mother died just before I entered high school and I was raised from that point on by my father. I was constantly teased and tormented growing up because I was so thin. My peers nicknamed me Anna (for "Anorexic"). What they did not know was that I suffered (and continue to suffer) from Crohn's disease, a life-threatening disability. Crohn's is an autoimmune disease that affects the gastrointestinal system and causes rashes, severe abdominal pain, arthritis, vomiting, and weight loss.

How did I survive? How did I become an honors student at one of the top high schools in the nation? How did I become a fashion model at the age of 15? I am blessed to have an amazing, supportive father who taught me that you never have to let your past or present dictate your future. He believed and taught me that no matter how humble one's beginnings, no matter where you were born or the circumstances of your life, the test of a person's character is knowing that he or she holds his or her destiny in his or her own hands.

He taught me that I had to take responsibility for my own life. I had to be my own savior. Further, he taught my siblings and me that "you may live

> My father taught me that "you may live in the ghetto, but the ghetto does not have to live in you."

184

# From Ordinary to Extraordinary

## REAL PEOPLE | REAL LIVES | REAL CHANGE

in the ghetto, but the ghetto does not have to live in you." He always told us that you do not have to think and act poor simply because you live in a lower-class neighborhood. He also taught us that in order to enjoy the finer things in life, you first have to experience hard times. He would say to us, "You have to ride in an old, ragged car before you can appreciate a Mercedes." His attitude helped guide and change my life.

After we moved to Virginia, I began working hard and taking college-level classes at Northern Virginia Community College while still in high school. My dream is to become a heart surgeon. I knew from the very beginning that I would have to study hard and give up many things I enjoyed doing. It paid off, however. By the end of my senior year in high school, I had over 30 college credits in math, science, anatomy, microbiology, calculus, and physiology, with a 4.0 grade point average. I won a full scholarship to Howard University and finished my first semester with a 3.92 GPA.

I write all of this to you to say, "Your life is what you make of it. You can let your past and present dictate and ruin your future, or you can get over it, work hard, believe in yourself, push yourself, and work toward your dreams." I wish you so much good luck and good fortune in your future.

## EXTRAORDINARY REFLECTION

**Read the following statement and respond in your online journal or class notebook.**

Sylvia mentions that her father would say to her, "in order to enjoy the finer things in life, you first have to experience hard times. You have to ride in an old, ragged car before you can appreciate a Mercedes." How do you plan to use your past experiences, positive or negative, to bring about positive change in your future?

of your conclusion and that some writers actually write their conclusions first. The main topic of this paragraph happens to be the first sentence. The remaining sentences simply add information and credibility to the topic sentence.

### Read and study the following paragraph.

*Do you remember where you were and what you were doing when you heard that Barack Obama had been elected the first African-American president of the United States? Chances are good that you remember some of the details surrounding what you were doing when you heard this historic news. Experts report that most people remember exactly where they were and what they were doing when a major event occurred. Depending on your age, you or your parents probably remember where you were when you heard about the World Trade Center attacks. Many people who were alive when John Kennedy was assassinated still remember vividly where they were when they heard the news, even though this event happened many years ago. Events of this magnitude seem to be seared into our memories.*

Circle the one option below that best describes the topic sentence of this paragraph.

1. The election of Barack Obama

2. John Kennedy's assassination

3. The fact that we tend to remember what we were doing when events of great magnitude happened

Which did you choose? Statements one and two have very little to do with the paragraph's intended message. They are simply prompts or examples. Statement three is the correct topic for this paragraph.

According to Dorothy Seyler (2003), professor and reading expert, you can identify the topic of a paragraph in four easy steps:

▶ The topic is the subject of the paragraph.

▶ You can identify the topic by answering the question, "What or who is the paragraph about?"

▶ The topic statement should be general enough to cover all of the specifics of the paragraph.

▶ The topic statement should be specific enough to exclude other paragraphs on related topics.

Finding the topic sentence or main idea of a paragraph, section, or chapter is not hard, but it does take concentration and a degree of analytical skills. If you approach each paragraph as a detective searching for clues, you will soon find out how easy and effortless it is to determine main points.

Read the following paragraph and identify the topic in your own words. Justify your answer. Then, identify the main idea of the paragraph. See if you can determine what the author really wants you to know.

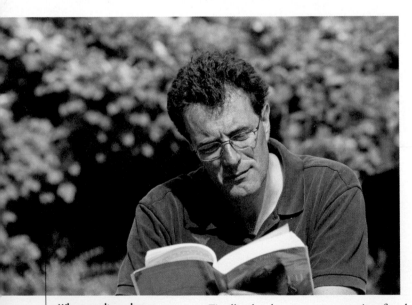

When reading, do you stop after each paragraph and think about the meaning?

Finally, develop one test question for the paragraph.

You *will not* have to do this for every paragraph you read in college. As you become a stronger reader, you will do this type of analysis after each heading or chapter section. But for now, as you work on building your skills as a reader, take the time to learn how to fully analyze a small portion of a chapter.

*The origin of emotion is the brain. You might say that there are two minds—one that thinks (the thinking mind) and one that feels (the emotional mind). Think of thoughts and emotions as two different mechanisms for knowing and making sense of the world. The two minds are not adversarial or physically separate; rather, they operate interactively to construct your mental life. Passion (the heart) dominates reason (the mind) when feelings are intense.*

—EMOTIONAL INTELLIGENCE, NELSON AND LOW

**VOCABULARY BUILDER (DEFINE THE FOLLOWING)**

*mechanism* _____

*adversarial* _____

*dominate* _____

*The* TOPIC of this paragraph is_____

_____

_____

*Who or what is the paragraph about (the* MAIN IDEA*)?* _____

_____

_____

_____

*What do the authors of the paragraph really want you* TO KNOW? _____

_____

_____

_____

_____

*Develop one* TEST QUESTION *from this paragraph using Bloom's Taxonomy test prompts.*

_____

_____

_____

BLOOM LEVEL 4 QUESTION

# SQ3R TO THE RESCUE

## How Can You Do it Right the First Time?

There are as many ways to approach a chapter in a textbook as there are students who read textbooks. One of the most effective and often-used reading and studying systems is the *SQ3R Method*, developed by Francis P. Robinson in 1941. This simple, yet highly valuable, system has proved to be a successful study tool for millions of students. SQ3R involves five steps: Scan, Question, Read, Recite, and Review. The most important thing to remember about SQ3R is that it should be used on a daily basis, not as a method for cramming. See Figure 7.5.

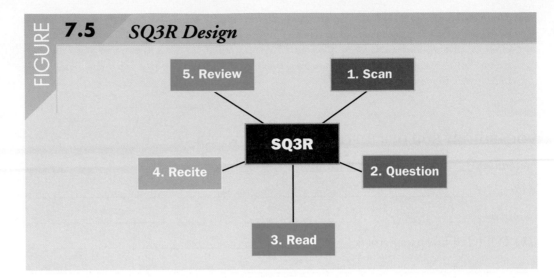

FIGURE **7.5** *SQ3R Design*

## Scan

The first step of SQ3R is to *scan*, or preread, an assigned chapter. You've been doing this since you began reading Chapter 1 of this text. You begin by reading the title of the chapter, the headings, and each subheading. Look carefully at the vocabulary, timelines, graphs, charts, pictures, and drawings included in each chapter. If there is a chapter summary, read it. Scanning also includes reading the first and last sentences in each paragraph. Scanning is not a substitute for reading a chapter. Reading is discussed later. Before going any further, scan Chapter 8 of this text using the following seven questions.

**Chapter Scan**

*What is the title of the chapter?*_____

*What is the subtitle of the chapter?*_____

*List the chapter's major headings.*_____

_____

_____

_____

*Who is introduced in the "Did You Know?" feature? List one thing you learned about him or her.*

_____

_____

_____

*If the chapter contains quotations, which one means the most to you? Why?*

_____

_____

_____

*What is the most important graph or chart in the chapter? Why?*

_____

_____

_____

*Without looking back, list five topics that this chapter will cover.*

_____

_____

_____

## Question

The second step is to ***question***. There are five common questions you should ask yourself when you are reading a chapter: Who? When? What? Where? and Why? As you scan and read the chapter, turn the information into questions and see if you can answer them. If you do not know the answers to the questions, you should find them as you read along. You have been doing this for each chapter in this book thus far.

Another way to approach the chapter is to turn the major headings of each section into questions (see an example in Figure 7.6). When you get to the end of the section, having carefully read the material, looked up unfamiliar words, taken notes, and highlighted important information, answer the questions that you wrote at the beginning of the section.

**FIGURE**

### 7.6  *Forming Questions from Headings*

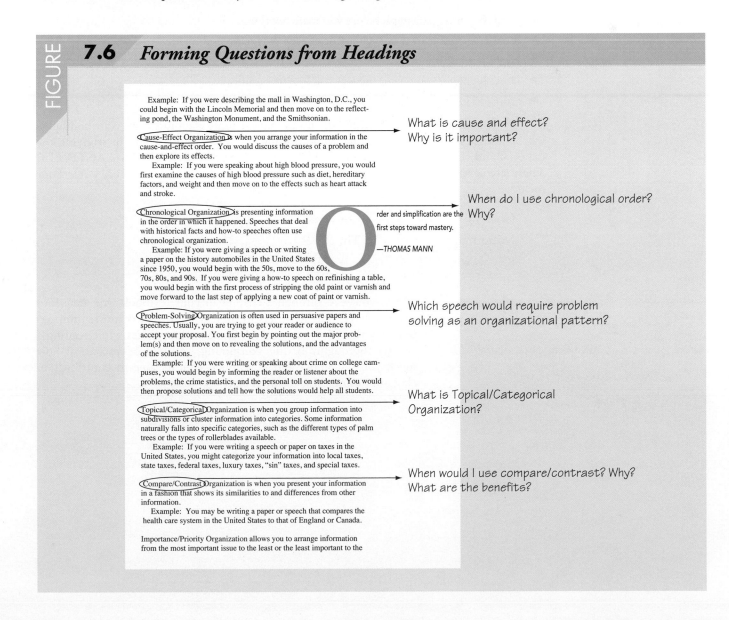

> "There are worse crimes than burning books. One of them is not reading them."
> —Joseph Brodsky

# Read

After you scan the chapter and develop some questions to be answered from the chapter, the next step is to *read the chapter*. Remember, scanning is not reading. There is no substitute for reading in your success plan. Read slowly and carefully. The SQ3R method requires a substantial amount of time, but if you take each step slowly and completely, you will be amazed at how much you can learn and how much your grades will improve.

Read through each section. It is best not to jump around or move ahead if you did not understand the previous section. Paragraphs are usually built on each other, and so you need to understand the first before you can move on to the next. You may have to read a chapter or section more than once, especially if the information is new, technical, or difficult.

Take notes, highlight, and make marginal notes in your textbook as you read along. You own your textbook and should personalize it as you would your lecture notes. Highlight areas that you feel are important, underline words and phrases that you do not understand or that you feel are important, and jot down notes in the margins. Refer to page xxii in the preface to see how a text page should look after using SQ3R.

As you begin to read your chapter, mark the text, and take notes, keep the following in mind:

▶ Read the entire paragraph before you mark anything.
▶ Identify the topic or thesis statement of each paragraph and highlight it.
▶ Highlight key phrases.
▶ Don't highlight too much; the text will lose its significance.
▶ Stop and look up words that you do not know or understand.

While reading, you will want to take notes that are more elaborate than your highlighting or marginal notes. Taking notes while reading the text will assist you in studying the material and committing it to memory. **This is a major part of LEARNING ACTIVELY.** There are several effective methods of taking notes while reading (see Figure 7.7). They include:

| | | |
|---|---|---|
| Charts | Outlines | Flash cards |
| Mind maps | Timelines | Summaries |
| Key words | | |

> "The man who does not read good books has no advantage over the man who can't read."
> —Mark Twain

As you read through a chapter in your textbook, you may find that you have to use a variety of these techniques to capture information. Try them for one week. Although taking notes while reading a chapter thoroughly is time consuming, you will be amazed at how much you remember and how much you are able to contribute in class after using these techniques. They work!

## 7.7    *Sample Note-Taking Methods*

**KEY WORDS**

**CHARTS**

Fat Soluble Vitamins: A, D, E & K (p. 237)

| | | |
|---|---|---|
| VitaminA | 1st to have been recognized; there are 3 forms: retinol, retinal & retinoic acid |
| VitaminD | Different from all other nutrients Body can't synthesize it w/out help of sunlight |

| | | |
|---|---|---|
| Aeschylus | Tragedy | * 7 Against Thebes<br>* Agamemnon<br>* The Persians |
| Sophocles | Tragedy | * Oedipus The King<br>* Antigone<br>* Electra |
| Euripides | Tragedy | * Medea<br>* Hippolytus<br>* The Cyclops |
| Aristophanes | Comedy | * The Clouds<br>* The Birds |
| Menander | New Comedy | * The Grouch<br>* The Arbitration<br>* The Shorn Girl |

**Key words help define terminology, phrases, names, and people.**

**Charts assist visual learners in seeing relationships and differences.**

**OUTLINES**

**Outlines organize information into clusters or under separate headings.**

Steps to Successful Speaking          p. 114

I. Select the Topic
  1.  What are your talents?
  2. Can you find sufficient materials?
  3. Is the topic appropriate for the audience?
II. Audience Analysis
  1. Conduct demographic study
  2. Use Maslow's Hierarchy of Basic Needs
III. Write a Purpose Statement
  1. What do you want your audience to understand?
  2. What is the main idea of your speech?
IV. Research Your Speech
  1. The Internet
  2. Personal interviews
  3. Electronic or print indexes
  4. Books
  5. Periodicals
V. Organize Your Speech
  1. Spatial organization
  2. Cause-effect
  3. Chronological
  4. Problem solving

# IT'S NOT OVER UNTIL IT'S OVER

## What Is Reading Piece by Piece and How Can It Help?

If you are reading material that is completely **new to you—difficult to understand** yet important to remember—you may have to disregard entire paragraphs or read pieces of certain paragraphs. When you get to a point where you have "read enough," or your mind begins to wander, put a tick mark at that point (see Figure 7.8). The placement of the tick marks will be different for every person reading based on individual skills and experience. After your first tick mark, continue reading until you get to another stopping point, putting tick marks in the places where you feel you have read a complete thought. You will not want to read an entire chapter at one time this way— only sections.

When you get to the end of a major section, reread the material in your first "ticked section." Out to the side, paraphrase that section (indicated in matching colors in Figure 7.8). Then go on to the next section. Figure 7.8 gives you a visual of this technique. The paragraph on criminal justice is shown with its original paragraph breaks. However, you will also see **"tick marks"** indicated with a "/" showing where the reader felt this was enough to try to comprehend at one time. The "ticked section" and paraphrased remarks are shown in corresponding colors.

Few techniques will assist your comprehension and retention more than this one because it requires you to be actively involved in the reading process.

---

**FIGURE**

**7.8**   *Original Paragraph Breaks and New "Tick Mark Breaks" Indicated with a "/"*

**A Brief History of Crime in America**
(from *Criminal Justice: A Brief Introduction, 6th Edition*. F. Schmalleger, Prentice Hall, 2006.)

What we call criminal activity has undoubtedly been with us since the dawn of history, and crime control has long been a primary concern of politicians and government leaders world-wide./ Still, the American experience with crime during the last half century has been especially influential in shaping the criminal justice system of today./

*Criminal activity has been around since the beginning of time and has been a concern to politicians and leaders.*

*Crime in Am. has greatly shaped our criminal justice system in the past 50 years.*

In this country, crime waves have come and gone, including an 1850-1880 crime epidemic, which was apparently related to social upheaval caused by large-scale immigration, and the spurt of widespread organized criminal activity associated with the prohibition years of the early twentieth century./ Following World War II, however, American crime rates remained relatively stable until the 1960s./

*Crime in Am. has come in waves including the 1850-1880 epidemic due to immigration and prohibition.*

*After WWII, crime in Am. remained stable until the '60's.*

The 1960s and 1970s saw a burgeoning concern for the rights of ethnic and racial minorities, women, the physically and mentally challenged, and many other groups. The civil rights movement of the period emphasized the equality of opportunity and respect for individuals, regardless of race, color, creed, or personal attributes./ As new laws were passed and suits filed, court involvement in the movement grew. Soon, a plethora of hard-won individual rights and prerogatives, based on the U.S. Constitution, the Bill of Rights, and the new federal and state legislation, were recognized and guaranteed. By the 1980s, the civil rights movement had profoundly affected all areas of social life—from education throughout employment to the activities of the criminal justice system./

*During the 60's and 70's, Am. saw the rise of individual rights regardless of race, creed, or attributes.*

*Due to laws based on the US Constitution the C.R. Movement profoundly impacted all aspects of life in Am. including the C.J. system.*

**Tips for Personal Success**

Consider the following strategies for making the most of your reading time:

▶ Reduce the distractions around you. Try to find an atmosphere that is comfortable and effective for you.

▶ Discover what time of day is best for you to read and concentrate on your material.

▶ Read in sections. Don't try to read an entire chapter in one sitting. Divide it up and take breaks.

▶ Never just skip over words or phrases that you don't understand. Look them up in a dictionary.

Now it is your turn. Make a list of three tips that you would share with a classmate to assist him or her in becoming a better reader.

1. _____

2. _____

3. _____

## Recite

Recitation is simple, but crucial. Skipping this step may result in less-than-full mastery of the chapter. Once you have read a section using one or more of the techniques already discussed, ask yourself this simple question: *"What was that all about?"* Find a classmate, sit down together, and ask questions of each other. Discuss with each other the main points of the chapter. Try to explain the information to each other without looking at your notes. If you are at home, sit back in your chair, recite the information, and determine what it means. If you have trouble explaining the information to your friend or reciting it to yourself, you probably did not understand the section and you should go back and reread it. If you can tell your classmate and yourself exactly what you just read and what it means, you are ready to move on to the next section of the chapter.

## Review

After you have read the chapter, immediately go back and read it again. **"What?!! I just read it!"** Yes, you did. And the best way to determine whether you have mastered the information is once again to survey the chapter; review marginal notes, highlighted areas, and vocabulary words; and determine whether you can answer the questions you posed during the *"Question Step"* of SQ3R. This step will help you store and retain this information in long-term memory.

CHANGING IDEAS TO *Reality*

**REFLECTIONS ON
READING
AND COMPREHENSION**

SQ3R can be a lifesaver when it comes to understanding material that is overwhelming. It is an efficient, comprehensive, and DOABLE practice that can dramatically assist you in your reading efforts. It may take more time than your old method, but you will begin to see the results almost immediately. Seriously considering and practicing the strategies outlined in this chapter will help increase your comprehension level and also help your ability to recall the information when you need it later on.

As you continue to work to become an active, engaged learner, consider the following tips for reading comprehension and retention:

▶ Approach the text, chapter, or article with an *open mind.*

▶ *Free your mind* to focus on your reading.

▶ Always read with your *"six pack"* at your side.

▶ Underline and look up words you do not *understand.*

▶ Write down your *vocabulary words,* and review them often.

▶ Use *SQ3R* to increase and test your comprehension.

▶ If you're having trouble, *get a tutor* to help you.

▶ Understand that *the more you read,* the better you'll become at it.

*"The knowledge of words is the gateway to learning."*
—W. Wilson

# KNOWLEDGE *in* BLOOM

## Reading for Comprehension

Each chapter-end assessment is based on *Bloom's Taxonomy of Learning.* See the inside front cover for a quick review.

### UTILIZES LEVELS 1–6 ON THE TAXONOMY

**PROCESS:** Read the following story carefully, looking up words that you do not understand, highlighting phrases that you think are important, and paraphrasing in the spaces provided. When reading the story, use the SQ3R method. We've done paragraph #1 for you as an example.

## The Life and Death of Harvey Milk.

| DIRECTIONS: READ THIS SECTION, IDENTIFY UNFAMILIAR WORDS WITH UNDERLINING, HIGHLIGHT IMPORTANT WORDS AND PHRASES | LOOK UP WORDS THAT NEED TO BE DEFINED | PARAPHRASE THE MAIN IDEA IN YOUR OWN WORDS |
|---|---|---|
| More <u>perplexing</u> things have happened, but a Twinkie caused the death of Harvey Milk. That's right. In 1978, defense lawyers using the "Twinkie Defense" explained an <u>inexplicable</u> murder away. This was the first mainstream trial to use the, "I am not responsible for my actions" defense. | *Unfamiliar words and definitions*<br><br>*Perplexing = confusing or puzzling*<br><br>*Inexplicable = not easily explained, unreasonable* | *The main idea of this paragraph is: In 1978, defense lawyers used a new strategy called "the Twinkie Defense" (I'm not responsible for my actions) to explain why someone murdered Harvey Milk.* |
| Harvey Milk was the first openly gay man elected to a significant office in America. In 1977, Milk was elected as a member of the San Francisco Board of Supervisors. This was quite arduous at this point in American history, when most people, including many psychologists and religious leaders, still classified homosexuality as deviant and a mental illness. | *Unfamiliar words and definitions* | *The main idea of this paragraph is:* |
| Harvey Milk is to the Gay Rights Movement what Martin Luther King, Jr. is to the Civil Rights Movement. Before King, little was happening with the CRM, and before Milk, little was happening with the GRM. He changed the face of California politics and paved the way for countless other gays and lesbians to enter the world of politics. | *Unfamiliar words and definitions* | *The main idea of this paragraph is:* |

| DIRECTIONS: READ THIS SECTION, IDENTIFY UNFAMILIAR WORDS WITH UNDERLINING, HIGHLIGHT IMPORTANT WORDS AND PHRASES | LOOK UP WORDS THAT NEED TO BE DEFINED | PARAPHRASE THE MAIN IDEA IN YOUR OWN WORDS |
|---|---|---|
| Dan White, a staunch antigay advocate, served on the board with Milk. They were constantly at odds with each other and often engaged in verbal confrontations. | *Unfamiliar words and definitions* | *The main idea of this paragraph is:* |
| White had been a policeman and a fireman in San Francisco before running for office. While running for office, he vowed to restore "family values" to the city government. He vowed to "rid San Francisco of radicals, social deviants, and incorrigibles." | *Unfamiliar words and definitions* | *The main idea of this paragraph is:* |
| Dan White was one of the most conservative members of the board, and many proposals brought to the board by Milk and the mayor of San Francisco, George Moscone, were defeated because of the heavily conservative vote led by White. | *Unfamiliar words and definitions* | *The main idea of this paragraph is:* |
| At that time, the Board of Supervisors was made up of 11 members; six of them, including Dan White, were conservative and had the power to defeat most, if not all, of the liberal measures brought before the board. This did not fare well with Harvey Milk and the other liberal members of the board. | *Unfamiliar words and definitions* | *The main idea of this paragraph is:* |
| Because the job offered diminutive wages, Dan White soon realized that he could not support his family on $9,800 per year, and he submitted his resignation to Mayor Moscone. This did not sit well with the people who'd elected him. They urged him to reconsider and when he tried to rescind his resignation, Mayor Moscone refused. This decision was made, in part, because Harvey Milk had convinced Moscone to deny White's reinstatement. | *Unfamiliar words and definitions* | *The main idea of this paragraph is:* |
| In a fit of wrath over the decision, Dan White entered the San Francisco City Hall on the morning of November 27, 1978, through a basement window. He went to Mayor Moscone's office and shot him in the chest, and as he lay dying, shot him again in the head. | *Unfamiliar words and definitions* | *The main idea of this paragraph is:* |
| He then walked calmly down the hall and asked to see Harvey Milk. Once inside the office, he slew Milk with two bullets to the brain. He then left City Hall, called his wife, spoke with her in person at St. Mary's Cathedral, and then turned himself in. | *Unfamiliar words and definitions* | *The main idea of this paragraph is:* |
| It is reported that policemen representing the city of San Francisco shouted, cheered, and applauded when news of the murders reached the police department. | *Unfamiliar words and definitions* | *The main idea of this paragraph is:* |

| Dan White's defense lawyers used a "diminished capacity" defense, suggesting that he was led to his actions by too much sugar from junk food. The lawyers convinced a jury that he was not himself and his senses were off-kilter. This became known as the "Twinkie Defense." | *Unfamiliar words and definitions* | *The main idea of this paragraph is:* |
|---|---|---|
| Dan White was convicted of second-degree manslaughter and was sentenced to only seven years for two premeditated murders. After serving only five years, he was released. The "Twinkie Defense" had worked. | *Unfamiliar words and definitions* | *The main idea of this paragraph is:* |
| In 1985, after being released from Soledad Prison, Dan White walked into his garage, took a rubber hose, connected it to his car's exhaust, and killed himself with carbon monoxide poisoning. He was 39 years old. His tombstone reads, *"Daniel J. White (1946–October 21, 1985), Sgt. U. S. Army, Vietnam. Cause of death: Suicide."* | *Unfamiliar words and definitions* | *The main idea of this paragraph is:* |

*Sources:* "He Got Away with Murder" at www.findagrave.com; "The Pioneer Harvey Milk" at www.time.com; "Remembering Harvey Milk" at www.lambda.net.

In 100 words or less, thoroughly summarize this entire article. Be certain to include dates, names, places, and circumstances. Pretend that you have to explain this entire story to a 10-year-old. This exercise will help you become more adept at the ESSENTIAL CORNERSTONE skill of KNOWLEDGE.

_____
_____
_____
_____
_____
_____
_____
_____
_____
_____
_____
_____
_____
_____
_____

# SQ3R *Mastery* Study Sheet

| | | |
|---|---|---|
| **EXAMPLE QUESTION:** *(from page 182)*<br>Describe the process of fixation. | | **ANSWER:** |
| **EXAMPLE QUESTION:** *(from page 180)*<br>Why is comprehension more important<br>than speed? | | **ANSWER:** |
| **AUTHOR QUESTION:** *(from page 177)*<br>Differentiate between passive<br>and active reading. | | **ANSWER:** |
| **AUTHOR QUESTION:** *(from page 181)*<br>Why is having a dictionary on hand important<br>to developing good reading comprehension? | | **ANSWER:** |
| **AUTHOR QUESTION:** *(from page 191)*<br>What are some of the effective methods<br>to take notes while reading? | | **ANSWER:** |
| **AUTHOR QUESTION:** *(from page 192)*<br>How can you use tick marks to help<br>you improve your reading ability? | | **ANSWER:** |
| **AUTHOR QUESTION:** *(from page 193)*<br>Why is recitation an important part<br>of reading comprehension? | | **ANSWER:** |
| **YOUR QUESTION:** *(from page ___)* | | **ANSWER:** |
| **YOUR QUESTION:** *(from page ___)* | | **ANSWER:** |
| **YOUR QUESTION:** *(from page ___)* | | **ANSWER:** |
| **YOUR QUESTION:** *(from page ___)* | | **ANSWER:** |
| **YOUR QUESTION:** *(from page ___)* | | **ANSWER:** |

Finally, after answering these questions, recite this chapter's major points in your mind. Consider the following general questions to help you master this material.

- ▶ What was it about?
- ▶ What does it mean?
- ▶ What was the most important thing I learned? Why?
- ▶ What were the key points to remember?

# CHAPTER 8
# RECORD

CULTIVATING YOUR LISTENING SKILLS AND DEVELOPING A NOTE-TAKING SYSTEM THAT WORKS FOR YOU

"To listen well is as powerful a means of communication as to talk well."

—Chinese Proverb

# WHY READ THIS CHAPTER?

## What's in it for me?

WHY do I need to become a better listener? WHY will a chapter on listening and note taking help me become a better student? WHY do instructors make such a big deal about note taking anyway? WHY is listening so important to my overall quality of life?

Why? Because listening is considered by many communication experts to be one of the, if not THE, most essential skills for building healthy relationships, solving problems, becoming open-minded, learning new information, and getting along in life. Listening will help you in terms of note taking, retaining information, and becoming actively involved in the learning process. The ability to listen in a variety of situations will also help you become a more efficient note-taker. Listening and note taking are important because well-designed notes create a history of your time in class, what you have read in your text and various articles, and what you might have studied with a group. You will find that there are different listening styles and note-taking styles and you will have to experiment to find which work best for you.

*By carefully reading this chapter and taking the information provided seriously, you will be able to:*

1. Understand the difference between listening and hearing.
2. Define the four listening styles.
3. Overcome the obstacles to listening and how to listen in different situations.
4. Discuss the importance of note taking and list specific tips to increase effectiveness.
5. Identify, discuss, and use the three types of note-taking systems: Cornell, outline, and mapping.

# CHAPTER 8 / RECORD

*"You cannot truly listen to anyone and do anything else at the same time."*

—M. Scott Peck

## . . . FROM MY PERSPECTIVE

**NAME:** Griffin Jones
**INSTITUTION:** Point Park University, Pittsburgh, PA
**MAJOR:** Cinema
**AGE:** 20

When you're making big decisions in your life, you will always have people who are older and more experienced than you bursting at the seams to give you "life lessons" and other advice. There is no point in your life where this will be more prevalent than when you first begin college. You will be bombarded with advice on sex, classes, drinking, relationships, and so on. A lot of it is just a rehash of all of the stuff you heard going into high school. However, many of the things we're asked to listen to can be helpful. Figuring out which ones are helpful is the hardest part. This is where listening comes in handy.

For most college students, listening to others is a ludicrous concept. We tend to want to try everything for ourselves. As someone who is quite stubborn, I completely understand, but over the past couple of years since enrolling in college, I've found that it's good to find a middle ground with these things. First, many people do actually know what they are talking about because they have "lived it," and we're just better off listening to their hard-earned advice and taking their word on it. On the other hand, trying something new for yourself isn't always a bad idea either. There are those people who don't know what they're talking about, either because they're completely oblivious to the real world or because they're trying to tell you stuff that doesn't necessarily apply to you. Again, this is where critical listening can come in very handy. Sometimes, you have to listen for what is not said. Also, trying something for yourself and failing is a great way of learning. Trial and error shouldn't be a forbidden activity.

What I have discovered is this: Find people who you know to be level-headed and in touch with the present and listen to them. Really listen to them. And even if you determine that they're not level-headed, take their advice and consider what they have to say anyway . . . store it away for another time; you never know when you will need their guidance. They may know what they're talking about but just don't know how to present it rationally. Just don't be afraid to step out of your boundaries and listen to others' viewpoints, listen to their lives, and use others' advice to live for yourself. This chapter on listening and note taking can help you become a much more active listener.

# SCAN & QUESTION

In the preface of this book (page xix), you read about the **SQ3R Study Method**. Right now, take a few moments, **scan this chapter**, and on page 223, write **five questions** that you think will be important to your mastery of this material. In addition to the two questions below, you will find five questions from your authors. Use one of your *"On The Test"* stickers to flag this page for easy reference.

**EXAMPLES:**

▶ **What are the four components of the Chinese verb "to listen"?** (from page 203)

▶ **Why is it important to identify key words during a lecture?** (from page 207)

# THE IMPORTANCE OF LISTENING

## Why Does Listening Really Matter in Classes and Relationships?

Listening is a survival skill. Period! It is that simple! *"I know listening is important,"* you might say, but few ever think of the paramount significance listening has in our everyday lives. It is necessary for:

How can becoming a critical listener help you in and out of the classroom?

▶ establishing and improving relationships,

▶ personal growth,

▶ showing respect to others,

▶ professional rapport,

▶ showing empathy and compassion,

▶ learning new information,

▶ understanding others' opinions and views,

▶ basic survival,

▶ entertainment, and

▶ health.

How much time do you think you spend listening every day? Research suggests that we spend almost 70% of our waking time communicating, and **53% of that time is spent in listening situations** (Adler et al., 2006). Effective listening skills can mean the difference between A's and F's, relationships and loneliness, and in some cases and careers, success and failure.

# LISTENING DEFINED

## Is There Really a Difference Between Listening and Hearing?

No doubt you've been in a communication situation in which a misunderstanding takes place. Either you hear something incorrectly or someone hears you incorrectly OR it could be that someone hears your message but misinterprets it. These communication blunders arise because we tend to view listening (and communicating in general) as an automatic response, when in fact it is not.

**Listening is a learned, voluntary activity. You must choose to do it.** It is a skill just like driving a car, painting a picture, or playing the piano. Becoming an active listener requires practice, time, mistakes, guidance, and active participation. **Hearing, however, is not learned; it is automatic and involuntary.** If you are within range of a sound, you will probably hear it even though you may not be listening to it. Hearing a sound does not guarantee that you know from where the sound comes. Listening actively, though, means making a conscious effort to focus on the sound you heard and to determine what it is.

According to Ronald Adler (Adler et al., 2006), the drawing of the Chinese verb "to listen" provides a comprehensive and practical definition of listening. (See Figure 8.1.)

In this figure, listening involves the ears, the eyes, undivided attention, and the heart. Do you make it a habit to listen with more than your ears? The Chinese view listening as a whole-body experience. At its core, listening is "the ability to hear, understand, analyze, respect, and appropriately respond to the meaning of another person's spoken and nonverbal messages" (Daly and Engleberg, 2006). Although this definition involves the word "hear," listening goes far beyond just the physical ability to catch sound waves.

FIGURE **8.1**   *Chinese Verb "To Listen"*

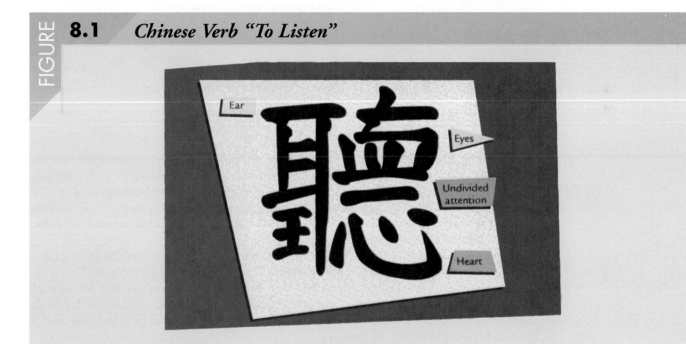

## Categories of Listening

The first step of listening *is* hearing, but true listening involves one's full attention and the ability to filter out distractions, emotional barriers, cultural differences, and religious biases. Listening means that you are making a conscious decision to understand and show reverence for the other person's communication efforts. Listening involves being open-minded as well. To understand listening as a whole-body experience, we can divide it into three different categories:

1. Listening with a **purpose**
2. Listening **objectively**
3. Listening **constructively**

**Listening with a purpose** suggests a need to recognize different types of listening situations—for example, class, worship, entertainment, and relationships. People do not listen the same way in every situation.

## THINKING FOR CHANGE: An Activity for Critical Reflection

Jennifer greatly disliked her biology instructor. She could not put her finger on exactly WHY she disliked her; she just knew that Dr. Lipmon rubbed her the wrong way. This had been the case since the first day of class. Other students seemed to like her and were able to carry on conversations with her—but Jennifer could not. "Why?" she thought. "Why do I dislike her so much? She's not a bad teacher," she reasoned, "but I just can't stand to listen to her."

Jennifer decided to sit in class for the next week and really try to figure out what the main problem was. As she sat in class and listened, she finally put her finger on the problem: She and Dr. Lipmon had completely different views on many things including evolution and women's reproductive rights. Every time Dr. Lipmon made a statement contrary to Jennifer's core beliefs, Jennifer cringed.

She "shut down" and refused to listen any further. She then transferred her dislike of Dr. Lipmon's lectures and opinions onto her as a person. She knew this was affecting her grade and her knowledge base in class, but did not know how to manage or change the situation.

In your own words, what would you suggest that Jennifer do at this point? Pretend that she is enrolled at your institution. List at least three things that she could do to ensure her success in her biology class. Think about what services are offered and what people might be of assistance to her.

1. _____

2. _____

3. _____

**Listening objectively** means listening with an open mind. You can give yourself few greater gifts than the gift of knowing how to listen without bias or prejudice. This is perhaps the most difficult aspect of listening. If you have ever been cut off in mid-conversation or mid-sentence by someone who disagreed with you, or if someone has left the room while you were giving your opinion of a situation, you have had the experience of talking to someone who does not know how to listen objectively.

**Listening constructively** means listening with the attitude: "How can this be helpful to my life, my education, my career, or my finances?" This type of listening involves evaluating the information you are hearing and determining whether it has meaning to your life. Sound easy? It is more difficult than it sounds because, again, we all tend to shut out information that we do not view as immediately helpful or useful. To listen constructively, you need to know how to listen and store information for later.

# THE FOUR LISTENING STYLES

## What Is Your Orientation?

According to Steven McCornack (2007), interpersonal communication expert, author, and educator, there are *four different listening styles*: action-oriented, time-oriented, people-oriented, and content-oriented. Study Figure 8.2 to determine which style best describes you as a listener.

Which style best describes you? _____

What are the "pros" of being this type of listener? _____

_____

_____

_____

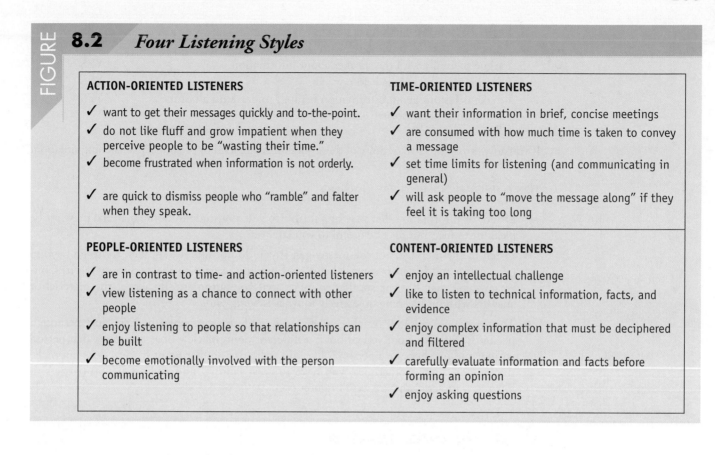

FIGURE **8.2** *Four Listening Styles*

**ACTION-ORIENTED LISTENERS**

✓ want to get their messages quickly and to-the-point.

✓ do not like fluff and grow impatient when they perceive people to be "wasting their time."

✓ become frustrated when information is not orderly.

✓ are quick to dismiss people who "ramble" and falter when they speak.

**TIME-ORIENTED LISTENERS**

✓ want their information in brief, concise meetings

✓ are consumed with how much time is taken to convey a message

✓ set time limits for listening (and communicating in general)

✓ will ask people to "move the message along" if they feel it is taking too long

**PEOPLE-ORIENTED LISTENERS**

✓ are in contrast to time- and action-oriented listeners

✓ view listening as a chance to connect with other people

✓ enjoy listening to people so that relationships can be built

✓ become emotionally involved with the person communicating

**CONTENT-ORIENTED LISTENERS**

✓ enjoy an intellectual challenge

✓ like to listen to technical information, facts, and evidence

✓ enjoy complex information that must be deciphered and filtered

✓ carefully evaluate information and facts before forming an opinion

✓ enjoy asking questions

What are the "cons" of being this type of listener? _____

_____

_____

_____

# LISTENING CAN BE SO HARD

## Can You Really Overcome the Obstacles to Listening?

Several major obstacles stand in the way of becoming an effective listener. To begin building active listening skills, you first have to remove some barriers.

## Obstacle One: Prejudging

*Prejudging*, the act of automatically shutting out what is being said, is one of the biggest obstacles to active listening. You may prejudge because you don't like or agree with the information or the person communicating it. You may also have prejudging problems because of your environment, culture, religion, social status, or attitude.

**DO YOU PREJUDGE INFORMATION OR ITS SOURCE?**

Answer yes or no to the following questions:

|   |     |    |
|---|-----|----|
| 1. I tune out when something is boring. | YES | NO |
| 2. I tune out when I do not agree with the information. | YES | NO |
| 3. I argue mentally with the speaker about information. | YES | NO |
| 4. I do not listen to people I do not like. | YES | NO |
| 5. I make decisions about information before I understand all of its implications or consequences. | YES | NO |

If you answered yes to two or more of these questions, you tend to prejudge in a listening situation.

### TIPS FOR OVERCOMING PREJUDGING

▶ Listen for information that may be valuable to you as a student. Some material may not be pleasant to hear but may be useful to you later on.

▶ Listen to the message, not the messenger. If you do not like the speaker, try to go beyond personality and listen to what is being said, without regard to the person saying it. Conversely, you may like the speaker so much that you automatically accept the material or answers without listening objectively to what is being said.

▶ Try to remove cultural, racial, gender, social, and environmental barriers. Just because a person is different from you or holds a different point of view does not make that person wrong; and just because a person is like you or holds a similar point of view does not make that person right. Sometimes, you have to cross cultural and environmental barriers to learn new material and see with brighter eyes.

## Obstacle Two: Talking

Not even the best listener in the world can listen while he or she is talking. The next time you are in a conversation with a friend, try speaking while your friend is speaking—then see if you know what your friend said. To become an effective listener, you need to learn the power of silence. Silence gives you the opportunity to think about what is being said before you respond. The first rule of listening is: Stop talking. The second rule of listening is: Stop talking. And, you guessed it, the third rule of listening is: Stop talking.

### ARE YOU A TALKER RATHER THAN A LISTENER?

Answer yes or no to the following questions:

|   |     |    |
|---|-----|----|
| 1. I often interrupt the speaker so that I can say what I want. | YES | NO |
| 2. I am thinking of my next statement while others are talking. | YES | NO |
| 3. My mind wanders when others talk. | YES | NO |
| 4. I answer my own questions. | YES | NO |
| 5. I answer questions that are asked of other people. | YES | NO |

If you answered yes to two or more questions, you tend to talk too much in a listening situation.

### TIPS FOR OVERCOMING THE URGE TO TALK TOO MUCH

▶ Avoid interrupting the speaker. Force yourself to be silent at parties, family gatherings, and friendly get-togethers. You should not be unsociable, but force yourself to be silent for 10 minutes. You'll be surprised at what you hear. You may also be surprised how hard it is to do this. Test yourself.

▶ Ask someone a question and then allow that person to answer the question.

▶ Too often we ask questions and answer them ourselves. Force yourself to wait until the person has formulated a response. If you ask questions and wait for answers, you will force yourself to listen.

▶ Concentrate on what is being said at the moment, not on what you want to say next.

## Obstacle Three: Becoming Too Emotional

Emotions can form a strong barrier to active listening. Worries, problems, fears, and anger can keep you from listening to the greatest advantage. Have you ever sat in a lecture and before you knew what was happening, your mind was a million miles away because you were angry or worried about something? If you have, you know what it's like to bring your emotions to the table.

### DO YOU BRING YOUR EMOTIONS TO THE LISTENING SITUATION?

Answer yes or no to the following questions:

1. I get angry before I hear the whole story.                                          YES   NO
2. I look for underlying or hidden messages in information.                             YES   NO
3. Sometimes, I begin listening on a negative note.                                     YES   NO
4. I base my opinions of information on what others are saying or doing.                YES   NO
5. I readily accept information as correct from people whom I like or respect.          YES   NO

If you answered yes to two or more of these questions, you tend to bring your emotions to a listening situation.

### TIPS FOR OVERCOMING EMOTIONS

▶ Know how you feel before you begin the listening experience. Take stock of your emotions and feelings ahead of time.

▶ Focus on the message; determine how to use the information.

▶ Create a positive image about the message you are hearing.

▶ Avoid overreacting and jumping to conclusions.

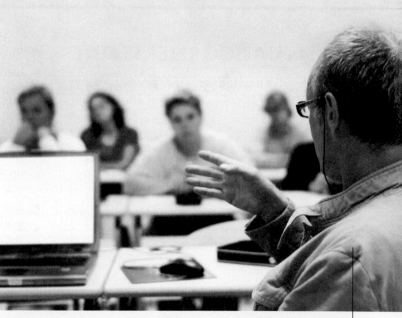

# LISTENING FOR KEY WORDS, PHRASES, AND HINTS

## Do Professors Really Offer Test Clues in Their Lectures?

Do you find it easy or hard to pick up on a professor's clues in class that may indicate important test information?

Learning how to listen for key words, phrases, and hints can help you become an active listener and an effective note-taker. For example, if your English instructor begins a lecture by saying, "There are 10 basic elements to writing poetry," jot down the number 10 under the heading "Poetry" or write the numbers 1 through 10 on your notebook page, leaving space for notes. If at the end of class you find that you listed only six elements to writing poetry, you know that you missed part of the lecture. At this point, you need to ask the instructor some questions.

## ESSENTIAL CORNERSTONE

**Knowledge:**
How can learning to take more effective notes help you master knowledge and learn more?

**Social Networking Moment:**
Share your response to this Essential Cornerstone with peers in your social network. Choose two responses from your peers and respond to their postings.

---

Here are some key phrases and words to listen for:

| | | |
|---|---|---|
| in addition to | another way | above all |
| most important | such as | specifically |
| you'll see this again | therefore | finally |
| for example | to illustrate | as stated previously |
| in contrast | in comparison | nevertheless |
| the characteristics of | the main issue is | moreover |
| on the other hand | as a result of | because |

Picking up on *transition words* such as these will help you filter out less important information and thus listen more carefully to what is most important.

# LISTENING IN DIFFICULT SITUATIONS

## What Do You Do When English Is Your Second Language?

For students whose first language is not English, the college classroom can present some uniquely challenging situations. One of the most pressing and important challenges is the ability to listen, translate, understand, and capture the message on paper in a quick and continuous manner. According to Lynn Forkos, professor and coordinator of the Conversation Center for International Students at the College of Southern Nevada, the following tips can be beneficial:

▶ Don't be afraid to stop the instructor to ask for clarification. Asking questions allows you to take an active part in the listening process. If the instructor doesn't answer your questions sufficiently, make an appointment to speak with him or her during office hours.

▶ If you are in a situation where the instructor can't stop or you're watching a movie or video in class, listen for words that you do understand and try to figure out unfamiliar words in the context of the sentence. Jot down questions to ask later.

▶ Enhance your vocabulary by watching and listening to TV programs such as *Dateline, 20/20, Primetime Live, 60 Minutes,* and the evening news. You might also try listening to radio stations such as National Public Radio as you walk or drive.

▶ Write down everything that the instructor puts on the board, overhead, or PowerPoint slide. You may not need every piece of this information, but this technique gives you (and hopefully your study group) the ability to sift through the information outside of class. It also gives you a visual history of what the instructor said.

▶ Join a study group with people who speak English well and have the patience to assist you.

▶ Finally, if there is a conversation group or club that meets on campus, take the opportunity to join. **By practicing language**, you become more attuned to common words and phrases. If a conversation group is not available, consider starting one of your own.

# TAKING EFFECTIVE NOTES

## Is It Just a Big, Crazy Chore?

Go to class, take notes. Listen, take notes. Read a text, take notes. Watch a film, take notes. Jeez! Is it really that important? Actually, knowing how to take useful, accurate notes can dramatically improve your academic life. If you are an effective listener and note-taker, you have two of the most valuable skills any student could ever use. There are several reasons why it is important to take notes:

▶ You become an active part of the listening process.

▶ You create a history of your course's content when you take notes.

▶ You have written criteria to follow when studying.

▶ You create a visual aid for your material.

▶ Studying becomes much easier.

▶ You retain information at a greater rate than non-note-takers.

▶ Effective note-takers average higher grades than non-note-takers (Kiewra and Fletcher, 1984).

# TIPS FOR EFFECTIVE NOTE TAKING

## How Can I Write It Right?

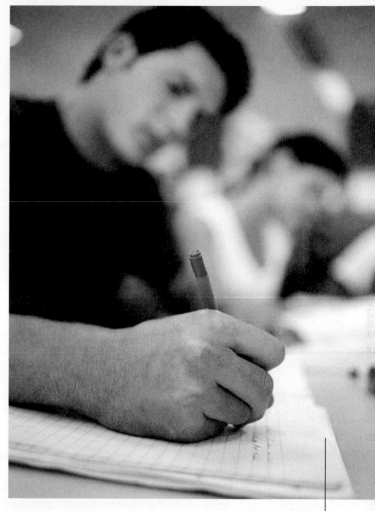

You have already learned several skills that you will need to take notes, such as cultivating your active listening skills, overcoming obstacles to effective listening, and familiarizing yourself with key phrases used by instructors. Next, prepare yourself mentally and physically to take notes that are going to be helpful to you. Consider the following ideas as you think about expanding your note-taking abilities.

▶ **Physically AND mentally attend class.** This may sound like stating the obvious, but it is surprising how many college students feel they do not need to go to class. Not only do you have to physically show up, you also have to be there mentally and emotionally—ready to listen, take notes, question, scrutinize, and interpret.

▶ **Come to class prepared.**   Scan, read, and use your textbook to establish a basic understanding of the material before coming to class It is always easier to take notes when you have a preliminary understanding of what is being said. Coming to class prepared also means bringing the proper materials for taking notes: lab manuals, pens, a notebook, and a highlighter.

▶ **Bring your textbook to class.**   Although many students think they do not need to bring their textbooks to class if they have read the homework assignment, you will find that many instructors repeatedly refer to the text while lecturing. The instructor may ask you to highlight, underline, or refer to the text in class, and following along in the text as the instructor lectures may also help you organize your notes.

▶ **Ask questions and participate in class.**   Two of the most critical actions you can perform in class are to ask questions and to participate in the class discussion. If you do not understand a concept or theory, ask questions. Don't leave class without understanding what has happened and assume you'll pick it up on your own.

> Good note-taking skills help you do more than simply record what you learn in class or read in a book so that you can recall it. These skills can also help reinforce that information so that you actually know it.

# YOU'LL BE SEEING STARS

## What Is the L-STAR System and How Can I Use It?

One of the most effective ways to take notes begins with the **L-STAR system**.

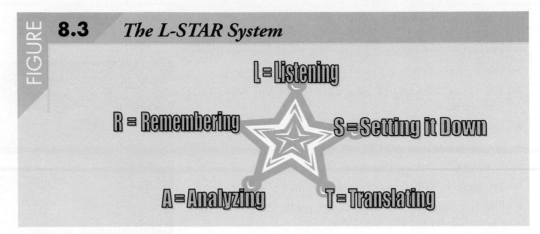

FIGURE

**8.3**    *The L-STAR System*

L = Listening

R = Remembering          S = Setting it Down

A = Analyzing          T = Translating

This five-step program will enable you to compile complete, accurate, and visual notes for future reference. Along with improving your note-taking skills, using this system will enhance your ability to participate in class, help other students, study more effectively, and perform well on exams and quizzes.

## L—Listening

One of the best ways to become an effective note-taker is to become an active listener. A concrete step you can take toward becoming an active listener in class is to sit near the front of the room, where you can hear the instructor and see the board and overheads. Choose a spot that allows you to see the instructor's mouth and facial expressions. If you see that the instructor's face has become animated or expressive, you can bet that you are hearing important information. Write it down! If you sit in the back of the room, you may miss out on these important clues.

## S—Setting It Down

The actual writing of notes can be a difficult task. Some instructors are organized in their delivery of information; others are not. Some stick to an easy-to-follow outline and others ramble around, making it more difficult to follow them and take notes. Your listening skills, once again, are going to play an important role in determining what needs to be written down. In most cases, you will not have time to take notes verbatim. Some instructors talk very fast. You will thus have to be selective about the information you choose to set down. One of the best ways to keep up with the information being presented is to develop a shorthand system of your own. Many of the symbols you use will be universal, but you may use some symbols, pictures, and markings that are uniquely your own. Some of the more common symbols are:

| | | | |
|---|---|---|---|
| w/ | with | w/o | without |
| = | equals | ≠ | does not equal |
| < | less than | > | greater than |
| % | percentage | # | number |
| & | and | ^ | increase |
| + | plus or addition | – | minus |
| * | important | etc. | and so on |
| e.g. | for example | vs. | against |
| esp | especially | " | quote |
| ? | question | . . . | and so on |

These symbols can save you valuable time when taking notes. Because you will use them frequently, it might be a good idea to memorize them.

## T—Translating

Translating can save you hours of work as you begin to study for exams. Many students feel that this step is not important, or is too time consuming, and leave it out. Don't. Often, students take notes so quickly that they make mistakes or use abbreviations that they may not be able to decipher later.

After each class, go to the library or some other quiet place and review your notes. You don't have to do this immediately after class, but before the end of the day, you will need to rewrite and translate your classroom notes. This process gives you the opportunity to put the notes in your own words and to incorporate your text notes into your classroom notes. This practice also provides a first opportunity to commit this information to memory.

Translating your notes helps you make connections among previous material discussed, your own personal experiences, readings, and new material presented. Translating aids in recalling and applying new information. Few things are more difficult than trying to reconstruct your notes the night before a test, especially when they were made several weeks previously.

## A—Analyzing

This step takes place while you translate your notes from class. When you analyze your notes, you are asking two basic questions: (1) What does this mean? and (2) Why is it important? If you can answer these two questions about your material, you have almost mastered the information. Though some instructors will want you to spit back the exact same information you were given, others will ask you for a more detailed understanding and a synthesis of the material. When you are translating your notes, begin to answer these two questions using your notes, textbook, supplemental materials, and information gathered from outside research. Once again, this process is not simple or quick, but testing your understanding of the material is important. Remember that many lectures are built on past lectures. If you do not understand what happened in class on September 17, you may not be able to understand what happens on September 19. Analyzing your notes while translating them will give you a more complete understanding of the material.

## R—Remembering

Once you have listened to the lecture, set your notes on paper, and translated and analyzed the material, it is time to study, or remember, the information. Some effective ways to remember information include creating a visual picture, speaking the notes out loud, using mnemonic devices, and finding a study partner. Chapter 9 will help you with these techniques and other study aids.

# THREE COMMON NOTE-TAKING SYSTEMS

## Why Doesn't Everyone Take Notes the Same Way?

There are three common note-taking systems: (1) the **outline** technique; (2) the **Cornell**, or split-page, technique (also called the T system); and (3) the **mapping** technique. You may find each technique useful or you may find that one is more effective for you than the others.

**Tips for Personal Success**

Consider the following tips for improving your listening skills and taking notes more effectively:

▶ Sit near the front of the room and establish eye contact with the instructor.

▶ Read the text or handouts beforehand to familiarize yourself with the upcoming information.

▶ Come to class with an open mind and positive attitude about learning. Listen purposefully, objectively, and constructively.

Now, it is your turn. Create a list of at least three more tips that you would offer a fellow classmate to assist him or her with bringing about positive change in his or her listening and note-taking skills.

1. _____
2. _____
3. _____

# IT'S AS SIMPLE AS A, B, C—1, 2, 3

## The Outline Technique

The outline system uses a series of major headings and multiple subheadings formatted in hierarchical order (Figure 8.4). The outline technique is one of the most commonly used note-taking systems, yet it is also one of the most misused systems. It can be difficult to outline notes in class, especially if your instructor does not follow an outline format while lecturing.

When using the outline system, it is best to get all the information from the lecture and, afterward, combine your lecture notes and text notes to create an outline. Most instructors would advise against using the outline system of note taking during class, although you may be able to use a modified version. The most important thing to remember is not to get bogged down in a

FIGURE **8.4** *The Outline Technique*

October 20

Topic: Maslow's Hierarchy of Basic Needs

I. Abraham Maslow (1908–1970)
- American psychologist
- Born - Raised Brooklyn, N.Y.
- Parents = Uneducated Jewish immigrants
- Lonely - unhappy childhood
- 1st studied law @ city coll. of N.Y.
- Grad school - Univ of Wisconsin
- Studied human behavior & experience
- Leader of humanistic school of psy.

II. H of B. Needs (Theory)
- Written in A Theory of Human Motivation in 1943
- Needs of human arranged like a ladder
- Basic needs of food, air, water at bottom
- Higher needs "up" the ladder
- Lower needs must be met to experience the higher needs

III. H of B. Needs (Features)
- Physiological needs
  - Breathing
  - Food
  - Air & water
  - Sleep
- Safety needs
  - Security of body
  - Employment

system during class; what is critical is getting the ideas down on paper. You can always go back after class and rearrange your notes as needed.

If you are going to use a modified or informal outline while taking notes in class, you may want to consider grouping information together under a heading as a means of outlining. It is easier to remember information that is logically grouped than information that is scattered across several pages. If your study skills lecture is on listening, you might outline your notes using the headings "The Process of Listening" and "Definitions of Listening."

After you have rewritten your notes using class lecture information and material from your textbook, your notes may look like those in Figure 8.4.

# IT'S A SPLIT DECISION

## The Cornell (Modified Cornell, Split-Page, or T) System

The basic principle of the Cornell system, developed by Dr. Walter Pauk of Cornell University, is to split the page into two sections, each to be used for different information (see Figure 8.5). Section B (the larger section) is used for the actual notes from class or your text. Section A (the smaller section) should be used for headings OR questions. Review Figure 8.5 to see an example of Cornell note taking. An example of outline notes using the Cornell system appears in Figure 8.6.

**FIGURE 8.5**   *Cornell Note-Taking System Example*

October 23

| | Used for:<br>Actual notes from class or textbook |
|---|---|
| Used for:<br>Headings<br>or<br>Questions | |
| Who was <u>Abraham Maslow</u> ? | – Born in 1908 – Died 1970<br>– American psychologist<br>– Born - raised in Brooklyn N.Y.<br>– Parents - uneducated Jewish imm.<br>– Lonely unhappy childhood<br>– 1$^{st}$ studied law at city coll. of N.Y. |

FIGURE   **8.6**    *Outline Using a Cornell Frame*

October 30

Topic: Maslow's Hierarchy of Basic Needs

| | |
|---|---|
| What is the theory of basic needs ? | I. <u>Published</u> in 1943 in<br>– "A Theory of human <u>motivation</u>"<br>– Study of human motivation<br>– Observation of innate <u>curiosity</u><br>– Studied <u>exemplary</u> people |
| | II. Needs arranged like <u>ladder</u><br>– <u>Basic</u> needs at the bottom<br>– <u>Basic</u> needs = deficiency needs<br>– <u>Highest</u> need = aesthetic need |
| What are the <u>Steps</u> in the Hierarchy ? | I. <u>Physiological</u> needs<br>– Breathing<br>– Food, water<br>– Sex<br>– Sleep |
| | II. <u>Safety</u> needs<br>– Security of body<br>– Security of employment<br>– Resources of<br>        – Family<br>        – Health |
| | III. <u>Love</u> - <u>Belonging</u> needs<br>– Friendships<br>– Family<br>– Sexual intimacy |

# GOING AROUND IN CIRCLES

## The Mapping System

If you are a visual learner, the mapping system may be especially useful for you. The mapping system of note taking generates a picture of information (Figure 8.7) by creating a map, or web, of information that allows you to see the relationships among facts or ideas. Figure 8.8 shows how to use the mapping system in a Cornell frame.

FIGURE **8.7**   *The Mapping System*

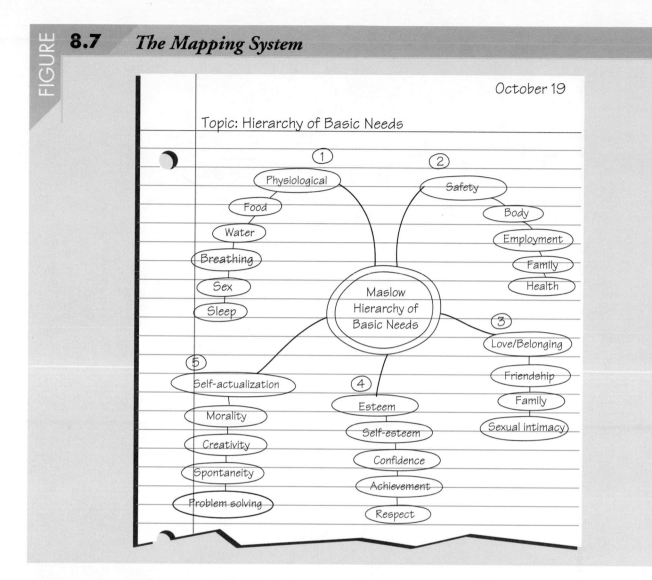

A note-taking system *must work for you*. Do not use a system because your friends use it or because you feel that you should use it. Experiment with each system or combination to determine which is best for you.

Always remember to keep your notes organized, dated, and neat. Notes that cannot be read are no good to you or to anyone else.

# TMI! TMI! (TOO MUCH INFORMATION)

## What Do I Do if I Get Lost While Taking Notes During the Lecture?

Have you ever been in a classroom trying to take notes, but the instructor is speaking so rapidly that you cannot possibly get all of the information? And just when you think you're caught up, you realize that he or she has made an important statement and you missed it. What do you do? How can you handle, or avoid, this difficult note-taking situation? Here are several hints:

## ESSENTIAL CORNERSTONE

**Adaptability:**

How can the skill of adaptability help you if you get lost while taking notes during a lecture?

**Social Networking Moment:**

Share your response to this Essential Cornerstone with peers in your social network. Choose two responses from your peers and respond to their postings.

**8.8** *The Mapping System in a Cornell Frame*

October 19

Who was Abraham Maslow?

- Studied law @ city college NY
- Born in 1908
- American psychologist
- Died 1970
- Parents uneducated
- Unhappy childhood
- Born-Raised Brooklyn, NY

What is the Theory of Basic Needs?

- Lower needs must be met first
- Studied exemplary people
- Published in "Theory of Hum Mot." 1943
- Esteem needs at top
- Human needs arranged like ladder
- Basic needs of air, food sleep at bottom

▶ Raise your hand and ask the instructor to repeat the information.

▶ Ask your instructor to slow down.

▶ If he or she will do neither, leave a blank space with a question mark in the side margin (Figure 8.9). You can get this information after class from your instructor, a classmate, or your study buddy. This can be a difficult task to master. The key is to focus on the information at hand. Focus on what is being said at the exact moment. Don't give up!

▶ Meet with your instructor immediately after class or at the earliest time convenient for both of you.

▶ Form a note-taking group that meets after each class. This serves two purposes: (1) you can discuss and review the lecture, and (2) you will be able to get the notes from one of your note-taking buddies.

FIGURE **8.9** *What To Do if You Get Lost*

> October 20
>
> Topic: Maslow's Hierachy of Basic Needs
>
> I. Abraham Maslow (1908–1970)
> - American psychologist
> - Born - Raised Brooklyn, N.Y.
> - Parents - Uneducated Jewish immigrants
> - Lonely - unhappy childhood
> - $1^{st}$ studied law @ city coll. of N.Y.
> - Grad school - Univ of Wisconsin
> - Studied human behavior & experience
> - Leader of humanistic school of psy.
>
> II. H of B. Needs (Theory)
> - written in 19 ?
> ?
> Ask
>
> } leave a blank space to fix in your notes later
>
> III. H of B. Needs (Features)
> - Physiological Needs
>   - Breathing
>   - Food
>   - Air & water
>   - Sleep
> - Safety Needs
>   - Security of body
>   - Employment

► Never lean over and ask questions of another student during the lecture. This will cause that person to miss information as well. It will probably also annoy your peers and the instructor.

► Rehearse your note-taking skills at home by taking notes from TV news magazines or channels like the History Channel.

► Ask the instructor's permission to use a tape recorder during the lecture. Do not record a lecture without permission. We suggest that you try to use other avenues, such as the ones listed above, instead of taping your notes. It is a time-consuming task to listen to the lecture for a second time. However, if this system works for you, use it.

# From Ordinary to Extraordinary

## REAL PEOPLE | REAL LIVES | REAL CHANGE

**CATHERINE SCHLEIGH**
Customer Service Coordinator, Kinkos-FedEx, Inc.
Philadelphia, PA

I don't like to speculate, but I would say that few college students in America have to take a bus two and a half hours each way, five days a week, to attend classes. I did. I would also speculate that few college students became the primary caregiver for his or her mother at the age of seven. I did. I might also speculate that few people feel lucky, proud, and honored to simply be able to hold his or her head high and say, "I made it." I do. My name is Catherine Schleigh and despite my past family history and personal strug-

gles, I am a first-generation college graduate and hold a professional position with a major corporation in one of the most wonderful cities in America.

Growing up, I had no real family to speak of. My dad left my mom and me when I was young, and from the age of seven, I was left to care for my mother, who is a diagnosed paranoid schizophrenic. Growing up, I received no help, no support, and no encouragement from her or any other members of my family. Often, she would not take her

> I was left to care for my mother, who is a diagnosed paranoid schizophrenic.

medications (or the medications had been improperly prescribed) and would thus be physically, emotionally, and verbally abusive to me. It was hard to watch her talk to herself or invisible people. We lived in a very poor, drug-infested, gang-populated area of Philly and many times, I could not see how I would ever survive.

I managed to complete high school and I began attending Job Corps, studying business. From there, I began my college studies and majored in business administration. I had to work very hard, and the adjustment from high school to college was massive. I had to learn how to motivate myself, but the most important thing I learned was that there are people in this world who will help you if you let them.

# From Ordinary to Extraordinary

## REAL PEOPLE | REAL LIVES | REAL CHANGE

Some of my instructors did not understand my situation at first. I cried a lot in class, did not have my projects completed from time to time, and basically lived the life of an introvert. Once everyone learned that I was caring for my mother, traveling five hours a day to class, and struggling just to eat, they became my family. They taught me that I had to put my education first. They taught me that without an education, I would most likely have to work in dead-end jobs for the rest of my life. I began to really look at all of the people in my neighborhood, and I made a committed decision that I was not going to fall prey to the temptations of alcohol, sex, unemployment, and drugs.

As I began to succeed in my classes, my self-esteem became healthier. I began to understand how to support myself, take pride in my successes, and help others in any way possible. I still struggle with my mother as she seeks therapy and better medical care, but I also know that I must take care of my own life and keep working toward my own goals. My life is my first priority.

Today, I am an honors graduate. I completed my Bachelor of Arts in business administration with a GPA of 3.50. At the graduation ceremony, I was presented an award by the faculty and staff for my dedication, hard work, and overcoming all odds to obtain my degree. I hope in some small way that my story can help you "hold on" and reach your dreams. Happiness and success are possible for you.

## EXTRAORDINARY REFLECTION

**Read the following statement and respond in your online journal or class notebook.**

Ms. Schleigh had no family support in college. As a matter of fact, because her father was gone, she was the primary caregiver for her mother. How has your family support (or lack of support) affected your college studies? Do you think it is important to have your family's support to succeed?

**CHANGING IDEAS TO** *Reality*

Yes, listening is a learned skill, but it is more than that. It is a gift that you give to yourself. It is a gift that promotes knowledge, understanding, stronger relationships, and open-mindedness. Good listening skills can help you manage conflicts, avoid misunderstandings, and establish trusting relationships. Perhaps most importantly at this point in your life, listening can help you become a more successful student. Once you learn how to listen with your whole body and mind, you will begin to see how your notes, your grades, your attitude, your relationships, and your learning processes change. As you work toward improving your listening skills and developing your note-taking system, consider the following:

▶ When listening, evaluate the content before you judge the messenger.

▶ Keep your emotions and preconceived notions in check while listening.

▶ Sit where you can see and hear the instructor.

▶ Listen for "how" something is said.

▶ Listen to the "entire story" before making a judgment call.

▶ Listen for major ideas and key words.

▶ Use a separate notebook for every class.

▶ Use abbreviations whenever possible.

▶ Write down what the instructor puts on the board or PowerPoint slide.

Becoming adept at listening and developing your own note-taking system are two essential skills that can help you become a more active learner.

> *"Listening is an attitude of the heart, a genuine desire*
> *to be with another person."*
>
> —S. Isham

# KNOWLEDGE *in* BLOOM

## Listening with an Open Mind

Each chapter-end assessment is based on *Bloom's Taxonomy of Learning.* See the inside front cover for a quick review.

### UTILIZES LEVELS 4 AND 5 ON THE TAXONOMY

**EXPLANATION:** Seldom (if ever) would you pop in a CD, click a song on your iPod, or tune your radio to a station that you strongly disliked. It just does not seem like a good use of time, and it is not something that you would probably enjoy doing on a daily basis. However, for this exercise, we are going to ask that you do precisely what we've described above and then apply what you've experienced and learned to several questions and four **ESSENTIAL CORNERSTONES** from Chapter 1.

**PROCESS:** Over the course of the next few days, find a song from your *least favorite* genre. If you are a huge fan of R&B, move away from that genre and choose something from a genre of which you are not particularly fond. You might choose an old country song or a song from rap or bluegrass. If you enjoy listening to "Easy Love Songs," try something different such as metal or swing. The only stipulation is that the **song must have lyrics**.

  You will have to listen to the song several times to answer the questions. HOWEVER, it is important that you read the questions BEFORE you listen to the song—particularly question #2. The key to this exercise is to practice listening with an open mind, listening for content, and listening to words when barriers are in the way (the barrier in this case would be the music itself).

1. What is the song's title and artist? _____

_____

2. What emotional and mental responses did you have to the song the first time you listened to it? Why do you think you had this response? _____

_____

_____

_____

_____

3. While listening to the song, what happened to your appreciation level? Did it increase or decrease? Why?

_____

_____

_____

_____

4. In your opinion, what was the message (theme) of the song? _____

_____

_____

_____

_____

5. What about the song most surprised you? The lyrics? The actual music? Your like or dislike of the song? The artist's voice? Etc. . . . _____

_____

_____

_____

_____

6. If you HAD to say that you gained or learned one positive thing from this song, what would it be? _____

_____

_____

7. From memory, list at least two statements, comments, or quotes from the song. _____

_____

_____

_____

_____

Now, using the following **ESSENTIAL CORNERSTONES from page 8 of Chapter 1** consider how becoming a more effective listener can help you with each.

By enhancing my listening skills, I can become more **OPEN-MINDED** by

_____

_____

_____

_____

By enhancing my listening skills, I can become more **CREATIVE** by _____

_____

_____

_____

_____

By enhancing my listening skills, I can become more **KNOWLEDGEABLE** by _____

_____

_____

_____

_____

By enhancing my listening skills, I can increase my **RESOURCEFULNESS** level by

_____

_____

_____

_____

# SQ3R *Mastery* STUDY SHEET

| | |
|---|---|
| **EXAMPLE QUESTION:** *(from page 203)*<br>What are the four components of the Chinese verb "to listen"? | **ANSWER:** |
| **EXAMPLE QUESTION:** *(from page 207)*<br>Why is it important to identify key words during a lecture? | **ANSWER:** |
| **AUTHOR QUESTION:** *(from page 204)*<br>What is objective listening? | **ANSWER:** |
| **AUTHOR QUESTION:** *(from page 205)*<br>List and define the four listening styles. | **ANSWER:** |
| **AUTHOR QUESTION:** *(from page 210)*<br>Discuss the five steps in the L-STAR note-taking system. | **ANSWER:** |
| **AUTHOR QUESTION:** *(from page 212)*<br>Discuss the benefits and drawbacks of using outline technique to take notes during class. | **ANSWER:** |
| **AUTHOR QUESTION:** *(from page 214)*<br>When would be the best time to use the mapping system of note taking? Justify your answer. | **ANSWER:** |
| **YOUR QUESTION:** *(from page ____)* | **ANSWER:** |
| **YOUR QUESTION:** *(from page ____)* | **ANSWER:** |
| **YOUR QUESTION:** *(from page ____)* | **ANSWER:** |
| **YOUR QUESTION:** *(from page ____)* | **ANSWER:** |
| **YOUR QUESTION:** *(from page ____)* | **ANSWER:** |

Finally, after answering these questions, recite this chapter's major points in your mind. Consider the following general questions to help you master this material.

► What was it about?
► What does it mean?
► What was the most important thing I learned? Why?
► What were the key points to remember?

# CHAPTER 9
# UNDERSTAND

EMPOWERING
YOUR MEMORY,
STUDYING
EFFECTIVELY,
AND TAKING
TESTS WITH
CONFIDENCE

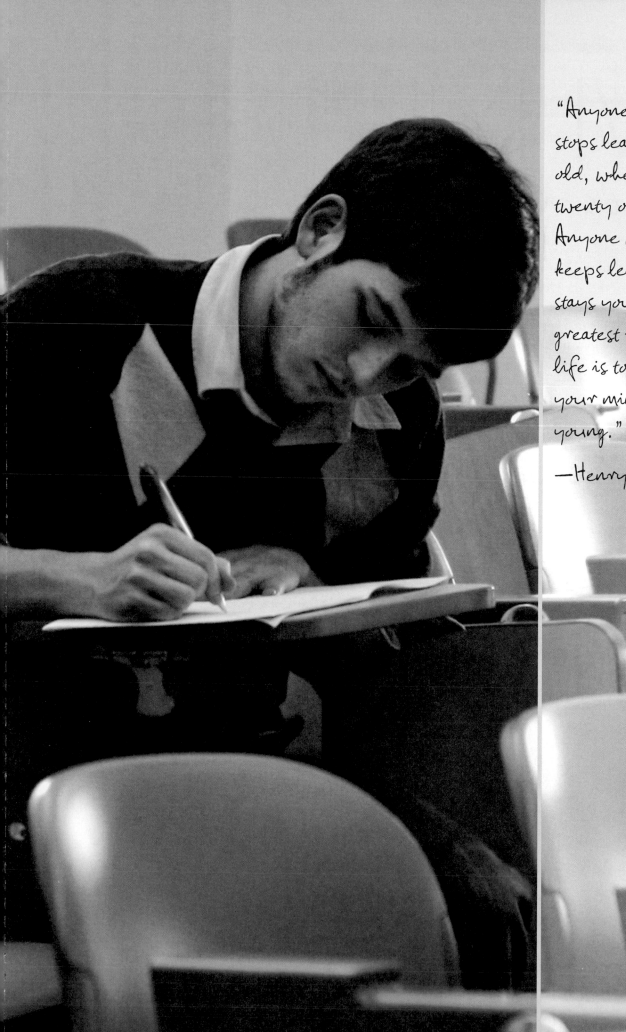

"Anyone who stops learning is old, whether at twenty or eighty. Anyone who keeps learning stays young. The greatest thing in life is to keep your mind young."

—Henry Ford

# WHY READ THIS CHAPTER?

## *What's in it for me?*

Why? Because when you read and study information, you learn amazing things. You may learn that Whoopi Goldberg has dyslexia, or that the Oedipus complex you read about in psychology class has its roots in a 2,500-year-old Greek tragedy, or that the first copying machine was invented in 1778. While you may not be tested on this material, you will certainly have many tests in college and beyond.

You will most likely be studying and taking tests for years to come. When you accept your first job, management may have you study their way of doing business and, in some cases, they will require you to pass an exam. If you go to graduate school, you will have to pass a test such as the G-MAT or the GRE or the MAT. Learning to study well and prepare for and take tests will be valuable lessons for you all your life. That is what this chapter is all about—learning how to study, how to increase your memory capacity, and how to take assessments more effectively.

*By carefully reading this chapter and taking the information provided seriously, you will be able to:*

1. Understand the importance of studying, how your memory works, and how to help it work better.

2. Identify the differences between short-term and long-term memory and how to commit information to long-term memory by using VCR3.

3. Use mnemonics to help you remember information.

4. Identify and use three different study strategies and apply these strategies to all your classes including math and science.

5. Identify the causes of your test anxiety and how to reduce anxiety by predicting test questions and formulating appropriate responses.

*WHY do I need to keep remembering information and cramming my brain full? WHY will a chapter on studying and remembering help me pass my classes? WHY is it so important, since I'm not going to be in school forever, to learn how to take tests? WHY will learning how to use mnemonic devices help me in all my courses?*

# CHAPTER 9 / UNDERSTAND

*"We can learn something new at any time we believe we can."*

*—Virginia Satir*

**NAME:** Fernando Machado
**INSTITUTION:** El Paso Community College, El Paso, TX
**MAJOR:** Electrical Engineering
**AGE:** 19

I have had to learn to how to study and how to develop a note-taking system that works for me. I found that the freshman experience course and the *Cornerstone* textbook helped me become a much better student because they gave me a much better insight into how to better myself, how to organize, and how to study. I also learned about many differences between high school and college.

When I study, I first skim the chapter and make notes on major headings and bolded words. I then read the chapter carefully, highlighting important information. I always read with a dictionary close by to be sure I am grasping the correct meaning of words.

Being able to take good notes is imperative to succeed in college. Professors usually talk fast, and they don't spoon-feed students as much as teachers do in high school. You'll soon learn that you really are on your own, and you have to learn how to listen, write clear notes, and keep up with the professor. I try to get the main topics and important ideas down on paper during the professor's lecture. I use bulleted subheadings to emphasize certain ideas. It really helps me if I have read the chapter before the lecture and have taken notes as I read the chapter.

When I study for a test, I mainly review my notes rather than read the chapters again. I also like to study with a study group. Together we know much more than I know alone. I try to find a group that is serious about making good grades and learning and I am always sure that I am a contributor to the group. It is very important, however, to be self-reliant because you may not always be able to find a group or to make the meetings.

Finally, I would advise you to do your own work even if others are cheating. If you cheat now, you will most likely cheat the rest of your life. The way you are performing in school today is the way you will perform all your life.

## SCAN & QUESTION

In the preface of this book (page xix), you read about the **SQ3R Study Method.** Right now, take a few moments, **scan this chapter**, and on page 251, write **five questions** that you think will be important to your mastery of this material. In addition to the two questions below, you will find five questions from your authors. Use one of your *"On The Test"* stickers to flag this page for easy reference.

**EXAMPLES:**

▶ **Discuss three strategies for studying math.** (from page 239)

▶ **Why are mnemonics important?** (from page 233)

# I FORGOT TO REMEMBER!

## Do You Understand the FACTS and MYTHS about Memory Function?

"My brain is full." ***MYTH***
"Certain foods can help with memory development." ***FACT***
"Proper sleep and exercise can help you retain more information." ***FACT***
"I can't remember another thing." ***MYTH***
"Being closed-minded can hurt your memory development." ***FACT***
"Drugs and alcohol can help me remember more." ***MYTH***

What study techniques have you used in the past to help you commit information to long-term memory?

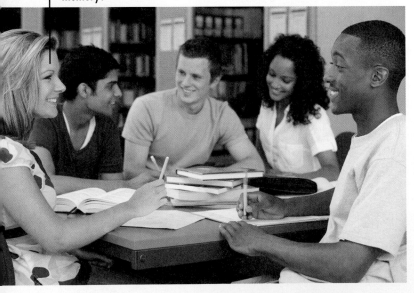

Several studies suggest that it is impossible to fill our brains completely. One study in the 1970s concluded that if our brains were fed 10 new items of information every second for the rest of our lives, we would never fill even half of our memory's capacity (Texas A&M University).

At times, you may feel that if you study or read or learn any more, you'll forget everything. Some researchers suggest that we never forget anything—that the material is simply "covered up" by other material, but it is still in our brain. The reason we can't recall that information is that it was not important enough, not stored properly, or not used enough to keep it from being covered up. According to the German philosopher Friedrich Nietzsche (1844–1900), "The ***existence of forgetting has never been proved***; we only know that some things don't come to mind when we want them."

So, why is it so hard to remember the dates of the Civil War or who flew with Amelia Earhart or how to calculate the liquidation value of stocks or the six factors in the communication process? The primary problem is that we never properly filed or stored this information.

What would happen if you typed your English research paper into the computer and did not give it a file name? When you needed to retrieve that paper, you would not know how to find it. You would have to search through every file until you came across the paper you needed. Memory works in much the same way. We have to store it properly if we are to retrieve it easily at a later time.

This section will detail how memory works and why it is important to your studying efforts. Below, you will find some basic facts about memory.

▶ Everyone remembers some information and forgets other information.

▶ Your senses help you take in information.

▶ With very little effort, you can remember some information.

▶ With rehearsal (study), you can remember a great deal of information.

▶ Without rehearsal or use, information is forgotten.

▶ Incoming information needs to be filed in the brain if you are to retain it.

▶ Information stored, or filed, in the brain must have a retrieval method.

▶ Mnemonic devices, repetition, association, and rehearsal can help you store and retrieve information.

Psychologists have determined that there are three types of memory: **sensory** memory; **short-term,** or **working,** memory; and **long-term** memory.

**Sensory memory** stores information gathered from the five senses: taste, touch, smell, hearing, and sight. Sensory memory is usually temporary, lasting about one to three seconds, unless you decide that the information is of ultimate importance to you and make an effort to transfer it to long-term memory.

**Short-term,** or **working, memory** holds information for a short amount of time. Consider the following list of letters:

*jmplngtoplntstsevng*

Now, cover them with your hand and try to recite them.

It is almost impossible for the average person to do so. Why? Because your working memory bank can hold a limited amount of information, usually about five to nine separate new facts or pieces of information at once (Woolfolk, 2006). However, consider this exercise. If you break the letters down into smaller pieces and add MEANING to them, you are more likely to retain them. Example:

*jum  lng  to  plnts  ts  evng*

This may still not mean very much to you, but you can probably remember at least the first two sets of information, "jum" and "lng."

Now, if you were to say to yourself that this sentence means "Jump Long To Planets This Evening," you would be much more likely to begin to remember this information. Just as your memory can "play tricks" on you, you can "play tricks" on your memory.

Although it is sometimes frustrating when we "misplace" information, it is also useful and necessary to our brain's survival that every piece of information that we hear and see is not in the forefront of our minds. If you tried to remember everything, you would not be able to function. As a student, you would never be able to remember all that your instructor had said during a 50-minute lecture. You have to take steps to help you to remember important information. Taking notes, making associations, drawing pictures, and visualizing information are all techniques that can help you move information from your short-term memory to your long-term memory bank.

Long-term memory stores a lot of information. It is almost like a computer disk. You have to make an effort to put something into your long-term memory, but with effort and memory techniques such as rehearsal, practice, and mnemonic devices, you can store anything you want to remember there. Long-term memory consists of information that you have heard often, information that you use often, information that you might see often, and information that you have determined necessary and/or important to you. Just as you name a file on a computer disk, you name the files in your long-term memory. Sometimes, you have to wait a moment for the information to come to you. While you are waiting, your brain disk is spinning; if the information you seek is in long-term memory, your brain will eventually find it if you stored it properly. You may have to assist your brain in locating the information by using mnemonics and other memory devices.

## DID YOU KNOW

**MICHAEL JORDAN** was born in Brooklyn, NY, in 1963. During his sophomore year in high school, Jordan tried out for the varsity basketball team. However, because he was only 5'11" he was considered too short to play and he was cut from the team. He was devastated but this experience only increased his determination to make the team and excel.

The following summer, he grew by four inches and with this growth spurt and intense training, he not only made the team but averaged over 25 points per game during his last two years in high school. Jordan then attended the University of North Carolina, where he was named ACC Freshman of the Year. In 1984, he was the NBA draft pick of the Chicago Bulls. He led the NBA in scoring for 10 seasons, holds the top career and playoff scoring averages, and is today considered by many to be THE most accomplished basketball player ever to hit the court.

# THIS ISN'T YOUR DADDY'S VCR

## How Can You Use VCR3 to Increase Memory Power?

Do you find that studying in the library, at home, or somewhere else is most effective for you? Why?

"If a man is given a fish, he eats for a day. If a man learns to fish, he eats forever."
—Chinese Proverb

BLOOM LEVEL 1 QUESTION

Countless pieces of information are stored in your long-term memory. Some of them are triggered by necessity, some by the five senses, and some by experiences. The best way to commit information to long-term memory and retrieve it when needed can be expressed by:

**V** Visualizing
**C** Concentrating
**R** Relating
**R** Repeating
**R** Reviewing

Consider the following story:

*As Katherine walked back to the dorm room after her evening class, she heard someone behind her. She turned to see two students holding hands walking about 20 feet behind her. She was relieved. This was the first night that she had walked back to the residence hall alone.*

*Katherine pulled her book bag closer to her as she increased her pace along the dimly lit sidewalk between the Salk Biology Building and the Horn Center for the Arts. "I can't believe that Shana didn't call me," she thought to herself. "She knows I hate to leave class alone."*

*As Katherine turned the corner onto Suddith Street, she heard someone else behind her. She turned but did not see anyone. As she continued to walk toward the residence hall, she heard the sound again. Turning to see if anyone was there, she saw a shadow disappear into the grove of hedges along the sidewalk.*

*Startled and frightened, Katherine crossed the street to walk beneath the streetlights and sped up to get closer to a group of students about 30 feet in front of her. She turned once more to see if anyone was behind her. Thankfully, she did not see anyone.*

*By this time, she was only one block from her residence hall. The lighting was better and other students were around. She felt better, but vowed never again to leave class alone at night.*

**To visualize** information, try to create word pictures in your mind as you hear the information. If you are being told about a Revolutionary War battle in Camden, South Carolina, try to see the soldiers and the battlefield, or try to paint a mind picture that will help you to remember the information. You may also want to create visual aids as you read or study information.

As you read Katherine's story, were you able to visualize her journey? Could you see her walking along the sidewalk? Did you see the two buildings? What did they look like? Could you see the darkness of her path? Could you see the shadow disappearing into the bushes? Could you see her increasing her pace to catch up to the other students? What was she wearing?

If you could see all of this, then you were using your visual skills—your mind's eye. This is one of the most effective ways to commit information to long-term memory. See it, live it, feel it, and touch it as you read and study it, and it will become yours.

**Concentrating** on the information given will also help you commit it to long-term memory. Don't let your mind wander. Stay focused. If you find yourself having trouble concentrating, take a small break (two to five minutes) and then go back to work.

**Relating** the information to something that you already know or understand will assist you in filing or storing the information for easy retrieval. Relating the appearance of the African zebra to the American horse can help you remember what the zebra looks like. You may not know

## 9.1 *Remembering Katherine*

Without looking back, answer the following questions about Katherine. Use the power of your visualization and concentration to recall the information.

1. What was the name of the biology building? _____

2. Did she see the shadow before or after she saw the two people behind her? _____

3. What were the two people behind her doing? _____

4. What was the name of the arts building? _____

5. Why did she cross the street? _____

6. How far ahead of her was the group of students? _____

7. When she saw the group of students in front of her, how far was she from her residence? _____

8. What was Katherine's friend's name? _____

BLOOM LEVEL 3
QUESTION

3

what the buildings in Katherine's story looked like, but try to see her in front of a building on *your campus*. Creating these types of relationships increases memory retention.

**Repeating** the information out loud to yourself or to a study partner facilitates its transfer to long-term memory. Some people have to hear information many times before they can commit it to long-term memory. Memory experts agree that repetition is one of the STRONGEST ways to increase the retention of material.

**Reviewing** the information is another means of repetition. The more you see and use the information, the easier it will be to remember it when the time comes. As you review, try to remember the main points of the information.

Walter Pauk (2007), educator and inventor of the Cornell note-taking method, concluded from a research study that people reading a textbook chapter forget 81% of what they had read after 28 days. With this in mind, it may behoove you to review Katherine's story (and other material in your texts) on a regular basis. Reviewing is a method of keeping information fresh.

# THE CAPABILITY OF YOUR MEMORY

## What Is the Difference Between Memorizing and Owning?

Why don't you forget your name? Why don't you forget your address? The answer is that you KNOW that information. *You OWN it.* It belongs to you. You've used it often enough and repeated it often enough that it is highly unlikely that you will ever forget it. Conversely, why might you have trouble remembering the details of Erickson's Stages of Development or Maslow's Hierarchy of Basic Needs? Most likely because you memorized it and never "owned" it.

Knowing something means that you have made a personal commitment to make this information a part of your life. For example, if you need to remember the name "Stephen" and his phone number of 925-6813, the likelihood of your remembering this information depends on *attitude*. Do you need to recall this information because he is in your study group and you might need to call him, or because he is the caregiver for your infant daughter while you are in class? How badly you need that name and number will determine the commitment level that you make to either *memorizing* it (and maybe forgetting it) or *knowing* it (and making it a part of your life).

Take a moment and refer to The Learning Process Chart in Chapter 6, "Learn" (Figure 6.1 on page 151). This will give you a good reminder of what it takes to learn new information and how to adjust your attitude about the value of that information.

**FIGURE**

## 9.2 *Seeing Clearly*

Consider the first picture. Study it carefully.
Look at everything from left to right, top to bottom.

Now, notice the picture and pay close attention to the areas marked.

Notice the number of people on the trampoline

Notice the storage building

Notice the color of the protective padding

Notice the green foliage

Notice the utility meter

FIGURE

## 9.2 *Seeing Clearly (continued)*

Now, cover this picture and answer the following questions:

1. How many people are on the trampoline? _____

2. What color is the protective padding on the edge? _____

3. What is the season of the year based on the foliage color? _____

4. What colors are used on the storage building? _____

5. Is there one utility meter or two? _____

6. How many children are in the air? _____

7. Are the children all male, female, or mixed? _____

8. How many people are wearing striped shirts? _____

9. What type of fence surrounds the house? _____

10. What colors are used on the house? _____

11. Is the house made of one material or more? _____

12. What color are the flowers on the bush? _____

*"NOT FAIR!"* you may be saying right now. "We were not asked to look at the fence, the colors on the house, or what people are wearing." Regardless, could you answer all of the questions without looking? The purpose of this exercise is to help you understand the real difference between casually looking at something and REALLY looking at something. To truly know something, you have to go beyond what is on the surface—even going beyond reading and studying what was asked of you. You have to look and examine more than you are told or more than what is pointed out to you. In order to own information, you have to be totally committed to examining every detail, every inch, and every angle of it. You will need to practice and master the technique of "going beyond."

The Greek goddess of memory, Mnemosyne.

# USING MNEMONIC DEVICES

## What Does a Greek Goddess Have to Do with My Memory?

The word "mnemonic" is derived from the name of the Greek Goddess of Memory, **Mnemosyne** (pronounced Ne-MO-ze-knee). She was considered one of the most important goddesses of all time because it was believed that memory separates us from lower animal life forms. It was believed that memory is the very foundation of civilization (The Goddess Path, 2009). Memory was so very important because most of the transmission of human history depended on oral stories and parables committed only to memory, not on paper.

In modern times, a mnemonic (pronounced ni-MON-ik) device is a memory trick or technique that assists you in putting information into your long-term memory and pulling it out when you need it. According to research into mnemonics and their effectiveness, it was found that mnemonics can help create a phenomenon known as the *bizarreness effect*. This effect causes us to remember information that is "bizarre" or unusual more rapidly than "normal," everyday facts. "The bizarreness effect occurs because unusual information and events trigger heightened levels of our attention and require us to work harder to make sense of them; thus we remember the information and its associated interaction better" (McCornack, 2007). The following types of mnemonics may help you with your long-term memory.

**JINGLES/RHYMES.** You can make up rhymes, songs, poems, or sayings to assist you in remembering information; for example, "Columbus sailed the ocean blue in fourteen hundred and ninety-two."

As a child, you learned many things through jingles and rhymes. You probably learned your ABC's, as well as your numbers, through a song pattern. If you think about it, you can probably still sing your ABC's, and maybe your numbers through the "Ten Little Indians" song. You can probably also sing every word to the opening of *The Brady Bunch, Scooby Doo,* or *Gilligan's Island* because of the continual reruns on TV. Some advertisements and commercials seem to stick with us even if we find them annoying. Jingles and rhymes have a strong and lasting impact on our memory—especially when repetition is involved.

**SENTENCES.** You can make up sentences such as "Some men can read backward fast" to help you remember information. Another example is "**P**lease **e**xcuse **m**y **d**ear **A**unt **S**ally," which corresponds to the mathematical operations **p**arentheses, **e**xponents, **m**ultiplication, **d**ivision, **a**ddition, and **s**ubtraction.

Other sentences in academic areas include:

1. **M**y **V**ery **E**lderly **M**other **J**ust **S**aved **U**s **N**icely. This is a sentence mnemonic for the eight planets **in order from the sun**: Mercury, Venus, Earth, Mars, Jupiter, Saturn, Uranus, Neptune.

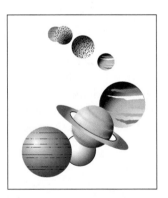

2. **E**very **G**ood **B**ird **D**oes **F**ly is a sentence mnemonic for the line notes in the treble clef in music.

3. **S**ome **M**en **H**elp **E**ach **O**ther is a sentence mnemonic for the Great Lakes from **west to east**: Superior, Michigan, Huron, Erie, Ontario.

**WORDS.** You can also create words. For example, **Roy G. Biv** may help you to remember the colors of the rainbow: **r**ed, **o**range, **y**ellow, **g**reen, **b**lue, **i**ndigo, and **v**iolet. Other word mnemonics include:

1. **HOMES** is a word mnemonic for the Great Lakes in no particular order: **H**uron, **O**ntario, **M**ichigan, **E**rie, **S**uperior.

2. **FACE** is a word mnemonic for the space notes in the treble clef.

**STORY LINES.** If you find it easier to remember stories than raw information, you may want to translate the information into a story that you can easily tell. Weave the data and facts into a creative story that can be easily retrieved from your long-term memory. This technique can be especially beneficial if your instructor gives essay exams, because the "story" that you remember can be what was actually told in class.

**ACRONYMS.** An acronym is a word that is formed from the first letters of other words. You may see reruns for the famed TV show *M*A*S*H*. This is an acronym for "Mobile Army Surgical Hospital." If you scuba dive, you know that *SCUBA* is an acronym for "Self-Contained Underwater Breathing Apparatus." Other common acronyms include:

*NASA* (**N**ational **A**eronautics and **S**pace **A**dministration)
*NASCAR* (**N**ational **A**ssociation for **S**tock **C**ar **A**uto **R**acing)
*NASDAQ* (**N**ational **A**ssociation of **S**ecurities **D**ealers **A**utomated **Q**uotations)
*NATO* (**N**orth **A**tlantic **T**reaty **O**rganization)
*BART* (**B**ay **A**rea **R**apid **T**ransit)

**PEGGING.** The pegging system uses association, visualization, and attachment to aid in memory. With this system, you literally "attach" what you want to remember to something that is already familiar to you—the pegs that you create. This is a visual means of remembering lists, sequences, and even categories of information.

# From Ordinary to Extraordinary

## REAL PEOPLE | REAL LIVES | REAL CHANGE

**H. P. RAMA**
CEO, JHM Hotels
Greenville, SC

I have led a life filled with a great variety of experiences, trials, challenges, and triumphs. Born in Africa, I was sent to India to live with my grandparents and go to school when I was just five years old. I lived away from my parents, whom I missed greatly, in a little farming village in India, where I finished school and ultimately earned an undergraduate degree. I knew I wanted to go to America and pursue the American dream, so at age 21 I left India and arrived in this country with only $2 in my pocket.

I had to get a job quickly, so I took the first job offered to me, a dishwasher, which I quit after just four hours. My next job was as a waiter at a Howard Johnson's restaurant in Manhattan. While I worked as a waiter to support myself, I attended Xavier University to pursue my MBA. My life was primarily one of work and sacrifice as I worked hard to pay my expenses and to graduate with this degree I prized so much. While working at Howard Johnson's, I paid attention to everything that happened around me because I had no intention of remaining a waiter all my life. I was absorbing knowledge of the hotel and restaurant business, which I would put to use later. At the time, I had no intention of becoming a hotelier. My goal was to go into banking. I always say that I became an accidental hotelier, but this field has served me well and offered me many opportunities. I was pursuing the American dream, and that was all that mattered.

> "At age 21 I left India and arrived in this country with only $2 in my pocket."

I considered myself fortunate to have this great opportunity to be in America, to be going to school, and to have a job that supported me.

After receiving my MBA from Xavier, I worked as a staff accountant for 14 months. In 1973 I had an opportunity to buy my first hotel in Pomona, California. My brother and I bought the hotel, and we had only two employees other than the two of us. We worked 24/7 and lived behind the office. There was no job that we did not do. But we were chasing the dream, and we were off and running with no idea of how many opportunities we would have.

# From Ordinary to Extraordinary

## REAL PEOPLE | REAL LIVES | REAL CHANGE

Then I moved East, still focused on achieving the American dream, and bought a 36-room hotel in Buffalo, Tennessee. My wife and I did everything—front desk, night duty, all the maintenance. We both worked very hard, long hours. In 1977 we moved to Greenville, South Carolina, and bought a foreclosed property from a bank. In 1983 I bought four Howard Johnson's hotels—just 13 years after working for HJ as a waiter. Over the years my brothers and I have owned and developed 78 hotels and still own 38 today.

We developed a five-star hotel in India in 1990, and today we are expanding and adding other hotels. We are most proud of the fact that we are developing a mixed-use development in India that will include a Hospitality College campus, a retailing and entertainment campus, a hospital campus, and luxury accommodations. We are using our knowledge learned in this wonderful country to continue the dream in India.

In 1999, I was named chairman of the American Motel and Hotel Lodging Association, which was a significant honor for me. Because I wanted to give back to the field that has done so much for me, I donated $1 million for scholarships for hospitality students. In 1989 I was the founding member of the Asian American Hotel Owners Association. Today I serve on several boards of advisors for hospitality programs and was named an executive ambassador by Cornell University, a position in which I speak to graduate students about my experiences.

My advice to students today is this: Anything is possible if you have the vision, pay the price, work hard, and take risks. I have been very blessed, but I have also worked very hard. And I am living proof that the American dream is alive and well.

## EXTRAORDINARY REFLECTION

### Read the following statement and respond in your online journal or class notebook.

Mr. Rama worked his way up the ladder and became chairman of the American Motel and Hotel Lodging Association, a major organization. What top honors do you hope to achieve in your own career? Why? How would they change your life?

FIGURE

**9.3** *The Pegging System*

Pretend that you are looking at a coat rack mounted on the wall, with 10 pegs sticking out of it. Just as you would hang a hat or coat on the pegs of a rack, you can hang information there, too.

For the sake of explaining this technique more thoroughly, we have named the 10 pegs for you with corresponding rhyming words. You, however, can name your pegs anything that would be easy for you to remember. Once you memorize these peg names, you can attach anything to them with visualization and imagination. The key to using the pegging mnemonic system is to name your pegs ONCE and use those names each time you hook information to them. This way, they become second nature to you. For our example, our 10 pegs are named:

| | | | |
|---|---|---|---|
| 1 | = sun | 6 | = sticks |
| 2 | = shoe | 7 | = heaven |
| 3 | = bee | 8 | = gate |
| 4 | = shore | 9 | = line |
| 5 | = alive | 10 | = pen |

Repeat these until you have memorized them.

Let's use an example from your *Cornerstone* text. In Chapter 1 you were introduced to the **Ten Essential Cornerstones for Personal and Professional Success** (passion, motivation, knowledge, resourcefulness, creativity, adaptability, open-mindedness, communication, accountability, and vision). Using visualization, attach one of the cornerstones to each peg.

| | |
|---|---|
| 1 - sun | I look at the **sun** on a beautiful day with **passion**. |
| 2 - shoe | I walk in my **shoes** with **motivation**. |
| 3 - bee | I see a **bee** flying around that seems to be very **knowledgeable**. |
| 4 - shore | The **shore** washes many **resources** to the beach. |
| 5 - alive | My brain is **alive** because I use **creativity**. |
| 6 - sticks | I see a **stick** bending into a half circle, making it very **adaptable**. |
| 7 - heaven | Believing in **heaven** takes **open-mindedness**. |
| 8 - gate | Many **gates** open for people who know how to **communicate**. |
| 9 - line | If you walk a straight **line,** you are **accountable**. |
| 10 - sin | Use a **pen** to write your **vision**. |

Read these over one more time, and then cover the list. You'll be amazed at how easy it is to repeat it. You will, of course, need to study each one to know what it means, but now, you have the list memorized, in order.

FIGURE

## 9.4 *A Quick Reference Guide to Studying Math and Science*

© **Robert M. Sherfield, Ph.D.**

### Before Class

▶ **NEVER** take a math or science course (or any course for that matter) for which you are not prepared. If you think you need, or test into a basic, remedial, or transitional class *take it*!!! Look at it as a chance to start over with new hope and knowledge.

▶ **UNDERSTAND** that most math and science classes build on previous knowledge. If you begin the class with a weak background, you must work very hard to learn missed information.

▶ **AVOID** taking math or science classes during "short" terms if possible. The more time you spend with the material, the better, especially if math and/or science are not your strong suits.

▶ **KNOW** your own learning style. If you're visual, use colors, charts, and photos. If you're auditory, practice your listening skills. If you're tactile, work to create situations where you can "act out" or touch the material.

▶ **PREPARE** yourself *before class* by reading the chapter. EVEN if you don't understand all of it, read through the material and write down questions about material you did not understand.

▶ **SCAN** all of the introductory and summation materials provided in the text or study guides.

▶ **JOIN** a study group. If there is not one, start one. Cooperative learning teams can be life savers.

▶ **SEEK** tutorial assistance on campus from the first day. Go visit the center and get familiar with how it operates. Get to know the people who work there. Don't wait until you get behind to seek assistance.

### During Class

▶ **COME to EVERY** class, study group, or lab.

▶ **CONTROL** your own anger and frustration. The past is the past and you can't change any part of it—but you can change YOUR future. Learn to make your negative self-talker "be quiet!"

▶ **ASK** questions. **ASK** questions. **ASK** questions. **ASK** questions. . . . and be specific in your questioning. Don't just say, "I don't understand that." Ask detailed and specific questions such as, "*I don't understand why $f(x + h)$ doesn't equal $f(x) + f(h)$*. Or, "*I don't understand the difference between 'algia' and 'dynia.' Why are two different words used for pain?*"

▶ **SLOW DOWN** and read the material carefully.

▶ **FIND** the formulas and write them down on note cards.

▶ **WRITE** down the explanatory remarks made by the instructor such as:

  ▶ How do you get from one step to the next?

  ▶ How does this problem differ from other problems?

  ▶ Why do you need to use formula "x" instead of formula "y"?

  ▶ Were any steps combined—why or why not?

▶ **TRY** to learn from a *general to specific* end. That is, try to get a feeling of the overall goal of the material before you hone in on smaller problems.

▶ **WRITE** down any theorem, formula, or technique that the instructor puts on the board, overhead, or PowerPoint.

▶ **LEAVE** a space in your notes for any material you missed or did not understand. This will help you keep your notes organized when you go back after class and add the explanation.

▶ **BRING** Post-it ® Notes, strips of paper, or bookmarks to class with you so that you can "tag" pages with important information and concepts. Use the tabs included with your text to help you mark important information.

### After Class

▶ **VISIT** your instructor's office (make an appointment to visit during office hours).

▶ **FILL** in the missing information in your notes by reviewing the text, going to your study group, or getting clarification from your instructor.

*(continued)*

## FIGURE 9.4    *A Quick Reference Guide to Studying Math and Science (continued)*

▶ **PRACTICE** the problems in your text or study guide and then practice them again, and again, and again until they become second nature. Much of Math and Science is learned by DOING . . . so DO . . . and then DO again.

▶ **APPLY** what you learned in class or lab. Find a way to make it "speak" to your life in a practical way.

▶ **CONTINUALLY** review all of the theorems, formulas, concepts, and terms from each chapter so they become second nature to you.

▶ When doing practice tests, **PRETEND** that you are in an actual test and adhere to the timelines, rules, and policies of your instructor. This helps replicate the actual testing situation.

### Before the Test

▶ **ASK** questions that will reduce your anxiety such as:

  ▶ What is the point value of each question?

  ▶ How many questions will be on the test?

  ▶ Will the questions be multiple choice, etc. . . . ?

  ▶ What materials do I need to bring to class?

  ▶ Will I be allowed to use a calculator or any other technology?

  ▶ Is there a time limit on the test?

  ▶ What is the overall grade value of the test?

▶ **MAKE** every effort to attend any study or review sessions offered by the instructor or peers.

### During Tests

▶ **READ** the directions carefully.

▶ **QUICKLY** glance over the test to determine the number of questions and the degree of difficulty as related to the time you have to complete the test.

▶ **WORK** by the clock. If you have 60 minutes to take a test that has 120 questions, this means you have about 30 seconds per question.

▶ **BEGIN** by solving the problems that are easiest or most familiar to you.

▶ **READ** the questions on the test carefully and MORE than once and don't jump to conclusions.

▶ **DETERMINE** which formulas you will need to use.

▶ **DECIDE** how you want to solve the problem.

▶ **CHECK** your work by using multiple solving techniques. (If the problem is division, can it be rechecked with multiplication? This is called Opposite Operations).

▶ **DRAW** pictures if you encounter word problems. Visualization is very important.

▶ **SHOW** all of your work, even if it is not required. This will help the instructor (and you) see what you did correctly and/or incorrectly.

▶ **RECHECK** every answer if you have time.

▶ **WORK** backward if at all possible. This may help answer the question and catch mistakes.

▶ After you've completed the answer, **reread** the question to determine if you did everything the question asked you do to.

▶ **NEVER** erase your margin work or mistakes. This wastes time and you may erase something that you need (or worse, something that was correct).

### After Tests

▶ **IMMEDIATELY** after the test, try to determine if the majority of test questions came from classroom notes, your textbook, your study guide, or from your homework. This will help you prepare for the next test.

▶ **THINK** about the way you studied for this test and how you could improve your techniques for the next time. Consider the amount of time spent studying for this test.

▶ Once the test is graded, **DETERMINE** what caused you to lose the most points: Simple errors? Applying incorrect formulas or theorems? Misunderstanding of the questions asked? Intensified test anxiety? Poor study habits in general?

# HAKUNA MATATA

## How in the World Can I Study with Small Children in the House?

For many college students, finding a place or time to study is the hardest part of studying. Some students live at home with younger siblings; some students have children of their own. If you have young children in the home, you may find the following hints helpful when it comes time to study.

**STUDY AT SCHOOL.** Your schedule may have you running from work to school directly to home. Try to squeeze in even as little as half an hour at school for studying, perhaps immediately before or after class. A half hour of pure study time can prove more valuable than five hours at home with constant interruptions.

**CREATE CRAFTS AND HOBBIES.** Your children need to be occupied while you study. Choose projects your children can do by themselves, without your help. Explain to your children that you are studying and that they can use this time to be creative; when everyone is finished, you'll share with each other what you've done. Give them little rewards for their work and for helping you have quiet time to study.

> Do you think it is a good idea to involve your children (or younger siblings) in your education? Why or why not?

**STUDY WITH YOUR CHILDREN.** One of the best ways to instill the value of education in your children is to let them see you participating in your own education. Set aside one or two hours per night when you and your children study. You may be able to study in one place, or you may have separate study areas.

**RENT MOVIES OR LET YOUR CHILDREN WATCH TV.** Research has shown that viewing a limited amount of educational television, such as *Sesame Street, Reading Rainbow,* or *Barney and Friends,* can be beneficial for children. If you do not like what is on television, you might consider renting or purchasing age-appropriate educational videos for your children.

**INVITE YOUR CHILDREN'S FRIENDS OVER.** What?! That's right. A child who has a friend to play or study with may create less of a distraction for you. Chances are your children would rather be occupied with someone their own age, and you will gain valuable study time.

**HIRE A SITTER OR EXCHANGE SITTING SERVICES** with another student. Arrange to have a sitter come to your house a couple of times a week if you can afford it. If you have a classmate who also has children at home, you might take turns watching the children for each other. You could each take the children for one day a week, or devise any other schedule that suits you both best.

**FIND OUT IF YOUR COLLEGE HAS AN ON-SITE DAY-CARE** center such as the Boys and Girls Club. Some colleges provide day-care facilities at a reduced cost, and some provide day care at no charge. It is certainly worth checking out.

**TALK TO THE FINANCIAL AID OFFICE** on your campus. In some instances, there will be grants or aid to assist you in finding affordable day care for your child.

## ESSENTIAL CORNERSTONE

**Adaptability:**
How can learning to be more adaptable help you study with your children or with distractions all around you?

**Social Networking Moment:**
Share your response to this Essential Cornerstone with peers in your social network. Choose two responses from your peers and respond to their postings.

# STUDYING IN A CRUNCH
## TOMORROW? What Do You Mean the Test Is Tomorrow?

Let's be straight up front. No study skills textbook will ever advise you to cram. It is simply a dangerous and often futile exercise in desperation. You will **never read the words**, "Don't waste your time studying, just CRAM the night before so you can party harder and longer!" in a study skills textbook. Cramming is the complete opposite of what this whole chapter is about—knowing versus memorizing. Cramming will not help you own the material; it can only help you memorize a few things for storage in short-term memory. You may spend several hours cramming, and shortly after the test, the information is gone, evaporated, vanished! If you find yourself in this spot, consider the following tips and suggestions for cramming. These probably won't get you an A, but they may help you with a few questions.

**DEPRESSURIZE.** Just tell yourself up front what you are doing. Don't pretend that cramming is going to save you. Let yourself realize that you are memorizing material for short-term gain and that you won't be able to keep it all. With this admission, your stress will diminish.

**KNOW THE SCORE.** When cramming, it is important to know what you're cramming for. If you're cramming for a multiple-choice test, you'll need different types of information than for an essay test. Know what type of test it is for which you are studying.

**READ IT QUICKLY.** Think about **H2 FLIB.** This is a mnemonic for: read the **h**eadings, **h**ighlight the important words, read the **f**irst sentence of every paragraph, read the **l**ast sentence of every paragraph, read the **i**ndented and **b**oxed material. This can help you get through a chapter when pinched for time.

> "Don't just learn something from every experience, learn something positive."
> —Al Neuharth

**MAKE CONNECTIONS.** As you are reading, quickly determine if any of the information has a connection with something else you know. Is there a relationship of any kind? Is there a cause and effect in motion? Can you pinpoint an example to clarify the information? Is there a mnemonic that can help you with this information? These questions can help you with retention and long-term memory commitment.

**USE YOUR SYLLABUS OR STUDY GUIDE.** If your instructor lists questions in the syllabus that you should know the answers to (mastery questions), or if he or she gave you a study sheet (or you developed your own study sheet, like the one you have created at the end of each *Cornerstone* chapter), this is the place to start. Answer those questions. If you don't have either, look to see if the text gives study questions at the end of the chapter.

**SEE IT.** Visualizing the information through mapping, diagrams, photos, drawings, and outlines can help you commit this information to short-term memory.

**CHECK YOUR NOTES.** Did the professor indicate that certain things are important to know for the test?

**CHOOSE WISELY.** If you're cramming, you can't do it all. Make wise choices about which material you plan to study. This can be driven by your study sheet, your lecture notes, or questions in your syllabus (if they are listed).

Information you've crammed is going to leave you after the test. Don't rely on it for the next test or the final. You will need to go back and relearn (truly understand) the information you "crammed" in order to commit it to long-term memory.

# THINKING ABOUT TESTING

## Can Changing My Attitude and Reducing Stress Really Help?

Yes, both are necessary to help you get through tests. A positive or negative attitude can truly mean the difference between success and failure. With an attitude adjustment from negative to positive and some basic preparation, you can overcome a good deal of your anxiety about tests and do well. You can reduce anxiety when you are in control of the situation, and you can gain control by convincing yourself that you *can be* and *will be* successful. If you think positively and can honestly say that you have done everything possible to prepare for a test, then the results will most likely be positive.

**Silencing *your negative self-talk*** is one of the most powerful things you can do for yourself. Consider the following tips for reducing test anxiety during your next test. You will not be able to employ them all, but if you learn and use a few new ones each time, before you know it, you'll be a testing pro!

- ▶ Prepare yourself emotionally for the test, control your self-talk, and be positive.
- ▶ Study and learn the material—NO! You can't study too much.
- ▶ Ask peers who have had a certain professor what type of tests he or she gives.
- ▶ Arrive early for the test (at least 15 minutes early).
- ▶ Go to the test with everything you need: pencils, calculator, and other supplies.
- ▶ Listen to the instructor before the test begins, know his or her rules about testing, and READ the instructions.
- ▶ Keep an eye on the clock during the test so that you can finish on time. However, don't let time cause you undue stress or anxiety.
- ▶ Answer what you know first, the questions that are easiest for you.
- ▶ Check your answers, but remember, your first response is usually correct.
- ▶ Find out ahead of time exactly what the test will cover.
- ▶ Ask the instructor for a study sheet; you may not get one, but it does not hurt to ask!
- ▶ When you get the test, jot down on the back or at the top of a page any mnemonics you might have developed.

**Tips for Personal Success**

Consider the following tips for making time for studying and committing information to long-term memory:

- ▶ Study daily to avoid having to "cram" the night before your test.
- ▶ Form a study group with people who are motivated and keep you on track.
- ▶ Keep up with your daily readings and homework.

Now, it is your turn. Create a list of at three more tips that you would offer a fellow classmate to assist him or her in making time in his/her life to study.

1. _____
2. _____
3. _____

What techniques have you found help you reduce your anxiety and negative self-talk during quizzes and exams?

# QUIZZING YOUR INSTRUCTOR AND KNOWING YOUR RESPONSE TYPE

## What Are Some Techniques I Can Use to Help Me During Tests?

Several classes before the test is scheduled to be given, **quiz your instructor** about the logistics and specifics of the test. This information can help you study more effectively and eliminate the anxiety that comes with uncertainty. If you don't know whether the test is going to be true-false or essay or both, it is much more difficult to study. Some questions you need to ask are:

1. What types of questions will be on the test?

2. How many questions will be on the test?

3. Is there a time limit on the test?

4. Will there be any special instructions, such as "use pen only" or "use a number 2 pencil"?

5. Is there a study sheet?

6. Will there be a review session?

7. What is the grade value of the test?

8. What chapters or sections will the test cover?

Asking these simple questions will help you know what type of test will be administered, how you should prepare for it, and what supplies you will need.

## What Do I Do When I Can't Remember the Answer?

Almost every test question will elicit one of three types of responses from you as the test taker:

▶ Quick-time response

▶ Lag-time response

▶ No response

Your response is a ***quick-time response*** when you read a question and know the answer immediately. You may need to read only one key word in the test question to know the correct response. Even if you have a quick-time response, however, always read the entire question before answering it. The question may be worded in such a way that the correct response is not the one you originally thought of.

You have a ***lag-time response*** when you read a question and the answer does not come to you immediately. You may have to read the question several times or even move on to another question before you think of the correct response. Information in another question will sometimes trigger the response you need. Once you've begun to answer other questions, you usually begin to remember more, and the response may come to you.

***No response*** is the least desirable situation when you are taking a test. You may read a question two or three times and still have no response. At this point, you should move on to another question to try to find some related information. When this happens, you have some options:

1. Leave this question until the very end of the test.

2. Make an intelligent guess.

3. Try to eliminate all unreasonable answers by association.

4. Watch for modifiers within the question.

It is very difficult to use intelligent guessing with essay or fill-in-the-blank questions. Remember these important tips about the three types of responses:

1. Don't be overly anxious if your *response is quick*; read the entire question and be careful not to make a mistake.

2. Don't get nervous if you have a *lag-time response*; the answer may come to you later, so just relax and move on.

3. Don't put down just anything if you have *no response*; take the remaining time and use intelligent guessing.

## THINKING FOR CHANGE: An Activity for Critical Reflection

After the second week of classes, Jose was devastated by his first test score. The instructor put the range of grades on the board, and he was shocked to see that many people passed the test and that his score was in the bottom 10%.

He began asking classmates if they did well or not and found some who had made A's and others who had made D's. When he spoke with one classmate, Letty, she told him that he should just chill and take a "cheat sheet" to class. "The instructor never looks, man, and she left the classroom twice. She'll never know. That's how I got my A."

"Cheat," Jose thought, "I don't think I can do that." He knew that others had made better grades than

he over the years, but he also knew that he had never once cheated on an exam. Never.

Jose went to the Tutoring Center and worked with a tutor on content and on how to take a test more effectively. On the next test, Jose scored a C. "It may not be the best grade in the class," he thought, "but it is all mine. I did it."

In your own words, what two suggestions would you give Jose to improve his grades without cheating?

1. _____

2. _____

# TEST-TAKING STRATEGIES AND HINTS FOR SUCCESS

## What Are Some Tips for Taking Tests?

Before you read about the strategies for answering these different types of questions, think about this: *There is no substitute for studying!* You can know all the tips, ways to reduce anxiety, mnemonics, and strategies on earth, but if you have not studied, they will be of little help to you.

## Strategies for Matching Questions

Matching questions frequently involve knowledge of people, dates, places, or vocabulary. When answering matching questions, you should:

▶ Read the directions carefully.

▶ Read each column before you answer.

▶ Determine whether there is an equal number of items in each column.

▶ Match what you know first.

▶ Cross off information that is already used.

▶ Use the process of elimination for answers you might not know.

▶ Look for logical clues.

▶ Use the longer statement as a question; use the shorter statement as an answer.

## Strategies for True-False Questions

True-false questions ask whether a statement is true or not. True-false questions can be some of the trickiest questions ever developed. Some students like them; some hate

---

*Sample Test #1* MATCHING

**DIRECTIONS:** Match the information in column A with the correct information in column B. Use uppercase letters.

**GOALS, MOTIVATION, & SELF-ESTEEM**

A

_____ They can be long or short, social, academic, religious, or financial

_____ They bring out the worst in you

_____ I CAN'T Syndrome

_____ Your "true self"

_____ Listening with an open mind

B

A. Child within

B. Objectivity

C. Contaminated people

D. Negative thoughts

E. Goals

---

them. There is a 50/50 chance of answering correctly, but you can use the following strategies to increase your odds with true-false questions:

▶ Read each statement carefully and watch for key words in each statement.

▶ Read each statement for double negatives such as "not untruthful."

▶ Pay attention to words that may indicate that a statement is true, such as "some," "few," "many," and "often."

▶ Pay attention to words that may indicate that a statement is false, such as "never," "all," "every," and "only."

▶ Remember that if any part of a statement is false, the entire statement is false.

▶ Answer every question unless there is a penalty for guessing.

---

*Sample Test #2* TRUE/FALSE

Place "T" for true or "F" for false beside each statement.

**NOTE-TAKING SKILLS**

1. _____ Note taking creates a history of your course content.
2. _____ "Most importantly" is not a key phrase.
3. _____ You should always write down everything the instructor says.
4. _____ You should never ask questions in class.
5. _____ The L-STAR system is a way of studying.

---

## Strategies for Multiple-Choice Questions

Many college instructors give multiple-choice tests because they are easy to grade and provide quick, precise responses. A multiple-choice question asks you to choose from among, usually, two to five answers to complete a sentence. Some strategies for increasing your success when answering multiple-choice questions are the following:

▶ Read the question and try to answer it before you read the answers provided.

▶ Look for similar answers; one of them is usually the correct response.

▶ Recognize that answers containing extreme modifiers, such as *always, every,* and *never,* are usually wrong.

▶ Cross off answers that you know are incorrect.

▶ Read all the options before selecting your answer. Even if you believe that A is the correct response, read them all.

▶ Recognize that when the answers are all numbers, the highest and lowest numbers are usually incorrect.

▶ Understand that the most inclusive and longest answers are often correct.

▶ If you cannot answer a question, move on to the next one and continue through the test; another question may trigger the answer you couldn't come up with previously.

▶ Answer every question unless there is a penalty for guessing.

---

## *Sample Test #3* MULTIPLE CHOICE

**DIRECTIONS:** Read each statement and select the best response from the answers given below.

### STUDY SKILLS

1. Which statement is true according to the 2007 Labor Statistics, Bureau of Census?
   A. Men earn more than women.
   B. Women earn more than men.
   C. People with a professional degree earn the most money of any education level.
   D. Unemployment is greatest among those with a doctorate degree.

2. To calculate a GPA, you would:
   A. Divide quality points by the number of semester hours.
   B. Multiply total points by quality points.
   C. Divide total points by the number of semester hours.
   D. Multiply the quality points by the total points.

3. To be an effective priority manager, you have to:
   A. Be very structured, organized, and self-disciplined.
   B. Be very unstructured and disorganized.
   C. Be mildly structured and organized.
   D. Know what type of person you are avoid working from that perspective.

---

# Strategies for Short-Answer Questions

Short-answer questions, also called fill-in-the-blanks, ask you to supply the answer yourself, not select it from a list. Although "short answer" sounds easy, these questions are often very difficult. Short-answer questions require you to draw from your long-term memory. The following hints can help you answer this type of question successfully:

▶ Read each question and be sure that you know what is being asked.

▶ Be brief in your response.

▶ Give the same number of answers as there are blanks; for example, _____ and _____ would require two answers.

▶ Never assume that the length of the blank has anything to do with the length of the answer.

▶ Remember that your initial response is usually correct.

▶ Pay close attention to the word immediately preceding the blank; if the word is "an," give a response that begins with a vowel (a, e, i, o, u).

▶ Look for key words in the sentence that may trigger a response.

---

*Sample Test #4* SHORT ANSWER

**DIRECTIONS:** Fill in the blanks with the correct response. Write clearly.

**LISTENING SKILLS**

1. Listening is a _____ act. We choose to do it.
2. The three elements of listening involve listening objectively, _____, and _____.
3. _____ is the same as listening with an open mind.
4. Prejudging is an _____ to listening.
5. Leaning forward, making eye contact, being patient, and leaving your emotions at home are characteristics of _____ listeners.

---

## Strategies for Essay Questions

Most students look at essay questions with dismay because they take more time. Yet essay tests can be one of the easiest tests to take because they give you a chance to show what you really know. An essay question requires you to supply the information. If you have studied, you will find that once you begin to answer an essay question, your answer will flow more easily. Some tips for answering essay questions are the following:

▶ More is not always better; sometimes more is just more. Try to be as concise and informative as possible. An instructor would rather see one page of excellent material than five pages of fluff.

▶ Pay close attention to the action word used in the question and respond with the appropriate type of answer. Key words used in essay questions include the following:

| | | | |
|---|---|---|---|
| discuss | illustrate | enumerate | describe |
| compare | define | relate | list |
| contrast | summarize | analyze | explain |
| trace | evaluate | critique | interpret |
| diagram | argue | justify | prove |

▶ Write a thesis statement for each answer.

▶ Outline your thoughts before you begin to write.

▶ Watch your spelling, grammar, and punctuation.

▶ Use details, such as times, dates, places, and proper names, where appropriate.

▶ Be sure to answer all parts of the question; some essay questions have more than one part.

▶ Summarize your main ideas toward the end of your answer.

▶ Write neatly.

▶ Proofread your answer.

Learning how to take a test and learning how to reduce your anxiety are two of the most important gifts you can give yourself as a student. Although tips and hints may help you, don't forget that there is no substitute for studying and knowing the material.

## Sample Test #5 ESSAY

**DIRECTIONS:** Answer each question completely. Use a separate paper if you wish.

### STUDY SKILLS

1. Identify and discuss two examples of mnemonics.
2. Justify why it is important to use the SQ3R method when reading.
3. Compare an effective study environment with an ineffective study environment.

## CHANGING IDEAS TO *Reality*

**REFLECTIONS ON NOTE TAKING AND TESTING**

Just as reading is a learned skill, so are memory development, studying, and learning how to take assessments. You can improve your memory, but it will take practice, patience, and persistence. You can improve your study skills, but it will take time and work. And you can increase your ability to do well on tests, but it will take a commitment on your part to study smarter and put in the time and dedication required. By making the decision "I CAN DO THIS," you've won the battle, for when you make that decision, your studying and learning become easier.

Your challenge is to focus on developing excellent memory techniques, study patterns, and test-taking abilities while earning the best grades you can. When you have done this, you can look in the mirror and be proud of the person you see without having to be ashamed of your character or having to worry about being caught cheating or wondering if you really did your best. When studying for your next class or taking your next test, consider the following:

▶ Study the hardest material first.

▶ Review your classroom and textbook notes frequently.

▶ Use mnemonics to help you remember lists.

▶ Learn the material from many different angles.

▶ *Ask* questions of the instructor before the test.

▶ Glance at the entire test *before* beginning.

▶ *Ignore* the pace of your classmates.

▶ Watch *time* limits.

▶ Use academic integrity.

As you study and learn to enter your chosen profession, remember this: "You are building your character for the long haul—not just a few short years."

*"Change occurs, progress is made, and difficulties are resolved if people merely do the right thing—and rarely do people NOT KNOW what the right thing is."*
*—Father Hessburg*

# KNOWLEDGE in BLOOM

## Using and Evaluating your GUIDING STATEMENT

Each chapter-end assessment is based on *Bloom's Taxonomy of Learning.* See the inside front cover for a quick review.

UTILIZES LEVELS 3 AND 6 OF THE TAXONOMY

**EXPLANATION:** Now that you have read and studied this chapter and, no doubt, taken a few tests this semester, you have a better understanding of what happens to you physically and mentally during an exam.

Below, you will find listed six of the common physical or mental symptoms of anxiety reported by students while testing.

**PROCESS:** Beside each symptom, **create a list** of at least three concrete, doable, realistic strategies to overcome this physical or emotional anxiety symptom before or during a testing situation.

| SYMPTOM | HOW TO REDUCE IT |
|---|---|
| Fatigue | 1.<br><br>2.<br><br>3. |
| Frustration | 1.<br><br>2.<br><br>3. |
| Fear | 1.<br><br>2.<br><br>3. |
| Anger | 1.<br><br>2.<br><br>3. |
| Nervousness/Nausea | 1.<br><br>2.<br><br>3. |
| Uncertainty/Doubt | 1.<br><br>2.<br><br>3. |

# SQ3R *Mastery* STUDY SHEET

| | | |
|---|---|---|
| **EXAMPLE QUESTION:** <br> Discuss three strategies for studying math. | *(from page 239)* | **ANSWER:** |
| **EXAMPLE QUESTION:** <br> Why are mnemonics important? | *(from page 233)* | **ANSWER:** |
| **AUTHOR QUESTION:** <br> What is the difference between short-term <br> and long-term memory? | *(from page 229)* | **ANSWER:** |
| **AUTHOR QUESTION:** <br> Discuss the five steps in VCR3. | *(from page 230)* | **ANSWER:** |
| **AUTHOR QUESTION:** <br> What is H2 FLIB and how can it help you? | *(from page 242)* | **ANSWER:** |
| **AUTHOR QUESTION:** <br> Discuss five ways to reduce test anxiety. | *(from page 230)* | **ANSWER:** |
| **AUTHOR QUESTION:** <br> Discuss one strategy for each type <br> of testing situation. | *(from page 243)* | **ANSWER:** |
| **YOUR QUESTION:** | *(from page ___)* | **ANSWER:** |
| **YOUR QUESTION:** | *(from page ___)* | **ANSWER:** |
| **YOUR QUESTION:** | *(from page ___)* | **ANSWER:** |
| **YOUR QUESTION:** | *(from page ___)* | **ANSWER:** |
| **YOUR QUESTION:** | *(from page ___)* | **ANSWER:** |

Finally, after answering these questions, recite this chapter's major points in your mind. Consider the following general questions to help you master this material.

► What was it about?
► What does it mean?
► What was the most important thing I learned? Why?
► What were the key points to remember?

# PROSPER

MANAGING
YOUR MONEY
AND DEBTS
WISELY

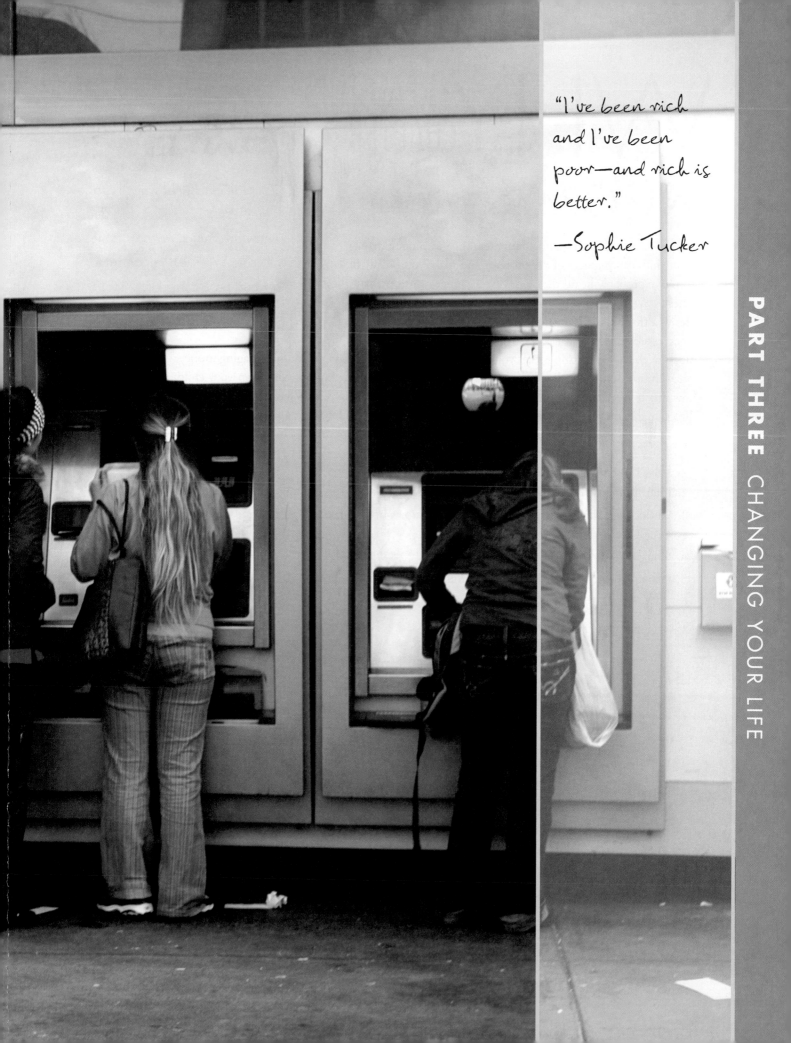

"I've been rich and I've been poor—and rich is better."
—Sophie Tucker

# WHY READ THIS CHAPTER?

## What's in it for me?

WHY is learning to manage money so important at this stage of my life? WHY does it matter if I have big student loans and credit card debt when I graduate? WHY is it such a big deal to know how much my next semester will cost? WHY is it important to know and protect my FICO score?

Why? Because changing and strengthening your money management skills can impact your life forever and make you fiscally fit! You have probably heard the old saying, "Money won't buy happiness." Well, neither will poverty. As in many areas of your life, wealth accumulation needs to be balanced with a solid work experience, physical health, good relationships, hobbies, travel, and other things that you enjoy. Managing money—or the lack of managing money—will impact what kind of house you live in, what kind of car you drive, what kind of education your children will have, how much you can give to charities, and what kind of retirement you will have. Few skills will have more of a direct impact on your quality of life than managing your personal finances.

*By carefully reading this chapter and taking the information provided seriously, you will be able to:*

1. Understand the ramifications and the pitfalls of crushing, overwhelming debt.
2. Identify the types of financial aid available to you and identify how each type differs from the others.
3. Understand the importance of your credit history, how to keep it healthy, and how to protect your FICO score.
4. Construct and use a budget.
5. Protect your credit cards and other vital information from identity theft.

# CHAPTER 10 / PROSPER

*"Millions of Americans live paycheck to paycheck. More than half said they would need $500 more per paycheck to live comfortably."*

—Careerbuilder.com, 2007

# WHY READ THIS CHAPTER?

## . . . FROM MY PERSPECTIVE

**NAME:** Melissa VonAschen
**COLLEGE:** Oklahoma State University, Stillwater, OK
**MAJOR:** Geography
**AGE:** 24

Learning to manage money, budget carefully, and pay your bills on time are some of the most important lessons students can learn, and the sooner you learn all this, the better. When I was much younger, I had some large medical bills, and I had no insurance. Since I am supporting myself, I was responsible for these bills. I couldn't pay the bills so I just ignored them and later had a collection agency calling me. The lesson I can pass on to you about not being able to pay your bills is to call the company to which you owe money and make an arrangement for a payment schedule that you can manage. If you don't do this, you may damage your credit score.

I think everyone needs to budget for large and small items, and be sure you can make payments on things like rent, cell phones, car payments, and groceries. One word of caution—I've found that the small miscellaneous items are the ones that cause me the most problems. Small expenditures add up in a hurry so I suggest that you keep track of what you are spending and try to stay within limits for each item.

I have totally stayed away from credit cards because I have heard too many horror stories from my friends. Now that I am close to graduation, I am going to open up two credit card accounts and use them to establish credit. I'll charge small amounts and pay them off early for several months to help establish a good FICO score. You should really pay attention to your credit rating because it will be very important to you when you graduate and try to buy a car or rent an apartment.

My biggest concern about money is paying off student loans. Since I am self-supporting, I had no choice but to borrow money. When I was a first-year student, I was awarded several scholarships and really didn't need all the money that was given to me in student loans, but I took the money anyway. Now, I wish I had taken only the amount I needed to pay for my tuition and books because I am now looking at paying off a considerable amount in student loans. My advice to you is to borrow only what you must have to make it because a day of reckoning will be coming.

# SCAN & QUESTION

In the preface of this book (page xix), you read about the **SQ3R Study Method**. Right now, take a few moments, **scan this chapter**, and on page 276, write **five questions** that you think will be important to your mastery of this material. In addition to the two questions below, you will also find five questions from your authors. Use one of your "*On The Test*" stickers to flag this page for easy reference.

**EXAMPLES:**

▶ **What are four types of financial aid?** (from page 258)

▶ **How does a grant differ from a loan?** (from page 258)

FIGURE

## 10.1 *Types of Aid*

| TYPE | DESCRIPTION |
|------|-------------|
| Federal and state loans | Money that must be repaid with interest—usually beginning six months after your graduation date. |
| Federal and state grants | Monies you do not have to repay—often need-based awards given on a first-come, first-served basis. |
| Scholarships (local, regional, and national) | Money acquired from public and private sources that does not have to be repaid. Often, scholarships are merit based. |
| Work study programs | Money earned while working on campus for your institution. This money does not have to be repaid. |

The most well-known sources of financial assistance are from federal and state governments. Federal and state financial aid programs have been in place for many years and are a staple of assistance for many college students. Figure 10.1 indicates the sources of aid.

Not every school participates in every federal or state assistance program. To determine which type of aid is available at your school, you need to contact the financial aid office.

One of the biggest mistakes students make when thinking about financial aid is forgetting about scholarships from private industry and social or civic organizations. Each year, millions of dollars are unclaimed because students do not know about these scholarships or where to find the necessary information about them. Speak with someone in your financial aid office regarding all types of scholarships.

## Federal Financial Aid Eligibility And Types

**PELL GRANT.** This is a need-based grant awarded to qualified undergraduate students who have not been awarded a previous degree. Amounts vary based on need and costs.

**FEDERAL SUPPLEMENTAL EDUCATIONAL OPPORTUNITY GRANT (FSEOG).** This is a need-based grant awarded to institutions to allocate through their financial aid offices to students.

**STAFFORD LOAN (FORMERLY KNOWN AS THE GUARANTEED STUDENT LOAN).** The Stafford Direct Loan Program is a low-interest, subsidized loan. You must show need to qualify. The government pays the interest while you are in school, but you must be registered for at least half-time status. You begin repayments six months after you leave school.

> How can learning about different loans, scholarships, and work study help you reach your goals?

**UNSUBSIDIZED STAFFORD LOAN.** This Stafford Loan is a low-interest, nonsubsidized loan. You DO NOT have to show need to qualify. You are responsible for the interest on the loan while you are enrolled. Even though the government does not pay the interest, you can defer the interest and the payment until six months after you have left school.

**PLUS LOAN.** This is a federally funded, but state-administered, low-interest loan to qualified parents of students in college. The student must be enrolled at least half-time. Parents must pass a credit check and payments begin 60 days after the last loan payment.

**WORK STUDY.** Work study is a federally funded, need-based program that pays students an hourly wage for working on (and sometimes off) campus. Students earn at least minimum wage.

**HOPE SCHOLARSHIP TAX CREDIT.** This tax credit is for students in their first two years of college who are enrolled at least half-time in a degree or certifi-

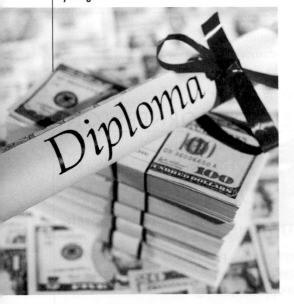

## FIGURE 10.2  *Student Eligibility for Federal Financial Aid\**

To receive aid from the major federal student aid programs, you must:

▶ Have financial need, except for some loan programs.

▶ Hold a high school diploma or GED, pass an independently administered test approved by the U.S. Department of Education, or meet the standards established by your state.

▶ Be enrolled as a regular student working toward a degree or certificate in an eligible program. You may not receive aid for correspondence or telecommunications courses unless they are a part of an associate, bachelor, or graduate degree program.

▶ Be a U.S. citizen.

▶ Have a valid Social Security number.

▶ Make satisfactory academic progress.

▶ Sign a statement of educational purpose.

▶ Sign a statement of updated information.

▶ Register with the Selective Service, if required.

▶ Some federal financial aid may be dependent on your not having a previous drug conviction.

*\*Source: Adapted from The Student Guide: Financial Aid from the U.S. Department of Education. U.S. Dept. of Education, Washington, DC, 2008–2009.*

cate program. Each student taxpayer may receive a 100% tax credit for each year for the first $1,000 of qualified out-of-pocket expenses. They also may claim a 50% credit on the second $1,000 used for qualified expenses (U.S. Bank, 2002).

**PERKINS LOAN.** This is a need-based loan in which the amount of money you can borrow is determined by the government and the availability of funds. The interest rate is 5%, and repayment begins nine months after you leave school or drop below half-time status. You can take up to 10 years to repay the loan. (Note: The federal government may have eliminated this program by the time this book is published.)

## Tips for Applying for Financial Aid

▶ You MUST complete a Free Application for Federal Student Aid (FAFSA) to be eligible to receive ANY federal or state assistance. *You AND your parents* must apply for and obtain a PIN number to complete the FAFSA *if you are considered a dependent*. Because much federal and state money is awarded on a first-come, first-served basis, it is advisable to complete your application as soon after January 1 as possible—even if you have to use the previous year's tax returns and update your application later. Your college's financial aid office can assist you with this process. You can also log onto *www.fafsa.ed.gov* to learn more.

▶ *Do not miss a deadline.* There are *no* exceptions that allow you to make up for missing deadlines for federal financial aid!

▶ *Read all instructions* before beginning the process, always fill out the application completely, and have someone proof your work.

▶ If documentation is required, submit it according to the instructions. Do not fail to do all that the application asks you to do.

▶ Never lie about your financial status.

▶ Begin the application process as soon as possible. Do not wait until the last moment. Some aid is given on a first-come, first-served basis. Income tax preparation time is usually also financial aid application time.

▶ Talk to the financial aid officer at the institution you will attend. Person-to-person contact is always best. Never assume anything until you get it in writing.

FIGURE

## 10.3 *Financial Aid Glossary*

**Borrower**—The person who borrows the funds and agrees to repay them.

**COA**—Cost of attendance. This is the total amount it will cost you to go to college.

**Cosigner**—A person who signs a promissory note and agrees to repay the debt should the borrower default.

**Default**—The term used when you do not repay your student loan. This will prevent you from receiving any further funding. Your wages can be garnished until full restitution is made. Your tax refunds will also be held until full payment is made. This default will also be reported to credit agencies and your credit will be scarred for 7 to 10 years.

**Deferment**—A period of time when you do not have to make loan payments. This period usually applies to education loans and usually lasts only six to nine months.

**EFC**—Expected Family Contribution. The amount of money your family contributes to your educational costs.

**FAFSA**—Free Application for Federal Student Aid. The application that you (or your parents) fill out to determine your financial needs. This is the first step in any financial aid process.

**FAT**—Financial Aid Transcript. A record of your financial assistance from all institutions.

**Gross income**—Your income before taxes and deductions.

**Interest**—The fee (or amount of money) charged to you to borrow money.

**Late fee**—A fee charged to you if you do not make your payment on time.

**Need analysis**—A formula established by Congress to determine your financial need. This is based on your FAFSA form.

**Net income**—Your income after taxes and deductions.

**Payoff**—The total amount owed on a loan if you were to pay it off in one lump sum.

**Principal**—The exact dollar amount that you borrowed and the amount on which interest is charged.

**Promissory note**—A legal document that obligates the borrower to repay funds.

**Selective Service Registration**—If you are required by law to register with Selective Service, you must do so before you can qualify for federal student aid.

---

Have you allotted enough time in your schedule to fill out your financial aid application completely and accurately?

▶ Take copies of fliers and brochures that are available from the financial aid office. Private companies and civic groups will often notify the financial aid office if they have funds available.

▶ Always apply for admission as well as financial aid. Many awards are given by the college to students who have already been accepted.

▶ If you are running late with an application, find out if there are electronic means of filing.

   ▶ Always keep a copy of your tax returns for each year!

   ▶ To receive almost any money, including some scholarships, you must fill out the FAFSA form.

   ▶ Apply for everything possible. You will get nothing if you do not apply.

# STUDENT LOANS

## A Day of Reckoning Will Come. Will You Be Ready?

The high cost of college makes tuition out of reach for many families. In recent years, "college tuition has risen at twice the rate of consumer prices. Tuition has soared much faster than pay has for the kinds of low-wage jobs that students tend to hold" (Block, 2006), making it much more difficult for students to work in the summer and pay for the coming year of college. Today a student would have to work an entire year to pay for one year of public college education, and that assumes that he or she saved every penny of his or her earnings. For many students, the only way they can attend college is with student loans. If this is the only way you can go to college, borrow the money—but borrow no more than you absolutely must. Try not to borrow anything but tuition and perhaps room and board. Get a job, budget, cut out extras, work in the summers, attend college via a

**FIGURE 10.4** *Total Interest Paid*

| AMOUNT OF MONEY BORROWED BY YOU | YOUR INTEREST RATE (AVERAGE) | TOTAL YEARS TO REPAY (20 YEARS IS THE AVERAGE) | YOUR MONTHLY PAYMENT | TOTAL INETREST PAID BY YOU (YOUR COST TO BORROW THE MONEY) |
|---|---|---|---|---|
| $ 5,000 | 7% | 10 | $ 58.05 | $ 1,966.00 |
| | | 20 | $ 38.76 | $ 4,302.40 |
| | | 30 | $ 33.27 | $ 6,977.20 |
| $ 10,000 | 7% | 10 | $ 116.11 | $ 3,933.20 |
| | | 20 | $ 77.53 | $ 8,607.20 |
| | | 30 | $ 66.53 | $ 13,950.80 |
| $ 15,000 | 7% | 10 | $ 174.16 | $ 5,899.20 |
| | | 20 | $ 116.29 | $ 12,909.60 |
| | | 30 | $ 99.80 | $ 20,928.00 |
| $ 20,000 | 7% | 10 | $ 232.22 | $ 7,866.40 |
| | | 20 | $ 155.06 | $ 17,214.40 |
| | | 30 | $ 133.06 | $ 27,901.60 |
| $ 30,000 | 7% | 10 | $ 348.33 | $ 11,799.60 |
| | | 20 | $ 232.59 | $ 25,821.60 |
| | | 30 | $ 199.59 | $ 41,852.40 |

cooperative program, enroll in online courses, take fewer credits even though it delays graduation, live at home—do everything possible not to borrow more money than you must.

Many students are finding it necessary to extend their student loans over a period of 30 years just to keep their heads above water; of course, if one does that, the interest paid is also higher. For example, a student who takes 30 years to pay off a $20,000 loan at 6.8% will pay about $27,000 in interest plus the principal, compared to $7,619 interest on a loan paid off in 10 years (Block, 2006). You will have to repay the money that you have borrowed. Period! ***Even bankruptcy will not relieve you of this debt*** because student loans are not subject to bankruptcy laws; so again, don't borrow any money that you don't absolutely need. Consider the examples in Figure 10.4.

# KNOW THE SCORE

## Why Is Understanding Your Credit History Important to Your Future?

Many college students don't even know they have a credit score, yet this score is the single most important factor that will determine if you get approved for a mortgage, car loan, credit card, insurance, etc. Furthermore, if you get approved, this credit score will determine what rate of interest you have to pay (Broderick, 2003). You can order one free credit score online by accessing the Web site *https://www.annualcreditreport.com*.

## Range of Scores and What FICO Means for You

This information may seem trivial right now, and you might not want to be bothered with more information, but the truth is, you must pay attention to this because your FICO score has long-lasting implications for almost everything you want to do. The sooner you understand the importance of this score and take steps to keep it healthy, the better off you will be.

ESSENTIAL CORNERSTONE

**Resourcefulness:**
How can being resourceful help me reduce the amount I have to borrow in student loans?

**Social Networking Moment:**
Share your response to this Essential Cornerstone with peers in your social network. Choose two responses from your peers and respond to their postings.

FIGURE

## 10.6 *Economic Readiness Assessment*

In the spaces below, please read each question carefully, respond with Yes or No, and then answer the question based on your financial research for **next semester.** Be specific. You may have to visit the financial aid office, bookstore, or other campus resource center to answer the questions.

| QUESTION | ANSWER | RESPONSE |
|---|---|---|
| I know exactly how much my tuition will cost next semester. | YES  NO | Answer: $_____ |
| I know the cost of lab fees, technology fees, and other fees associated with my courses. | YES  NO | Answer: $_____ |
| I know how much my textbooks will cost next semester. | YES  NO | Answer: $_____ |
| I know how much my transportation will cost next semester (car payment, gas, insurance, bus passes, etc.). | YES  NO | Answer: $_____ |
| I know how much I need to spend on supplies for next semester. | YES  NO | Answer: $_____ |
| I know how much child care will cost next semester. | YES  NO | Answer: $_____ |
| I know where my GPA must remain to keep my financial aid. | YES  NO | Answer: _____ |
| I know how much money I can borrow through the Guaranteed Student Loan Program in one academic year. | YES  NO | Answer: $_____ |
| I know how much money I need to manage my personal budget in a single semester. | YES  NO | Answer: $_____ |
| I have estimated miscellaneous and unexpected costs that might occur during the semester. | YES  NO | Answer: $_____ |
| I know what a FAFSA is and how and WHEN to apply. | YES  NO | Answer: _____ |
| I know how a drug arrest could affect my financial aid. | YES  NO | Answer: _____ |
| I know the scholarships available to me, how, when, and where to apply for them. | YES  NO | Answer: _____ |
| I know how and where to apply for work study. | YES  NO | Answer: _____ |
| I know how a felony charge affects my ability to get a job after graduation. | YES  NO | Answer: _____ |
| | | TOTAL $_____ |

> Can you imagine paying for a piece of pizza for 12 years?

you are spending. According to the article "Live Without Plastic" (Rosato, 2008), after McDonald's started accepting credit and debit cards in 2004, diners who paid with plastic spent $7 a visit on average compared to $4.50 when they paid in cash. The article also suggests that you are less aware of what you spend if you use plastic. For example, 68% of cash-paying students exiting a college bookstore knew how much they'd spent. Conversely, only 35% of students using plastic knew what they'd spent. Rosato also reports that you are willing to pay more for the same stuff if you are using plastic instead of real money.

"Imagine being 30 years old and still paying off a slice of pizza you bought when you were 18 and in college. Sounds crazy, but for plenty of people problems with credit card debt can lead to that very situation" (Collegeboard, 2008). If you borrow excessively and pay only the minimum each month, it will be very easy to find yourself over your head with credit card problems. Take the case of Joe. "Joe's average unpaid credit card bill over a year is $500, and his finance charge is 20 percent. He pays a $20 annual fee plus a $25 late fee (he was up late studying and forgot to mail in his check). Joe ends up owing $145 to his credit card company, and he still hasn't paid for any of his purchases" (Collegeboard, 2008).

**FIGURE**

## 10.7 *Important Facts You Need To Know About Credit Cards*

What you don't know can wreck your credit rating and can ruin your life. Listed below are some of the most important things you can learn about managing credit card debt.

✔ Understand that credit cards are nothing more than high interest loans—in some cases, very high! The system is designed to keep you in debt.

✔ Be aware that companies often add on new fees and change policies after customers already have signed up.

✔ If you fall behind on payments to one creditor or if your credit score drops for any reason, your rates can be raised on all your credit cards.

✔ Banks can and will abruptly switch your due date so pay attention. Always check your bill to see if any fees or charges have been added.

✔ Avoid cards that charge an annual fee just for the privilege of carrying their card. This fee can be as high as $100–$400 per year. If you charge this fee, it will be automatically added to your card and then you begin paying interest on the fee.

✔ Be sure your card allows for a grace period before interest is charged.

✔ Carry only one or two credit cards so you can manage your debt and not get in over your head. Do not accept or sign up for cards that you don't need.

✔ When you accept a card, sign it right away and keep records of your credit card numbers (in a secure location) and the phone number to contact in case they are lost or stolen. If you lose your card, report it immediately to avoid charges.

✔ Avoid the temptation to charge. You should use credit cards only when you absolutely must and only when you can pay the full amount before interest is added. "Buy now, pay later" is a dangerous game.

✔ When you pay off a card, celebrate and don't use that as a reason to charge again. Lock that card in a safe place and leave it there.

✔ Each month, always try to pay more than the "minimum payment due."

✔ Send the payment at least five days in advance. Late fees now represent the third-largest revenue stream for banks.

✔ Call the credit card company and negotiate a better rate. If they won't give you a better rate, tell them you are going to transfer the debt.

✔ If you have several credit card debts, consolidate all the amounts on the card where you have the lowest balance. Don't cancel your cards because it helps your credit score if you have cards on which you have no debt. Just don't use them again!

✔ Do not leave any personal information (credit cards, Social Security numbers, checking accounts) in places where roommates or other students have access to them. Purchase a metal file box with a lock and keep it in a secure place.

✔ Consider using a debit card. Money is deducted directly from your bank account and you cannot spend more than you actually have.

✔ If you have already gotten into credit card trouble, get *reputable* counseling. One of the best agencies is the National Foundation for Credit Counseling (NFCC).

✔ Be aware that using a credit card carelessly is similar to a drug addiction. Credit card use is habit forming and addictive!

✔ Ask yourself these questions: "If I can't pay this credit card in full this month, what is going to change next month? Will I have extra income or will I reduce my spending enough to pay for this purchase?" If the answers are "No," you don't need to make the purchase.

✔ Realize that you are building your future credit rating even though you are a student.

*Once you get a credit card, immediately write, "CHECK ID" across the back in RED, permanent ink.*

Most credit card companies charge a very high rate of interest—18 to 21% or higher. If you are late with a payment, the interest rate can go even higher. For every $1,000 you charge, you will pay from $180 to $210 in interest each year, states Konowalow (2003). Don't be fooled by the ploy of "1.5% interest." This means 1.5% each month, which equates to 18% per year. The best practice is to charge no more than you can pay off each month while avoiding high interest rates. Consider the tips in Figure 10.7.

# THE PITFALLS OF PAYDAY LOANS, CAR TITLE LOANS, AND RENT-TO-OWN CONTRACTS

## Did You Know There's Someone Lurking on Every Corner to Take Your Money?

Many unsuspecting consumers have been duped into signing car title loans, payday loans, or rent-to-own contracts that resulted in very high monthly payments and penalties. Some were told by their title loan broker before they signed the contract that they could make a partial payment if they needed to and this would be OK. Unfortunately, the unsuspecting victims find out too late that their car is going to be repossessed due to one late or partial payment. Others realize too late that on a loan of

## THINKING *for* CHANGE: An Activity for Critical Reflection

Jonathon is having a great time at college. He has joined a fraternity, is loving going to football games, and is managing to keep his grades up. But he's already got a major problem—keeping up with his expenses. He is spending much more money than he has coming in. His parents told him he could join a fraternity, but that he would have to pay these expenses from the allowance they provide him every month. He and his parents made the decision for him not to work his first year, so he is in a bind.

To compound his problems, he has met a great girl, and he has tried hard to impress her by taking her to expensive clubs and out to dinner. He took her to his frat dance and that cost a bundle. He didn't have the funds so he charged everything on his new credit card. Jonathon is getting very stressed about his money situation. He's having trouble sleeping well. Fraternity dues are coming up again soon. There is a big interfraternity/

sorority dance at the end of the semester that is high on his new girlfriend's list. Now she is talking about going on a cruise for spring break. He is very worried because he has already maxed out one credit card and has heavy charges on the other one. Jonathon has calculated that if he charges $1,000 on his card and makes only the minimum payment, it will take 15 ½ years for him to pay for the cruise. He doesn't want to disappoint his girlfriend and fears losing her if he doesn't go on the cruise. But clearly, he has to make some changes.

What are two things you would advise Jonathon to do right away?

1. _____
2. _____

List two other suggestions that you would make to Jonathon to help him get control of his expenses.

1. _____
2. _____

$400, they must pay back over $500 that month. According to recent reports from consumer affairs groups, some institutions have been charging as much as 250% interest on an annualized basis (Cojonet, 2003). In some instances, interest rates as high as 900% have been charged due to poor government regulatory policies. Some states have recently enacted laws to prevent this.

Payday loans are extremely expensive compared to other cash loans. For example, a $300 cash advance on the average credit card, repaid in one month, would cost $13.99 in finance charges and an annual interest rate of almost 57%, which is very high. By comparison, however, a payday loan costing $17.50 per $100 for the same $300 would cost $105 if renewed one time or 426% annual interest (Pay Day Loan Consumer Information, 2008). As bad as credit card debt is, it pales in comparison to the pitfalls of payday loans.

# SMALL COSTS ADD UP!

## How Much Money Will You Throw Down the Drain in 10 Years?

Many people pay more money for convenience. If you are on a tight budget, you might want to give up some of the conveniences so that you can hold onto more of your money. Although we want you to really live and enjoy life, we also want you to take a hard look at where your money goes. Those dimes, quarters, and dollars add up quickly. In fact, small-amount money drains for the typical person can add up to $175,000 over a 10-year period. What if you could hold onto some of that money and invest it? What would that money be worth to you when you are 65 and want to retire? Is having sausage biscuits and orange juice from a fast-food restaurant really worth $3.50 a day or $1,274 if you have that *every day for one year*? Did you ever stop to think that if you spend $3.50 every day on fast food or coffee or whatever for 10 *years*, you would be spending $12,740?

## The 10-Year Plan

According to the Web site The Digerati Life (2008), some other prime causes of money drain are:

▶ **Gum**—a pack a day will cost you $5,488 in 10 years.

▶ **Bottled water**—One bottle a day will cost you almost $5,500 in 10 years. (Most bottled water comes from no special source and is no better than tap water.)

▶ **Eating lunch out daily**—Even if you spend only $9, this will cost you over $35,000 in 10 years. If you can eat lunch at home, you will save so much money.

▶ **Junk food, vending machine snacks**—This will cost you at least $4,000 in 10 years if you are a light snacker, and they are empty calories.

▶ **Unused memberships**—Those gym memberships that look so enticing and, for many people, go unused will total over $7,500 in 10 years.

▶ **Expensive salon visits**—Fake nails along with the salon visit can cost over $30,000 in 10 years. Is that really how you want to spend your money?

▶ **Cigarettes**—Not only will this terrible habit kill you and make people want to avoid you, it will cost you over $25,000 in 10 years if you smoke a pack a day.

These are just a few of the drains that take our money and keep us from being wealthy when we are older. Maybe you want to splurge at times and go for the convenience, but day in and day out, you can really save a lot of money if you budget your time and do some of these things for yourself.

Examine the following information about *The Latte Factor*™ (Figure 10.8), and apply it to your own spending habits.

FIGURE

## 10.8    *The Latte Factor*™

In his book *The Finish Rich Notebook* (2003), Bach states, "How much you earn has no bearing on whether or not you will build wealth." As a rule, the more we make, the more we spend. Many people spend far more than they make and subject themselves to stress, exorbitant debt, fear, and an ultimate future of poverty.

Bach uses the Latte Factor™ to call people's attention to how much money we carelessly throw away when we should be saving and investing for the future. He uses the story of a young woman who said she could not invest because she had no money. Yet, almost every day she bought a large latte for $3.50 and a muffin for $1.50. If you add a candy bar here, a drink there, a shake at the gym, you could easily be spending $10 a day that could be invested.

If you take that $10 per day and invest it faithfully until retirement, you would have enough money to pay cash for a home and a new car, and have money left over. This is the power of compound interest! If you are a relatively young person, you will probably work that many years and more, so you could retire with an extra $1 million in addition to any other savings you might have accumulated.

The point is that most of us have the ability to become rich, but we either lack the knowledge or the discipline to do so. Remember the Latte Factor™ as you begin your college career and practice it, along with other sound financial strategies, if you want to become a millionaire.

### DID YOU KNOW

**WARREN BUFFET** is worth over $62 BILLION and still lives in the home he bought in 1958 for $31,500.

Born in 1930, Mr. Buffett, a native Nebraskan, is not only one of the world's wealthiest people, most savvy investors, most successful businessmen, and financial intellectuals, but also one of the most philanthropic. He recently announced that he is leaving 83% of his wealth to the Bill and Melinda Gates Foundation.

Having always been "financially smart," he filed his first income tax return at the age of 13 so that he could deduct the cost of his bicycle as a business expense. At age 15, he and a friend spent $25 to purchase a pinball machine, which they placed in a barber shop. A few months later, they owned three machines in different locations.

He applied to Harvard in 1950 but was denied entrance. He attended and graduated from Columbia University and began working as a stockbroker. His first real business venture, the purchase of a Texaco gas station, did not work out very well. He then decided to enroll in a public speaking course and began teaching an investment class at the University of Nebraska.

**Calculate your own Latte Factor™.** For example, if you buy one diet soda each morning for $1.81, then your Latte Factor™ is $685.84 per year ($1.81 × 7 days/week × 52 weeks/year).

My daily "have to have it" is _____
It costs $ _____ per day
My Latte Factor™ is $ _____

Small expenditures add up. What you do today may inhibit your ability to buy a car, purchase a house, and even get certain jobs!

# PROTECT YOURSELF FROM IDENTITY THEFT

## Why Are College Campuses Ground Zero?

"Amid all the back-to-school activities and tasks that college students face, one of the most important is to protect their identities. You have such busy schedules that you may unknowingly expose yourself to identity theft and fraud, particularly when you're making online purchases or engaging in social-networking web sites. We're all living in an extremely open environment where free flow of information is the norm, as opposed to the exception," said Adam Levin, cofounder of Identity Theft 911 (Yip, 2008). Because college students tend to move often, their mail service may be interrupted if they don't follow through with change-of-address cards. By the time their information catches up to them, they may have already suffered from identity theft. "All these things make this group vulnerable," said Thomas Harkins, chief strategy officer of Secure Identity Systems (Yip, 2008).

People who may steal your identity are roommates, relatives, friends, estranged spouses, restaurant servers, and others who have ready access to your papers. They may steal your wallet, go through your trash, or take your mail. They can even legally photocopy your vital information at the courthouse if, for example, you have been divorced. The Internet provides thieves many other opportunities to use official-looking e-mail messages designed to obtain your personal information. Do not provide personal information over the Internet no matter how official the Web site might look. Reputable businesses will not inquire about your personal information in this manner.

It is very difficult, if not impossible, to catch identity thieves. While you may not be liable, you still have to spend your time filing expensive legal affidavits, writing letters, and making telephone calls to clear your good name.

## How to Minimize Identity Theft Risk

Criminals are very clever, and many are adept at using electronic means to steal your personal information. According to a variety of financial sources, there are a number of ways to avoid having your identity stolen:

▶ Carry only the ID and cards you need at any given time.

▶ Do not make Internet purchases from sites that are unsecured (check for a padlock icon to ensure safety).

▶ Do not write your PIN number, Social Security number, or passcode on any information that can be stolen or that you are discarding. Do not keep this information in your wallet or exposed in your living space.

▶ Try to memorize your passwords instead of recording them on paper or in the computer.

▶ Buy a shredder and use it.

▶ Avoid providing your Social Security number to any organization until you have verified its legitimacy.

▶ Check your credit file periodically by requesting a copy of your report.

▶ Do not complete credit card applications at displays set up on campus. This exposes your personal information to people you don't know.

▶ Use your home address as your permanent mailing address rather than a temporary address while in school.

▶ Do not provide personal information on a social network that can be accessed by an identity thief. You don't know these people!

▶ Carry your wallet in your front pocket instead of your back pocket.

▶ Place security freezes on your credit scores. This prevents anyone from looking at your credit report except the companies that already have a financial relationship with you. Lenders who can't pull your credit report are unlikely to grant new credit to someone else in your name.

▶ Opt out of preapproved credit offers, which are easy ways for identity thieves to steal your personal identity. This stops credit bureaus from selling your name to lenders. Go to the opt-out Web site at *www.optoutprescreen.com* or call 888-567-8688.

▶ Don't use obvious passwords like your birthday, your mother's maiden name, or the last four digits of your Social Security number.

(Adapted from Consumer Response Center brochure, *Identity Theft and Fraud*, 2003; *ConsumerReport, Money Advisor*, 2008; *The State* Newspaper, August 31, 2008)

He later became a major shareholder in the firm Berkshire Hathaway, which purchased major shares in The *Washington Post* Company, ABC, Geico, Dairy Queen, and Coca-Cola. The most he has ever taken as an actual salary from all of his ventures and investments is $100 per year. It was reported in 2006 that Mr. Buffett does NOT carry a cell phone, does NOT have a computer at his desk, and drives his own car.

Upon his death, his children will NOT inherit much of his wealth. He has been quoted as saying, *"I want to give my kids just enough so that they would feel that they could do anything, but not so much that they would feel like doing nothing."*

*(Adapted from Forbes, Wikipedia, and About.com)*

**Tips for Personal Success**

Consider the following suggestions for improving your financial status during the semester:

▶ Practice delayed gratification.

▶ Reduce your Latte Factor™.

▶ Talk to an advisor about taking a personal finance course next semester as an elective.

Now, it is your turn. What three things could you implement to change your financial management practices?

1. _____

2. _____

3. _____

# From Ordinary to Extraordinary

## REAL PEOPLE | REAL LIVES | REAL CHANGE

**LEO G. BORGES**
Founder and Former CEO
Borges and Mahoney, San Francisco, CA

Tulare, California, is still a farming community today, but in 1928 when I was born, it was totally agricultural and an exceptionally rural, detached part of the world. My parents had immigrated to California from the Azore Islands years earlier in search of a better life—the American dream. My father died when I was 3 years old and when I was 11, my mother passed away. Even though I lived with and was raised by my sisters, the feelings of aloneness and isolation were the two primary feelings I had growing up. We were orphans. We were poor. We were farm kids. We were Portuguese—not Americans. Every day, someone reminded us of these realities. One positive thing remained, however. My mother always told us that we could be anything or

> We were orphans. We were poor. We were farm kids. We were Portuguese—not Americans.

have anything if we believed in it and worked hard for it.

I left home at 17 to attend a program in advertising in San Francisco. Later that year, I moved to Los Angeles and began working for a major advertising firm. From there I enlisted in the Coast Guard, and when my duty was over, I worked for an oil company and then a major leasing firm. In each position, I worked my way up the ladder, strove to do my very best, and proved that I was capable of doing anything regardless of my background.

When I was in my early forties, my best friend, Cliff, and I decided to start our own business. We were tired of working in "middle management" and knew that we could be successful if we worked hard. After much research and consulting with companies across the

country, we determined that we would start a company in the water treatment business.

You may be asking yourself, "What experience did an advertising agency, an oil company, and a leasing firm give him to start a business in water treatment?" The answer is none. However, Cliff was an excellent accountant and I was an excellent salesman. We found a third partner who was one of the leading water treatment experts in the world and we were off. It was not easy and we had to eat beans for many meals, but Borges and Mahoney, Inc. was born.

Our first office was a small storefront in San Francisco. Through the development of our superior products, expert advice to clients, and outstanding customer service, we grew and grew, finally moving to our largest location in San Rafael, California. By the time we sold our business some 20 years later, we had 15 full-time employees and annual revenues in the millions of dollars.

270

# From Ordinary to Extraordinary

## REAL PEOPLE | REAL LIVES | REAL CHANGE

To this day, I attribute my success to the fact that I was determined to show everyone—my sisters, cousins, aunts and uncles, former co-workers, friends and foes—that I would never let my past, my heritage, my economic background, or my history hold me back. I knew that I could be a success. Through hard work, determination, and surrounding myself with supportive, brilliant people, I proved that the American dream my parents sought years earlier is truly possible for anyone who works hard, believes in him- or herself, and doesn't give up. It is possible for you, too.

## EXTRAORDINARY REFLECTION

**Read the following statement and respond in your online journal or class notebook.**

Mr. Borges states that through "hard work, determination, and surrounding himself with supportive, brilliant people," he and his partner, Cliff, were able to become very successful in business and beyond. Who can you call upon in your life to offer you support, advice, and provide you with solid, smart advice? What questions do you need to ask them?

How careful are you when it comes to protecting your financial and medical records?

# BATTLING THE BIG "IF'S"

## Do You Know What to Do When You Need Something?

Below, you will find some helpful tips for managing some important financial decisions in your life and protecting yourself when things get tough.

### IF YOU NEED TO PURCHASE A CAR

▶ Do not purchase a new car. We know it is tempting, but the value will plummet 20 to 40% the moment you drive off the lot. It is just not worth it! Purchase a two- to three-year old car from a reputable dealer.

▶ DON'T fall in love with a car before you know everything about it. Love is blind when it comes to people . . . and cars, too!

▶ Purchase an extended warranty, BUT read the terms carefully.

▶ Always ask for a "Car-fax" and a title search and make the dealer pay for them.

▶ Check to see if your state has a "Lemon Law" and if so, read it carefully.

▶ Don't be pressured into a sale by lines such as: "This is our last one like this," or "I've got several people interested in this car." Let them have it!

▶ Make sure the car has passed the smog test if one is required in your state.

### IF YOU NEED TO SAVE ON FUEL

▶ Consider carpooling.

▶ Make sure your car is in good running condition and that your tires are inflated properly. Get your car tuned up often.

▶ Drive slower and at a constant speed when possible. Driving 74 mph instead of 55 mph increases fuel consumption by as much as 20%.

▶ Check your car's air filter and fuel filter and replace them if they are dirty.

▶ Do not use "Jack Rabbit" starts. Accelerate easily after red lights and stop signs. "Flooring it" costs money.

▶ When stuck in traffic, try to drive at a steady pace and not stop and start. Watch how the large trucks do this—they seldom come to a complete stop.

▶ Plan your trips so that you can make the most number of right turns, thus saving time at lights. Also, combine your errands so that you can make fewer trips.

- ▶ Clean out your car. Carrying around just a few extra pounds in the trunk or backseat costs fuel.

- ▶ Stick with the wheels and tires that came with your car. Using larger wheels and tires than recommended creates more drag and weight on your car and costs you more fuel.

- ▶ Use the telephone. Often, many things can be accomplished without personal visits.

### IF YOU FEEL THE URGE TO MAKE AN IMPULSE PURCHASE

- ▶ Use the 72-hour rule. Wait 72 hours to make any purchase over $50.

- ▶ If you still feel the need to purchase the item after 72 hours, consider your budget and how you are going to pay for the item.

Do you work hard to control everyday and impulse spending?

- ▶ Consider waiting until you can pay cash for the item, or consider putting the item on lay-away. Do not charge it!

- ▶ Purchase the item later as a reward to yourself for getting all A's in your classes.

- ▶ Think about how purchasing this item will affect your family's budget.

- ▶ Make as few trips out shopping as possible to lower your temptation to purchase things you can't afford.

### IF YOUR GROCERY BILL IS OUT OF CONTROL

- ▶ Shop with a calculator and enter each item as you place it into your cart. This will give you a great idea of what you're spending.

- ▶ Create a menu for each day of the week and shop only for the items on your list. Do not shop when you are in a hurry, tired, or after working all day.

- ▶ Consider purchasing generic brands—often they are the same product as brand-name items, just with a different label.

- ▶ Clip coupons. They actually work. Go online to your favorite product's Web site and print out their online coupons. Try to shop when stores double or triple coupons' value.

- ▶ Consider cooking in bulk and then freezing leftovers for later in the week.

- ▶ Look for placement of the product in the store. Items at chest level are the most expensive. Look up and down on the shelves to find less expensive items.

- ▶ Do not shop for convenience items such as premade meals, bakery items, or boneless chicken breasts. Purchase an entire chicken and cut it up. You'll save a lot of money this way.

- ▶ Buy in bulk at one of the major warehouse stores. Often this can save a lot of money if you are buying for a large family.

CHANGING IDEAS TO *Reality*

**REFLECTIONS ON FINANCIAL RESPONSIBILITY**

Although many young people fail in the management of their personal finances, there is no reason that you cannot manage your financial business well. You should think about personal finance and the management of money and investments as basic survival skills that are very important to you now, as well as for the rest of your life.

Since only 10% of high school students graduate from high school with any kind of instruction in personal finance, learning to budget your money, make wise investments, and avoid credit card debt are priority needs of all college students. As you move toward establishing yourself in a career, it is important to remember that to get what you want out of life, a significant part of your success will depend on your ability to make sound money decisions. We hope you will learn to make money work for you instead of your having to work hard for money because of poor decisions made early in life. En route to becoming a good money manager, the following tips will assist you:

▶ Don't get caught in the credit card trap.

▶ Know exactly how you are spending your money.

▶ Protect your credit rating by using wise money management strategies.

▶ Learn all you can about scholarships and grants.

▶ Understand the regulations about repaying student loans.

▶ Don't borrow any more money than you absolutely have to.

▶ Ask for your credit score at least once a year and be sure you have a good one.

▶ Use only one or two credit cards.

▶ Try to pay off your credit card each month before any interest is charged.

▶ Write down your credit card numbers and keep them in a safe place in case your cards are lost or stolen.

▶ If you get into credit card trouble, get counseling.

▶ Learn everything you can about investments and retirement plans.

Learning to manage your money and protecting your credit rating will be as important to you as getting your degree. It is never too early to learn about money management. If you can do it when you have just a little money, it will be easier when you have more money.

*"Never work just for money or for power. They won't save your soul or help you sleep at night."*

*—Marian Wright Edelman*

# KNOWLEDGE in BLOOM

## Improving Your Money Management Skills

Each chapter-end assessment is based on *Bloom's Taxonomy of Learning*. See the inside front cover for a quick review.

### UTILIZES LEVELS 1–6 ON THE TAXONOMY

**PROCESS:** As a beginning college student, it is not too early for you to map out your financial future. In this exercise, you will be asked to list some of your pressing financial concerns and discuss how you might spend more wisely. You will be asked to apply principles of financial management as you analyze your overall current financial management profile, design a plan for improvement, and critique your plan after practicing it for a week.

**Level 1 Question:** List three of your most pressing financial concerns:

1. _____
2. _____
3. _____

**Level 2 Question: Give examples** of how you might improve your money management techniques relative to these three concerns and spend more wisely.

_____
_____
_____

**Level 3 Question: Prepare** a plan for improving how you spend your money in these three areas only.

_____
_____
_____

**Level 4 Question: Analyze** your current financial management practices using the information you have studied in this chapter. Discuss your income, your expenses, student loans, credit card debt, impulse-buying habits, and overall financial situation at the moment. Be sure to list financial concerns.

_____
_____
_____

**Level 5 Question:** Now that you have been honest with yourself and have identified current financial practices and concerns, **design** a plan for improvement by listing steps that you will employ to practice better financial management.

_____
_____
_____

**Level 6 Question:** Follow your plan for a week. Write down everything you spend, the things you resist that you might have typically bought, and strategies you have employed to improve. After a week, **evaluate your plan and your ability to stick with this plan at this point.**

_____
_____
_____
_____

# CHAPTER 11

# PLAN

## FOCUSING ON YOUR PROFESSIONAL CAREER AND LIVING WELL

# SCAN & QUESTION

In the preface of this book (page xix), you read about the **SQ3R Study Method**. Right now, take a few moments, **scan this chapter**, and on page 302, write **five questions** that you think will be important to your mastery of this material. In addition to the two questions below, you will find five questions from your authors. Use one of your **"On The Test"** stickers to flag this page for easy reference.

**EXAMPLES:**

▶ **Why is it important to write an excellent resume?** (from page 291)

▶ **What does R.E.W.A.R.D.S. stand for?** (from page 297)

# PLANNING FOR THE FUTURE

## What's Change Got to Do with It?

Change has got everything to do with it! One of the things that human beings have the most difficulty handling is change. Yet, never before in the history of the world have people been bombarded with so many changes—and they are not likely to slow down anytime soon. If you look at technology, for example, you know that you hardly learn to use one version of a cell phone or computer before a newer and greater version is on the market. Because change is going to be a watchword for your generation, your authors have interwoven one central theme—**change**—throughout your text, and nowhere does it apply more powerfully than in planning for a career and your future.

The very first chapter of this book focused on change, which shows you how important change is to your future. The entire book is based on the changes you may need to make as you move through your college career, as well as the multitude of changes that are coming your way in every aspect of your life. We have focused so much attention on change because it is real, now, and in your face.

What changes do you foresee coming in your chosen career field in the next five years?

# WHAT AM I GOING TO DO FOR THE REST OF MY LIFE?

## How Do I Make Such an Awesome Decision?

"What am I going to do for the rest of my life?" is an overwhelming question for anyone, much less a beginning college student, especially in a dramatically changing global environment. What was true last year—and sometimes even last week—is no longer true. Your generation has a wonderful opportunity to be the first generation that truly functions in a world economy; at the same time, you have the concern of having few guidelines to follow.

While many things that worked for your parents and grandparents are still important and relevant today—things like ethics, integrity, hard work, education, honesty, teamwork—many practices that were true in their time are no longer valid. Your grandfather may have gone to work for a company and stayed there all his life. Back then, employers were loyal to employees, and employees were loyal to the company. Work stayed pretty much the same from one year to the next. All that has changed. You will have many different jobs during your lifetime—you will most likely have three or four different careers, and what constitutes your work will be constantly changing.

## What Is the Difference Between a Career and a Job?

A job is just a place you go to earn a paycheck or a task that an employer assigns to you. It could be making hamburgers at a fast-food restaurant. A career could be owning a chain of fast-food restaurants, which allows you to be the entrepreneur you always wanted to become. A career is something you own. Employers will be looking for people who can fill a job; you should be looking for a career that enhances your life. You need to use jobs to progress within your career choice. You might use your current or future job to move forward in a career progression, applying skills, experience, and knowledge to advance. The ideal career will provide internal rewards as well as monetary satisfaction.

# 10 BABY STEPS THAT WILL BECOME GIANT SUCCESSES TOMORROW

> What unique interests, skills, and talents do you possess to give you that "cutting edge" in today's workforce?

## What Strategies Can I Use to Successfully Prepare for My Future?

You might consider what you are doing today and the rest of your college career as baby steps that will lead to giant steps in being prepared for the future. The following strategies will help you as you move toward your goals.

**1. Master the material and make good grades.** Grades do matter! While not everyone can graduate with a 4.0 GPA, you need to be one of those people who earns a respectable GPA. Not only do good grades show that you have gained knowledge in certain areas, they also indicate the work ethic and sense of responsibility that employers are seeking.

**2. Come to grips with your abilities, interests, values, and personal characteristics.** You might be telling people that you want to be a corporate attorney or a businesswoman. Do you really know what these careers entail? How many years of education are required? What kind of GPA does it take to get into a really good business school?

Specifically, what do you want to do? Where will the jobs be? What kind of preparation does it take? Do you have the ability and perseverance to become what you dream about becoming?

**3. Fine-tune your computer skills.** Most first-year students today have good computer skills, but these skills need to be very strong. Your skills need to include the ability to work with spreadsheets, databases, and PowerPoint. Some careers will require knowledge and expertise of industry software—you need to be an expert if this is true in the field you want to work in. Learn to develop Web pages, and create your own Web site that reflects a professional, career-oriented person.

**4. Hone your communication (speaking and writing) skills.** By now, you are tired of hearing this, but it's true. Enroll in classes that are writing and speaking intensive, even if you hate the thought of doing so, because many recruiters point out the weaknesses of applicants' writing and speaking skills. Good communications skills could be a major asset to you in a job search in the future. You have to pay the price to become a good writer and speaker!

> "A study has shown that first and second year students spend more time deciding on a movie to watch than on what they might want for a career, even though a movie lasts two hours and a career lasts a lifetime."
> —Bob Orndorff

# From Ordinary to Extraordinary

REAL PEOPLE | REAL LIVES | REAL CHANGE

**MARK JONES**
SCANA Senior Customer Service Trainer
Columbia, SC

*My proudest moment?* Finally coming to the realization that I am a functional member of a highly dysfunctional family. *"I know. I know. Many people say they have a dysfunctional family,"* but in my case, it is the raw, inescapable truth. My realization may not sound like much to an outsider, but when you finally realize that you do not have to be a victim of your family or your past, it is a proud moment! I can confidently say, *"I am not like them."*

I don't have any memories of a time when my family was "normal." My mother, who has been clinically depressed my entire life, attempted suicide when I was four years old. I have never known a day when she was not heavily medicated. My father had the first of four heart attacks when I was six. My parents divorced when I was 11 and I went to live with my father. My mother remarried when I was 13. When I was 15—my father died, leaving us very little. Even the mobile home in which we lived was repossessed.

My new stepfather was legally blind and has never driven a car. My mother did not drive either. They never wanted me to get my permit or drive and fought my attempts to do so for years. They thought walking everywhere was perfectly normal. My stepfather did not have any children of his own and did not have any parenting skills. I was treated more as a tenant than a son or stepson. As a matter of fact, I had to pay rent to live with him and my own mother. Due to my father's death, I drew a small Social Security check until I graduated from high school. Every month, much of that money had to be turned over to my stepfather. I even had to buy my own bed to sleep in. Of course, we had our share of good times, too. But I knew this situation was far from "normal"—whatever that was.

When I was in my early twenties, I begged a dear friend, Stella, to let me use her car so I could try for my driver's license. I had practically no driving experience, but somehow, I passed the test. I paid $200 for my first car in two installments of $100 each. It was a 1973 Buick LeSabre that was wrecked down one entire side and had been used in demolition donut field races. But, it was much better than walking everywhere. This was a turning point in my life. I was in my early twenties and working in a local grocery store. I had enrolled in the university right after high school, but I

> I paid $200 for my first car . . . a 1973 Buick LeSabre that was wrecked down one entire side and had been used in demolition donut field races.

# From Ordinary to Extraordinary

## REAL PEOPLE | REAL LIVES | REAL CHANGE

had to drop out because I could not get a grant and did not make enough money to pay tuition. I later enrolled in the local community college but after one semester, I realized I could not afford this either.

Basically, I had to make a hard, life-altering decision. I did not want to live my life in debt as my father had, so I made up my mind that I would have to take a few steps back to eventually go forward. I began to look for a job that offered educational benefits. I scanned the phone book for hospitals, utility companies, banks, and government agencies that offered this benefit. Every Monday night, their job lines would be updated and I would call, fill out an application, and wait. Nothing!

Finally, I learned how to properly fill out an application. I would call the job lines many times and write down every word in their advertisements. Then, I would craft my application and letter based on *their needs,*

not *my experiences.* I had to learn to apply for a job as if I already had it. After two years and many attempts to secure a suitable position, a utility company hired me—AND they had educational benefits. Finally, I could go back to school and get another car! I began working toward my degree and after six long, hard years, I graduated with a Bachelor of Science in business management. It was not easy, as I am sure you know. I had to take some courses online, and I was in class every Friday night for years and years.

During my time in college, I worked my way up in the company and today, 17 years later, I am a senior trainer for SCANA, an $11 billion Fortune 500 utility holding company founded in 1846. I design training programs and development materials for new hires, system enhancements, and employee upgrades.

I look back on my childhood and early adulthood and I am proud of the

fact that I did not let my past or my family dictate my future. I survived. I refused to succumb to their life. I knew that I had to have my own life with my own fate. You can have this too. Never let your past or your family tell you what you're capable of doing. Take chances. Take risks. And, if you have to take a step backward to go forward, never be ashamed to do that, too.

## EXTRAORDINARY REFLECTION

**Read the following statement and respond in your online journal or class notebook.**

Mr. Jones came from a family that did not support him financially, emotionally, or educationally. What advice would you give to someone who might be experiencing the same type of environment? Does your family have to play a role in your life for you to be successful?

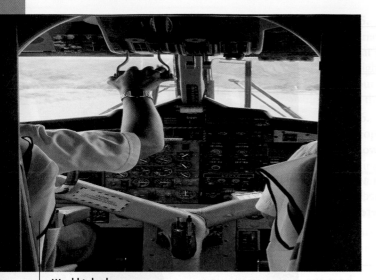

Would it bother you (or would you love it) to travel two to four days per week for your career?

*Is your major goal in choosing a profession money or something else? What?* _____

_____

*What does your goal mean to your career path?*

_____

_____

## Where Do You Want to Live?

Although this question may sound strange, many careers are limited by geography. If you are interested in oceanography, you would be hard-pressed to live in Iowa; if you love farming, New York City would be an improbable place for you to live. If you like small towns, you might not be happy in Atlanta. Some people simply prefer certain parts of the United States (or the world) to others. You need to ask yourself, "What climate do I really enjoy?" "Where would I be the happiest?" "Do I want to live near my family or away from them?"

*Where do you eventually want to live? Why?* _____

_____

*What does your preference mean for your career path?* _____

_____

## Do You Want to Travel?

Some jobs require travel; some people love to travel, some hate it. Ask yourself whether you want to be away from your home and family four nights per week, or whether you want a job that does not require any travel.

*Do you enjoy travel? Do you want to do a lot of traveling?* _____

_____

*What does this mean for your career path?* _____

_____

## What Motivates You and What Do You Value?

Do you value relationships, possessions, money? Are you motivated by love, security, challenges, or power? Once you have identified what you value and what motivates you, you can identify careers that closely match your personal value system and eliminate careers that don't motivate you. If you have to constantly compromise your values just to get a paycheck, you may be unhappy, and motivation will be hard to find on a daily basis.

*What do you truly value in your life and what motivates you?* _____

_____

*How might these two things affect your career decisions?* _____

_____

## What Are Your Skills?

Are you especially good at one or two things? Are you good with computers, a good manager of money, a good carpenter, a good communicator? Employers still stress the importance of three basic skills: writing, speaking, and listening. If you have these skills, you are ahead of the pack. If not, you need to enroll in a class that will help you become better at all three.

*What are your skills? What do you do well?* _____

_____

*How could your strongest skills help you make a career decision?* _____

_____

## Do You Like Routine?

The answer to this question will narrow down your choices tremendously. If you like routine, you will want a career that is conducive to routine and provides structure. If you do not like routine and enjoy doing different things each day, certain careers will be unrealistic for you.

*Do you like routine or do you prefer variety? Why?* _____

_____

*How does this affect your career path?* _____

_____

**DREAM JOB**

Using the answers you provided to the previous questions and a variety of additional resources such as Web sites, shadowing, and interviews, write a description of your dream job—the job you would have if you could do anything you want to do.

_____
_____
_____
_____
_____

BLOOM LEVEL 5 QUESTION

**DID YOU KNOW**

**MAYA ANGELOU** was born in St. Louis, MO, in 1928. By the time she was in her twenties, she had been a cook, streetcar conductor, cocktail waitress, dancer, madam, high school dropout, and unwed mother. As a young girl, she had been raped by her mother's boyfriend and did not speak again for four years.

Today, Dr. Angelou is a world-renowned poet, civil rights activist, historian, screenwriter, and director. She is only the second poet *in history* to write and deliver an original poem at a Presidential Inauguration (for former President Clinton).

She has won three Grammy® awards in the spoken-word category and has been nominated twice for Broadway's prestigious Tony® award.

# HELP ME: I'M UNDECLARED

## Is It Awful that I Don't Know What I Want to Do?

No, it is not. And being undeclared is not a fatal disease. It is not a disgrace or a weakness. It is a temporary state of mind, and the best way to deal with it is to stop and think. You should not declare a major because you are ashamed to be undeclared, and you shouldn't allow yourself to be pressured into declaring a major. Instead, you can take measures to work toward declaring a major and being satisfied with your decision. It is better to be undeclared than to spend several semesters in a field that is wrong for you, wasting hours that won't count toward a degree. On the other hand, the sooner you declare a major, the less likely you will be to take courses that do not count toward your eventual decision. While you do need to take your time and make a good decision, you don't have forever!

THINKING *for* CHANGE: **An Activity for Critical Reflection**

LaKeisha has been trying to plan for her future, but she really has no idea what she would like to do with her life. Her grades are excellent, and she loves college, but she doesn't have a clue of what she wants to declare as a major. She has read her textbooks carefully, listened to her most forward-thinking professors, and talked to her parents, but so far she has come up with a blank slate. Her parents didn't go to college, so LaKeisha can get very little guidance at home.

LaKeisha knows that she needs to declare a major—and that means she has to have some idea of what she wants to do with her life. Her biology professor, Dr. Margaret Palmer, has made quite an impression on her. In fact, she has suggested to LaKeisha that she consider majoring in biology, with plans of becoming a medical researcher or doctor. Her words to LaKeisha were, "You are a very bright young woman. Students don't come along every day who can grasp science and

math concepts like you can. I could help you apply for scholarships if you are interested."

LaKeisha is interested in finding out more from Dr. Palmer. She thinks she might love being a doctor or a researcher, but she believes that she needs to know more before going down that path. How can LaKeisha go about getting Dr. Palmer to become her mentor? How might she get Dr. Palmer to let her work with her as an assistant so she can get some hands-on experience?

_____

_____

What kinds of long-term plans will LaKeisha need to make if she decides to pursue a career as a doctor or medical researcher?

_____

_____

## 10 Steps To Career Decision Making

**STEP 1—DREAM!** If money were not a problem or concern, what would you do for the rest of your life? If you could do anything in the world, what would you do? Where would you do it? These are the types of questions you must ask yourself as you try to select a major and a career. Go outside, lie on the grass, and look up at the sky; think silently for a little while. Let your mind wander, and let the sky be the limit. Write your dreams down. These dreams may be closer to reality than you think.

**STEP 2—GO WHERE THE PUCK IS GOING!** Sound crazy? The great hockey champ Wayne Gretzky made the comment that *this ONE STEP* had been his key to success. What does it mean? He said that when he was playing hockey, he did not skate to where the puck was at the moment, he skated to where the puck was GOING. He anticipated the direction of where it was going to be hit, and when it came his way, he was already there—ready to play. Think of your career in this light. Go to where the future will be bright, not necessarily where the present is bright at this moment. Look ahead and try to determine what is going to be "hot" in the future, not what is hot right now. Plan ahead. Look at trends. Read. Ask questions. Think in the future, not the moment.

**STEP 3—TALK TO YOUR ADVISOR.** Academic advisors are there to help you. But don't be surprised if their doors are sometimes closed. They teach, conduct research, perform community service, and sometimes advise hundreds of students. Always call in advance; make an appointment to see your advisor. When you have that appointment, make your advisor work for you. Take your college catalog and ask questions, hard questions. Your advisor will not make a career decision for you, but if you ask the proper questions, he or she can be of monumental help to you and your career decisions.

Use students in your program as advisors, too. They will be invaluable to you as you work your way through the daily routine of college. Experienced students can assist you in making decisions about your classes, electives, and work-study programs. They can even help you join and become an active member of a preprofessional program.

**STEP 4—USE ELECTIVES.** The accreditation agency that works with your school requires that you be allowed at least one free elective in your degree program. Some programs allow many more. Use your electives wisely! Do not take courses just to get the hours. The wisest students use their electives to delve into new areas of interest or take a block of courses in an area that might enhance their career opportunities.

> "It's a sad day when you find out that it's not an accident—or time—or fortune, but just YOURSELF that kept things from you."
> —Lilian Hellman

**STEP 5—GO TO THE CAREER CENTER.** Even the smallest colleges have some type of career center or a career counselor. Use them! Campus career centers usually provide free services. The same types of services in the community could cost from $200 to $2,000. The professionals in the career center can provide you information on a variety of careers and fields, and they can administer interest and personality inventories that can help you make career and other major decisions.

**STEP 6—READ, READ, READ!** Nothing will help you more than reading about careers and majors. Ask your advisor or counselor to help you locate information on your areas of interest. Gather information from colleges, agencies, associations, and places of employment. Then read it!

**STEP 7—SHADOW.** Shadowing describes the process of following someone around on the job. If you are wondering what engineers do on the job, try calling an engineering office to see whether you can sit with several of their engineers for a day over spring break. Shadowing is the very best way to get firsthand, honest information regarding a profession in which you might be interested.

**STEP 8—JOIN PREPROFESSIONAL ORGANIZATIONS.** One of the most important steps you can take as a college student is to become involved in campus organizations and clubs that offer educational opportunities, social interaction, and hands-on experience in your chosen field. Preprofessional organizations can open doors that will help you make a career decision, grow in your field, meet professionals already working in your field, and, eventually, get a job.

**STEP 9—GET A PART-TIME JOB.** Work in an area that you may be interested in pursuing as a career. Get a part-time job while you are in school or work in a related field in the summer.

**STEP 10—TRY TO GET A SUMMER PRACTICUM OR INTERNSHIP.** Work in your field of interest to gain practical experience and see if it really suits you. Some programs require a practicum or internship, and this experience often leads to your first full-time job.

By working through this 10-step plan, you will come closer to finding what you really want and need in your life's work. Take your time, study, read, ask questions, shadow others, and most importantly, make your own decisions. Yes, you may change majors or even careers along the way, but that is a part of life's journey.

# WORKIN' 9 TO 5—OR TRYING TO

## Is It Really Possible to Sell Yourself Through a Cover Letter and Resume?

Remember the old saying, "You are what you eat"? When searching for any position, you could change that to read, ***You are what you write.*** Your resume and cover letter are your first marketing tools and in many cases must stand alone when a recruiter is determining whether or not to interview you. Just as a well-designed and well-written resume and cover letter can be a wonderful first step, a poorly designed and poorly written resume and cover letter can doom you before you even leave your house. A good thing to remember is this: A resume and cover letter get you the interview; the interview gets you the job.

A cover letter is basically an expansion of your resume. A cover letter gives you the chance to link your resume, skills, and experience together with your interest in *a specific company's* position and their advertising. You will need to write many cover letters to make this link work properly; in other words, you will most likely need to write a cover letter designed for each position for which you apply. Your cover letter will often be the stepping stone to get an employer to even look at your resume. Consider it "a teaser," if you will, of all of your talents and experience. Just as you would never send someone a greeting card and not sign it, you would never send a resume and not tell the person or committee *why* you sent it. Your cover letter tells why.

# WRITE A POWERFUL AND CONCISE COVER LETTER

## How Do You Get Your Foot in the Door?

The most important part of the job search process is the preparation that must be done *prior to starting* the interview process. A carefully crafted letter and resume communicate your past history (education, skills, and experience) that makes you the ideal candidate for the position. They are the first marketing pieces a recruiter sees when determining whether or not to interview you. Consider the general tips outlined in Figure 11.1

Figure 11.2 provides a sample cover letter and indicates the correct format and spacing to the left of the letter's content.

---

**FIGURE 11.1** *General Tips for the Cover Letter and Resume*

- ▶ Both your resume and cover letter *MUST be typed*. There are no exceptions to this rule. Ever! Seriously, EVER!
- ▶ Your cover letter and resume must be printed on the same *type and color* of *fine-quality paper*. Cheap paper sends the message that you don't care. This is not the place or time to pinch pennies; buy excellent quality, 100% cotton stock, resume-quality paper.
- ▶ Check your printer and be sure that the print quality is impeccable. Never send a cover letter or resume with smudges, ink smears, or poor print quality.
- ▶ When you print your cover letter and resume, be certain that the watermark on the paper is turned in the correct direction. Hold it up to the light and you will see the watermark embedded in the paper. This may sound silly and picky, but people notice attention to detail.
- ▶ Do not fold your cover letter or resume. Purchase a packet of 9 x 13 envelopes in which to send your materials.
- ▶ Do not handwrite the address on the envelope. Use a label or type the address directly on the envelope. Remember, first impressions are important.
- ▶ Never send a generic photocopy of a cover letter or resume, even on the finest paper.
- ▶ Layout, design, font, spacing and color must be considered in the building of your cover letter and resume.
- ▶ Unless you are specifically asked to do so, NEVER discuss money or salary history in either your cover letter or resume. This could work against you. When asked for a salary history, use ranges.
- ▶ Your resume and cover letter MUST be error-free. That's right, not one single error is acceptable including grammar, spelling, punctuation, layout/spacing, dates, or content.
- ▶ Each cover letter must be signed in black or blue ink.

FIGURE **11.2** *Sample Cover Letter with Formatting Information*

| | |
|---|---|
| Your name and address on high-quality paper. Your name should be larger and/or in a different font to call attention. → | **CARSON SCOTT**<br>1234 Lake Shadow Drive,<br>Maple City, PA 12345 |
| | (123) 555-1234<br>Scott@bl.com |
| The date (then double space) → | January 3, 2011 |
| The specific person, title, and address to whom you are writing (then double space) → | Mr. James Pixler, RN, CAN<br>Director of Placement and Advancement<br>Grace Care Center<br>123 Sizemore Street, Suite 444<br>Philadelphia, PA 12345 |
| The formal salutation followed by a colon (then double space) → | Dear Mr. Pixler: |
| Paragraph 1 (then double space) → | Seven years ago, my mother was under the treatment of two incredible nurses at Grace Care Center in Philadelphia. My family and I agree that the care she was given was extraordinary. When I saw your ad in today's *Philadelphia Carrier,* I was extremely pleased to know that I now have the qualifications to be a part of the Grace Care Team as a Medical Assistant. |
| Paragraph 2 (then double space) → | Next month, I will graduate with an Occupational Associate's Degree from Victory College of Health and Technology as a certified Medical Assistant. My resume indicates that I was fortunate to do my internship at Mercy Family Care Practice in Harrisburg. During this time, I was directly involved in patient care, records documentation, and family outreach. |
| Paragraph 3 (then double space) → | As a part of my degree from Victory, I received a 4.0 in the following classes: |
| | ✓ Management Communications<br>✓ Microsoft Office (Word, Excel, Outlook, PowerPoint)<br>✓ Business Communications I, II, III<br>✓ Anatomy and Physiology I, II, III<br>✓ Medical Coding I, II<br>✓ Principles of Pharmacology<br>✓ Immunology I, II, III, IV<br>✓ Urinalysis and Body Fluids<br>✓ Clinical Practicum I, II, III |
| | This, along with my past certificate in Medical Transcription and my immense respect for Grace Care Center, makes me the perfect candidate for your position. |
| Final paragraph or closing (then double space) → | I have detailed all of my experience on the enclosed resume. I will call you on Monday, January 24 at 11:30 a.m. to discuss how my education and experiences can help streamline operations and continue superior patient care at Grace. In the meantime, please feel free to contact me at the number above. |
| The complementary close (then four spaces) → | Sincerely, |
| Your handwritten signature in black or blue ink within the four spaces → | *carson scott* |
| Your typed name → | CARSON SCOTT |
| Enclosure contents → | Enclosure: Resume |

## 11.3    *Chronological Resume*

CARSON SCOTT

1234 Lake Shadow Drive, Maple City, PA 12345          (123) 555-1234
Scott@bl.com

OBJECTIVE:    To work as a medical assistant in an atmosphere that uses my organizational skills, compassion for people, desire to make a difference, and impeccable work ethic.

PROFESSIONAL EXPERIENCE:

| | |
|---|---|
| January 2007–Present | Medical Assistant Intern<br>Mercy Family Care Practice, Harrisburg, PA<br>▶ Responsible for completing patient charts<br>▶ Took patient's vitals<br>▶ Assisted with medical coding |
| February 2003–December 2006 | Medical Transcriptionist<br>The Office of Brenda Wilson, MD, Lancaster, PA<br>▶ Interpreted and typed medical reports<br>▶ Worked with insurance documentation<br>▶ Assisted with medical coding<br>▶ Served as Office Manager (1/05–12/06) |
| March 1998–February 2003 | Ward Orderly<br>Wallace Hospital, Lancaster, PA<br>▶ Assisted nurses with patient care<br>▶ Cleaned patient rooms<br>▶ Served patient meals |
| August 1995–March 1998 | Administrative Assistant<br>Ellen Abbot Nursing Care Facility<br>▶ Typed office reports<br>▶ Organized patient files |

EDUCATION:

*Occupational Associate's Degree—Medical Assistant*
Victory Health Institute, Harrisburg, PA
May 2008 (with honors)

*Certificate of Completion—Medical Transcription*
Philadelphia Technical Institute
December 2002

*Vocational High School Diploma—Health Sciences*
Philadelphia Vocational High School
August 1995

As you begin to prepare for your interview, consider the following mnemonic. If you confidently *carry* **R E W A R D S** with you to an interview, you will most likely *get* rewards after the interview such as a job offer, benefits, and a career in which you can grow and prosper.

**R = Rapport**

Rapport is basically your "relationship" (intended or unintended) with another person—the emotional alliance you establish with someone. Consider how you come across to others. Rapport involves your verbal and nonverbal communication efforts. You should strive to establish a positive relationship with potential employers and future colleagues.

**E = Education and Training**

Be confident about what you know and eloquently promote your abilities, skills, and talents to the interviewer. Remember, if you don't promote yourself, it is unlikely that anyone else will.

**W = Willingness**

Project a sense of willingness to learn new things, to become a team member, to assist the company with growth and new projects, and to keep up with advancements and changes in the modern world of work. Potential employers enjoy seeing an attitude of willingness and engagement.

**A = Appearance**

Dress for success. Pay close attention to your grooming, your hygiene, your hair, your clothing, and, yes, even your shoes and socks (or hosiery). It all matters—and it is all noticed. Never make the mistake of thinking that appearance is not important.

**R = Response**

Project positivity and optimism in your responses to the questions asked in the interview. Even if you have to talk about your weaknesses or past experiences of conflict and turmoil, put a positive spin on them. Let the interviewer know that you have learned from adversity.

**D = Demeanor**

Project a quality of confidence (not cockiness), intelligence, professionalism, and positivity. Carrying yourself with confidence during the interview will not go unnoticed. Pay attention to your handshake, your eye contact, your posture, your mannerisms, and your facial expressions.

**S = Sincerity**

No one likes phony people, especially a potential employer. Be yourself and strive to be sincere in your answers, your emotions, and your passion.

# WIN, LOSE, OR DRAW, *ALWAYS* SAY "THANK YOU" IN WRITING

## Do I Have to Say "Thank You" Even If I Don't Get the Job?

Indeed, it is safe to say that sending a thank you note is *"the most overlooked step in the entire job search process"* (Bolles, 2008). Yes, this is a mandatory step for every interview, and it is also mandatory that you send one to every person who interviewed you. Period. In today's world of high-tech and run, run, run, this one act will set you apart from the thousands who interview on a daily basis. And yes, you must send a thank you note even if you DO NOT get the job. "When do I send the thank you note?" you might ask. *Immediately after the interview.*

Sending a simple thank you note does many things. It lets the employer know that you have good manners, that you respect other people's time and efforts, that you are considerate, that you really do care about the position, and that you have positive people and communication skills. Yes, all of that from a card and a stamp that can cost less than $2.

In Figures 11.4 and 11.5, you will find examples of two thank you notes. Review them and consider using them as templates to build your own notes.

FIGURE

## 11.4 *Thank-You Note: After the Interview*

CARSON SCOTT
1234 Lake Shadow Drive
Maple City, PA 12345
Scott@bl.com

January 20, 2011

Mr. James Pixler, RN
Director of Placement
Grace Care Center
123 Sizemore Street
Philadelphia, PA 12345

Dear Mr. Pixler,

I wanted to thank you for the wonderful opportunity to meet with you and the team at Grace Care Center on Monday. Your facilities are amazing, and the new wing is going to be a remarkable addition to your center.

I enjoyed learning more about the new position in Medical Assisting, and I think that my qualifications and experiences have prepared me for this challenging opportunity. I would consider it an honor to answer any further questions that you might have or to meet with you again if you consider it necessary.

I look forward to hearing from you at your convenience. If you need any additional information, you can reach me at 123-555-3454.

Thank you,

*carson scott*

CARSON SCOTT

FIGURE

## 11.5 *Thank-Your Note: After a Position Rejection*

CARSON SCOTT
1234 Lake Shadow Drive
Maple City, PA 12345
Scott@bl.com

January 20, 2011

Mr. James Pixler, RN
Director of Placement
Grace Care Center
123 Sizemore Street
Philadelphia, PA 12345

Dear Mr. Pixler,

I wanted to thank you for the opportunity to meet with you and the team at Grace Care Center on Monday. I enjoyed learning more about your center and the planned addition.

While I was not offered the position, I did want to let you know that I appreciate your time and I would like for you to contact me if you have any future openings where you feel my qualifications and experiences would match your needs. Grace is an incredible facility, and I would consider it an honor to hold a position there.

If you need to contact me in the future, you can reach me at 123-555-3454.

Thank you for your time and assistance and good luck to you and your colleagues.

Sincerely,

*carson scott*

CARSON SCOTT

CHANGING IDEAS TO *Reality*

**REFLECTIONS ON
CAREER AND LIFE
DEVELOPMENT**

Making a decision about your major or career can be difficult, but, fortunately, you still have a few months before you have to make this choice. Use this time to explore all avenues that will expose you to different possibilities. This is a growing time for you and you might discover new interests and directions that you had never considered before. Follow your heart, and pursue your dreams. If there is something you have always wanted to do or be, chances are your desires will not change even after you study other options.

This is your one lifetime! You need to prepare to do something you love. No matter how much money you make, you won't be happy unless you are doing something that matters to you, something that allows you to keep learning and becoming, something that provides you opportunities to give back—perhaps the best gift of all.

As you reflect on this chapter, keep the following pointers in mind:

▶ Identify the assets you can offer a company.

▶ Learn to promote and sell yourself in an interview.

▶ Discover your personality type and make it work for you.

▶ *Shadow* and do volunteer work to learn as much as you can about the profession.

▶ Realize that life is *more* than money.

▶ Know your own *value* system and what motivates you.

"If you follow your bliss, doors will open for you that wouldn't have opened for anyone else."

—Joseph Campbell

# KNOWLEDGE *in* BLOOM

**DEVELOPING SKILLS and Knowledge to Make Wise Career Decisions**

Each chapter-end assessment is based on *Bloom's Taxonomy of Learning*. See the inside front cover for a quick review.

UTILIZES LEVEL 4 OF THE TAXONOMY

### Applying the 10 Essential Cornerstones

On page 8 in Chapter 1, "Change," you will find a list of **10 ESSENTIAL CORNERSTONES.** These cornerstones are the foundation for a successful life and career. Although you are a first-year student and have time to make decisions about your career, ways you plan to change, and how you want to live your life, now is a good time to start thinking about these heavy decisions. You have one life . . . this is not a trial run!

After researching several Web sites about a career you might be interested in and talking with people who are pursuing this career, apply the 10 Cornerstones to this possible choice to see if it meets the criteria for a lasting, rewarding career.

## Passion

How does this career possibility make you feel when you think about going to work and doing this every day for many years? How would this choice enable you to give back to others and feel rewarded?

_____

_____

_____

_____

## Motivation

How does this career choice relate to goals and objectives you might have already set for yourself? Will this career help you keep growing and learning? Will it help you further develop your inner strengths? Discuss your responses in the space below.

_____

_____

_____

_____

## Knowledge

Will you be able to master the knowledge that is required to be successful in the field that you are exploring? How will this field require you to keep learning and growing? Will the knowledge you have to master be challenging and exhilarating to you?

_____

_____

_____

_____

## Resourcefulness

Is this a field that will allow you to be resourceful? Will this field challenge you to seek new and different opportunities? Will you need to be a problem solver?

_____

_____

_____

_____

## Creativity

Will this career allow you to be creative? Will you be able to implement innovative ideas? Will you have an opportunity to grow in ways that allow you to solve complex problems?

_____

_____

_____

_____

## Adaptability

Will you be required to use adaptive techniques? Will you be able to grow by constantly reinventing yourself?

_____
_____
_____
_____

## Open-Mindedness

Will this career give you an opportunity to work in a diverse work community? Will you be required to learn to appreciate differences in cultures? Would learning a new language be valued, appreciated, and useful?

_____
_____
_____
_____

## Communication

Will you work in an environment that supports networking among colleagues and clients? Will this career enable you to develop mentors and to become a mentor yourself?

_____
_____
_____
_____

## Accountability

Will this career enable you to be accountable for the overall development of your well-being? Will it provide opportunities to develop solid relationships? Will it offer you resources to learn more about financial development and responsibility?

_____
_____
_____
_____

## Vision

Will this career provide opportunities to continue growing as the global economy keeps bringing about major changes to the workplace? Will the company's management be visionary in their approach to keeping up with competition?

_____
_____
_____
_____

# SQ3R *Mastery* STUDY SHEET

| | | |
|---|---|---|
| **EXAMPLE QUESTION:** *(from page 297)*<br>What does R.E.W.A.R.D. stand for? | | **ANSWER:** |
| **EXAMPLE QUESTION:** *(from page 291)*<br>Why is it important to write<br>an excellent resume? | | **ANSWER:** |
| **AUTHOR QUESTION:** *(from page 283)*<br>Discuss the differences between<br>a career and a job. | | **ANSWER:** |
| **AUTHOR QUESTION:** *(from page 286)*<br>Why does personality type matter when<br>deciding on a major or a job? | | **ANSWER:** |
| **AUTHOR QUESTION:** *(from page 290)*<br>Discuss three of the steps to declaring a major. | | **ANSWER:** |
| **AUTHOR QUESTION:** *(from page 292)*<br>Why is it important to write a compelling cover letter<br>to accompany your resume or application? | | **ANSWER:** |
| **AUTHOR QUESTION:** *(from page 297)*<br>Why do you need to write a thank you note even<br>if you do not get the position? | | **ANSWER:** |
| **YOUR QUESTION:** *(from page ___)* | | **ANSWER:** |
| **YOUR QUESTION:** *(from page ___)* | | **ANSWER:** |
| **YOUR QUESTION:** *(from page ___)* | | **ANSWER:** |
| **YOUR QUESTION:** *(from page ___)* | | **ANSWER:** |
| **YOUR QUESTION:** *(from page ___)* | | **ANSWER:** |

Finally, after answering these questions, recite this chapter's major points in your mind. Consider the following general questions to help you master this material.

- ▶ What was it about?
- ▶ What does it mean?
- ▶ What was the most important thing I learned? Why?
- ▶ What were the key points to remember?

Adler, R., Rosenfeld, L., & Towne, N. (2006). *Interplay. The Process of Interpersonal Communication* (2nd ed.). New York: Holt, Rinehart and Winston.

Altman, I., & Taylor, D. (1973). *Social Penetration: The Development of Interpersonal Relationships.* New York: Holt.

American Library Association. (1989). *Presidential Committee on Information Literacy. Final Report.* Chicago: American Library Association.

American Psychological Association. (2008). *For a Better Understanding of Sexual Orientation and Homosexuality.* Retrieved August 12, 2008, from http://www.apa.org/topics/orientation.html.

Anderson, L., & Bolt, S. (2008). *Professionalism: Real Skills for Workplace Success.* Upper Saddle River, NJ: Pearson Prentice Hall.

Bach, D. (2003). *The Finish Rich Notebook.* New York: Broadway Books.

Barrett, D. (2008). *Average Student Loans Top $19,000.* Retrieved September 2, 2008, from http://encarta.msn.com/encnet/departments/financialaid/?article=averagestudentloans.

Beebe, S., Beebe, S., & Redmond, M. (2008). *Interpersonal Communication: Relating to Others* (5th ed.). Boston: Allyn and Bacon.

Block, S. (February 22, 2006). Students Suffocate Under Tens of Thousands in Loans. *USA Today.*

Bolles, R. N. (2008). *What Color Is Your Parachute? A Practical Manual for Job-Hunters and Career-Changers, 2008 Edition.* Berkeley, CA: Ten Speed Press.

Bosack, J. *Fallacies.* Dubuque, IA: Educulture Publishers, 1978.

Britton-Whitcomb, S. (2003). *Resume Magic: Trade Secrets of a Professional Resume Writer.* Indianapolis, IN: JIST Works Publishing, Inc.

Broderick, C. (2003). *Why Care About Your Credit Score?* InCharge Education Foundation, Inc.

Bureau of Labor Statistics. (2006). *How Americans Spend Time.* Washington, DC: Department of the Census. Retrieved February 9, 2009, from www.bls.gov.

Chronicle of Higher Education. (August 29, 2008). *Almanac Edition, 2008–2009,* 55(1), 18.

Cojonet (City of Jacksonville, FL). (2003). *Consumer Affairs Gets New Tough Law on Car Title Businesses.* Accessed from www.coj.net/Departments/Regulatory+and+Environmental+Services/Consumer+Affairs/TITLE+LOANS.htm.

Collegeboard. (2008). *College Prices Increase in Step with Inflation: Financial Aid Grows but Fewer Private Loans Even Before Credit Crisis.* Accessed at http://www.collegeboard.com/press/releases/201194.html.

Consumer Response Center. (2003). *Identity Theft and Fraud,* 2003; *ConsumerReport, Money Advisor,* 2008; *The State* Newspaper, August 31, 2008.

Consumer Reports. (September 2008). *Protect Yourself Online: The Biggest Threats and the Best Solutions.*

Consumer Reports. Money Advisor. (September 2008). *Protecting Your Identity.*

Cooper-Arnold, A. L. (2006). *Credit Card Debt: A Survival Guide for Students.* www.youngmoney.com/credit_debt/credit_basics/050804-02.

Daly, J., & Engleberg, I. (2006). *Presentations in Everyday Life: Strategies for Effective Speaking.* Upper Saddle River, NJ: Allyn and Bacon.

Department of the Census, Department of Labor. (2008). *Education and Training Pay.* Washington, DC: U.S. Government Printing Office.

DeVito, J. A. (2007). *Interpersonal Messages: Communication and Relationship Skills.* Boston: Pearson Education.

The Digerati Life. (2008). *Lost Money: How Money Drains Add Up to $175,000 in 10 Years.* Retrieved September 5, 2008, from http://www.thedigeratilife.com/blog.index.php/2008/07/31/lost-money-how-money-drains-.

Donatelle, R., & Davis, L. (2002). *Health: The Basics.* Upper Saddle River, NJ: Prentice Hall.

Drugs of Abuse: National Institute on Drug Abuse website, accessed at http://www.nida.nih.gov/.

Dunn, R., & Griggs, S. (2000). *Practical Approaches to Using Learning Styles in Higher Education.* New York: Bergin & Garvey.

Feagin, J. R., & Feagin, C. B. (2008). *Racial and Ethnic Relations.* Upper Saddle River, NJ: Pearson/Prentice Hall.

Gamble, T., and Gamble, M. (1978). *Public Speaking in the Age of Diversity.* Upper Saddle River, NJ: Prentice Hall.

Gardner, H. (1983). *Frames of Mind: The Theory of Multiple Intelligence.* New York: Basic Books.

*Get More Done.* (2009). Retrieved January 3, 2009, from www.getmoredone.com.

Girando, D., Dusek, D., & Everly, G. (2009). *Controlling Stress and Tension* (8th ed.). Boston: Benjamin Cummings.

Glenn, J. M. L. (October 2007). Generations at Work: The New Diversity. *Business Education Forum,* 62(1).

The Goddess Path. (2009). *Mnemosyne, the Goddess of Memory.* Accessed from www.goddessgift.com.

Goleman, D. (2006). *Emotional Intelligence: Why It Can Matter More than IQ* (10th Anniv. Ed.). New York: Bantam.

Gordon, E. E. (2005). *The 2010 Meltdown: Solving the Impending Jobs Crisis.* Westport, CT: Praeger.

Hall, E. (1966). *The Hidden Dimension.* Garden City, NY: Doubleday.

Housden, R. (2007). Taking a Chance on Joy. *O's Guide to Life: The Best of the Oprah Magazine.* Birmingham, AL: Oxmoor House.

Ireland, S. (2003). *The Complete Idiot's Guide to the Perfect Resume.* Indianapolis, IN: Alpha Publishing Company.

Jung, C. (1921). *Psychology Types.* In *Collected Works of C.G. Jung* (Volume 6; R. Hull, Translator). Princeton, NJ: Princeton University Press, 1976.

Kallock, A. (April 16, 2009). Sunstein: Lack of Ideological Diversity Leads to Extremism. *The Harvard Law Review.*

Kiewra, K., & Fletcher, H. (1984). The Relationship Between Note Taking Variables and Achievement Measure. *Human Learning, 3,* 273–280.

Kirszner, L., & Mandell, S. (1995). *The Holt Handbook.* Orlando, FL: Harcourt Brace College Publishers.

Konowalow, S. (2003). *Planning Your Future: Keys to Financial Freedom.* Columbus, OH: Prentice Hall.

Lane, H. (1976). *The Wild Boy of Aveyron.* Cambridge, MA: Harvard University Press.

Lane, S. (2008). *Interpersonal Communication: Competence and Contexts.* Boston: Pearson/Allyn and Bacon.

Leinwood, D. (September 23, 2002). Ecstasy-Viagra Mix Alarms Doctors. *USA Today.*

Light, R. (2001). *Making the Most of College: Students Speak Their Minds.* Cambridge, MA: Harvard University Press.

Maslow, A. (1943). A Theory of Human Motivation. *Psychological Review. 50,* 370–396.

McCornack, S. (2007). *Reflect and Relate: An Introduction to Interpersonal Communication.* Boston: Bedford-St. Martin's Press.

National Leadership Council for Liberal Education and America's Promise. (2008). *College Learning for the New Global Century.* Washington, DC.

Nellie Mae Study. (2005). *Credit Cards 101,* p. 1.

Nelson, D., & Low, G. (2003). *Emotional Intelligence: Achieving Academic and Career Excellence.* Upper Saddle River, NJ: Prentice Hall.

1 on 1 health. (2006). *You Can Stop Smoking: Tips to Help You Quit for Good.* GlaxoSmithKline Group.

Ormondroyd, J., Engle, M., & Cosgrave, T. (2001). *How to Critically Analyze Information Sources.* Cornell University Libraries, www.library.cornell.edu.